SOCIAL WORK IN WALES

Edited by
Wulf Livingston, Jo Redcliffe and Abyd Quinn Aziz

With a foreword by
Mark Drakeford

P

First published in Great Britain in 2023 by

Policy Press, an imprint of
Bristol University Press
University of Bristol
1–9 Old Park Hill
Bristol
BS2 8BB
UK
t: +44 (0)117 374 6645
e: bup-info@bristol.ac.uk

Details of international sales and distribution partners are available at
policy.bristoluniversitypress.co.uk

British Library Cataloguing in Publication Data
A catalogue record for this book is available from the British Library

ISBN 978-1-4473-6719-2 paperback
ISBN 978-1-4473-6720-8 ePub
ISBN 978-1-4473-6721-5 ePdf

The right of Wulf Livingston, Jo Redcliffe and Abyd Quinn Aziz to be identified as editors of
this work has been asserted by them in accordance with the Copyright, Designs and Patents
Act 1988.

Cover design: Robin Hawes
Front cover image: Eluned Plack

Contents

Contents

Contents

List of figures and tables

Figures

Tables

List of abbreviations

BASW	British Association of Social Workers
BME	Black and minority ethnic
CCETSW	Central Council for the Education and Training of Social Workers
CCW	Care Council for Wales
CJS	criminal justice system
CPD	Continuing Professional Development
CPEL	Continuing Professional Education and Learning
EYST	Ethnic Minorities and Youth Support Team Wales
DipSW	Diploma in Social Work
DWP	Department for Work and Pensions
ECM	Enhanced Case Management
EHRC	Equality and Human Rights Commission
FtP	Fitness to Practise
GBV	gender-based violence
HEI	higher education institution
MASW	Masters in Social Work programme
NHS	National Health Service
PLO	practice learning opportunity
PQ	post-qualifying
PSHE	personal, social, health and economic education
RISCA	Regulation and Inspection of Social Care (Wales) Act, 2016
SCW	Social Care Wales
SROI	Social Return on Investment
SSWWA	Social Services and Well-being (Wales) Act 2014
UNHCR	United Nations High Commissioner for Refugees
WFGWA	Well-being of Future Generations (Wales) Act 2015
YJ	youth justice
YJB	Youth Justice Board
YJS	Youth Justice Service

Notes on contributors

Penny Alexander is Artist Practitioner and Masters student at Bangor University. Penny came into the creative ageing field through her arts background. Her BA (Hons) in Visual Arts and passion for working with older people led her into working in care homes as a cARTrefu Artist in Residence. She remained with the cARTrefu programme from Phase 2 (2017–19) and throughout Phase 3 (2019–22), but in 2020 also applied to undertake a KESS II East funded Masters by Research. Her thesis investigated embedding and sustaining the cARTrefu programme.

Katherine Algar-Skaife is Postdoctoral Fellow at the Norwegian University of Science and Technology. She has over 12 years of experience in research into improving health, well-being and support for older people, people living with dementia, and family/professional caregivers. Throughout her research career, she has collaborated with organisations such as Age Cymru and Flintshire Social Services to ensure that her research has a real-life impact. She led the cARTrefu research partnership at the Dementia Services Development Centre Wales, Bangor University, between 2015 and 2021 before moving to NTNU to begin a Postdoctoral Fellowship in Dementia Care and Welfare Technology.

Graham Attenborough was an Outside In representative at Glyndŵr University. A former lecturer in history at the University of Portsmouth, and expert through experience of using probation and rehabilitation services, Graham brought a 360-degree understanding of social work and university education to students' learning. His unique contributions were always expressed with thoughtful compassion and gentle humour. We miss him.

Helena Barlow is Lecturer in Social Work at Glyndŵr University. Helena is a registered and qualified social worker, who has practised in a variety of settings, including children, adults and youth justice. Helena leads on modules at Glyndŵr University on Law and Safeguarding in social work. She is currently undertaking a PhD on women's experiences of ex-partner stalking, with research interests including domestic abuse and coercive control.

Kelly Barr is Arts and Creativity Programme Manager with Age Cymru. Kelly manages creative ageing projects including Gwanwyn, a Wales-wide festival celebrating creativity in later life. She has an MA in Arts Management from the Royal Welsh College of Music and Drama and has worked with a range of organisations on participatory projects, including National Dance Company Wales, Earthfall and Sherman Theatre.

Tegan Brierley-Sollis is Lecturer in Policing, Criminology and Trauma-Informed Approaches at Glyndŵr University. Tegan has recently completed her PhD in Criminal Justice which explored the trauma-informed culture within the North Wales Youth Justice Service. Tegan is a member of Cyfiawnder: The Social Inclusion Research Institute at Wrexham Glyndŵr University and has experience working and volunteering with children and adults involved in the criminal justice system, across both statutory and voluntary services.

Sarah Buckley is an Outside In representative at Glyndŵr University. Sarah is a valued member of the group who, due to her complex mental health issues, has extensive experience of social and mental health services, both good and bad. She is happy to share these experiences with students so they can gain understanding and empathy. Sarah's ability and confidence in herself has grown since participating with the group. Among her many talents, Sarah has shown herself to be a very gifted artist.

Jenny Burgess is an Outside In representative at Glyndŵr University. Jenny is transgender, which is a small part of her life but an important part of her story from childhood till now. It has had an impact on her life that is valuable to those in the caring services and those caring for transgender people. Since retiring from her employment as an engineer, Jenny has been involved in volunteer work and is an unpaid carer. Jenny likes to share her experience as a carer and the impact it can have, and the support needed. Sadly, Jenny died in November 2022. She will sorely be missed by all those who knew her.

Daniel Burrows is a tutor at Cardiff University. Dan practised as a social worker in Wales for seven years before moving into higher education and is now a tutor on the MA Social Work at Cardiff University. His research interests include social work with older people, hospital social work and unpaid carers.

Ceryl Teleri Davies is Lecturer in Social Work at Bangor University. Ceryl is a qualified solicitor and social worker. Ceryl has practised across social care, criminal justice and learning disability services at practitioner, middle and senior management level. Ceryl's research interests are focused on exploring social norms, the nature of young people's intimate relationships, domestic abuse and healthy relationships. Ceryl also has interest in exploring issues across adult social care, including dementia and learning disabilities. Ceryl has taught at undergraduate and postgraduate levels on education, law, criminology and social work matters.

James Deakin is founder and organisational lead for North Wales Recovery Communities. James has worked in addiction and criminal justice services for approaching 20 years. A strong advocate for peer-led recovery, James has helped support the growth of recovery in north-west Wales for over a decade.

Hayley Douglas is Senior Lecturer at Wrexham Glyndŵr University. Hayley is a Joint Negotiating Committee professionally qualified youth worker with nearly 20 years' experience of youth and community work. This has involved working in a range of settings across both the statutory and voluntary sector with people of all ages, and often taking the lead on safeguarding issues. Hayley currently teaches at Wrexham Glyndŵr University, including modules on safeguarding, and is the safeguarding officer for a local organisation.

Mark Drakeford is First Minister of Wales. Mark is a former probation officer, youth justice worker and Barnardo's project leader. He has been a Professor of Social Policy and Applied Social Sciences at Cardiff University and previously at Swansea University.

Anna-Louise Edwards is an Outside In representative at Glyndŵr University. Anna-Louise believes the ultimate goal of social services is the need not to exist one day and chooses to bring her experience of the looked after children's system and the stories of others to the BA Social Work, Wrexham Young People's Care Council, Leaders Unlocked, Senedd yr Ifanc and anywhere else she feels it is necessary that people understand the experiences of looked after children and young people. Her contributions to lectures, workshops, role play, interviews, group discussions and students are highly valued for the ways in which they give insight into the impacts of social work practice on young people's lives.

Rhoda Emlyn-Jones OBE is Director of Achieving Sustainable Change Ltd. Rhoda has been a qualified social worker practising in Wales since 1979. She has designed and delivered a wide range of services straddling Adults and Children's Services and Health and Social Care. Since retiring in 2013 she continues to work across Wales in an independent capacity, alongside Social Care Wales, helping public services meet the ambitions of the Social Services and Well-being (Wales) Act 2014. Rhoda was awarded an OBE in 2009.

Miriam Ennis is a registered social worker with 25 years' practice experience working in various child and family settings and is a bilingual (Welsh) senior lecturer. Miriam's research interests within social work education are in the law, the Welsh context, intersectionality, philosophy and language, learning theory and model design.

Jade Forbes is a Locum Senior Social Work Practitioner and Approved Mental Health Professional. Jade has 11 years' experience and postgraduate studies in mental health and practice education. She is currently working in emergency out-of-hours services and acute mental health services for adults and children. Her experience spans across direct work and implementation of new practice initiatives within adult services. Her interests are in anti-racism, human rights and least restrictive practices for recipients in mental health care.

Hefin Gwilym is Lecturer in Social Policy at Bangor University. Hefin has lectured at Bangor University since 2006, initially in Social Work and since 2012 in Social Policy. He has published peer-reviewed articles in academic journals on social work, poverty and neoliberalism. His doctoral thesis completed in 2016 explores social work biographies within a neoliberal era. He teaches on social policy modules at undergraduate and postgraduate levels at Bangor. He also supervises PhD students in social policy in areas including food banking, carers' resilience and the link between social welfare and public transport in Wales. He regularly contributes to BBC Radio Cymru and BBC Radio Wales news programmes.

Christian Kerr is a social worker and Lecturer in Social Work and Social and Community Studies at Leeds Beckett University. He has been a mental health support worker and community worker, and has practised as a social worker with adults with physical disabilities, mental health issues, learning disabilities, neurological conditions and brain injuries. His research so far has been mainly in the area of reform and networks of power and influence in children's services. He was a member of the editorial collective of SW2020/21 under *COVID-19* magazine.

Hope Lawrence is an Outside In representative at Glyndŵr University. Since joining Outside In in 2019, Hope has developed her understanding of social work, and of working together in a non-judgemental way to change the misunderstandings and stigma associated with the profession.

Natacha Leao de Silva is a Qualified Social Worker. Natacha is undertaking her PhD, exploring the transitional experiences of unaccompanied care leavers in Wales. She is a qualified AMHP, who has practice experience of fostering, and is currently a social worker in a Community Mental Health Team.

Liz Lefroy is Senior Lecturer in Social Care at Glyndŵr University. Since 2006, Liz's role within the social work degree programme has focused on facilitating the participation of experts through experience, particularly working with the Outside In focus group. Her previous experience of managing support services for adults with complex needs, and her skills as an award-winning poet, have proved invaluable in finding creative ways of building learning communities.

Wulf Livingston is Professor in Alcohol Studies at Glyndŵr University. Wulf actively researches and is widely published within a range of alcohol, other drug, mental health and social work arenas. He is a registered and qualified social worker, whose current activities focus on: participation methodologies, policy and practice evaluation, and recovery communities.

Sarah Lord is Arts Development Manager at Arts & Business Cymru. Sarah worked as a photographer for seven years prior to taking over the management of the cARTrefu project from January 2019 until the project's conclusion in March 2022. Sarah spoke at numerous conferences during her time with cARTrefu, recruited and maintained strong working relationships with care homes across Wales and the social care sector, and worked closely with the KESS research team on Embedding and Sustaining the cARTrefu programme, before moving to Arts & Business Cymru in 2022.

Jen Lyttleton-Smith is Lecturer in Education at Cardiff Metropolitan University. Jen's research explores well-being and participation in public policy, with a particular focus on the experiences of children and young people.

Gillian Macintyre is Senior Lecturer in Social Work at the University of Strathclyde. Gillian is programme lead for the Postgraduate Certificate in Mental Health Social Work. She has a particular interest in research with people with learning disabilities and with those with lived experience of mental illness with a strong focus on participation, rights and citizenship. Recent research has explored the experiences of parents with learning disabilities and survivors of domestic abuse with learning disabilities.

Tracey Maegusuku-Hewett is Senior Lecturer and Programme Director of the BSc in Social Work at Swansea University. Tracey practised as a social worker in a variety of settings including community development, youth and outreach work with children, young people and families seeking sanctuary or with refugee status. Tracey's research interests relate mainly to immigration policy, children's rights and their well-being.

Jaime Ortiz is Professor of Global Economies and Markets at the University of Texas at Rio Grande Valley, USA. Jaime has worked for international organisations and universities. At the latter he has held senior executive leadership positions with a remit to campus-wide globalisation engagement. Jaime also holds Visiting Professorship appointments at Chinese and Welsh universities. He has been Fulbright Scholar and MSI Fellow with the W.K. Kellogg Foundation. Jaime's international experience ranges from Azerbaijan to Vietnam.

Naomi Parry is a qualified social worker and studied the DipSW/MA programme at Bangor University. Naomi has experience working with children, families and adults. Naomi's research interest is in the development of social work practice with transgender individuals in Wales and the impact of stigma and discrimination on well-being.

Beth Pearl is Senior Lecturer in Social Work at Swansea University. Beth has a particular interest in social work education and disenfranchised grief and ambiguous loss. She is passionate about coproduction and hearing the voices of experienced people in social work education.

Eluned Plack is an Outside In representative at Glyndŵr University. A former operating theatre nurse with over 38 years' experience and a prolific artist, Eluned has contributed widely to the social work degree including contributions to publications, most recently in Ghisoni, M. and Murphy, P. (2020) *Study Skills for Nursing, Health and Social Care*, Lantern Publishing. Eluned is passionate about providing students with a well-informed holistic perspective that combines health and social care models. Her expertise by experience is established upon the foundations of being both a provider and recipient of health and social care services.

Rhiana Povey graduated with a BA (Hons) in Social Work from Glyndŵr University in 2022. When Rhiana was made redundant from a 15-year career in the radio industry, she decided to turn this into a positive and follow her lifetime desire to become a social worker. The three years of her qualification were the hardest of her life: the pandemic and losing her only child impacted her like nothing she had ever experienced. The support she was given has given Rhiana even greater motivation to be there for others. Working with poetry as part of *The Creative Practitioner* module, Rhiana found it helped her to offload the weight of the griefs on her shoulders in a way that is less personally intrusive than some more traditional approaches.

Gwenan Prysor is Director of the MA in Social Work programme at Bangor University. Gwenan is a registered social worker, with a professional social work background mainly in children and families' services, undertaking both short- and longer-term interventions, including safeguarding. Before joining the MA Social Work Programme as Director in 2012, Gwenan managed the North Wales Social Work Practice Learning Centre. Gwenan was recently given a prestigious award by the Coleg Cymraeg Cenedlaethol in recognition of her outstanding contribution to Welsh-medium education.

Joanne Pye is Senior Lecturer in Social Work at Swansea University. Joanne is a registered social worker with over 20 years' experience of working with children and families within the voluntary, private and statutory setting, as both a residential and field social worker (including working with unaccompanied young people). The primary focus of Joanne's area of interest is upon children who are looked after and care leavers, with a particular interest upon promoting positive outcomes for children within the care system.

Abyd Quinn Aziz is Programme Director and Reader in the MA in Social Work programme at Cardiff University. Abyd is a registered social worker, having practised for 25 years in residential, field work, family centres, independent chairing and family group conferencing. His interests are citizen involvement, activism and anti-racism and he is a member of BASW Cymru National Committee.

Jo Redcliffe is Associate Professor at Swansea University and University of Texas Rio Grande Valley, USA. Jo practised as a social worker in a variety of settings, including mental health and substance misuse. She is currently the Swansea University lead for post-qualifying social work education and social work internationalisation link, with research interests including post-qualifying social work, disability, citizen involvement and substance misuse.

Haddy Sallah is a qualified social worker. Haddy has supported sanctuary seekers and refugees before and after her post-graduation. Haddy is a member of Llais Swansea University, Trustee for Cardiff Muslim School and also teaches spirituality to BME women. Haddy's interests are community involvement, building and supporting the Siffoe Orphanage in Gambia, Islamic integrated psychotherapy, social work, social justice and culturally sensitive practice.

Diane Seddon is Reader in Social Care at Bangor University. Diane has developed a successful programme of social care research with a particular focus on the experiences and support needs of older adults, people living with dementia and their unpaid carers. Diane is a member of the Welsh Government's Ministerial Advisory Group for Unpaid Carers.

Robin Sen is Lecturer in Social Work at the University of Edinburgh. Robin formerly practised as a child and family social worker in Glasgow. He has also worked as an academic in England. He is the author of *Effective Practice with Looked after Children* (2018) and has been co-editor of the journal *Practice: Social Work in Action* since 2020. Robin was also a member of the editorial collective behind SW2020/21 under *COVID-19* magazine.

Ian Thomas practised as a social worker, approved social worker and manager for 12 years before moving into education and training in South Wales. He chaired several national groups including the Post Qualifying Consortium for Wales before being appointed to the Care Council for Wales and Social Care Wales where he led on the regulation of social work training until he retired in 2019. He maintains an active interest in social work training in Wales.

Neil Thompson is an independent writer, educator and adviser and a Visiting Professor at the Open University. He is also a BASW Cymru ambassador. He is currently working with Vigrooom, a sophisticated employee wellness platform (www.vigroom.co.uk). His website, with his acclaimed Manifesto for Making a Difference, is at www.NeilThompson.info.

Gill Toms is Research and Practice Development Officer at Bangor University. Gill has an academic background in psychology and has worked on several applied research projects in fields including mental health and dementia. She is currently involved in research exploring short breaks for unpaid carers.

Sarah Vaile is Founder and Director of Recovery Cymru. Sarah has nearly 20 years' experience in the substance use sector and is a passionate champion of the peer movement and recovery community approach. A psychology graduate, she is also experienced in training and community development, with an interest in system and culture change and policy, having co-written the National Recovery Framework for Wales.

Fiona Verity is Professor in Social Work at Swansea University. Fiona has a practice background in community development. She has been active in community research in areas such as risk management and public liability insurance, community capacity building, community care and participatory evaluations.

Tim Versey is a social worker for Flintshire Local Authority. Tim has 15 years' experience working in the field of multiple exclusion homelessness. He has been an advocate for visible recovery and publicly raising awareness of the stigma and discrimination attached to addiction. He is at present a practising social worker with Flintshire Local Authority within the Substance Misuse team. His current (PhD) research is around the UK addiction recovery movement.

Sarah-Jane Waters is Chair of the Coproduction group at Cardiff University. Sarah-Jane is a great believer in looking beyond the immediate problem to understand what led to it. She has an interest in the involvement of people who will use a service or project from its conception, creation and delivery. She is from Rhiwbeina, Cardiff but spent many years in Derby and is currently between terriers.

David Wilkins is a Reader at Cardiff University. David is a qualified social worker, with practice experience primarily in the fields of disability and child protection. David was one of the first Principal Child and Family Social Workers appointed in England following the Munro review of child protection. David now works for Cardiff University, lecturing on the MA Social Work programme, and undertaking research in relation to professional supervision, good judgement and decision-making.

Sandra Williams is a founding member of Outside In at Glyndŵr University. Sandra has been involved in all types of play provision in north Wales since 1973. She retired as a play provider in 2012 but continues to be involved in community regeneration as a community councillor and as director of a community interest company that manages a building as an advice/information centre, community café and meeting place.

Tim Wynn is a long-standing member of Outside In at Glyndŵr University. During his time with the group, he has greatly enjoyed participating in many areas of the social work degree. Due to an acquired neurological condition, Tim's career in physiotherapy was curtailed. However, his involvement in the group has been invaluable in maintaining Tim's sense of well-being and worth. He first started writing poetry during the 2020 lockdown.

Foreword

Mark Drakeford

A quarter of a century into the devolution story, it is absolutely fitting to draw together a series of key themes and developments in one of the core, foundational responsibilities transferred to Wales in 1999.

In the run up to the first Assembly (as it was then) election, a book was published with the aim of setting an agenda across the range of policy areas to be taken up at the start of devolution. It included chapters on services for children, older people, mental health and learning disability: in short, some of the service areas which are reflected in this text.

As we look back, much has changed, but the ambition – for the state to take the leading role in the development and delivery of welfare services; for services to be produced collaboratively rather than in competition and as a partnership between workers and users, based on high levels of trust; for a shift to prevention rather than cure; for collaboration to be entrenched between local government and the health service; for the significance of the third sector to be properly recognised; for the linguistic and other diversities of Wales to be celebrated and promoted – remains remarkably intact.

For some, these continuities might amount to an argument that not enough has been achieved over the first two decades of devolved government. For me, they demonstrate, rather, the tenacity with which progressive principles have been sustained in bad times, as well as good, and the continuing relevance of these ambitions in contemporary Wales.

Of course, one of the lessons any new social work student has to learn is that good intentions, by themselves, are not good enough. Just because a worker sets out to help is not a guarantee, by itself, that help will result. The same is true for government. Principles are essential, but the hard work is to translate those underlying purposes into practical policy. Many of the chapters in this book weigh up that journey, and come to conclusions as to where success has been achieved, and where further ground remains to be gained. As a snapshot of what has been a huge amount of activity, inside and outside government, the book provides a really valuable milestone in our understanding of issues and services which remain essential in the lives of so many of our fellow citizens.

I want to end this brief Foreword by highlighting the work of new and emerging scholars in the field of social work studies and, as the book does, also the diverse voices of social workers, social work students and people who use services. One of the genuine strides of the devolution era, in its first two decades, has been the emergence of new voices and new perspectives in many of the responsibilities now discharged on a distinctive Welsh geography. Nowhere is that truer than in the study of social work, and that sense of freshness and innovative thinking is apparent throughout the volume. It should give us all confidence that the future of the profession and the discipline lies in strong and committed hands.

Preface

Sometimes it is difficult to pinpoint the exact moment an idea came to life. While some are considered lightbulb realisations, others are gestated over longer periods of time. The journey of this book has origins rather than any obvious single starting point. Perhaps the most overt of these is that all three of us, as editors, had often sat in meetings between Social Care Wales (the regulator for social work and social work education in Wales) and those Higher Education Institutes (universities teaching social work), where one of the regular conversations was about the need for resources that specifically captured the increasingly Welsh nature of social work practice. This distinct nature has accelerated since 2016 and the enactment of the Social Services and Well-being (Wales) Act 2014 (SSWWA). It was, however, already emerging through separate matters of culture, devolution, economics, language and legislative deviation.

One of the editors (Wulf) had been deliberating on these thoughts for some time, and during one such focused musing (Christmas 2020) he concluded that he would try to see if it was possible to get a Welsh dedicated social work book off the ground, and if not he would let the matter leave him and be for others to take up in due course. His mind set up, he chose to approach the other two editors (Abyd and Jo) to see if they were interested, and if they said no, again the idea for him would probably be laid to rest. They both instantly said yes. Still not 100 per cent convinced we had a 'goer', we then agreed to approach our first few thoughts for possible author contributors and gauge whether there was any wider appetite and support. They all instantly said yes too.

It is from these speculative origins and such positive responses, that the idea rapidly turned itself into a reality. A quick serendipitous conference bumping into Isobel Bainton (Commissioning Editor at Policy Press) confirmed some potential publisher interest. From here, we just snowballed. Every potential author we approached said yes, each with a belief in the need to tell the collective story, and to our pleasant surprise we ended up with a structure and abstracts that resonated well with the publisher's peer review process. From this point there was no turning back, and this huge wave of energy and positivity has meant here we are.

While working through the starting points, it became clear to us that we wanted to bring together a text with three core aims.

First, we knew quite early on that in capturing the formative journey of social work in Wales, we wanted an *edited volume* and not a textbook per se. This book had to and does tell of early passages of devolved practice rather than describing a finished scenario. We would argue, anyway, that social work is always evolving rather than has reached any conclusive definitive understanding of itself and those it works with. In encompassing the first decade of practice leading up to and following the SSWWA, we wanted to afford space to selected accounts of things that are important and could be told now, rather than any forced formulaic consideration across the lifespan or all client groups/services. The story to be told in the future will be different from this current one. We want this to be a text that offers something to help people think about their practice rather than being told how to practice.

Second, and critically, we wanted a text that captured a diversity of voices, and this in turn meant a diversity of styles and messages. In part we hope this text reflects the ambitions inherent in the SSWWA, of coproduction, inclusion and partnership. This edition, therefore, includes contributions from those identifying as people with lived experience, practitioners, students, researchers, and social work lecturers. It is deliberately a *collection* of perspectives.

Finally though, and given the starting points, the book had to be and aims to capture something that we have chosen to coin as 'the Welsh way'. It has an explicit understanding of how social work in Wales is developing its own way of being. Our journey as social workers, educators and writers has, in a way, been a mirror of the Welsh journey identified by the First Minster in his preface. In doing so, we have encouraged authors to consider some comparisons with international social work, and in particular the departures from England/UK, the previous and current areas of shared jurisprudence. This said, we have also been keen to produce a text and its content that also speaks to those beyond Offa's Dyke, and have kept a continual regard for the international social work practice and writing communities.

In delivering this aim we have set out a book in three distinct sections. The book's three structures are those of (i) broader contextual considerations, (ii) applied practice perspectives and (iii) emerging and critical conversations. The majority of the chapters have some common elements to provide the reader with some consistency in the navigation. However, within this framework are contributions that have deliberately retained very distinct voices and styles.

In Part I, the broad scene is set in terms of policy by Hefin Gwylim, law by Miriam Ennis and regulation by Ian Thomas. This is followed by an intriguing exploration of the often vexing Welsh Context by Gwenan Prysor, before Jo Redcliffe, Jaime Ortiz, Sarah-Jane Waters and Liz Lefroy explore the intersections of social work education and coproduction.

In being conscious of not providing an ABC of how to do social work and alongside whom, we have specifically curated, in Part II, a diverse range of applied practice examples. It begins with David Wilkins' reflections on child and family social work in Wales and Hayley Douglas and Helena Barlow's exploration of the Welsh joint children and adult approach to safeguarding. This is then followed by the reflections of Sarah Buckley, Graham Attenborough, Hope Lawrence, Tim Wynn, Jenny Burgess, Eluned Plack, Anna-Louise Edwards, Rhiana Povey and Sandra Williams on their own experiences of social work, education and involvement. We then have explorations of unpaid carers, youth justice, and alcohol and other drug recovery from Daniel Burrows, Jen Lyttleton-Smith, Tim Versey, Sarah Vaile, James Deakin, Wulf Livingston and Tegan Brierley-Sollis. The final particular practice example examines social care practice with older people and comes from another large collective of Penny Alexander, Diane Seddon, Katherine Algar-Skaife, Sarah Lord, Gill Toms and Kelly Barr.

Arriving at Part III, we wanted to give regard to the developing and ongoing nature of a number of critical challenges that reflect modern social work practice. While not unique to Wales, each of these considerations has, in turn, its own strong Welsh flavour in their messages for social work practice. These start with Thompson's application of a holistic approach to well-being. Two chapters than look at emerging issues for young people; Naomi Parry and Ceryl Davies' examination of transgender children and families, and Davies' research on young women's intimate relationships. It is unsurprising that our ongoing considerations also include those of racism by Jade Forbes and Abyd Quinn Aziz and migration by Tracey Maegusuku-Hewett, Haddy Sallah, Joanne Pye, Natacha Leao de Silva and Beth Pearl. And, given the emphasis in SSWWA on communities that we also include chapters about community development by Fiona Verity and the COVID-19 pandemic by Christian Kerr, Robin Sen, Gillian Macintyre and Abyd Quinn Aziz. It is fitting that the final chapter in this book comes from Rhoda Emlyn-Jones, in which she reflects how many of the previous chapters' messages are being translated into an emerging and specific Welsh way of doing social work practice.

We hope the reader will find this content informative and stimulating. We want the diversity of the considerations and narratives to resonate with the variety of social workers and social work practice within Wales. We recognise that this is a book of the here and now and that what it describes and aspires to can only be fully achieved over the years to come. By consequence it is likely it will be other contexts, practices and challenges that will need to be captured in future editions.

This book is not ours, we have merely been the curators of others' work and the recipients of huge amounts of generosity. We would like to say thanks to all those who have enabled the idea to come to fruition. I (Wulf) would like to thank Abyd and Jo for saying yes, coming along on the ride and helping an old man with one of his swansong ambitions. We cannot really express enough thanks to all the authors who have contributed. Their willingness to work with us, provide positive responses to editorial feedback and mindfulness of timelines have made our job so much easier. We have been, throughout this process, especially conscious of those for whom writing or publishing is not their everyday fare, many of whom have produced their fabulous contributions despite the intense difficulties and pressures of COVID-19, family life and work (case) load demands. Thank you. We would also like to say additional thanks to Ceryl Davies and Liz Lefroy for taking on a first-level editorial role in regard to Chapters 10 and 16. We have been superbly encouraged and supported by Policy Press and in particular Isobel Bainton in the early stages, and Jay Allan in the composing stage. There have been moments when getting the book over the line has been all consuming for three of us, and we would like to pay special thanks to our colleagues and families for their continued supporting and understanding during these moments.

Wulf Livingston, Jo Redcliffe and
Abyd Quinn Aziz

PART I

Context

Introduction

Eluned Plack, Wulf Livingston, Jo Redcliffe and Abyd Quinn Aziz

Our preface lays out how this book is a collection of voices, capturing diverse perspectives of personal and shared journeys. Imperative to this and the Welsh approach is the giving and hearing of all voices. We felt that, as an introduction, one of the best ways for us to reflect this flavour of the book and 'the Welsh way' was to begin with some words from Eluned about her picture, *The Quilt of Life*. Eluned's picture provides us with the image for the book's cover design and is presented in full in Figure 0.1.

In many ways we could or should have produced a bilingual text, as this is the demand and spirit of living and working in Wales and The Welsh Language Act 1993 and The Welsh Language (Wales) Measure 2011 (see Chapters 3 and 4). However, the practicalities of publishing page limitations, cost and the unwieldy nature of what would become such a large volume do not easily support such a consideration. We therefore invited Eluned to give voice to her picture and in doing so offer you a flavour of how the same message looks and feels in the two different languages. *(The side by side presentation, with Welsh on the left is the standard expectation.)* This book is accompanied by a set of additional resources: (i) further Welsh translations of some sections; (ii) supplementary resources for certain chapters; and (iii) recorded video interviews between the editors and some chapter authors. These can be found at https://policy.bristoluniversitypress.co.uk/social-work-in-wales/companion-website.

We hope you enjoy the journey of reading the book and hearing its many voices, *mwynhau* (Welsh for enjoy).

Figure 0.1 *The Quilt of Life*, Eluned Pack

Yn aml, pan fyddaf yn dechrau arni gyda fy mheintiadau, bydd fy hwyliau'n ymgolli yn y papur. Serch hynny, mae'r papur yn ogystal a'r arddull a'r strwythur dyluniad yn aros yr un fath – ond yr hyn sy'n allweddol yw bod y paentiad yn dangos newid, mae yna wahaniaeth ac mae hynny yn fy meddylfryd. Gofynnais y cwestiynau hyn i mi fy hun, "Pwy ydw i? Beth ydw i?" Pwy yw'r fi newydd?" Ar adegau, rwy'n teimlo fel Elton John yn dod i Marks and Spencer; mae pobl yn syllu, sibrwd, a gwrando'n astud ar fy sgyrsiau preifat. Profais drawsnewidiad poenus a gwelaf fod pobl yn rhyfeddu at y fi newydd hon mewn cadair olwyn drydan.

Mae *The Quilt of Life* yn cynrychioli cylch y tymhorau: dechreuodd y paentiad gyda siâp unigol ac yna amsugnwyd fy meddwl gan y pensil ac aeth ati i ddarlunio fy emosiynau. Coch yw lliw poen corfforol, ac mae hyn yn treiddio drwy'r paentiad, gan bortreadu pwysigrwydd y darlun a'r ymdeimlad corfforol sy'n gwefreiddio ac atgyfnerthu fy mhrofiadau. Mae bob darn yn cynrychioli agweddau o'm meddylfryd ac o fewn y broses o beintio rwyf yn archwilio ac yn ailddatgan fy hunaniaeth newidiol. Mae'n rhaid i mi beintio: fy diazepam i yw e, fy Yin a Yang – fy therapi. Rhai dyddiau, rwy'n parhau'n ddisymud mewn rhyw fath o swyngwsg ac mae'n ymdrech enfawr i mi allu symud. Mae'r symbol atomig yn y paentiad hwn yn tynnu ar yr ofn sydd gen i o'r perygl hollbresennol y bydd fy symudiadau'n creu ffrwydrad o boen, ac mae'r ysgolion yn mynd i fyny ac i lawr rhwng fy realiti o hunan-niweidio i dawelwch myfyriol fy adegau mwyaf creadigol.

Rwy'n cynnig y cyfle gwerthfawr i chi gael cipolwg ar fy mywyd fel ag y mae.

Often, when I start my paintings, my mood becomes immersed in the paper. However, the paper remains the same, and the style, and the design structure – but crucially this painting shows a shift, there is a difference and it's my mindset. I asked myself these questions, "Who am I? What am I? Who have I become?" Sometimes, I feel like Elton John arriving in Marks and Spencer; people stare, whisper, and listen intently to my private conversations. I have experienced a painful transformation and I find people are fascinated by this new me in an electric wheelchair.

The Quilt of Life represents the cycle of the seasons: the painting began with a single shape and then the pencil absorbed my mind and drew my emotions. Red is the colour of physical pain, and this permeates the painting, depicting the importance of the image and the physical sensation that electrifies and amplifies my experiences. Each segment represents aspects of my mindset and within the process of painting I am exploring and reaffirming my changing identity. I have to paint: it is my diazepam, my Yin and Yang – my therapy. Some days, I remain trance-like and immobile and it takes a huge effort to make a move. The atomic symbol in this painting draws on my fear of the ever-present danger of my movements causing an explosion of pain, and the ladders ascend and descend my reality of self-harming to the meditative calmness of my most creative moments.

The Quilt of Life represents the cycle
I am offering you the precious opportunity to look into my life as it is.

1

The social policy context for social work in Wales

Hefin Gwilym

Chapter objectives

- To delineate social policy developments since devolution in 1999.
- To look at key legislative and social policy developments.
- To address key policy changes for social work practice.

Introduction

This chapter is about the key devolutionary developments which have created a new social policy context in Wales since the establishment of the Senedd (then known as the Welsh Assembly) in 1999. It will summarise the key stages in the devolutionary process including the reasons why Wales voted for devolution in 1997 and the key developments that have happened since, including the gaining of legislative powers. Then it will focus on the importance of key policy developments and key legislation for social workers practising in Wales, including the Social Services and Well-being (Wales) Act 2014 and the Well-being and Future Generations (Wales) Act 2015. The context of social work practice in Wales has radically changed during the devolution era. Social workers near retirement today will recall a very different context when they started their careers many years ago. The newly qualified social worker, unlike their predecessor, practises within a legislative framework made in Wales to meet the needs of the people of Wales who need social services. The chapter will set these changes in the context of a Welsh political tradition that has fostered collectivism and a commitment to a statutory approach to social services in Wales.

Devolution process and the Welsh political tradition

Devolution in Wales has been described as a process rather than an event (see key quotes later in the chapter). The critical moment along that process was the referendum on the establishment of the Welsh Assembly in 1997 (Welsh Parliament, 2022). By a narrow victory and with a low turnout, the people of Wales voted for devolution. Up to that point Wales had been governed centrally by Westminster, often regarded as remote from Wales where Welsh issues were not appropriately addressed. The Welsh Office was established as part of the central state in the 1950s and the post of Secretary of State for Wales was created in 1964 (Davies, 2007). In the subsequent years, a series of politicians from both the Labour and Conservative parties occupied the post of Secretary of State for Wales with some of the Conservative postholders having their parliamentary constituencies in England. In 1979, there had been an unsuccessful attempt to establish a Welsh Assembly when the people of Wales overwhelmingly voted against the Wales Act 1978 which had been brought before the people of Wales at the rump end of the unpopular Labour Government of 1974–79. This begs the question why did the opinion of the people of Wales change by the time of the 1997 referendum? The referendum had been a manifesto commitment of the Labour Government led by Tony Blair, elected to power in 1997. The answer to this question lies in the modern history of Wales and, in particular, to the effects the Conservative Governments of 1979–97, led by Margaret Thatcher and John Major, had on Welsh society and economy. These were the years of mine closures, deindustrialisation and unemployment in Wales. Communities experienced economic decline as traditional industries closed, scarring what once had been thriving working-class communities (Day, 2010). This period exposed the vulnerability of Welsh society and economy and the realisation that Wales lacked political powers to defend itself from policies that most of the people of Wales had not voted for.

Wales has a rich political heritage encompassing radicalism and innovation (see key quotes). Before devolution, Lloyd George introduced the first state pension paid to the over seventies in 1908. A year later he delivered the People's Budget which raised taxes to tackle poverty and squalor. Aneurin Bevan was inspired by the Tredegar Workmen's Medical Aid Society on which he based the National Health Service which he founded in 1948. Welsh social radicalism has many roots, not least the influence of its nonconformist chapels which were more influential than Marxism in the Welsh coalfields (Greenleaf, 1983). Wales is widely regarded as being a nation of strong communities influenced by nonconformity and socialist politics.

The Welsh way

Wales has had a radical political tradition with emphasis on social issues and tackling economic disadvantages and inequalities.

Decade after decade the Welsh people have consistently voted in more Labour MPs than any other party. Indeed, in the post-devolution era, the Labour Party has led every government in the Senedd since its creation. It has had to share power in a coalition government on only two occasions. There are many pros and cons to this degree of consistency in the governance of Wales. The chief advantage is consistency in policy direction without the pendulum swings that happen at Westminster. The disadvantage is the danger of a government becoming stale and the wider issue of one-party rule in Wales. However, the Welsh Labour Party has shown remarkable skill in acquiring and maintaining autonomy from the UK Labour Party and in developing a clear Welsh identity. Indeed, the Welsh Labour Party has justifiable reasons for defining itself as the party of Wales because of its broad appeal. Indeed, according to one survey 50 per cent of supporters of Welsh independence vote Welsh Labour.

The significance of the process of devolution started in 1999 and the heritage of the Welsh political tradition for social work is that Wales has retained a social work profession within the public sector (see key quotes). This state collectivist approach is in stark contrast to England where the social work profession has experienced far greater privatisation. Most social workers in Wales continue to work for a local authority. According to the Care Council for Wales in 2016, 76 per cent worked in the public sector (Care Council for Wales, 2016). In contrast, according to Social Work England, of the social workers on their register, 48.5 per cent were employed by a local authority in England in 2021. Since 1999, a body of Welsh policy and legislation for social services has built up creating a distinct Welsh approach to social problems. Social work in Wales has navigated these policy and legislative changes in the post-devolution era by being reconstructed in the image of a Welsh social work.

The Welsh way

Social work in Wales is largely a state sector activity, reflecting the continued commitment in Wales to public sector provision.

The passing of the Wales Act 2006 enabled the Welsh Assembly to seek powers from the UK Government to pass laws in Wales for the first time in modern history. These powers were enhanced after another referendum in 2011 allowing Wales to draft laws in devolved areas without having to seek the permission of the UK Government. The referendum approved the granting of full legislative powers for Wales with 63.5 per cent of those voting doing so in favour but with a very low turnout of just 35 per cent of the Welsh electorate. Another Wales Act was passed in 2014 giving Wales tax-raising powers in some areas, including the power to vary income tax in Wales by ten pence in every pound, a power that has not yet been used but might be used in the future to help tackle Wales' chronic problems with poverty. The most recent constitutional change in Wales has been the Senedd and Elections (Wales) Act 2020 changing the name of the Assembly to Senedd or Welsh Parliament and lowering the voting age for the Senedd and local government elections in Wales to 16. These constitutional changes have enabled Wales to legislate in social policy areas and thus create a legislative framework for social work practice in Wales. The next two sections of this chapter will explore some of these key legislative and social policy areas.

Key quotes from the devolution era

'Devolution is a process. It is not an event and neither is it a journey with a fixed end-point. The devolution process is enabling us to make our own decisions and set our own priorities, that is the important point. We test our constitution with experience and we do that in a pragmatic and not an ideologically driven way.' (Rt Hon Ron Davies, 1988, Secretary of State for Wales)

'I want now to turn to my second main theme, the social policy achievements of the Welsh Assembly Government and, in particular, the principles which have grounded our actions in this field. In doing so, I will wish to say a little more about the issue of distinctiveness, the so-called "clear red water", as the Guardian inevitably put it and which has emerged over the lifetime of my administration between the way in which things are being shaped in Wales and the direction being followed at Westminster for equivalent services. There are always going to be those ideological fault-lines in the approaches to social welfare in post-war social policy in Britain – universalism against means-testing and the pursuit of equity against pursuit of consumer choice.' (Rt Hon Rhodri Morgan, 2002, First Minister of Wales)

'As someone who has been lucky enough to play a part in every Welsh Government, I believe that the strongest thread in social policy making has been the strength of the great Welsh radical tradition: a belief in the power of government to craft solutions which reach deepest into the lives who need that help the most.' (Rt Hon Mark Drakeford, 2021, First Minister of Wales)

Welsh social policy development

With the Welsh Assembly attaining more powers, particularly legislative powers, there was a period of contemplation regarding the provision of social services in Wales. In 2007 the Welsh Government produced a new strategy for social services called *Fulfilled Lives, Supportive Communities: A Strategy for Social Services in Wales Over the Next Decade*. The strategy set a path towards modernising social services in Wales and reflected a similar process that was going on in England. There would be a new emphasis on partnerships and collaboration between agencies. Consistency in standards would be fostered across Wales and services would be sustainable and cost effective. The strategy recognised the increasing ageing population in Wales and the requirement for social services to do more with the same or even less resources. Commissioning and the remodelling of services based on partnerships between the statutory, voluntary and private sectors was seen as the best approach and this would generate greater efficiency and better value for money.

The Welsh way

Welsh social policy emphasises partnership, collaboration and sustainability.

In a more austere financial climate following the credit crunch crisis of 2008 and the start of an era of austerity, the Welsh Assembly Government established the Independent Commission on Social Services in Wales to address how to deliver social services in a new era which reported in 2010. In its report *From Vision to Action* the Commission acknowledge the bleak outlook for public spending and the need for increased efficiency. The report supported the goals of *Fulfilled Lives, Supportive Communities*, but wanted to see an acceleration of the modernisation process with planning, commissioning and collaboration enhanced. Private and voluntary providers would be more involved in planning, designing and commissioning of services, demonstrating a steer towards the direction of privatisation.

The pre-legislative White Paper called *Sustainable Social Services for Wales: A Framework for Action* brought together the recommendations of these reports and other reports on the social care workforce and safeguarding in one document in 2011. The context remained the same – ambitious plans in an economically difficult time. Thus, the theme of modernisation was ever present, with aims to do more for less with collaborative and partnership working in an integrated care service being the main vehicle for progress. This against a background of an ageing society, diverse types of families, and increasing demands on social services. The choice was viewed as between retrenchment and renewal or between carrying on as before and going backwards or modernising through collaboration and innovation. There would be more regional level collaboration and commissioning and joined up services to offset the unfortunate position of having 22 local authorities across Wales often duplicating their tasks at wasteful costs. The White Paper set the scene for Welsh legislation in social care which is the subject of the next section of this chapter.

At the time of writing, the UK Government has announced plans for dealing with what has become known as the social care crisis of providing decent and dignified care in old age at affordable costs to both the state and the individual. The principal report in this area is the Dilnot Report in England (2011) which recommended that no one should pay more than £35,000 for care across their lifetime and that assets up to £100,000 could be protected. This would provide security in old age against the loss of savings and the loss of one's house to pay for social care costs such as residential care. The proposals put forward at the time of writing are far less generous than Dilnot, with assets protected up to £86,000 in England. The proposals were always going to be means tested and the lack of universality has caused division, with savers and life-long earners feeling disadvantaged compared to what they perceive as those who have not saved for a rainy day. However, the issue has been addressed after years of procrastination and the principle of paying for social care through an extension of income tax has been confirmed.

Other key Welsh social policy initiatives include Designed for Life (2005), the Welsh Assembly Government document setting out a ten-year strategy for improving health and social services in Wales. The emphasis was on rebalancing of services towards the community and shaped around service users. Making the Connections: Delivering Beyond Boundaries (2006), is the Welsh Assembly Government response to a review of public services in Wales by Sir Jeremy Beecham in 2006. The report sets out to transform public services in Wales through greater efficiencies, training, partnership, and performance improvements with the citizen at the centre. Strategy for Older People 2013–23 (2013), is a strategy to meet the needs of older people for family and community life, and to influence decisions. The strategy restates the principle of well-being as a sense of purpose and control over individuals' lives. Strategy for Unpaid Carers, what we will do to improve the recognition of and support of unpaid carers (2021), addresses the need for renewing recognition and support for unpaid carers. It supports carers' rights, including the right to an assessment.

Key Welsh legislation

The legislative framework for social work practice in Wales is defined by two major pieces of Welsh legislation, these are the Social Services and Well-being (Wales) Act 2014 and the Well-being of Future Generations (Wales) Act 2015, as previously mentioned. Both acts together encompass and promote the social policy values and principles of Welsh Government which are broadly defined as collectivist and social democratic with a commitment to a positive role for the state and public sector. The Social Services and Well-being (Wales) Act 2014 sets out the functions of local social services departments in Wales and the governance role of Welsh Government ministers. The Act applies to both adults and children and is the principal legislation in Wales for safeguarding and looked after children. It sets out the duty to assess and the principle of promoting well-being is defined in the Act as healthy personal development, security of family life and accommodation, access to education and training and the right to contribute to society (see Table 1.1). The values of the Act are reflected in its commitment to support partnership working and individual rights. However, the Act makes no attempt to reverse elements of privatisation introduced before devolution, including direct payments and the duty to carry out a financial assessment and charge for services.

Table 1.1 Social Services and Well-being (Wales) Act 2014, Part 1: Introduction, key terms

---

Meaning of 'well-being'
(1) This section applies for the purpose of this Act.
(2) 'Well-being', in relation to a person, means well-being in relation to any of the following
    (a) physical and mental health and emotional well-being;
    (b) protection from abuse and neglect;
    (c) education, training and recreation;
    (d) domestic, family and personal relationships;
    (e) contribution made to society;
    (f) securing rights and entitlements;
    (g) social and economic well-being;
    (h) suitability of living accommodation.
(3) In relation to a child, 'well-being' also includes
    (a) physical, intellectual, emotional, social and behavioural development;
    (b) 'welfare' as that word is interpreted for the purposes of the Children Act 1989.
(4) In relation to an adult, 'well-being' also includes
    (a) control over day-to-day life;
    (b) participation in work.

Table 1.2 Well-being of Future Generations (Wales) Act 2015, Part 2

The well-being goals	
A prosperous Wales	An innovative, productive, and low carbon society which recognises the limits of the global environment and therefore uses resources efficiently and proportionately (including acting on climate change); and which develops a skilled and well-educated population in an economy which generates wealth and provides employment opportunities, allowing people to take advantage of the wealth generated through securing decent work.
A resilient Wales	A nation which maintains and enhances a biodiverse natural environment with healthy functioning ecosystems that support social, economic, and ecological resilience and the capacity to adapt to change (for example climate change).
A healthier Wales	A society in which people's physical and mental well-being is maximised and in which choices and behaviours that benefit future health are understood.
A more equal Wales	A society that enables people to fulfil their potential no matter what their background or circumstances (including their socioeconomic background and circumstances).
A Wales of cohesive communities	Attractive, viable, safe, and well-connected communities.
A Wales of vibrant culture and thriving Welsh language	A society that promotes and protects culture, heritage and the Welsh language, and which encourages people to participate in the arts, and sports and recreation.
A globally responsible Wales	A nation which, when doing anything to improve the economic, social, environmental, and cultural well-being of Wales, takes account of whether doing such a thing may make a positive contribution to global well-being.

Table 1.3 Other key Welsh (social policy) legislation

Children's Commissioner for Wales Act 2001	Established by the Care Standards Act 2000, this Act amends the 2000 Act and defines the purpose and remit of the Commissioner's role in promoting children's rights in Wales.
Commissioner for Older People (Wales) Act 2006	To promote and safeguard the interest of older people in Wales including challenging discrimination and endorse best practice.
Children and Families (Wales) Measure 2010	Established the Integrated Family Support Teams. It had ambitious plans to eradicate child poverty in Wales by 2020. Other areas covered in the measure include day care and participation in local authority decision making.
Housing (Wales) Measure 2011	Suspension of right to buy in Wales.
Rights of Children and Young Persons (Wales) Measure 2011	Made it a duty for social workers to have due regard for the United Nations (UN) Convention on the Rights of the Child. The measure placed Wales at the forefront of children's rights.
Human Transplantation Act 2013	Introduced the concept of assumed consent in organ transplantation to address the chronic shortage of donated organs in Wales.
Housing (Wales) Act 2014	Major legislation addressing homelessness and homelessness prevention in Wales.
Regulation and Inspection of Social Care (Wales) Act 2016	Established Care Wales as a powerful institution to regulate social care in Wales, replacing the Care Council for Wales, the Social Services Improvement Agency and Social Care Wales.
The Public Health (Minimum Pricing of Alcohol) (Wales) Act 2018	Introduced a minimum price for a unit of alcohol in Wales to address cheap prices for alcohol in supermarkets. There was concern about harmful drinking and strong low-cost alcohol products.
Abolition of the Right to Buy and Associated Rights (Wales) 2018	To preserve Wales' social housing stock and help address the problem of chronic homelessness in Wales.

The Well-being of Future Generations (Wales) Act 2015 is widely admired as an innovative and forward-looking piece of legislation. It incorporates the principle of sustainable development and establishes the post of the Future Generations Commissioner for Wales. The Act sets out well-being goals for Wales which are a prosperous, resilient, healthier, more equal Wales, with cohesive communities, a vibrant culture and globally responsible (see Table 1.2). The Act defines the sustainable development principle as a duty on public bodies to act in a manner that does not compromise the interest of future generations by meeting the needs of the present generation. Both these pieces of legislation can be viewed as legislative frameworks which set out the legislative and professional setting in which professional social work is practised in Wales.

Table 1.3 sets out other Welsh legislation important to the field of Welsh social work.

Key challenges

The legislative and policy developments post-devolution can be contextualised as a response to some of the most entrenched and long-lasting social and economic problems that Wales faces. The Welsh economy consistently underperforms compared to the wider UK economy and the economies of the other nations within the UK as well as most regions of England. Production levels in Wales are well below the UK levels of wealth creation. For every hour worked, Wales produces on average 4.4 per cent less than all other parts of the UK except for Northern Ireland which performed 9.6 per cent less than the UK average (Office for National Statistics, 2019). Wales has too few medium sized industries and is too dependent on small businesses. Like other parts of the UK there is a high dependence on low-pay and seasonal employment. The landscape of traditional industries has been replaced by the precarity of low paid work in supermarkets and call centres. The effects of post-industrialisation have marred Welsh society, including chronic ill health. The economic problems are not helped by poor transport infrastructure with inadequate trunk roads and poor railway links.

The Welsh way

Wales takes a collectivist and public sector approach to tackling long-standing problems of poverty and disadvantage which every social worker will encounter.

Wales has a chronic problem with poverty and one that appears to be intractable, having remained at the same level for a generation despite flagship policies to address it, including the shelved Communities First initiative. Relative poverty is defined as living below 60 per cent of the median household income, or below the poverty line. In Wales, 23 per cent of the population are in this sorry position. In comparison the figure for England is 22 per cent and for Scotland it is 19 per cent and Northern Ireland it is 18 per cent. Significantly, 22 per cent of working adults in Wales are living in poverty, reflecting the high level of in-work poverty due to low pay. Children living in these poor households account for 31 per cent of children living in poverty in Wales. At the time of writing, the Welsh economy is dealing with the economic shock of Brexit and the effects of the COVID-19 pandemic and lockdowns and, for this reason, the number of people and children in poverty will increase for the foreseeable future. In comparison in England the portion of children living in poverty is 30 per cent; in Scotland and Northern Ireland it is 24 per cent. Poverty is not only about data but is the lived experience of these adults and children. It is always accompanied by poor housing, lower educational attainment, increased illnesses and a shorter life span. There is psychosocial stress and often stigma about using food banks – the use of which has increased enormously during the lockdowns (Beck and Gwilym,

2021). Outside the city urban areas in the south there are very real problems of rural poverty, including deep rural poverty in isolated parts of Powys where running a car is essential because of poor public transport. But there is cause for optimism about the scourge of pensioner poverty in Wales. In recent times this has been reducing because of UK-wide government initiatives to help pensioners, including the triple-lock. The level of pensioner poverty in Wales has decreased to 18 per cent because of these measures and others.

The era of austerity started following the credit crunch crisis of 2008 when the world economy went into free fall following irresponsible subprime mortgages particularly in the United States and, significantly, the inability of ordinary people to pay them back. It led to the collapse of banks and the saving of others by the state including the Royal Bank of Scotland which was nationalised and Lloyds Bank which was rescued by massive state bailouts. In 2012 the UK Government passed the Welfare Reform Act which is the centrepiece legislation of the austerity era. It introduced the Universal Credit (UC) and Personal Independence Payment (PIP), replacing legacy benefits and tax credits for people of working age including replacing Disability Living Allowance. The Act set out to simplify the benefit system and make it easier for people to move from welfare to work. However, it also introduced a benefit cap and restricted housing benefit in what became known as the 'bedroom tax'. The overall effect of austerity has been to increase poverty and social insecurity among people of working age so that the national deficit can be reduced and a return to a balanced budget can be achieved by the mid-2020s. According to the House of Commons Library (2021), the reduction in the generosity of the social security system resulted in savings of £26 billion UK-wide between 2010 and 2016/17, 10 per cent of what the spending would have been with no cuts. The biggest savings occurred because of measures taken by the government to make working age benefits considerably less generous. Social security remains the policy prerogative of the UK Government, limiting the ability of the Welsh Government to address problems of economic decay and poverty.

Messages for practice

- Social workers practising in Wales need to be aware of the social policy framework and social policy legislation which has been created since the establishment of the Welsh Senedd (previously Welsh Assembly) in 1999.
- The landscape is radically different from England, with made in Wales policy and legislation informed by a social collectivist approach within the public sector for the delivery of social work services. In Wales the values of partnership and collaboration are important within a context of sustainability and the well-being of future generations.
- At the time of writing, the Welsh Government is working towards a National Care Service, free at the point of need. Although there are limitations to the

powers of the Welsh Senedd, particularly in tackling poverty and in the legal field, it is noted that devolution is a process and not an event and more powers are sure to follow and the Welsh approach to social work advanced further in the future. There is for example, pressure to devolve the criminal justice system and the social security system to Wales which would increase the powers of the Senedd. Another Scottish independence referendum would be watched closely and could strengthen the resurgent independence movement in Wales. There is then the potential for an ever-increasing social work practice that is distinctively Welsh.

Conclusion

Wales has changed greatly because of the developments brought about by devolution since 1999. It can legislate and develop its own Welsh social policy. It has income tax-raising powers which, so far, the Welsh Government has chosen not to use. The developments have not changed its commitment to a collectivist approach to social policy with a central role for the state and public services. Although it has sought to modernise in difficult economic times, unlike England it has largely not pursued privatisation of public services. The legislation and policies in place are long term and are designed to deal with the challenges facing Wales in the future. They aim to build a better and sustainable Wales. But the challenges remain great and will require both vision and determination to overcome. The social work profession will practise in a very uncertain socioeconomic environment for the foreseeable future because of a perfect storm formed by the uncertainty about Brexit, the economic effects of COVID and lockdowns, the increasing cost and demands of social care, and the intractable problem of poverty in Wales. Social work will have a very important role to play in supporting people and communities through these difficult times and in building a better Wales for future generations.

Further resources
1. Davies, J. (2007) *A History of Wales*, London: Penguin.
2. Day, G. (2010) *Making Sense of Wales: A Sociological Perspective*, Cardiff: University of Wales Press.
3. Gwilym, H. and Williams, C. (2021) *Social Policy for Welfare Practice in Wales*, Birmingham: British Association of Social Workers.

References
Beck, D. and Gwilym, H. (2021) 'The food bank: a safety-net in place of welfare security in times of austerity and the Covid-19 crisis', *Social Policy and Society*, Online First, 1–17.

Care Council for Wales (2016) *The Profile of Social Workers in Wales 2016: A Report from the Care Council for Wales Register of Social Care Workers*. Cardiff: Care Council for Wales.

Davies, J. (2007) *A History of Wales*, London: Penguin.

Davies, Ron (1998) 'Devolution: a process not an event'. Address to the Institute of Welsh Affairs Gregynog Seminar, p 15.

Day, G. (2010) *Making Sense of Wales: A Sociological Perspective*, Cardiff: University of Wales Press.

Drakeford, Mark (2021) 'Foreword', in H. Gwilym and C. Williams (eds), *Social Policy for Welfare Practice in Wales*. Birmingham: BASW.

Greenleaf, W.H. (1983) *The British Political Tradition, Vol. 1: The Rise of Collectivism*, London: Methuen.

House of Commons Library (2021) 'Welfare Savings 2010–11 to 2020–21'. Briefing Paper, Number CBP 7667, 26 July 2016.

Morgan, Rhodri (2002) 'Clear Red Water'. Speech to National Centre for Public Policy Swansea. https://www.sochealth.co.uk/the-socialist-health-association/sha-country-and-branch-organisation/sha-wales/clear-red-water/

Office for National Statistics (2019) 'Regional labour productivity, including industry by region, regional output per hour and output per job, and an experimental analysis of the performance of output per hour levels and growth by industry and region UK:2019'. Office for National Statistics.

Welsh Parliament (2022) 'History of devolution'. https://senedd.wales/how-we-work/history-of-devolution/)

2

A rights-based approach: the new social work legislation in Wales

Miriam Ennis

Chapter objectives

- To outline the rights-based concept design within Welsh law.
- To identify the language and philosophy of the law, and its impact.
- To evaluate narratives drawn from people.
- To consider an intersectional approach to the law, and the implementation gap.

Introduction

A rights-based narrative within the legislation of the past decade has defined the road map to legal and practice changes in Wales. When we survey the language and the intended outcomes of the legislation, there are some shared themes, which collectively, provide a consistent and justifiable narrative. Until 2020, the Welsh Government's focus has been to legislate according to the rights-based approach. This provides welcome codes and regulations, and a workable reference grid for both the student social worker and the seasoned practitioner. However, the Coronavirus (Wales) Act 2020 distorted the road map for the practitioner and, along with the wider impact of the pandemic, has served to undermine and derail the confidence, trust and rights of the population. The positivist language within the pre-existing legislation has the potential to transform practice; nevertheless, we have seen that narrative and discourse in themselves are not enough to protect and promote a citizen's well-being. It rests with the social worker to map out coordinates to their practice and choose a sustainable approach.

   This chapter will seek to explain how student social workers and qualified practitioners may develop their understanding and application of the legal framework; to improve their traction to the road and the efficiency of their model design. To bridge the divide between the intention of the law and the person's lived experience of care and support, attention will be given to some of the structures and approaches, which best protect and actualise the rights of people in Wales. This chapter will draw on the themes shared by the Social Services and Well-being (Wales) Act (SSWWA) 2014, the Well-being of Future Generations (Wales) Act (WFGWA) 2015, the Data Protection Act 2018, the Human Rights

Act 1998, the Equality Act 2010, the Welsh Language Measure 2011, the Mental Health Act 1987/2007, the Mental Health Wales Measure 2010, and the Mental Capacity Act 2005 and their detailed Codes.

The Welsh way: minding the gap

The Welsh Government has ambitious intentions in relation to equality and human rights and is committed to embedding UN conventions and treaties throughout its devolved legislation. These reflect both the Welsh Government's own political agenda and the values held by Welsh society. Welsh law is characterised by this rights-based conceptual design, and this design seeks to reconcile a rights-based narrative within the legal framework, and the lived experience of people requiring care and support. The law's language and philosophy assist our understanding and evaluation of the law's conceptual design and its efficacy.

The Welsh way is journeying towards this reconciliation, and the rights-based conceptual design has yet to gain traction. There remains an implementation gap or misalignment between the intention of the law and that which is realised, in practice. The Welsh way requires organisations to realign agile processes and tailor care and support services to these conceptual frameworks and well-being goals. This reconciliation may be considered as 'minding the implementation gap' and requires the social worker in Wales to consider their role in reconciling the law and practice outcomes, and to adopt a rights-based, intersectional approach and method, that is responsive to the powerful, contextual, intersecting inequalities and disadvantages impacting people in Wales.

Making sense of the current rights-based narratives

The Government of Wales Act 2006 requires the Welsh Government to improve the social, economic and environmental well-being of Wales, and to act in a way that is compatible with Human Rights Conventions (1998). The Welsh Government is also required to comply with the Equality Act 2010 in relation to its duties under section 149, and give due regard to the prevention of discrimination, harassment and victimisation of its population. The Welsh Government has carved out a distinct Welsh identity to its legal framework and has made a particular commitment to promoting and protecting the human rights and equal treatment of people in Wales. However, there remains some confusion concerning the relationship between human rights and equality, and how they scaffold well-being and there is a need to progress our understanding and use of these concepts, in practice (Equality and Human Rights Commission (EHRC), 2020, 2021a, 2021b; Future Generations Commissioner for Wales (FGCW), 2021; Children's Commissioner for Wales, 2021a, 2021b; Hoffman et al, 2021; Older People's Commissioner for Wales, 2021).

Given that the SSWWA 2014 is concerned with the lives of individuals, families and carers, and the Well-being of Future Generations (Wales) Act 2015 extends this commitment to individuals, groups and communities, there exists an individual, local and national concurrent interpretation of human rights and equality in Wales. Before the arrival of COVID-19, the population of Wales had long been voicing its concern over the diversity in practice outcomes. Despite the government's limited autonomy, the White Paper *Sustainable Social Services for Wales: A Framework for Action* (Welsh Government, 2011), and later the Parliamentary Review of Health and Social Care in Wales (Hussey et al, 2018) outlined the same strategic aims for Wales and provided an authentic narrative proposing to improve the well-being of people in Wales (Welsh Government, 2018; Hussey et al, 2018). Given its historic backdrop, it is not surprising that the SSWWA 2014 detailed a progressive commitment to securing well-being, with the Codes attached to the Act providing more guidance to the social worker on processes, principles and outcomes, under section 145. Both the WFGWA 2015, the SSWWA 2014 and its Codes of Practice, dovetail with the Mental Capacity Act 2005 Code of Practice (2013) and the Mental Health 1983 Code of Practice for Wales Review (2016) as they each advocate a coproductive model of engagement with people and share similar principles and concepts.

The Equality Act 2010 (Statutory duties) (Wales) Regulations 2011 outlines the rights of people who have protected characteristics under the Equality Act (2010), and the social worker's responsibilities to challenge direct and indirect discrimination, victimisation and harassment, with socioeconomic inequality being one of the most prominent obstacles to a person's equal treatment (FGCW, 2021). The EHRC's reports 'Is Britain Fairer?' (2018b) and 'Is Wales Fairer?' (2018a), make plain the disconnect between the human rights framework and people's lived experiences. The EHRC has recommended that the Welsh Government undertake a review of the equality agenda in Wales (EHRC, 2018a). The research provides a cross-population assessment of inequality and human rights issues, and outlines the progress made in each of its six domains (EHRC, 2018a), and the Commission has since progressed its research, with particular attention to the centrality of rights and equality in social care processes, standards, objectives and well-being indicators (EHRC, 2020b, 2021). The Welsh Government also commissioned a report into gender equality (Chwarae Teg, 2020) and later issued their Health and Social Care Strategy (2020), which broadened the scope of 'A Healthier Wales' (Welsh Government, 2021a), to achieve better outcomes. These along with the significant impact of Brexit and the pandemic, have continued to influence the design and construction of the anticipated human rights changes in Wales, with the government pledging to strengthen its commitment still further.

Some of the most significant sources which detail the disparity between the intentions of the legislation and the co-existing structural inequalities and oppressions in people's lives, have been the 'Measuring the Mountain' review report (Welsh Government, 2019), the FGCW's report (2020), Race Council

Cymru's report (2016) and EHRC research reports (2018a, 2018b, 2021), as well as the Welsh Government's commissioned works in relation to human rights (Hoffman et al, 2021; Welsh Government, 2021a, 2021b). Such reports are the equivalent to the telemetry of a Formula One car, and outline what changes are required to realise the human rights design, to realign practice and the legislation with the lived experience of people. A disconnect between indicators of measurement and the outcomes for people has long been established (Wallace, 2019) and even though the Welsh Government has chosen a unique approach to embedding human rights into its distinctive legislation, we have yet to see whether it will bridge 'the divide between policy and practice' (Miles, 2018), and progress beyond its conceptual design.

A further evaluation of the SSWWA 2014 was commissioned by the Welsh Government (Welsh Government, 2020a), and although some improvements had been observed, the findings identified key shortfalls such as the financial constraints and the unmet needs of the ageing population, the growing responsibilities and reliance on unpaid carers and the rising numbers of looked after children. Despite the Welsh Government increasing its funding to the Health and Social Care sector, there is a greater need to secure the sustainability of the provision and improve the consistency and uniformity of the commissioning practices and stabilise the workforce (FGCW, 2021). A further evaluation of the SSWWA 2014 (Hoffman et al, 2021), found that there exists some confusion concerning the meaning and interpretation of the concepts that characterise the SSWWA 2014 and WFGWA 2015, resulting in a delay in policy development, planning and service delivery. Each local authority's interpretation and implementation of the Acts is different across Wales and is in flux, and while this short-term, localised approach to embedding concepts in practice may produce more scope for creative practices, it also provides room for inconsistency and inequality (Hoffman et al, 2021).

The evaluations' narratives speak of the efforts being made to understand concepts, and how they can be translated to policy, commissioning and service delivery frameworks, and the difficulty in aligning processes, resources and ideologies. The concepts embodying the devolved legislation do not conform to the old Welsh ways, and this may be contributing to the inconsistency in how the Act is being outworked (FGCW, 2021). If social work practice is to be organic, it could be argued that inconsistent outcomes are inevitable, however there needs to be some consensus around the meaning of concepts, equality, rights, and well-being, and how they can be actualised (Al Faham et al, 2019; FGCW, 2021; Hoffman et al, 2021).

One of the fundamental issues with a positivist legislation built on a conceptual framework, is that it relies on the population's congruent understanding of the laws' principles and language. The lack of understanding expressed by decision makers, along with the population's voiced experiences suggests that this pervasive lack of understanding continues to dictate the speed and efficacy of change (Coyle, 2013; Hoffman et al, 2021). Guidance has been produced by the Children's Commissioner for Wales, the Older People's Commissioner for Wales, and the FGCW, in order to clarify meanings, in an attempt to conform local authority functions to the purpose of the legislation (Zifcack, 2009). The engagement of people in the impact assessment process and the evaluation of the legislation will enable more scrutiny of personal experiences and assessed needs, as well as the development of sustainable structures in data gathering, policy development, commissioning and allocation of resources (FGCW, 2021; EHRC, 2021).

Since March 2021, the Welsh Government has enacted the socioeconomic duty of Part 1 Section 1 of the Equality Act (2010), which will be used to set sustainable standards for the government and public bodies. This will require a genuine consideration of people's context, and an extended intersectional lens of discrimination, harassment and privilege (Banks et al, 2013; EHRC, 2018b, 2020b). This builds on the objectives of the SSWWA 2014, which has incorporated a more prominent development of children's rights, with ethnic groups being identified as requiring greater consideration and advocacy, and carers, survivors of domestic abuse, Gypsies, Roma and Travellers, refugees and asylum seekers, and people with disabilities requiring greater support, to advance equality and human rights in Wales (Hoffman et al, 2021).

One of the most common findings of the evaluation of the SSWWA 2014, WFGWA 2015, Human Rights Act 1993 and Equality Act 2010 are that there is an 'implementation gap' between language of the law and the lived experience of people (Children's Commissioner for Wales, 2021b; FGCW, 2021; Older People's Commissioner for Wales, 2021). The EHRC have consistently highlighted the need for increased resources to tackle inequality and protect human rights (EHRC, 2018a, 2018b). These inequalities have since been compounded and entrenched by austerity and socioeconomic conditions, and more recently, the pandemic (Audit Wales, 2020; Welsh Parliament Equality, Local Government and Communities Committee (WPELGCC), 2020). De-structuring the oppression, discrimination and disadvantage of people on a national scale, requires a greater provision of targeted and sustainable resources (EHRC, 2020b).

The narratives have been summarised in Table 2.1.

Minding the gap: understanding the law's philosophy and language

A positivist approach to the law considers that the law is core to society's function, without which the fabric of society would somehow unravel. Yet, it is this positivist stance that has created unease and dissatisfaction among the population, as the idealistic concepts have failed to gain traction (EHRC, 2021). An organisation's engagement with these concepts often creates its own phenomena; a hierarchy of prioritisation which often differs from the interpretation of the person. It rests therefore, for organisations to consistently and coproductively agree and apply concepts such as well-being, voice and control, to sustain its moral code (FGCW, 2021; Hoffman et al, 2021).

Table 2.1 Core legislation, and their themes

Social Services and Well-being (Wales) Act 2014	Well-being of Future Generations (Wales) Act 2015	Equality Act 2010	Human Rights Act 1998 (Convention Rights)	Data Protection Act 2018 and GDPR 2018	Welsh Language Measure 2011	Code of Professional Practice for Social Workers (SCW 2017)
Voice and control	A healthier Wales (well-being goal)	Protected characteristics: age; disability; gender reassignment; pregnancy and maternity; race; religion or belief; sex; sexual orientation	Article 2: Right to life Article 3: Freedom from torture Article 4: Freedom from slavery and forced labour Article 5: Right to liberty and security Article 6: Right to a fair trial	Lawfulness, fairness and transparency Purpose limitation	Standards in relation to: Service delivery; Policy making; Operational; Promotion; Record keeping; Promote and facilitate the Welsh language: the official status of the Welsh language in Wales	1. Respect the views and wishes, and promote the rights and interests of individuals and carers. 2. Strive to establish and maintain the trust and confidence of individuals and carers.
Prevention and early intervention	A prosperous Wales (well-being goal)					
Coproduction	A more equal Wales (well-being goal)	Responsibility to protect against direct discrimination, create inclusive culture, respond to or make complaints, training, make reasonable adjustments	Article 7: No punishment without law Article 8: Respect for your private and family life	Protecting privacy	The duty to use the Welsh and the rights which arise from enforcing those duties under the Welsh Language Standards. Well-being – according to Section 2 of the Act, refers to: the well-being of children and adults under SSWWA 2014, or welfare of a child under CA1989	3. Promote the well-being, voice and control of individuals and carers while supporting them to stay safe.

Table 2.1: Core legislation, and their themes (continued)

Social Services and Well-being (Wales) Act 2014	Well-being of Future Generations (Wales) Act 2015	Equality Act 2010	Human Rights Act 1998 (Convention Rights)	Data Protection Act 2018 and GDPR 2018	Welsh language Measure 2011	Code of Professional Practice for Social Workers 2017
Multi-agency working	Globally responsible (well-being goal)	Responsibility to protect against victimisation, create inclusive culture, respond to or make complaints, training, make reasonable adjustments	Article 9: Right to freedom of thought, conscience and religion Article 10: Freedom of expression	Accuracy – information is correct and up to date	The official status of the Welsh language in Wales: the principle that persons in Wales should be able to live their lives through the medium of the Welsh language if they choose to do so	4. Respect the rights of individuals while seeking to ensure that their behaviour does not harm themselves or other people.
Well-being	Cohesive communities (well-being goal)	reasonable adjustments	Article 11: Freedom of assembly and association	Length of time – must justify storage of information		5. Act with integrity and uphold public trust and confidence in the social care profession.
	Vibrant culture (well-being goal)	Responsibility to protect against harassment, create inclusive culture, respond to or make complaints, train, make reasonable adjustments	Article 12: Right to marry Article 13: Right to an effective remedy when a violation occurs (under the Act)	Integrity, confidentiality	Welsh is not to be treated less favourably than English in Wales	6. Be accountable for the quality of your work and take responsibility for maintaining and developing knowledge and skills.
	Thriving Welsh language (well-being goal)		Article 14: Protection from discrimination	Accountability		7. In addition to sections 1 – 6, if you are responsible for managing or leading staff, you must embed the Code in their work.

In order to understand the current debates in relation to the legal framework in Wales, it is beneficial to consider the philosophical nature and features of the law, known as the jurisprudence. For the social worker, the act of developing a narrative around the concepts and philosophies of the law may provide an insight into meanings and contexts in practice. Legal practices reflect the concepts and values of society; and the task of the social worker is to reflect on how these concepts impact our professional identity and conduct. One example would be our understanding of the concept of 'well-being', and our commitment to supporting people to achieve 'well-being', at a time when organisations are yet to establish its meaning (Hoffman et al, 2021; FGCW, 2021). Wittgenstein, and other philosophers, believe that there is a purpose in focusing on the concepts that would illuminate our practices and our values (Aparece, 2005), our positionality and role (Mattsson, 2014; Al-Faham et al, 2019), and the inherent ethical and moral conflicts (Jones and Wijeyesinghe, 2011).

Understanding the meaning of an individual word can best be achieved when it is placed within a system of words (Aparece, 2005: 22), and understanding the meaning of words and their use in language is core to interpreting the lived experience of people, in context (Aparece, 2005). Words are therefore fundamental to intersectional practice and to social work education (Bubar et al, 2016; Bernard, 2021). Furthermore, understanding concepts within their context, requires the practitioner to understand their current, historical and future meaning, which enables further reflection of the impact of past meanings on current understandings of such concepts as 'well-being', 'welfare', 'partnership', 'coproduction', 'eligibility' and 'need'. For example, the SSWWA established the eligibility framework, and the measurements to be used to establish eligibility for care and support, however due to the inconsistency in its application to practice, prior to and during the pandemic, the concept of eligibility and the classification of need has become rather elusive (Carers UK, 2020; EHRC, 2020a, 2020b; Children's Commissioner for Wales, 2021b; FGCW, 2021). It seems that the debasement of concepts by the Coronavirus Act (2020) has complicated our response to the rhetoric still further and has confused perceptions concerning the authority of the law (WPELGCC, 2020), individual rights, and subsequently the authority of the social work profession.

The modernist approach to the law considers that the law reflects the individual and shared beliefs of the population concerning their rights, and their collective decision-making (Al-Faham et al, 2019). The implementation of the SSWWA 2014 has revealed a distinction between the law as a rule-governing authority on the one hand, and the expression of societal belief and idealism on the other (Coyle, 2007). This may partially explain the chasm that continues to exist between people's experiences, and the principled ideals of the written law. The legal framework in Wales is reliant on the sustainability and uniformity of its conceptual design, in practice (Zifcack, 2009; Hoffman et al, 2021). However, people's experience of restrictive gatekeeping and scarce entitlement does not reflect the core principles of the legislation and has exposed flaws in the framework's conceptual design, in that its ideals are not sufficiently achievable and sustainable. It would seem that we have much to gain from an architect's commitment to conceptual design, in that an architect would determine that the development and execution of a concept is more important than the concept itself, in as much as the concept design must be functional, practical and sustainable and must stand the test of time, as a form of constructive alignment (Royal Institute Chartered Surveyors, 2022).

Addressing the implementation gap: an intersectional approach to the law

The WFGWA 2015 requires local authorities and organisations to consider the sustainability of their systems and services. The Act requires practitioners and their employers to implement preventative measures that will address the contextual realities, such as environmental factors, economic disadvantage, poverty and access to local services. The Act promotes an intersectional approach to assessing and meeting the care and support needs of individuals and local communities, within the context of sustainable development, improving the economic, social, environmental and cultural well-being of people in Wales, and advocates a shared responsibility to meeting personal outcomes (Audit Wales, 2020).

Hoffman et al (2021) advocate the need for the Welsh Government to explicitly embed the human rights and equality agendas in its information and communication systems, as well as data gathering, audit, inspection and regulation processes. One of the most significant recommendations is the potential benefit of an intersectional approach, to restructure systems, processes and provisions (Mattsson, 2014; EHRC, 2020b; Welsh Government, 2021c). Intersectionality is critical to resolving issues around the applied conceptual framework (Hoffman et al, 2021: 136), and how a more intersectional approach to human rights and equality legislation and guidance may improve outcomes. Hoffman et al (2021) further recommend that an intersectional method may be incorporated into the design and purpose of the Equality Impact Assessment on policy; that the objectives of the revised guidance should be aligned to the objectives of Section 4 of the Equality Act 2010; and that those qualitative indicators which relate to 'diverse and under-represented communities' should also be integrated within the monitoring mechanisms.

Intersectionality is a term that was first developed by Crenshaw (1991), to describe how different forms of oppression and disadvantage combine. It is a framework which conceptualises people's lived experiences of intersecting identities, discrimination, prejudice, disadvantage and privilege (Simon et al, 2022). Thus, intersectionality is the examination of interrelated elements of a person's identity and the combined impact of diverse sources of oppression, with 'mutually reinforcing systems of structural and situational inequalities' (Bernard, 2021: 4). A local authority's commitment to specific identities is usually reflected in the planning and delivery of its services, and in its flexibility in meeting person-centred needs (Nash, 2008; Parken, 2019; Carers UK, 2020; Iredele and Cooke, 2020; WPELGCC, 2020). An intersectional design questions power and the paradigms of privilege, towards social change (Murphy et al, 2009; Miller, 2012; Banks et al, 2013) and enables the social worker to analyse how a person intersects with their context (Bernard, 2021).

Although anti-discriminatory laws, such as the Human Rights Act 1993, and the Equality Act 2010 are enforced by certain universal categorisations, they do not incorporate the unique detail of a person's identity and experiences. Conversely, it is possible that the more general, universal application of the principles and concepts of the SSWWA 2014 and the WFGWA 2015 has widened the 'gap' further between the intention of the legislation and its outcome. It may be the case, as the FGCW has suggested, that a combination of greater individualism and intersectionality, and tailored, micro-level approaches are required to transcend organisational language, structures and processes (Al-Faham et al, 2019; FGCW, 2021), to provide a justice-oriented framework that has sufficient dexterity to tackle sociopolitical realities (Vygotsky, 1978; Hancock, 2016; Mattsson, 2014).

Maintaining an intersectional approach serves to critique norms and manifestations of power and offers a different world view of the real inequalities and disadvantages close to home (Grabham et al, 2008). Dhamoon (2011) provides four intersectional lenses by which the dimensions of an individual's experiences may be considered, which lend themselves well to the Assessment Framework located in Part 3 Code of Practice on Assessment and the subsequent social work engagement. These could be applied to the assessment and support of older adults and their carers, as this combination captures the context and systems within which the adult resides (Mehrotra, 2010; Hancock, 2016). This cannot be realistically achieved by surface-level assessments or the simplistic gathering of core data alone, under the Part 3 Code. Engagement with people requires the social worker to understand their own positionality, as it is critical to understanding privilege and power, and ethnocentric inequalities (Crenshaw, 1991; Murphy et al, 2009; Bubar et al, 2016). The process requires the social worker to consider how their involvement has influenced experiences and outcomes (Miller, 2012; García Bedolla, 2014; Huxley-Binns, 2014; Welsh Government, 2019), social justice and social change (Crenshaw, 1991; Ife, 2012; García Bedolla, 2014; Mattsson, 2014; Nayak and Robbins, 2018; Al-Faham et al, 2019; Hoffman et al, 2021; Simon et al, 2022). Aisha's story invites an intersectional approach to applying the legislation's conceptual design:

Aisha's story

Aisha is a 29-year-old Asian mother of two children, aged four and five years. Her husband has been charged and remanded in custody after causing her grievous bodily harm, which was witnessed by her children. Aisha has a strong sense of her identity, as an Asian mother, and is adjusting to life as a single mother. Despite having a degree, employment opportunities are scarce. Aisha has little understanding of your interpretation of 'well-being', but she has a strong cultural and religious identity, and she receives weekly support from her local mosque. She hasn't had much time to reflect on recent events but has mentioned 'the stigma' and her 'reputation' as both a victim and a troublemaker, due to the police's regular visits to her home. Aisha believes that her post-natal depression may have exacerbated her husband's behaviour. The children were impacted by the violence between their parents, but they are now settling, and seem happy at school. You might:

• consider the information which you have gathered during your initial engagement with Aisha;
• reflect on the intersections and their relevance to the Assessment Framework at Part 3 Code of Practice;
• consider what are the most relevant skills, knowledge, and theories to your engagement with Aisha.

Messages for practice

• The Welsh Government has ambitious intentions in relation to equality and human rights; to strengthen a 'tangible' and 'coherent' interlocking, interdependent infrastructure of UN conventions and treaties throughout its devolved legislation (Miles, 2018). Yet the positivist frame, which was originally intended to introduce this unique national political agenda, has failed to progress beyond its conceptual design.
• While the SSWWA 2014 and WFGWA 2015 were intended to coordinate, stabilise and sustain a moral identity, this will require a consistent understanding and application of the conceptual framework, the language and philosophy of the law, to dismantle the implementation gap and reconcile the lived experience with the rights of people (Wallace, 2019).
• Personal rights and privileges interconnect to create a fabric of rights, and it remains for the Welsh Government and the social work profession in Wales to continue to mill the legal framework – a 'brethyn' (a strong, milled Welsh wool fabric), that will sustain a rights-protecting approach, particularly 'in the small places, close to home' (Roosevelt, 1958; Miles, 2018).

The Older People's Commissioner for Wales (2021), the Children's Commissioner for Wales (2021b) and the FGCW (2021), and the EHRC (2020b), have all voiced their concern over how the legal concepts are being outworked in practice, and recent evaluations continue to highlight the inequalities, deprivation and marginalisation of people in Wales (EHRC, 2021; FGCW, 2021; Welsh Government, 2021b; Welsh Government, 2021c). There exists an 'implementation gap' (Hoffman et al, 2021), or shortfall (Children's Commissioner for Wales, 2021a), and misalignment between the intention of the law, and what is realised (Bevan, 1952). The constructive alignment between social work practice, the conceptual legal framework and people's lived experience are critical to the validity of the legal framework and, more importantly, to the protection and promotion of people's rights and freedoms.

There are both structural and cultural obstacles to reconciling the law with professional practice, which require a higher level of understanding (Vygotsky, 1978) and a duty to advocate (International Federation of Social Workers, 2014). The coproductive principles of voice and control need to be embedded within the social worker's language and method (Lutz, 2015); they must tend to the most silent and complex dimensions of a person's identity, to meet their needs, and attend to 'the smaller things that bring about the most significant change' (Carers UK, 2020; Hoffman et al, 2021: 84–88).

It rests with the local authorities to align their goals to the Act's objectives, to agree the meaning and purpose of its conceptual design (Welsh Government, 2019; FGCW, 2021), and be prepared to change at the required pace and level. This will require local authorities to understand and incorporate the concepts within their provisions, including 'the cultural pillar of well-being' (FGCW, 2021: 158), and the Welsh language (Welsh Government, 2019; Hoffman et al, 2021). There needs to be greater coherence between the implementation of the goals, which should ideally act as interdependent systems across the nation (FGCW, 2021, Hoffman et al, 2021), especially in relation to the assessment and planning for the needs of rural communities and the most disadvantaged in our society.

The concepts will therefore need to be embodied within the planning, commissioning, data, information and support systems, and the wider processes (FGCW, 2021; Hoffman et al, 2021). This requires local authorities, the voluntary sector, and local communities to jointly consider their shared responsibilities and socioeconomic duties under the well-being objectives, which are shared by the SSWWA 2014, WFGWA 2015 and the Domestic Abuse and Sexual Violence (Wales) Act 2015, Human Rights Act 1998, Equality Act 2010, the Welsh Language Measure 2011, the Mental Health Act 1987/2007, Mental Health Wales (Measure) 2010, and the Mental Capacity Act 2005 and their detailed Codes, so as to make 'the small places' sustainable and equal (EHRC, 2020b).

An intersectional outworking of the legislation, in practice, is essential to understanding a person's unique lived experience, and need for care and support. Intersectionality advocates a tailored, person–centred and agile approach to service planning, commissioning, delivery and evaluation, which is capable of actively identifying and targeting structural and contextual inequality and disadvantage (Bernard, 2021; FGCW, 2021; Hoffman et al, 2021). Intersectionality requires the social worker to reflexively consider and address their own power and positionality and its impact, and how their engagement with the law influences lived experiences, rights, freedoms and privileges, within the intersecting structural context of disadvantage and inequality, in Wales.

Further resources

1. Braye, S. and Preston-Shoot, M. (2016) *Practising Social Work Law* (4th edn), London: Palgrave.
2. Clements, L. (2022) 'The Social Services & Well-being (Wales) Act 2014: An overview'. http://www.lukeclements.co.uk/rhydian-social-welfare-law-in-wales/rhydian-online-journal/
3. Social Care Wales 'Social Care legislation in Wales: Overview of the Social Services and Well-being Wales Act 2014'. Information and learning Hub. https://socialcare.wales/hub/sswbact

References

Al-Faham, H., Davis, A.M. and Ernst, R. (2019) 'Intersectionality: from theory to practice', *Annual Review of Law and Social Science*, 15: 247–265.

Aparece, P.A. (2005) *Teaching, Learning and Community: An Examination of Wittgensteinian Themes Applied to the Philosophy of Education*, Rome: Gregorian University Press.

Audit Wales (2020) 'Better law making: the implementation challenge'. https://www.audit.wales/publication/better-law-making-implementation-challenge

Banks, C.A., Pliner, S.M. and Hopkins, M.B. (2013) 'Intersectionality and paradigms of privilege: teaching for social change', in K.A. Case (ed) *Deconstructing Privilege: Teaching and Learning as Allies in the Classroom*, New York: Routledge, pp 102–114.

Bernard, C. (2021) *Intersectionality for Social Workers: A Practical Introduction to Theory and Practice*, London and New York: Routledge.

Bevan, A. (1952) *In Place of Fear*, Melbourne/London: Heineman.

Bubar, R., Cespedes, K. and Bundy-Fazioli, K. (2016) 'Intersectionality and social work: omissions of race, class, and sexuality in graduate school education', *Journal of Social Work Education*, 52(3): 283–296.

Carers UK (2020) 'Caring behind closed doors: six months on. The continued impact of the coronavirus (COVID-19) pandemic on unpaid carers'. https://www.careknowledge.com/media/48383/caringbehindcloseddoorsoct20v4-003.pdf

Children's Commissioner for Wales (2021a) 'Children's Commissioner for Wales Annual Report 2020/2021'. https://www.childcomwales.org.uk/publications/annual-report-20–21/

Children's Commissioner for Wales (2021b) 'The Right Way: A Children's Rights Approach for Social Care in Wales'. https://www.childcomwales.org.uk/resources/the-right-way-a-childrens-rights-approach/

Chwarae Teg (2020) 'Women and Covid-19'. https://chwaraeteg.com/wp-content/uploads/2020/04/FINAL-UK-Briefing-on-Women-and-Covid-19.pdf

Coyle, S. (2007) *From Positivism to Idealism: A Study of the Moral Dimensions of Legality*, Surrey: Ashgate.

Crenshaw, K. (1991) 'Mapping the margins: intersectionality identity politics, and violence against women of color', *Stanford Law Review*, 43(6): 1241–1299.

Dhamoon, R. (2011) 'Considerations on mainstreaming intersectionality', *Political Research Quarterly*, 64(1): 230–243.

Equality and Human Rights Commission (2018a) 'Is Wales Fairer? The State of Equality and Human Rights'. https://www.equalityhumanrights.com/sites/default/files/is-britain-fairer-2018-is-wales-fairer.pdf

Equality and Human Rights Commission (2018b) 'Is Britain Fairer? The State of Equality and Human Rights'. https://www.equalityhumanrights.com/sites/default/files/is-england-fairer-2018.pdf

Equality and Human Rights Commission (2020a) 'How Coronavirus Has Affected Equality and Human Rights'. https://www.equalityhumanrights.com/en/publication-download/

Equality and Human Rights Commission (2020b) 'Rebuilding a More Equal and Fairer Wales: Focus on the Unequal Impact of the Coronavirus Pandemic'. https://www.equalityhumanrights.com/sites/default/files/parliamentary-briefing-paper-rebuilding-more-equal-fairer-wales-coronavirus-may-2020.pdf

Equality and Human Rights Commission (2021) 'Impact Report 2020–2021'. https://www.equalityhumanrights.com/en/publication-downloads/wales-impact-report-20202021

Future Generations Commissioner for Wales (2021) 'The Future Generations Report 2020'. https://www.futuregenerations.wales/public_info/annual-report-2020-2021/

García Bedolla, L. (2014) 'How an intersectional approach can help to transform the university', *Politics and Gender*, 10(3): 447–455.

Grabham, E., Cooper, D., Krishnadas, J. and Herman, D. (2008) *Intersectionality and Beyond*, Oxfordshire: Taylor & Francis.

Hancock, A.-M. (2016) *Intersectionality: An Intellectual History*, New York: Oxford University Press.

Hoffman, S., Nason, S., Beacock, R., Hicks, E. and Croke, R. (2021) 'Strengthening and Advancing Equality and Human Rights in Wales'. https://www.gov.wales/sites/default/files/statistics-and-research/2021-08/strengthening-and-advancing-equality-and-human-rights-in-wales.pdf

Hussey, R., Aylword, M., Berwick, D., Black, C., Dixon, J., Edwards, N., et al (2018) 'The Parliamentary Review of Health and Social Care in Wales'. Welsh Government OGL.

Huxley-Binns, R. (2014) 'Law', in H. Fry, S. Ketteridge and S. Marshall (eds) *A Handbook for Teaching & Learning in Higher Education: Enhancing Academic Practice* (4th edn), London and New York: Routledge, chapter 21.

Ife, J. (2012) *Human Rights and Social Work: Towards Rights-Based Practice* (3rd edn), New York: Cambridge University Press.

International Federation of Social Workers (2014) 'Global Definition of Social Work'. https://www.ifsw.org/what-is-social-work/global-definition-of-social-work/

Iredele, R. and Cooke, K. (2020) *Understanding What Matters in Social Care: Experiences of Care and Support Services and Being an Unpaid Carer in Wales. Story-Gathering Report 2020.* https://gov.wales/sites/default/files/publications/2020–12/understanding-what-matters-in-social-care.pdf

Jones, S.R. and Wijeyesinghe, C.L. (2011) 'The promises and challenges of teaching from an intersectional perspective: core components and applied strategies', *New Directions for Teaching and Learning*, 125: 11–20.

Lutz, H. (2015) 'Intersectionality as method', *Journal of Diversity and Gender Studies*, 2(12): 39–44.

Mattsson, T. (2014) 'Intersectionality as a useful tool: anti-oppressive social work and critical reflection', *Affilia*, 29(1): 8–17.

Mehrotra, G. (2010) 'Toward a continuum of intersectionality theorizing for feminist social work scholarship', *Affilia*, 25: 417–430.

Miles, J. (2018) 'Eileen Illtyd Memorial Lecture on Human Rights', Counsel General. Swansea University. https://www.swansea.ac.uk/media/The-Eileen-Illtyd-Memorial-Lecture-on-Human-Rights.Counsel-General-Nov-2018-FINAL-v28.11.18-(2).pdf

Miller, D. (2012) 'Grounding human rights', *Critical Review of International Social and Political Philosophy*, 15(4): 407–427.

Murphy, Y., Hunt, V., Zajicek, A.M., Norris, A.N. and Hamilton, L. (2009) *Incorporating Intersectionality in Social Work Practice,* Research, Policy, and Education, Washington, DC: NASW Press.

Nash, J.C. (2008) 'Re-thinking intersectionality'. *Feminist Review*, 89: 1–15.

Nayak, S. and Robbins, R. (eds) (2018) *Intersectionality in Social Work: Activism and Practice in Context*, Oxford: Routledge.

Older People's Commissioner for Wales (2021) 'State of the Nation'. https://www.olderpeoplewales.com/Libraries/Uploads/State_of_the_Nation_Report_2021.sfb.ashx

Parken, A. (2019) *Improving Well-Being and Equality Outcomes: Aligning Processes Supporting Implementation and Creating New Opportunities. Report of the Well-Being and Equality Working Group.* https://chwaraeteg.com/wp-content/uploads/2019/09/Aligning-and-Improving-Outcomes-for-Well-being-and-Equality.pdf

Race Council Cymru (2016) *Race Equality in Wales Report.* https://racecouncilcymru.org.uk/race-equality-in-wales-report/

Roosevelt, E. (1958) 'Where Do Human Rights Begin? Speech at the United Nations General Assembly'. https://www.amnesty.org.uk/universal-declaration-human-rights-UDHR

Royal Institute Chartered Surveyors (2022) 'Upholding professional standards'. https://www.rics.org/uk/upholding-professional-standards/sector-standards/valuation/redbook/

Simon, J.D., Boyd, R. and Subica, A.M. (2022) 'Refocusing intersectionality in social work education: creating a brave space to discuss oppression and privilege', *Journal of Social Work Education*, 58(1): 34–45.

Vygotsky, L. (1978) *Mind in Society: The Development of High Psychological Processes,* Cambridge, MA: Harvard University Press.

Wallace, J. (2019) *Wellbeing and Devolution: Reframing the Role of Government in Scotland, Wales and Northern Ireland*, London: Palgrave Macmillan.

Welsh Assembly Government (2011) 'Sustainable Social Services for Wales: A Framework for Action'. Number: WAG10-11086. https://www.basw.co.uk/system/files/resources/basw_10728-7_0.pdf

Welsh Government (2018) 'Parliamentary Review of Health and Social Care in Wales. A Revolution from within: Transforming Health and Social Care in Wales'. https://www.gov.wales/sites/default/files/publications/2018-01/Review-health-social-care-report-final.pdf

Welsh Government (2019) *Measuring the Mountain: What Really Matters in Social Care to Individuals in Wales? Final Report.* https://www.gov.wales/sites/default/files/publications/2019–03/measuring-the-mountainfinal-report.pdf

Welsh Government (2020a) *Measuring the Mountain. Response to Phase One Recommendations.* https://gov.wales/sites/default/files/publications/2020–02/measuring-the-mountain-responseto-phase-one-recommendations.pdf

Welsh Government (2020b) *Prosperity for All: The National Strategy. Taking Wales Forward.* https://www.wcva.cymru/wp-content/uploads/2020/01/Prosperity-for-all.pdf

Welsh Government (2021a) *A Healthier Wales: A Plan for Health and Social Care.* https://www.gov.wales/sites/default/files/publications/2021–09-a-healthier-wales-action-planfor-health-and-social-care

Welsh Government (2021b) *Evaluation of the Social Services and Well-being (Wales) Act 2014: Process Evaluation (Research Briefing).* https://gov.wales/evaluation-social-services-and-well-being-wales-act-2014-process-evaluation

Welsh Government (2021c) *The Future of Welsh Law: A Programme for 2021 to 2026.* https://gov.wales/the-future-of-welsh-law-accessibility-programme-2021-to-2026

Welsh Parliament Equality, Local Government and Communities Committee (2020) *Into Sharp Relief: Inequality and the Pandemic.* https://senedd.wales/laid%20documents/cr-ld13403/cr-ld13403-e.pdf

Zifcack, S. (2009) 'Towards a reconciliation of legal and social work practice', in P. Swain and S. Rice (eds) *In the Shadow of Law: Legal Context of Social Work Practice*, Sydney: The Federation Press.

3

The regulation of social work in Wales

Ian Thomas

Chapter objectives

- To consider the principles, purpose and practice of professional regulation.

- To explore its impact and what it might tell us about the state of the profession in Wales.

- To see how far we have come, and where professional regulation might develop in the future.

Introduction

It is often said change is the only constant in life. Despite it being such a feature of our lives, it can remain challenging and painful, frequently involving setbacks and beset by unintended consequences, but change can also be invigorating and help maintain a desire to keep going. It is only when we reflect on the changes we have made, helped instigate or had to respond to, that we can appreciate their impact and appreciate the point of them.

In terms of professional regulation, social work is still in its infancy. Doctors were first regulated with the General Medical Council established under the Medical Act 1858, nurses under the Nurses Registration Act 1919 (Shepherd, 2019). The system for registration of social workers was established through the Care Standards Act 2000 and became a requirement for social workers and social work students in Wales in 2004. Regulation of social work in Wales is therefore early in its journey and will continue to develop and mature, and it is probably helpful to reflect on its current state.

Consideration will be given to models of regulation, the nature of regulation of the social care workforce and education and the impact of regulation. This will be examined through reference to fitness to practise hearings in Wales. The chapter concludes with a review of some of the ways the regulator currently supports the profession and how regulation can strengthen professional identity.

The legislation (Regulation and Inspection of Social Care (Wales) Act, 2016) (RISCA) provides the statutory framework for three areas of regulation and inspection of social care in Wales, namely: (i) the regulation and inspection of care and support services, (ii) the regulation of education and training of social workers, and (iii) the regulation of the social care workforce, including social workers.

The regulation and inspection of care and support services is undertaken by Arolygiaeth Gofal Cymru/Care Inspectorate Wales which approves, registers and quality assures social care services provided for adults and children as well as early years childcare and play services. Gofal Cymdeithasol Cymru/Social Care Wales (SCW) is responsible for the regulation of social work education and training, and the social care workforce. In education and training, it sets standards for qualifications and approves, registers and quality assures social work courses at qualifying and post-qualifying levels.

In relation to the workforce, SCW sets standards for professional registration, conduct and practice (Social Care Wales, 2021a). SCW registers a wide range of social care workers including social workers and social work students. The requirements for registration are set out in the SCW website (Social Care Wales, 2022a) and registrants must demonstrate they continue to meet them throughout their professional careers. Additionally, SCW has Fitness to Practise (FtP) procedures to deal with concerns raised about a social worker's standard of practice, which can ultimately lead to removal from the register.

The principles and purpose of regulation

Section 68 of RISCA describes SCW's main function as to 'protect, promote and maintain the safety and well-being of the public in Wales'. Furthermore, in pursuing that goal it must promote and maintain high standards in the provision of care and support services, the conduct and practice among social care workers, in the training of social care workers and in public confidence in social care workers.

The public protection requirement is common to all professions operating in the health and social care sector (Professional Standards Authority, n.d.) and different professional regulators employ a variety of approaches to address this. For SCW, the legislation prescribes a wider role, and the organisation also has responsibility for research, development and improvement as well as ensuring conformity to given standards in order to contribute to supporting the people of Wales. SCW refers to this as 'regulation for improvement' in which regulation is not a bureaucratic process or a restrictive control mechanism but has the potential to be used proactively to make positive changes to the profession and the people it serves.

The extent to which the state is involved in regulation varies across different professions and services. Healey (2019) explores this in relation to social work accreditation bodies and identifies three types – first, a government accreditation body such as those in the UK and elsewhere, which is 'established and endorsed by government' (p 58). Second, self-regulation through a social work education council such as in the USA and Canada – where social work education is 'accredited and regulated by an authority developed by social work educators and is independent of government' (p 59). Third, self-regulation by the profession, such as in Australia where the voluntary professional body is responsible for setting and maintaining educational standards for the profession. Fundamentally, the question is who determines what knowledge, skills and values are required of social workers in their training and therefore in their practice? Is it the profession, existing educators, government or another body?

Which of these is most effective at promoting public protection is debatable, but the move towards state involvement in Wales, with a management board in which lay members are in the majority, reflects the concern for improving public confidence and public protection.

The regulation of the workforce

The British Association of Social Workers' campaign for the statutory regulation of the profession has continued for over 50 years (Jones, 2018). However, debate over the case for registration and what constitutes proportionate regulation continues. While there have been attempts to calculate a financial cost benefit analysis of professional registration (for example, see Deloitte Access Economics, 2016), achieving value for money is only one element of establishing a proportionate model of registration. In the UK, the catastrophic consequences of poor practice such as those highlighted through the inquiries into the Bristol Royal Infirmary (Bristol Royal Infirmary Inquiry, 2001) and the GP Harold Shipman (Smith, 2004) have remained key influencers in shaping the approach to regulation and this applies not only to doctors but other professional groups, especially those in contact with vulnerable people. As a result of these inquiries, the General Medical Council introduced changes that included the introduction of appraisal, continuing professional development and revalidation for all healthcare professionals to ensure they keep their skills up to scratch, and the creation of national standards of care, both in clinical care and for hospitals (Butler, 2002).

This model, with some differences, applies to social workers in Wales and elsewhere. So registered social care professionals in Wales must:

- uphold the standards in the Code of Professional Practice for Social Care at all times;
- keep their registration, contact and employment details up to date;
- participate in and record continuing professional development;
- achieve the qualification required for the role (where appropriate).

Additionally, section 111 of RISCA introduced Protection of Title for social workers so the public know who is qualified and has met the standards of competence.

The requirements for education and training

It is perhaps reasonable to expect that regulated training should produce people capable of delivering the standards of practice required by the workforce standards.

This is illustrated by the requirements for social work students in Wales to be registered with SCW, to provide evidence of competence in the standards for practice and apply the Code of Professional Practice.

It could be argued that, given its size, it is easier for SCW to engage with the social work profession than it is for other UK countries (as of April 2021, England had 96,315 registered social workers (Social Work England, 2021) compared with 6,470 in Wales (Social Care Wales, 2022b)). There are 22 local authorities in Wales and seven universities awarding social work degrees and it is therefore possible to get all local authority (and third sector) social work employers and training providers together in one room. It is perhaps this size which has contributed to the partnership approach to training whereby social work courses are delivered not by universities but through partnerships of university and local authorities with the additional involvement of people with experience of using social care services.

As a result, SCW's rules for social work education are specific to Wales and include bespoke learning outcomes such as the need to understand the impact of working in a Welsh context. All social workers need to be able to take account of people's culture and experience. As a multicultural country this is no less important for social workers in Wales. However, for many, living in Wales is something that binds people together, whether it be the distinct national structures arising from devolution, the history of Wales, its rurality, or the Welsh language. Students, therefore, need to demonstrate they 'can identify, understand, and respond to issues which are specific to or characteristic of the needs of Wales, its languages, legislation, culture, geography and institutions and the distinctive position of the Welsh language' (Social Care Wales, 2021b).

We have considered the nature of regulation, the varied role of the state and the situation in Wales regarding social work regulation. As with any change, its impact needs to be evaluated. While there has been no formal evaluation of the regulation of social workers in Wales, there may be other evidence to draw upon.

The impact of regulation

If the intention of regulation is to improve public protection from poor or abusive practice, to increase public confidence in the profession and contribute to the improvement of social care services, what evidence is there of this being delivered? Measurement will, of course, be difficult: we cannot know how many incidents of abuse or poor practice have been averted, nor how many training providers have changed their plans to meet regulatory requirements. Reference to FtP systems may, however, give some indication of the state of social work as a regulated profession.

Worsley, Shorrock and McLaughlin (2020) analysed the outcomes of UK FtP proceedings against social workers, doctors and nurses/midwives. The analysis raised several concerns. Men are overrepresented in cases across all three professions: 46 per cent of social worker cases concern men while just 17 per cent of social workers are men; 88 per cent of cases against doctors concern men (54 per cent of doctors are men); and 30 per cent of cases against nurses/midwives concern men (11 per cent of nurses/midwives are men). There were wide variations in attendance at FtP hearings where 10 per cent of social workers attended as opposed to 71 per cent of doctors and 46 per cent of nurses/midwives. Of those attending their hearings, 11 per cent of social workers were legally represented, compared to 58 per cent of doctors and 41 per cent of nurses/midwives. And, finally, in terms of FtP cases resulting in the registrant's removal, this occurred in 36 per cent of cases for social workers, 24 per cent for doctors and 29 per cent for nurses/midwives.

The authors also reported on the rationale given for the outcomes of hearings. They found that for social workers, 'seriousness of allegation' was the most common reason for a particular sanction. For doctors, it was 'evidence of remediation/insight/remorse' and for nurses/midwives the reason for a particular outcome was to allow 'time for remediation/insight'. They ask whether this difference could reflect a view of some professions being considered a more valuable public asset than others, who need to change their ways rather than face the ultimate sanction of de-registration. Further, given the differences in professions' engagement with FtP processes, whether more could be done through improvements in professional training and support to reduce discrepancies.

Another consideration is the extent to which poor or abusive practice is the result of a failing individual, a failing organisation or a combination of both. Kirkham, Leigh, McLaughlan and Worsley (2019) explore what constitutes a fair hearing in terms of FtP and conclude that procedural fairness is context dependent and that organisational issues, such as levels of supervision or staff shortages, which are considered in other arenas such as serious case reviews, are missing from FtP procedures. This, combined with low attendance rates by social workers and low levels of representation, may result in the context in which poor practice has occurred not being fully described. This is, in part, addressed in Wales through the publication of a Code of Practice for Social Care Employers which describes the 'standards required of employers to ensure a safe, skilled and appropriately supported social care workforce' (Social Care Wales, 2022c). The Code quotes sections of RISCA describing how Care Inspectorate Wales can take action against an employer if it fails to comply with the Code and how SCW (which has no authority in relation to employers) can give advice to employers following cases that have been subject to FtP investigation or hearing. In other words, where an investigation or hearing considers the extent to which an employer complied with the standards had a bearing on the practice of the registrant, it can give advice to the employer.

Attendance at a hearing by the social worker whose practice is being judged, especially with legal representation, may make the use of this power easier for SCW. Professionals are responsible for their social work practice which includes 'bringing to the attention of your employer or the appropriate authority, resource or operational difficulties that might get in the way of the delivery of safe social care and support' (Social Care Wales, 2017). While we must not underestimate the difficulties in an employee challenging their employer, it may ultimately be in their interests to do so if SCW is to reach a full and fair judgement about their practice.

The Professional Standards Authority (2017) has considered the definition and relevance of professional identity and its impact on patient safety. While the research focused on a number of health care professions, the principles may be transferable. They describe the complexity of what professional identity may mean which includes: a clear connection between professional identity and good quality care, a sense of community with others in the profession in which all are held to account, and status resulting from meeting requirements to become and remain registered and recognising the effort involved.

So, while measuring the impact of regulation can be difficult, we can use data and intelligence to direct our resources into areas that are shown to be of concern. This may lead us to explore how to promote attendance at hearings, ensure appropriate representation and develop resources to address concerns over common areas of practice in need of improvement. More broadly, to look 'upstream' and use data and intelligence to address the more common causes for concern. In this context, upstream may include thinking about how the profession is promoted, the student selection procedures in place, professional identity, whether the standards are appropriate, the assessment of students in both academic and practice settings, the transition from training to qualified practice, the requirements for renewal of registration, including Continuing Professional Development (CPD) and the organisational context in which practice occurs.

Despite this lack of hard or conclusive evidence, there are signs of efforts in Wales to use its remit for regulation and improvement to support the registered workforce.

These include:

- The promotion of working in the sector through a dedicated website promoting careers in social care (WeCare Wales, 2022).
- The development of a Health and Social Care Workforce Strategy for Wales (Health Education and Improvement Wales and Social Care Wales, 2020).
- A requirement that social work training programmes are provided through partnerships between a training provider (such as a university) and an employer, not by the training provider alone. Consequently, there is some limit over the number of students accepted as intake is restrained by the number of practice learning opportunities (PLO) an employer can arrange. One effect of this has been that in Wales, 90 per cent of social work students had their final practice learning opportunity in a local authority social services authority (and 77 per cent of their first long PLO) (Social Care Wales, 2021c).
- Practice guidance for social workers which builds on the Code of Professional Practice for Social Care and aims to describe what is expected of social workers and support them in delivering a good service.
- Further guidance on the duty of candour and the use of social media.

- Strengthening employer support of newly qualified social workers through a framework for post-qualifying training that includes guidance on the first three years in practice, and where completion of the Consolidation Programme for Newly Qualified Social Workers is required in order to renew professional registration.
- Engagement with the workforce through communities of practice.
- Training requirements for social workers wanting to return to practice after a period of absence so they are adequately prepared for contemporary practice.
- The commitment made by the Welsh Government in December 2021 (Welsh Government, 2021) that the employment terms and conditions of the registered social care workforce and personal assistants should improve through the payment of the real living wage.

This chapter has considered the model of regulation in social care and the education and training of social workers. We have seen evidence at UK level of the overrepresentation of men, and how social workers (compared with other professions) may be facing harsher sanctions at FtP hearings, and that there is lower attendance and less legal representation at hearings. While numbers in Wales may be small and therefore further research is required, there are questions about what more could be done to encourage greater engagement in the FtP systems and how the profession can be better supported to embrace professional registration. If there is a weaker professional identity, what could be done to strengthen it and is there more that could be done to further improve the quality and practice of social work in Wales?

The Welsh way

Within Wales, social work education is delivered through partnerships of a training provider and an employer, giving equal weight to practice and college-based learning. The regulatory body (SCW) has broad responsibilities, including setting research priorities, contributing to improvements in services, sharing good practice, improving workforce standards as well as regulating the workforce and social work education. The size of Wales makes it easier for the regulatory body to engage directly with the workforce and employers, and for the workforce to get involved in Wales-wide improvement and development projects. Social work students can submit work for assessment in either Welsh or English and must identify, understand and respond to the context of working in Wales.

Messages for practice

- This chapter has referred to some of the initiatives already taken by SCW and others to support social work and other social care professionals. However, the challenges facing social workers in practice and in their relationship with the regulatory body suggests there is a case for further improvement.

- Social workers, employers, trade unions, professional bodies and regulatory services will need to work together for regulation to be truly effective and beneficial to the people of Wales. It is not for a regulatory body to advocate on behalf of the profession but, given the wish to 'regulate for improvement' and to strengthen public confidence, regulation should be seen as part of the improvement plan not separate from it. A failure to make the connections is liable to undermine the profession. Social workers play a part in this and need to demonstrate their individual and collective commitment to their profession and the Code of Professional Practice. It is for each individual social worker, as well as their representatives and leaders of the profession, to determine how this commitment can be strengthened.

With social work regulation being only 18 years old, we will want to be sure that when we reflect and evaluate recent changes, we use the best knowledge and information we can, to ensure we keep a focus on our ultimate goals. According to the Social Care Wales website, for social workers in Wales that is protecting the public, securing public confidence and enabling people to 'live the life that matters to them' (https://socialc are.wales/about-us). Achieving that requires a workforce that is sufficient in number, appropriately skilled, confident in itself and proud of its regulated status.

Further resources
1. Professional Standards Authority (2016) *Regulation Rethought, Proposals for Reform.* https://www.professionalstandards.org.uk/publicationsebb
2. Webb, S.A. (ed) (2017) *Professional Identity and Social Work* (1st edn), Abingdon: Routledge.
3. van der Heijden, J. (2020) 'What makes a modern and entrepreneurial regulator?' 5 October. https://regulatoryfrontlines.blog/

References
Bristol Royal Infirmary Inquiry (2001) *Learning from Bristol: The Report of the Public Inquiry into Children's Heart Surgery at the Bristol Royal Infirmary 1984–1995.* London: HMSO.
Butler, P. (2002) 'The Bristol Royal Infirmary Inquiry: the issue explained'. https://www.theguardian.com/society/2002/jan/17/5
Deloitte Access Economics (2016) *The Registration of Social Workers in Australia.* https://www.aasw.asn.au/document/item/8806
Healey, K. (2019) 'Regulating for quality social work education: who owns the curriculum?', in M. Connolly, C. Williams and D.S. Coffey (ed) *Strategic Leadership in Social Work Education*, Cham: Springer, pp 53–66.
Health Education and Improvement Wales and Social Care Wales (2020) *Health and Social Care Workforce Strategy.* https://heiw.nhs.wales/programmes/health-and-social-care-workforce-strategy/

Jones, D. (2018) *Regulation of Social Work and Social Workers in the United Kingdom.* https://www.basw.co.uk/system/files/resources/Social%20Work%20Regulat ion%20-%20Contexts%20and%20Questions.pdf

Kirkham, R., Leigh, J., McLaughlan, K. and Worsley, A. (2019) 'The procedural fairness limitations of fitness to practise hearings: a case study into social work', *Legal Studies*, 39: 339–357.

National Assembly for Wales (2016) Regulation and Inspection of Social Care (Wales) Act, 2016. https://www.legislation.gov.uk/anaw/2016/2/contents/enacted

Professional Standards Authority (2017) *Professional Regulation: How Does it Affect the Identity of Health and Care Professionals.* https://www.professionalstandards. org.uk/docs/default-source/publications/infographics/professional-identity- may-17.pdf?sfvrsn=e7b7020_4

Professional Standards Authority (nd) *What We Do.* https://www.professionalst andards.org.uk/what-we-do

Shepherd, J. (2019) 'Timeline: the road to nurse registration in the UK'. *Nursing Times.* https://www.nursingtimes.net/

Smith, J. (2004) *The Shipman Inquiry Fifth Report, Safeguarding Patients, Lessons from the Past – Proposals for the Future.* London: HMSO.

Social Care Wales (2017) *Code of Professional Practice for Social Care Workers.* Cardiff: Social Care Wales.

Social Care Wales (2021a) *Social Care Wales: Registration Rules 2021.* https://soc ialcare.wales

Social Care Wales (2021b) *The Framework for the Degree in Social Work in Wales 2021.* https://socialcare.wales

Social Care Wales (2021c) *Quality Assurance of Social Work Education and Training – Annual Report.* https://socialcare.wales/learning-and-development/regulation- of-social-work-education-and-training

Social Care Wales (2022a) *How to Apply.* https://socialcare.wales/registration/ how-to-apply

Social Care Wales (2022b) *Workforce Reports 2021 Registration Data Reports.* https:// socialcare.wales/research-and-data/workforce-reports#section-40041-anchor

Social Care Wales (2022c) *Code of Practice for Social Care Employers.* Cardiff: Social Care Wales.

Social Work England (2021) *Annual Report and Accounts 2020 to 2021.* https:// www.socialworkengland.org.uk/about/publications/annual-report-and-accou nts-2020-to-2021/

WeCare Wales (2022) *WeCare Wales.* https://wecare.wales/

Welsh Government (2021) *Written Statement: A Real Living Wage for Social Care Workers in Wales.* https://gov.wales/written-statement-real-living-wage-soc ial-care-workers-wales

Worsley, A., Shorrock, S. and McLaughlin, K. (2020) 'Protecting the public? An analysis of professional regulation – comparing outcomes in fitness to practice for social workers, nurses and doctors', *British Journal of Social Work*, 50(6): 1871–1889.

4

The Welsh Context: we are what we know

Gwenan Prysor

Chapter objectives

- To explore the Welsh Context through the lens of threshold concepts and liminal spaces.
- To consider links between Welsh Context and critical reflection.

Introduction

To make life easier, the human mind tends to favour categorisation and binary thinking, so that things are either this or that, here or there. The problem with this is that things can slip through and become invisible, and as such, we can miss important stuff. When I started this chapter, I thought I knew exactly what I was going to write about and how I was going to present it all. This has not been the case. This chapter seemed to continually take on a new life – its own life – and ended up nothing like what I was expecting. Ironically, it turns out that the main focus of the chapter also reflects the process that I went through myself, which I am very happy to share with you as I invite you to join me on a parallel journey of discovery.

Writing this chapter has placed me in a liminal space. Liminal spaces are not feel-good places, as they are the spaces in between what is familiar and unfamiliar. There is inevitable discomfort in letting go of what was previously known and grappling, instead, with some new knowledge and meaning. Previous drafts of this chapter were based on what has now become my old way of thinking. I am therefore not asking the reader to do anything that I have not done or been through myself. This will hopefully engender an element of camaraderie between us as we embark on this journey together.

The Welsh Context

As part of their ongoing professional learning and development, students, newly qualified social workers, and those who support them, need to demonstrate their engagement with and understanding of what has come to be known as 'the Welsh Context', for their practice. Ironically, this is possibly not the most helpful of terms in assisting people to 'get it'. The Welsh Context, which is represented throughout the chapter as a proper noun to assist clarity, has developed into a shorthand term for what could be more accurately termed as 'the context of working in Wales'. The main problem may lay with the conflation of the 'Welsh' element of the context with the Welsh language. Although it cannot be denied that the Welsh language is an important and integral consideration in relation to living and working in Wales, the Welsh Context is not, and cannot sensibly be, attributed and limited to (the) language alone. Also worthy of note is the fact that the concept of considering context is not particular to Wales. Social work practice all over the world needs to consider the inherent political, economic, sociological, technological, legal and environmental context when working with individuals (Chartered Institute of Personnel and Development, 2021). In this regard, what better place to start than with the International Federation of Social Work (IFSW, 2014) definition of social work, and its core mandates, principles, knowledge and practice that can be amplified at national and/or regional levels?

The definition suggests that a key element of social work is to identify, unravel and minimise barriers preventing individuals from living their best lives. This provides background to understanding the context of individuals, as well as the context of the practice itself. Over years of involvement in social work education, I have found that while it may be possible to confidently state *when* the Welsh Context has been well-evidenced, it is much more difficult to articulate *how* the combination of particular components deem some to have managed to do this satisfactorily, while others have not. To further our understanding of this, and take it from a different angle, the lens of Meyer and Land's (2003) threshold concepts is explored. This will be followed by an appreciation of Foote's (2013) exploration of critical reflection as a specific social work threshold concept.

Threshold concepts

Since Meyer and Land's (2003) initial introduction, much work has been undertaken within various disciplines to identify threshold concepts (Heading and Loughlin, 2018). Atherton, Hadfield and Meyers (2008) suggest that understanding threshold concepts is a threshold concept in itself. Threshold concepts have been described as getting to grips with some key elements of a particular subject, and as part of the journey of mastering one's chosen field (Gaunt and Loffman, 2018). Such examples of threshold concepts include *metabolism* in Exercise Physiology, *opportunity cost* in Economics, and *gravity* in Physics (Meyer and Land, 2003). Similar to Winkler's (2018) claim that threshold concepts open up further learning, Stopford (2021) refers to threshold concepts as notions that have to be grasped to be able to partake effectively in a discipline, with Heading and Loughlin (2018) claiming that the learner's ability to understand the subject as a whole will be impaired if particular threshold concepts are not crossed. They have further been described as: cumulative learning (Irving et al, 2019), an induction to the discipline's way of thinking (Davies, 2006) and a process of shared understanding with others within the discipline (Natanasabapathy and Maathuis-Smith, 2019). However, despite their enticing offer, threshold concepts are not simple things. They can be hard to grasp, and they are not easy to teach (Chatterjee-Padmanabhan et al, 2019; Stopford 2021).

Although there appear to be no agreed rules per se in relation to threshold concepts, there has been a clear attempt to differentiate between them and core concepts. Core concepts help to build understanding, adding layers to existing knowledge (Barradell, 2013) but will not necessarily change the way a learner sees the subject, in the same way as threshold concepts do (Gaunt and Loffman, 2018). Reeping (2020: 67) suggests that being as 'plentiful as cubic zirconia' diminishes the potency of threshold concepts, defending more of a 'rare as diamonds' approach to their development. Being so open to interpretation, therefore, makes it harder to establish consistency within and across disciplines.

Meyer and Land (2003) identified five characteristics of threshold concepts, namely that they are (1) transformative, (2) irreversible, (3) integrative, (4) bounded and (5) troublesome. These characteristics are not without dispute, with Rowbottom (2007), for example, observing a lack of consensus about whether all five characteristics must be met or whether some characteristics are more important than others. Barradell (2013) believes that the 'troublesome' and 'transformative' characteristics are most influential in either inciting or inhibiting learning, while Winkler (2018) observes that the nature and extent of troublesome and transformative knowledge will vary for different individuals.

What follows is a brief explanation of the five characteristics, and their application to Welsh Context.

Transformative

Learning is messy and full of abstract realisations that may be difficult to track (Baillie et al, 2013; Smith et al, 2021). Heading and Loughlin (2018) suggest that threshold concepts are crossed in learning and realisations which often come through several smaller insights within a liminal space towards a deeper understanding, and are not necessarily epic or grandiose events. Alternatively, Meyer and Land (2006) suggest that transformative learning can take place suddenly and momentously or can be a more protracted and incremental affair.

When the penny drops and the threshold concept is understood, the transformation is not limited to knowledge of the subject. The world is seen anew, which can also impact the learner's identity and sense of self (Davies, 2006). The transition may even reach as far as a shift in the way the learner views society (Winkler, 2018). If thresholds have been crossed, the learner should be showing recognisable signs of fidelity to their profession/discipline in their day-to-day thinking and behaviour (Meyer and Land, 2005; Timmermans and Meyer, 2019). It is not impossible for crossing the threshold to bring with it feelings of shame and guilt for previous thoughts and actions. For some, however, understanding a threshold concept may bring with it a sense of relief, as reaching new understandings can clear up previous confusion and discomfort (Winkler, 2018). For the Welsh Context, this could mean seeing individuals in a different light, including the wider context and influence of their circumstances. It could lead us to becoming more open to trying to understand the lived-in experiences of others, not holding back from further exploring matters about which we may be ignorant, but not afraid to uncover.

Irreversible

Once a threshold concept is grasped, or even partly grasped, there is no going back. This is Pandora's Box territory. It is not possible to revert to our previous state of not knowing, and conscious effort would be needed to undertake a process of un-knowing (Clouder, 2005). Furthermore, once our existing knowledge is challenged with something new and different, it is difficult to pretend and act as if this knowledge does not exist and to not do anything about it (Hibbert and Cunliffe, 2015). This would explain the differing spaces occupied by teachers and learners as they relate to threshold concepts from different angles: the student not knowing what is ahead of them, with the teacher's previous understandings, before the threshold was crossed, long gone (Gaunt and Loffman, 2018). Our new learning of Welsh Context, therefore, shapes and becomes part of the new us – our new identity. Like a snowball effect or nesting dolls, it becomes an integral part of our discovery of further knowledge.

Integrative

Gaunt and Loffman (2018) refer to the fact that threshold concepts are integrative as new connections and relationships unfold within a subject. This inter-relatedness can extend the understanding and sense-making of other concepts, resulting in the integrated and wider development of knowledge across disparate elements of a discipline (Nicola-Richmond et al, 2018; Chatterjee-Padmanabhan et al, 2019). A highly integrative threshold concept demands much effort on behalf of the learner to grasp some potentially complex and difficult interrelated elements. This can make the world appear more problematic and knowledge acquisition more troublesome (Meyer and Land, 2003). In turn, this will have a gradual influence both on how we see the world as well as how we fit into that world (Land et al, 2014), like finding connecting pieces in a jigsaw. The interesting observation to make here is that gradually, we may realise that it is not a 50-piece jigsaw that we are trying to put together here, but more like a 1,000-piece one, without the picture on the box, as we come to realise that the more we learn the less we know.

In relation to the context of working in Wales, we will be aware that living in Wales brings with it its own uniqueness. However, themes such as rurality, post-industrialisation, recession, youth migration, poverty, health inequalities, digital divide, homelessness, living costs, adverse childhood experiences, immigration and bilingualism are, of course, found beyond Wales. These are themes about which others have written, and with whom we can relate, bringing our deepened learning and understanding back home, as it were.

Bounded

The easiest way to explain boundedness may be through Barradell and Fortune's (2020) analogy, which illustrates that, despite being neighbouring European countries, France and Spain each have their own distinct histories, languages and cultural and societal norms. Similarly, a range of professions may have similar foundational knowledge, but also distinct specialties and practice areas based on different approaches (Barradell and Fortune, 2020). Threshold concepts are instrumental in demarcating disciplines, inherently promoting a unique professional identity and worldview (Gaunt and Loffman, 2018). Notwithstanding the preceding claims, this may be where the tension lies with social work-specific threshold concepts, as social work's *raison d'être* requires appreciation and understanding of threshold concepts from several other disciplines, such as psychology, philosophy, sociology, law and education. This same boundedness, or lack of it, similarly relates to the context of working in Wales, where concepts from other disciplines remain essential to understand the micro, meso and macro elements of the Welsh Context. For example, we may need to explore a person's health circumstances through a health economics threshold concept, their capacity through a legal threshold concept, and so on.

Troublesome

Taylor (2008) and Cartensen and Bernhard (2008) consider this as the main defining characteristic of a threshold concept, that sets it apart from other thinking. This is because, without it, the other characteristics would not come into play. The search for trouble-free knowledge (Clouder, 2005) may explain why it is hard to find or place oneself in a liminal space. The learner will notice a disruption of current knowledge and understandings and face the fact that there are shortcomings to be addressed in their existing thinking (Hawkins and Edwards, 2015). This will mean letting go of previous thinking. Threshold concepts are therefore far from trouble-free.

There are various ways in which knowledge can be troublesome (Meyer and Land, 2003). Troublesomeness can be caused simply by not knowing for what one is looking (Land et al, 2014), or once found, that it is difficult or complicated to understand (conceptually difficult knowledge). It may conflict with previous understandings or come from a different value base or perspective to one's own, causing dissonance (foreign knowledge). Part of the human condition is that much of our acquired knowledge remains unused as we fail to make active connections to either everyday life or what is going on in the world around us (inert knowledge). Some knowledge may come in the form of personal wisdom that is too difficult to articulate and transfer (tacit knowledge) or considered mundane and meaningless (ritual knowledge). Learning new concepts and terms demands an extension of language – a further layer of potential troublesomeness (Meyer and Land, 2003).

Since the Welsh Context is often conflated with the Welsh language, as such, it becomes troublesome at the first hurdle. This is inevitable if the 'Welsh' element is linked to binary thinking of either being able to speak Welsh or not. This inevitably leads to a painful, possibly emotional space. Surely exploring the Welsh Context cannot be about making social workers feel lambasted for not speaking the Welsh language or feel inadequate and/or negative about themselves and their skills deficit – and, of course, it is not.

In practice

Despite a threshold concept seeming to be in accordance with all of Meyer and Land's (2003) characteristics, the ability to grasp a threshold concept does not automatically mean ability in practice. This could be linked to the earlier statement about the Welsh Context being more than references to a few context-related components. For example, citing Census data of Welsh speakers, practising in line with The Active Offer of the Welsh language (the upfront provision of services in the Welsh language without having to request it) (Social Care Wales, 2022), does not necessarily provide evidence of having crossed the concept threshold and practising in line with the new understanding. Heading and Loughlin (2018) use a tennis analogy to illustrate this point. They highlight that several concepts make up tennis, and understanding the game is not the same as the ability to play it. More is involved than merely learning a collection of separate ideas identified as a concept. Furthermore, unless a deeper understanding is reached, learners will find themselves remaining on the outside looking in and will not enjoy the benefits of the 'insider position' (Stopford, 2021: 164).

Care must also be taken to avoid implying that grasping a threshold concept involves all learners arriving at the same defined understanding and achieving total comprehension in due course. Learners may get stuck with aspects of a threshold concept within a liminal space, which does not equate to rejecting or struggling with the concept in its entirety (Morgan, 2012). Gaunt and Loffman (2018) advise that learners are more likely to embrace learning when they have been forewarned about the likely struggles involved in edging towards understanding. Furthermore, Land et al (2005) suggest that informing learners about the nature and purpose of threshold concepts early provides them with the opportunity to assess their own progress in understanding the subject matter, and is more likely to generate perseverance and patience required to sustain the journey.

Threshold concepts are usually of interest to academics and educators whose business is to design and deliver a subject-specific curriculum, that is, what is to be learned within a subject area (Barradell, 2013). However, there is ongoing debate about who decides what is considered a threshold concept within a particular discipline (Marshall and Wagner, 2019), and less explicitness about how to get there. Even if it was explicit, leading a horse to water remains to be the case, as educators cannot force learners to acquire the knowledge, or undertake the learning on their behalf (Heading and Loughlin, 2018). The student/learner has to come up with their own insights and find their own path to and through the threshold (Marroum, 2004). Threshold concepts are not the IKEA furniture equivalent of learning, and do not come with step-by-step assembly instructions. As such, there is no guaranteed transformation: it is only the opportunity to 'assemble the kit' that can be offered.

Land, Meyer and Baillie (2010) suggest that when a new threshold concept is introduced to a group of learners, even in the unlikely event that they all have similar baseline knowledge, there could still be the possibility of four various levels of understanding among the group – complete, partial, wrong and meaningless – as further confirmation of the idiosyncrasy of learning. Furthermore, Heading and Loughlin (2018) refer to the impact of bias, where learners may find difficulty in appreciating the different insights of others or any challenge to their own. This could result in a learner creating the world as they would like it to be, rather than as it is. This may explain the struggle with grappling with the context of working in Wales, where understandably, Welshness can be taken personally, making it difficult to move beyond this element, which is unhelpful, if not irrelevant.

Liminal spaces

Liminal spaces are not emotionally neutral spaces and can evoke feelings of anxiety, doubt, frustration and confusion (Hawkins and Edwards, 2015). In other words, they are troublesome. The word 'liminal' originates from the Latin word '*limen*', which means threshold, and threshold concepts are crossed in liminal spaces. Although threshold suggests a door or gateway and space suggests rooms, liminal spaces are best described as periods, and as times when learners are between old and familiar thinking and yet to grasp new understandings. There is a sense of being 'betwixt and between' (Turner, 1987) – in limbo – and of being neither here nor there, swinging back and forth in trying to fill gaps in understanding. There may be a glimmer of understanding here and there, only to be gone again, until further efforts of grasping are to be made, moving the learner towards increased understanding (Gaunt and Hoffman, 2018). Some oscillation may happen between knowledge about how to behave in the new state, and the wholesale adoption of such behaviours so that they become second nature. The significance of this space is that the learner is willing to struggle with mastering the concept, and is neither avoiding, oblivious to, nor choosing to refute the concept altogether and, as aforementioned, returning in full to the pre-liminal state is not possible (Land et al, 2005).

If what Meyer and Land (2003) are saying about threshold concepts is correct, it is reasonable to conclude that they are instrumental in what is also known as deep learning (Stopford, 2021). Some learners fully commit to learning, engaging in a 'deep' learning approach (Dyer and Hurd, 2016). Others will engage in just about enough 'surface learning' to do what is needed. Deep learning has an intrinsic drive, where such learners have an inner desire to go beyond minimum requirements as part of their motivation to learn as much as possible. For surface learners, the focus and drive are externalised, with efforts linked to achieving a particular mark or award, impressing someone else, or keeping out of trouble (Entwistle and Entwistle, 2003; Asikainen and Gijbels, 2017). Simplifying threshold concepts, albeit with good intentions to assist and accelerate understanding, risks learners settling for the initial introduction to the threshold as the threshold itself. This is more likely to be the case for the surface learner than for the deep learner. This could, at least partly, explain what can happen with learning/teaching the Welsh Context. The resultant effect may be ritualised learning and/or mimicry (intentional or non-intentional), and ultimately, failure to cross the threshold (Cousin, 2006). This could explain why citing populations statistics and referring to The Active Offer may appear to pay homage to the Welsh Context, but, as a threshold concept, it may not have been fully understood.

Although liminal spaces may be considered effective learning and development spaces, they can remain somewhat counter-intuitive. The knowledge may be troublesome in and of itself, causing discomfort and uncertainty. Some social workers may think that the examination of their values, beliefs and prejudices may get them into trouble, especially when their practice is being assessed. Ironically, they are more likely to get into 'trouble' for not being open and reflective, as the valued signs of commitment to professional learning and development. However, learning in this manner does require there to be an explicitly safe environment, where biographical discussions are directly linked to the practice issues at hand, and do not digress to irrelevant areas or by improper use of power (Foote, 2013).

Mimicry and fakery are also found in liminal spaces and can be considered manifestations of a learner's coping mechanisms or playing it safe in a state of liminality (Cousin, 2006). With possibly no intended deviousness, individuals may genuinely believe and state that that they 'do it' already and consider themselves to have crossed the threshold concept (Hawkins and Edwards, 2015), but may have only achieved partial, wrong or meaningless understanding (Land et al, 2014). This limits potential to recognise and learn further concepts, missing the integrative, irreversibility and transformative potential inherent in threshold concepts (Meyer and Land, 2005). Interestingly, Owen (2016) has established that there is a link between the well-being and performance levels of deep learners, whereas surface learners tend to underperform in relation to their abilities and may be anxious in their approach. As for other professions, this also has relevance for social work professionals.

Although I had come to understand, through the lens of threshold concepts, more about why learning about the Welsh Context may be difficult, I was also in a place where suggesting what could be done about it seemed to be slipping further away. I was in a liminal space, and I was stuck. Heading and Loughlin (2018) and Hawkins and Edwards (2015) are in agreement that threshold concepts are not located in neat silos and are not learned one by one in an orderly fashion, ending one before starting another. Understanding one threshold concept can bring others into view and within reach, highlighting areas for further exploration and understanding. Searching for 'threshold concepts in social work' did not result in a huge return, but what did come up was the work of Foote (2013), exploring critical reflection as a specific threshold concept to social work. This was a 'lightbulb moment' for me.

The troublesome knowledge within the liminal space had become transformational in that the two concepts became inextricably linked (integrated). This was a point of no return for me, as the context of working in Wales (or the Welsh Context) could never again be considered separate from critical reflection. This last section will hopefully explain why.

Critical reflection

As we have come to learn, although threshold concepts are troublesome to master, they are transformational with critical reflection being no exception (Foote, 2013). It calls for analysing social work practice at all levels. These levels are described by Bronfenbrenner (1979) as micro, meso and macro in considering the immediate circle, the community and wider society, which includes any policies and legislation that may have an impact on the individual and their situation. This has echoes of Thompson's (2005) Personal, Cultural and Societal Model, and its concern with analysing the power within a situation on a personal, cultural and structural level.

Over ten years ago, George, Coleman and Barnoff (2010) argued that social work had developed into an individual-based profession, with less focus on linking personal problems to structural and systemic factors, shoehorning individual needs to fit in with ever-decreasing services, and thus reducing social work to a brief, often inadequate intervention to the most acute and intense of situations. Fook (2002) and Mullaly and Dupré (2018) claim that individuals cannot be held solely responsible for their own problems, calling for links to be made between individual issues and broader societal issues in the quest of achieving a more equitable and fair society. The principles of the Social Services and Well-being (Wales) Act 2014 attempt to direct social work practice towards this notion, focusing more on prevention and early intervention, voice and control, and coproduction (Care Council for Wales, 2017). Whether such pieces of legislation and policies manage to deliver on the promise of tangible long-term individual and social change remains at the heart of critical reflection.

Critical reflection requires social workers to consider their own position in relation to the individual with whom they are working. This usually involves examining and challenging their own existing beliefs and assumptions, thoughts, feelings and actions, as well as power and assumptions implicit in organisational structures and discourses (Foote, 2013). In Fook's (2002) critical reflection model, this is the reconstitution stage that follows the telling the story and deconstruction stages. Overall, this should lead to a deeper understanding of the student's experience and impact of practice that informs future learning. Hibbert and Cunliffe (2015) also add reflexive practice to the mix. They distinguish between the examination of our own practices, as involved in self-reflexivity, that leads to changing and improving practice, and the questioning of wider organisational and social practices, as involved in critical reflexivity, to challenge oppression, injustice and inequality. Effective social work involves both, as we should not consider ourselves as separate from the context in which we practise our social work.

Messages for practice

- We need an appropriate critical reflective framework from which to explore the context of our social work practice, wherever we may be, and regardless of whether we are in Wales or not.
- The skill of critical reflection is as portable as driving skills. However, practising social work without engaging in critical reflection is like driving where there are no other cars. Put simply, there is no context to the driving. With nothing to impact it, it becomes routine and provides no opportunity to build our confidence and, most importantly, increase our safety on the roads. If driving is about mobility, independence and freedom to move from one place to another, driving where there are no other cars tends to miss the total point of driving. Practising (Welsh Context) without critical reflection is similarly futile.

Due to the potential for benefit and harm in social work, critical reflection is a non-negotiable concept in considering the impact of our whole selves and biographies as social workers on the individuals we come across and for whom we provide services. It is only by fully adopting critical reflection, self-reflexivity and critical reflexivity in our work with individuals that we can start to initiate real change and execute the inherent positive power of social work. In doing this, we will also have covered the context of working in Wales, without needing to make further considerations. Only then can we safely conclude that the Welsh Context is not *about* social work: the Welsh Context *is* social work.

Conclusion

Linking critical reflection to the Welsh Context takes us to a different space. 'Doing' the Welsh Context involves more than merely linking different 'Welsh/ Wales' stuff when reflecting on practice. Neither is it a case of bolting on a few relevant elements to tick the proverbial 'Welsh Context' box. Critical reflection of social work practice is inherently the Welsh Context.

The title of this chapter has echoes of the saying 'You are what you eat', which implies that what people eat consequently defines and influences their physical and mental states, and affects their lives. It could be argued that 'We are what we know' is relevant to our social work identity and the social work that we practise. Furthermore, the knowledge we 'feed' ourselves is not limited to defining and influencing ourselves, but also the people we come across in practice.

The story of writing this chapter created a liminal space for me. My hope is that it will do the same for you. Considering the context of working in Wales through the lens of threshold concepts identifies why the learning is often troublesome, but also how it can be transformative. What I have also found is that in the process of exploring and articulating the Welsh Context a good companion has been found within an existing social work threshold concept.

Further resources

1. Collingwood, P. (2005) 'Integrating theory and practice: the Three-Stage Theory Framework', *Journal of Practice Teaching*, 6(1): 6–23.
2. Torrance, D. (2022) *Devolution in Wales: 'A Process, Not an Event'*. (Research Briefing) House of Commons Library. https://researchbriefings.files.parliam ent.uk/documents/CBP-8318/CBP-8318.pdf
3. Welsh Government (2022) *More Than Just Words: Five Year Plan 2022–27*. https://gov.wales/sites/default/files/publications/2022–07/more-than-just-words-action-plan-2022–2027.pdf

References

Asikainen, H. and Gijbels, D. (2017) 'Do students develop towards more deep approaches to learning during studies? A systematic review on the development of students' deep and surface approaches to learning in higher education', *Education Psychological Review*, 29: 205–234.

Atherton, J., Hadfield, P. and Meyers, R. (2008) 'Threshold Concepts in the Wild'. Expanded version of a paper presented at Threshold Concepts: Theory to Practice Conference, Queen's University, Kingston, Ontario, 18–20 June 2008. https://www.doceo.co.uk/tools/Threshold_Concepts_Wild_expanded_70.pdf

Baillie, C., Bowden, J.A. and Meyer, J.H.F. (2013) 'Threshold capabilities: threshold concepts and knowledge capability linked through variation theory', *Higher Education*, 65: 227–246.

Barradell, S. (2013) 'The identification of threshold concepts: a review of theoretical complexities and methodological challenges', *Higher Education*, 65(2): 265–276.

Barradell, S. and Fortune, T. (2020) 'Bounded: the neglected threshold concept characteristic', *Innovations in Education and Teaching International*, 57(3): 296–304.

Bronfenbrenner, U. (1979) *The Ecology of Human Development*, Cambridge, MA: Harvard University Press.

Care Council for Wales (2017) 'Social Services and Well-being (Wales) Act 2014: the main principles underpinning the Act'. https://socialcare.wales/cms-assets/documents/hub-downloads/Principles-Resource-Guide_March-17.pdf

Cartensen, A.-K. and Bernhard, J. (2008) 'Threshold concepts and keys to the portal of understanding', in R. Land, J.H.F. Meyer and J. Smith (eds) *Threshold Concepts within the Disciplines*, Rotterdam: Sense Publishers, pp 143–154.

Chartered Institute of Personnel and Development (2021) *PESTLE analysis*. https://www.cipd.co.uk/knowledge/strategy/organisational-development/pes tle-analysis-factsheet#7986

Chatterjee-Padmanabhan, M., Nielsen, W. and Sanders, S. (2019) 'Joining the research conversation: threshold concepts embedded in the literature review', *Higher Education Research and Development*, 38(3): 494–507.

Clouder, L. (2005) 'Caring as a "threshold concept": transforming students in higher education into health(care) professionals', *Teaching in Higher Education*, 10(4): 505–517.

Cousin, G. (2006) 'An introduction to threshold concepts', *Planet*, 17: 4–5.

Davies, P. (2006) 'Threshold concepts: how can we recognize them?', in J. Meyer and R. Land (eds) *Overcoming Barriers to Student Understanding: Threshold Concepts and Troublesome Knowledge*, Abingdon: Routledge, pp 70–84.

Dyer, S. and Hurd, F. (2016) '"What's going on?" Developing reflexivity in the management classroom: from surface to deep learning and everything in between', *Academy of Management Learning and Education*, 15(2): 287–303.

Entwistle, N. and Entwistle, D. (2003) 'Preparing for examinations: the interplay of memorising and understanding, and the development of knowledge objects', *Higher Education Research and Development*, 22(1): 19–41.

Fook, J. (2002) *Social Work: Critical Theory and Practice*, London: Sage Publications.

Foote, W. (2013) 'Threshold theory and social work', *Social Work Education*, 32(4): 424–438.

Gaunt, T. and Loffman, C. (2018) 'When I say … threshold concepts', *Medical Education*, 52: 789–790.

George, P., Coleman, B. and Barnoff, L. (2010) 'Stories from the field: practicing structural social work in current times: practitioners' use of creativity', *Critical Social Work*, 11(2). https://doi.org/10.22329/csw.v11i2.5821

Hawkins, B. and Edwards, G. (2015) 'Managing the monsters of doubt: liminality, threshold concepts and leadership learning', *Management Learning*, 46(1): 24–43.

Heading, D. and Louglin, E. (2018) 'Lonergan's insight and threshold concepts: students in the liminal space', *Teaching in Higher Education*, 23(6): 657–667.

Hibbert, P. and Cunliffe, A.L. (2015) 'Responsible management: engaging moral reflexive practice through threshold concepts', *Journal of Business Ethics*, 127(1): 177–188.

International Federation of Social Work (2014) *Global Definition of Social Work*. https://www.ifsw.org/what-is-social-work/global-definition-of-social-work/

Irving, G., Wright, A. and Hibbert, P. (2019) 'Threshold concept learning: emotions and liminal space transitions', *Management Learning*, 50(3): 355–373.

Land, R., Cousin, G., Meyer, J.H.F. and Davies, P. (2005) 'Threshold concepts and troublesome knowledge (3): implications for course design and evaluation', in C. Rust (ed) *Improving Student Learning Diversity and Inclusivity*, Oxford: Oxford Centre for Staff Learning and Development, pp 53–63.

Land, R., Meyer, J.H.F. and Baillie, C. (2010) 'Editors' preface: threshold concepts and transformational learning', in *Threshold Concepts and Transformational Learning*, Rotterdam: Sense, pp ix–xlii.

Land, R., Rattray, J. and Vivian, P. (2014) 'Learning in the liminal space: a semiotic approach to threshold concepts', *Higher Education*, 67(2): 199–217.

Marroum, R.-M. (2004) 'The role of insight in science education: an introduction to the cognitional theory of Bernard Lonergan', *Science and Education*, 13(6): 19–40.

Marshall, A. and Wagner, S. (2019) 'A way through … troublesome knowledge: student research as threshold concept practice', *Portal: Libraries and the Academy*, 19(3): 393–406.

Meyer, J.H.F. and Land, R. (2003) 'Threshold concepts and troublesome knowledge: linkages to thinking and practising within the disciplines', in C. Rust (ed) *Improving Student Learning: Theory and Practice—Ten Years On*, Oxford: Oxford Centre for Staff and Learning Development, pp 412–424.

Meyer, J.H.F. and Land, R. (2005) 'Threshold concepts and troublesome knowledge (2): epistemological considerations and a conceptual framework for teaching and learning', *Higher Education*, 49(3): 373–388.

Meyer, J.H.F. and Land, R. (2006) *Overcoming Barriers to Student Understanding: Threshold Concepts and Troublesome Knowledge*, Abingdon: Routledge.

Morgan, H. (2012) 'The social model of disability as a threshold concept: troublesome knowledge and liminal spaces in social work education', *Social Work Education*, 31(2): 215–226.

Mullaly, B. and Dupré, M. (2018) *The New Structural Social Work: Ideology, Theory, and Practice* (4th edn), Oxford: Oxford University Press.

Natanasabapathy, P. and Maathuis-Smith, S. (2019) 'Philosophy of being and becoming: a transformative learning approach using threshold concepts', *Educational Philosophy and Theory*, 51(4): 369–379.

Nicola-Richmond, K., Pépin, G., Larkin, H. and Taylor, C. (2018) 'Threshold concepts in higher education: a synthesis of the literature relating to measurement of threshold crossing', *Higher Education Research and Development*, 37(1): 1–14.

Owen, S. (2016) 'Professional learning communities: building skills, reinvigorating the passion, and nurturing teacher wellbeing and "flourishing" within significantly innovative schooling contexts', *Educational Review*, 68(4): 403–419.

Reeping, D. (2020) 'Threshold concepts as "jewels of the curriculum": rare as diamonds or plentiful as cubic zirconia?', *International Journal for Academic Development*, 25(1): 58–70.

Rowbottom, D. (2007) 'Demystifying threshold concepts', *Journal of Philosophy of Education*, 41(2): 263–270.

Smith, W.L., Crowley, R.M., Demoiny, S.B. and Cushing-Leubner, J. (2021) 'Threshold concept pedagogy for antiracist social studies teaching', *Multicultural Perspectives*, 23(2): 87–94.

Social Care Wales (2022) 'Understanding language needs'. https://socialcare. wales/resources-guidance/improving-care-and-support/people-with-demen tia/understanding-language-needs#:~:text=The%20'active%20offer'%20me ans%20that,through%20the%20medium%20of%20Welsh

Stopford, R. (2021) 'Threshold concepts and certainty: a critical analysis of "troublesomeness"', *Higher Education*, 82: 63–179.

Taylor, C.E. (2008) 'Threshold concepts, troublesome knowledge and ways of thinking and practising', in R. Land, J.H.F. Meyer and J. Smith (eds) *Threshold Concepts within the Disciplines*, Rotterdam: Sense Publishers, pp 185–195.

Thompson, N. (2005) *Anti Discriminatory Practice* (4th edn), Basingstoke: Palgrave Macmillan.

Timmermans, J.A. and Meyer, J.H. (2019) 'A framework for working with university teachers to create and embed "Integrated Threshold Concept Knowledge" (ITCK) in their practice', *International Journal for Academic Development*, 24(4): 354–368.

Turner, V. (1987) 'Betwixt and between: the liminal period in rites of passage', in L.C. Mahdi, S. Foster and M. Little (eds) *Betwixt and Between: Patterns of Masculine and Feminine Initiation*, Chicago: Open Court Publishing, pp 3–19.

Winkler, E.N. (2018) 'Racism as a threshold concept: examining learning in a "diversity requirement" course', *Race, Ethnicity and Education*, 21(6): 808–826.

5

Social work education in Wales

Jo Redcliffe and Jaime Ortiz

Chapter objectives

- To recognise some of the opportunities and challenges in providing contemporary pre- and post-qualifying social work education and training, from a Welsh perspective.

- To consider how the regulation of social work education in Wales has attempted to raise standards to address criticisms and to work towards the reinstatement of public and political faith in the profession.

- To contemplate the future of social work education in Wales, both as impacted by the COVID-19 pandemic and relevant to contemporary economic pressures.

Introduction

The Welsh Government has a vision of a Wales-only social care model that is based on coproduction, grounded in culture and society, free at the point of contact and fits the long-term care needs of its growing and ageing population. However, despite Wales' reputation for innovation in social care delivery, particularly adult social care (Gwilym, 2011; Redcliffe, 2021), social work education continues to be criticised for its inability to match practice expectations (Healy, 2017), leading to lack of practitioner autonomy (Soldatic and Meekosha, 2012), an overly bureaucratic system and an overemphasis on professional power (Harris and Roulstone, 2011).

Social work education in context

This section focuses on the recent development of social work education in Wales, starting with the Diploma in Social Work and followed by the Degree in Social Work and post-qualifying education and concluding with an example of the Welsh way of social work education. Contemporary social work education in Wales and the wider United Kingdom comes under intense scrutiny and is subject to considerable regulation and regular reform aimed at improving both education and practice (Short et al, 2022). The Regulation and Inspection of Social Care Act 2016 places the task of regulating social work education in Wales at the door of Social Care Wales. This is alongside accountability for the regulation and development of the social care workforce and responsibility for leading improvement across the sector in general. Critics point at the succession of reorganisations, reforms, restructuring and student debt that have been imposed on social work education (Higgins et al, 2014; Short et al, 2022) as being somewhat to blame for its broad paradigm that is too general (Roulstone, 2012) and therefore falls short of practice expectations. The result is a public outcry over a series of safeguarding failures (Orme et al, 2009; Wilson and Campbell, 2012). In order to address these public and political concerns, social work education in Wales, as in other parts of the UK, has focused on raising its standards. These improvements are aimed at ensuring that social work education appropriately prepares students for practice upon qualification (Munro, 2011; Quality Assurance Agency for UK Higher Education, 2019).

The Diploma in Social Work

The Diploma in Social Work (DipSW) was the approved qualification of the then UK social work regulator, the Central Council for Education and Training in Social Work, between 1993 and 2002–03. It replaced both the work-based route (Certificate in Social Service) and the academic route (Certificate of Qualification in Social Work). Very soon after its introduction, the DipSW faced censure from a variety of stakeholders including students themselves, employers, the media and academics. Dominelli (1996) and Taylor and Bogo (2014) critiqued its overemphasis on competences, perceiving this approach as an attempt to decontextualise and reduce practice complexities into a prescriptive checklist of behaviours.

Research by Lyons and Manion (2004) into the experiences of newly qualified social workers during their DipSW education revealed high levels of dissatisfaction with the teaching of work-based skills including using information technology and recording. Similarly, Marsh and Triseliotis (1996) identified that over half of newly qualified social workers thought that they had not been taught well, with once again the teaching of skills being highlighted as a particular concern. Furthermore, the experiences of non-traditional students from diverse backgrounds who did not fit the typical white, mature female profile – for example, students with disabilities, Black and minority ethnic (BME) students, lesbian, gay, bisexual and transgender students – experienced lower progression rates than other students, indicating that systems were not in place to provide adequate support (Aymer and Bryan, 1996; Baron et al, 1996; Cropper, 2000; Crawshaw, 2002).

The DipSW was also criticised by employers. It was deemed to be of inadequate length (two years) and to emphasise training rather than education (Orme, 2000; Preston-Shoot, 2000). Employers of newly qualified social workers also bemoaned the lack of familiarity with routine procedural skills (recording, report writing, and so on) as well as poor links between theory and practice. The pathways model was disapproved of, with the preference being for a generic model. Its competence-based approach was perceived to inadequately prepare students for the application of professional judgements in practice (Dominelli,

1996; Lymbery, 2006). In addition, the way in which competence was assessed was perceived to be value laden and, as a result, potentially disadvantaged students from under-represented groups, for example, BME students (Kemshall, 1993). Combined with a curriculum that was perceived as being too statutory-biased, too open to interpretation and a lack of recognition of employer/practice input, plus the impact of student debt, the product of all this discontent was too much to bear and the DipSW was terminated in 2002 with resounding support for change (Department of Health, Social Services and Public Safety, 1999).

The Degree in Social Work

The challenges of the DipSW prompted the call for standards to be raised to at least degree level (Lyons and Manion, 2004). The overall rationale for this change was indicative of a more general drive for degree qualifications in other professions. The vision of the new regulator, the Care Council for Wales (CCW), was to increase the standard of social work education and practice with the intended consequence of an improvement in the quality of service for citizens. The introduction of the undergraduate social work degree was therefore intended to ensure that social workers were equipped with generic knowledge, practice skills and competency (CCW, 2004). In addition, the practice component of the qualification was expanded to better prepare newly qualified workers for the realities of contemporary practice (SCW, 2011).

The Care Standards Act 2000 and the Social Services Inspectorate for Wales brought together various rules and requirements in one place, including the 'Requirements for Social Work Training in Wales' (CCW, 2004, updated 2012), the learning outcomes and standards required at each level of the new degree (Quality Assurance Agency Subject Benchmark Statements for Social Work 2000, updated 2008 and 2016), the Code of Professional Practice for Social Care (CCW, 2002, updated SCW, 2015 and 2017), the National Occupational Standards in Social Work (CCW, 2002, updated 2011) and the 'Approval and Visiting of Degree Courses in Social Work (Wales) Rules' (CCW, 2004). The particular requirements of the new undergraduate degree were established by the regional Care Councils and required academic learning to be more relevant to better support practice learning, the length of practice learning to be increased overall, and improvements made in students' skills in critical reflection and application of theory (Wilson and Kelly, 2010). This represented the latest and biggest event in a parade of reforms to social work education since the introduction of the DipSW in 1993 (Blewett and Tunstill, 2007). The qualification was to emphasise the abilities of the students in practical knowledge, skills, critical analysis, communication, theoretical application and effective participation in multidisciplinary practice environments (Department of Health, 2003).

Transformation was not restricted to the level of qualification only – legislative and policy changes were also apparent. The introduction of the Care Standards Act 2000 resulted in new Codes of Practice for social care workers and employers, a register of people appropriately qualified to work in social care/social work and, in 2005, the restriction of the title 'social worker' (SCW, 2017).

Early indications revealed that the changes implemented by the introduction of the Degree in Social Work resulted in an increase in the number of applications to social work programmes, the creation of a larger pool of potential applicants with higher educational qualifications, and a more rigorous selection process which involved citizens who use services and their carers and comprised interviews and written tasks (Evaluation of the Social Work Degree Qualification in England Team, 2008). However, despite this seemingly promising start, public opinion was again dented by a series of highly publicised tragedies including the deaths of Victoria Climbié in 2000, Peter Connelly in 2007 and Khyra Ishaq in 2008. Enquiries and reports found social work practice to be wanting. The Laming Review (2009) and the subsequent report on social work in England (Social Work Task Force, 2009), found that the Degree in Social Work did not adequately prepare students for social work practice. Fifteen recommendations were made in total, with four focusing specifically on the education of social workers from point of entry to qualification. These recommendations called for strengthening of the entry criteria, overhaul of content and delivery of curricula, new arrangements for high-quality practice placements and more transparent regulation of education to ensure quality and consistency (Social Work Task Force, 2009). The Department of Health (2002) stipulated the involvement of citizens who used services and their carers as a basic requirement of social work education (CCW, 2001). In addition, it was stated that of all the stakeholders (employers, higher education institutions, students, citizens, practice educators, external examiners and the relevant regulator) only higher education institutions and citizens were required to participate in every one of the eight specified roles, ranging from student selection to programme design and delivery.

Post-qualifying social work

Increasingly stringent UK regulation requires qualified social workers to evidence post-qualifying (PQ) continuing professional development (Moriarty and Manthorpe, 2014). PQ education is subject to the same sort of demands as its pre-qualifying sibling, but is also affected by time-poverty resulting from employment. Additionally, the PQ emphasis on distance learning delivery methods that predated the COVID-19 pandemic requires an information technology framework that is fit for purpose.

The most recent iteration of PQ education across Wales was the Continuing Professional Education and Learning (CPEL) Framework. Commissioned in 2012 by SCW, it comprised a Level 6 (graduate level) Consolidation Programme that newly qualified social workers had to complete within their first three-year period of registration, plus an additional three higher programmes. These higher programmes were all Level 7 (Masters level), except for the first programme that learners could opt to study at either Level 6 or 7. The programmes were modular and were designed to be accessible, primarily work-based and delivered bilingually in order to strengthen the body of knowledge across the profession nationally. CPEL ended in 2020, and key messages that emerged from an independent review identified positives, including the innovative nature of the programmes, the quality of the learning materials and the excellent teamwork between the providers. It also identified that a rethink of overall design was necessary to address critical foundational factors that included student competence and satisfaction with online learning, and the requirement for practical employer support, for example ring-fenced study time (for a fuller discussion, see Rees et al, 2018).

Quality PQ education is essential for an informed workforce, but the very nature of it is challenging. Following a two-year PQ gap, partly due to the impact of COVID-19, the situation at the time of writing is that SCW is inviting tenders for the design and delivery of the successor to CPEL. The overall objectives of the new iteration are consistent with those of the original, focusing on raising standards of practice and assisting with the recruitment, retention and development of practitioners. Similarly, the requirement to address the Welsh context remains central, as does modular structure, flexibility of access and the achievement of academic qualifications. What currently lacks clarity is how this new version will address the shortcomings of the original CPEL design, namely the impact of time-poverty on practitioners, and the need for employer support in the form of ring-fenced time and back-fill. This is particularly concerning considering that this new version will come at a time when the pressure on practitioners is at a peak (Social Care Wales and Health Education and Improvement Wales, 2020).

Current themes in social work education

This section is concerned with current themes within social work education in Wales. It begins with a consideration of the impact of, and learning from, the COVID-19 pandemic, followed by descriptions of the inclusion of creativity and social entrepreneurship into the curriculum. It concludes with some key suggestions for future research and practice.

The COVID-19 pandemic

Professional education is responsible for ensuring that practitioners provide high-quality, ethical social work interventions (Asakura and Bogo, 2021), and social work education in Wales has a strong in-person pedagogical tradition. The COVID-19 pandemic 'revealed the fragility' of in-person services (Petružytė et al, 2022: 2). Even prior to the pandemic the profession had a 'problematic relationship' with technology, and this general lack of expertise within a digital environment has been accused of contributing to unpreparedness for practice (Taylor-Beswick, 2022: 15). The swift move to online teaching and assessment in March 2020, triggered by the COVID-19 lockdown, meant that there was no time to plan a smooth transition and contributed to the exacerbation of contemporary trends. Some students reported increased mental health support needs (Morris et al, 2021). Practitioners and educators alike had to act quickly to deliver services or materials that had been planned for in-person delivery via digital platforms (Bennett et al, 2021; Hatton et al, 2021). Hard work by all ensured that the impact on the individual, whether a citizen in receipt of services or a student, was as marginal as possible.

PLOs were also hit by the transition to online teaching and assessment (Lomas et al, 2022). In Wales, PLOs make up around 50 per cent of social work education, the essence of which is for students to demonstrate their ability to transfer classroom learning into real-life practice situations. The initial suspension of PLOs plus the subsequent move to virtual practices resulted in lost learning opportunities for students and made the assessment of them more challenging for practice educators. In-person practices between PLO hosts differed, as did students' individual circumstances which required some to self-isolate, resulting in an unavoidable inequality where some students were able to participate in limited in-person activities, while others had no in-person experience at all.

The disruption of COVID-19 required us all to rethink our practices in innovative ways. Ferguson, Pink and Kelly (2020) perceive as beneficial the combination of different forms of practice to incorporate in-person, digital and hybrid models. While it is imperative to take a pragmatic approach and update practices, it is also important to plan for sustained change and not be tempted to throw the baby out with the bathwater. Akuffi Pentini and Lorenze (2020, in Hatton et al, 2021) advise us to be alert to the risk of erosion of in-person practices purely due to costs. In contrast, Taylor-Beswick (2022: 2) warns against the gradual reinstatement of pre-pandemic practices that risk the return to 'analogue methods'. The most likely path forward may be a hybrid one, as Wallengren Lynch, Dominelli and Cuadra (2022) advise us that some in-person teaching and learning is essential. However, we must pay attention to well-being in order to avoid technological burnout (see Chapter 15).

Creativity

As contemporary social work practice faces increasing financial constraints, decreasing service availability and the ongoing effects of COVID-19, so social work education needs to recognise these issues and respond in non-traditional ways (Skoura-Kirk et al, 2021). Hatton (2020) suggests that a creative approach to the curriculum is required to recognise intersectionality and social activism and to foster democratic participation of citizens. This is not a new idea per se – the inclusion of citizens who use services in social work education is central to the international definition of social work adopted by the International Federation of Social Workers (IFSW, 2014), and in Wales it is a requirement of both Batchelor and Masters level qualifying programmes (Social Care Wales, 2017). However, the extent of citizen representation across higher education institutions varies and can, as such, lack a formal framework (Dorozenko et al, 2016) resulting in the voices of citizens often being perceived as less valuable than those of other more traditional academic stakeholders (Anka and Taylor, 2016). Effective citizen involvement is essential to shift the patterns of traditional polarising views of academia ('first place') and PLOs ('second place') into a 'third place' (Meredith et al, 2021).

Asakura and Bogo (2021), Keeney et al (2021) and Lee et al (2021) suggest that simulation-based learning and assessment that uses citizens or actors may offer a flexible, consistent solution and ameliorate somewhat the effects of a lack of equitable opportunities for students. Similarly, advancement of our understanding of coproduction within professional education will help ensure that future generations of social workers can practise responsibly, sustainably and creatively despite the effects of austerity (Beresford, 2019).

The Welsh way

Part Nine of the Social Services and Well-being (Wales) Act 2014 (SSWWA) concerns coproduction, the aim of which is to tilt the balance of power more towards citizens who use the services. 'Co-create' is an arts-based approach to education, based in Swansea University. It involves partnerships between members of the citizen involvement group Llais (*Voice* in English), social work students and creative advisers working coproductively to present an issue relevant to the citizen to peers through a creative medium.

Evaluation of the project revealed many practice positives, including: the realisation that development of the relationship between the different stakeholders was often tricky but was the important factor, not the quality of the resulting creative artefact; and that the participants felt both challenged and changed by their involvement in the project.

The project also revealed two contemporary citizen-led research priorities: research into factors that address barriers to coproduction, and cost-benefit outcomes research into the impact of coproduction on subsequent service delivery. For a fuller consideration of this project, including the theoretical underpinnings and findings, please refer to Hatton, Maegusuku-Hewett and Redcliffe (forthcoming, 2023).

Social entrepreneurship

The latter research priority identified by the Co-create project represents the challenge for social work educators in ensuring that qualifications optimise student preparedness for contemporary practice. Cherry et al (2021) have noted how countries where the governments have neoliberalist leanings and a focus on market-based factors, have had their commitment to social welfare whittled away at. It is noticeable that Wales currently has the highest poverty rate in the UK at 23 per cent, compared with 18 per cent for Northern Ireland, 19 per cent for Scotland and 22 per cent for England (Joseph Rowntree Foundation, 2022). Poverty can lead to negative impacts at any and all points in the life-cycle, and this is further impacted by the current rising rates of inflation and energy prices. Those likely to be most affected by rising costs are non-working families, those unable to work due to disabilities or caring responsibilities, single-parent families, large families with three or more children, children, older citizens and Bangladeshi, Pakistani and Black families (Joseph Rowntree Foundation, 2022). Social entrepreneurship differs from commercial entrepreneurship because it looks to address social problems (Boysen, 2021).

In the UK, the British Association of Social Workers (BASW) requires practitioners to ensure that resources are shared equitably and on a 'needs' basis, which is similar to the National Association of Social Workers in the US, which specifically compels practitioners to attend to the needs of citizens living in poverty. Furthermore, increases in life expectancy mean that finances need to be carefully planned so that they last longer. Frey et al (2017) report that, historically, social workers used to be involved in the support of citizens through their financial problems, but notes that this element of the professional role has been lost. An already shaky financial system was hit hard by the COVID-19 pandemic (Cherry et al, 2021; Wang et al, 2022). Despite this, and despite the BASW requirement to engage with citizens who may be financially vulnerable and who may lack financial skills (Fenge, 2011; Frey et al, 2017), the social work curriculum in Wales currently contains little economic content. Fenge (2011) has long advised that there is a role for educators in assisting both students and practitioners to develop their financial skills, and Frey et al (2017) report that doing so can better help citizens through a strengths perspective to assess and support them to feel empowered to make decisions regarding financial problems.

Messages for practice

The following are required.

- International participatory research on the outcomes resulting from the introduction of creativity into social work curricula from the perspectives of students, citizens and educators.
- International participatory research into experiences of using digital technology during the global pandemic, including the management of ethics and well-being in digital educational settings.
- Injection of social entrepreneurship into social work curricula to assist students to learn how to respond to citizens' financial difficulties and to promote economic well-being.

Further resources

1. Rees, J., de Villiers, T., Livingston, W., Maegusuku-Hewett, T. and Prysor, G. (2018) 'A new distance learning national framework for social work continuing education: critical reflections on the first phases of implementation', *Social Work Education*, 37(6): 761–774. https://doi.org/10.1080/02615479.2018.1479383
2. Social Care Wales (2019) *The Framework for the Degree in Social Work in Wales.* https://socialcare.wales/cms_assets/file-uploads/The-framework-for-the-degree-in-social-work-in-Wales-2018.pdf
3. Gwilym, H. and Williams, C. (eds) (2021) *Social Policy for Social Welfare Practice – New Directions* (3rd edn), Birmingham: British Association of Social Workers.

References

Anka, A. and Taylor, I. (2016) 'Assessment as the site of power: a Bourdieusian interrogation of service user and carer involvement in the assessments of social work students', *Social Work Education*, 35(2): 172–185.

Asakura, K. and Bogo, M. (2021) 'Editorial: the use of simulation in advancing clinical social work education and practice', *Clinical Social Work Journal*, 49(2): 111–116.

Aymer, C. and Bryan, A. (1996) 'Black students' experience on social work courses: accentuating the positives', *The British Journal of Social Work*, 26(1): 1–16.

Baron, S., Phillips, R. and Stalker, K. (1996) 'Barriers to training for disabled social work students', *Disability and Society*, 11(3): 361–378.

Bennett, B., Ross, D. and Gates, T. (2021) 'Creating spatial, relational and cultural safety in online social work education during COVID-19', *Social Work Education*. https://www.frontiersin.org/articles/10.3389/fsoc.2018.00041/full

Beresford, P. (2019) 'Public participation in health and social care: exploring the co-production of knowledge', *Frontiers in Sociology*, 41(3).

Blewett, J., Lewis, J. and Tunstill, J. (2007) *The Changing Roles and Tasks of Social Work: A Literature Informed Discussion Paper*. London: Social Care Institute for Excellence.

Boysen, M. (2021) 'The incorporation of entrepreneurship into social work education: combining social and commercial norms', *Social Work Education*, 41(6): 1367–1386.

CCW (Care Council for Wales) (2001) *Social Work: A People Profession*, Cardiff: Care Council for Wales.

CCW (2002) *The Codes of Practice for Social Care Workers*. Cardiff: Care Council for Wales.

CCW (2004/12) *The Framework for the Degree in Social Work in Wales*. Cardiff: Care Council for Wales.

Cherry, K., Leotti, S., Panichelli, M. and Wahab, S. (2021) 'Pandemic possibilities: confronting neoliberalism in social work education', *Social Work Education*. https://doi.org/10.1080/02615479.2021.1989397

Crawshaw, M. (2002) 'Disabled people's access to social work education: ways and means of promoting environmental change', *Social Work Education*, 21(4): 503–514.

Cropper, A. (2000) 'Mentoring as an inclusive device for the excluded Black students' experience of a mentoring scheme', *Social Work Education*, 19(6): 597–607.

Department of Health (2002) *Requirements for Social Work Training*. London: Department of Health.

Department of Health (2003) *The Victoria Climbie Inquiry: Report of an Inquiry by Lord Laming*. London: Department of Health.

Department of Health, Social Services and Public Safety (1999) *Review of the Diploma in Social Work: Report on the Content of the DipSW Conducted as Part of the Stage Two Review of CCETSW*. http://www.dhsspsni.gov.uk/review_of_the_dipl oma_in_social_work_%28jm_consulting_report%29_.pdf

Dominelli, L. (1996) 'Deprofessionalizing social work: anti-oppressive practice, competencies and postmodernism', *British Journal of Social Work*, 26(2): 153–175.

Dorozenko, K., Ridley, S., Martin, R. and Mahboub, L. (2016) 'A journey of embedding mental health lived experience in social work education', *Social Work Education*, 35(8): 905–917.

Evaluation of Social Work Degree Qualification in England Team (2008) *Evaluation of the New Social Work Degree Qualification in England. Volume 1: Findings*. London: King's College London.

Fenge, L. (2011) 'Economic well-being and ageing: the need for financial education for social workers', *Social Work Education*, 31(4): 498–511.

Ferguson, H., Pink, S. and Kelly, L. (2020) *How Social Work and Child Protection Are Being Creative and Helping Children and Families During COVID-19 and Can Do So Beyond It*. https://www.researchinpractice.org.uk/children/news-views/ 2020/august/how-social-work-and-child-protection-are-being-creative- and-helping-children-and-families-during-covid-19-and-can-do-so- beyond-it/

Frey, J., Sherraden, M., Birkenmaier, J. and Callahan, C. (2017) 'Financial capability and asset building in social work education', *Journal of Social Work Education*, 53(1): 79–83.

Gwilym, H. (2011) 'Social services for adults in Wales', in H. Gwilym and C. Williams (eds) *Social Policy for Social Welfare Practice in a Devolved Wales* (2nd edn). Birmingham: Venture Press.

Harris, J. and Roulstone, A. (2011) *Disability, Policy and Professional Practice*, London: Sage.

Hatton, K. (2020) 'A new framework for creativity in social pedagogy', *International Journal of Social Pedagogy*, 9(1). doi: 10.14324/111.444.ijsp.2020.v9.x.016

Hatton, K., Galley, D., Veale, F., Tucker, G. and Bright, C. (2021) 'Creativity and care in times of crisis: an analysis of the challenges of the COVID-19 virus experienced by social work students in practice placement', *Social Work Education*. https://doi.org/10.1080/02615479.2021.1960306

Hatton, K., Maegusuku-Hewett, T. and Redcliffe, J. (forthcoming, 2023) 'Co-creating experiences through the use of arts in social work education: a cross-national comparison', *Social Work Education*.

Healy, K. (2017) 'Regulating for quality social work education: who owns the curriculum?', in M. Connolly, C. Williams and D. Coffey (eds) *Strategic Leadership in Social Work Education*, Cham: Springer, pp 53–66.

Higgins, M., Popple, K. and Crichton, N. (2014) 'The dilemmas of contemporary social work: a case study of the social work degree in England', *British Journal of Social Work*, 46(3): 619–634.

International Federation of Social Workers (2014) *Global Definition of Social Work*. https://www.ifsw.org/what-is-social-work/global-definition-of-social-work/

Joseph Rowntree Foundation (2022) *UK Poverty 2022: The Essential Guide to Understanding Poverty in the UK*. https://www.jrf.org.uk/report/uk-poverty-2022

Keeney, A., Byrnes, E., Young, J. and Beecher, B. (2021) 'Beyond COVID-19: what's next for skill assessment practices in social work education?', *Social Work Education*. https://doi.org/10.1080/02615479.2021.2003321

Kemshall, H. (1993) 'Assessing competence: scientific process or subjective inference? Do we really see it?', *Social Work Education*, 12(1): 36–45.

Lee, E., Kourgiantakis, T. and Hu, R. (2021) 'Developing holistic competence in cross-cultural social work practice: simulation-based learning optimized by blended teaching approach', *Social Work Education*. https://doi.org/10.1080/02615479.2021.1892055

Lomas, G., Gerstenberg, L., Kennedy, E., Fletcher, K., Ivory, N., Whitaker, L., et al (2022) 'Experiences of social work students undertaking a remote research-based placement during a global pandemic', *Social Work Education*. https://doi.org/10.1080/02615479.2022.2054980

Laming, L.H. (2009) *The Protection of Children in England: A Progress Report*. London: The Stationery Office.

Lymbery, M. (2006) 'United we stand? Partnership working in health and social care and the role of social work in services for older people', *British Journal of Social Work*, 36(7): 1119–1134.

Lyons, K. and Manion, H. (2004) 'Goodbye DipSW: trends in student satisfaction and employment outcomes: some implications for the new social work award', *Social Work Education*, 23(2): 133–148.

Marsh, P. and Triseliotis, J. (1996) *Ready to Practise? Social Workers and Probation Officers: Their Training and First Year in Work*, Aldershot: Avebury/Ashgate Publishing.

Meredith, C., Heslop, P. and Dodds, C. (2021) 'Simulation: social work education in a third place', *Social Work Education*. https://doi.org/10.1080/02615479.2021.1991908

Moriarty, J. and Manthorpe, J. (2014) 'Post-qualifying education for social workers: a continuing problem or a new opportunity?', *Social Work Education*, 33(3): 397–411.

Morris, B., Short, M., Bridges, D., Crichton, M., Velander, F., Rush, E., et al (2021) 'Responding to student mental health challenges during and post-COVID-19', *Social Work Education*. https://doi.org/10.1080/02615479.2021.1962271

Munro, E. (2011) *The Munro Review of Child Protection: Final Report, a Child-Centred System* (Vol. 8062). London: The Stationery Office.

Orme, J. (2000) 'Social work: "the appliance of social science" – a cautionary tale', *Social Work Education*, 19(4): 323–334.

Orme, J., MacIntyre, G., Green Lister, P., Cavanagh, K., Crisp, B.R., Hussein, S. and Stevens, M. (2009) 'What (a) difference a degree makes: the evaluation of the new social work degree in England', *British Journal of Social Work*, 39(1): 161–178.

Petružytė, D., Gevorgianienė, V., Seniutis, M., Yamaguchi, M., Šumskienė, E. and Žalimienė, L. (2022) 'Envisioning the future of (techno) social work education: perspectives of Japanese and Lithuanian social work educators', *Social Work Education*. https://doi.org/10.1080/02615479.2021.2023492

Preston-Shoot, M. (2000) 'Stumbling towards oblivion or discovering new horizons? Observations on the relationship between social work education and practice', *Journal of Social Work Practice*, 14(2): 87–98.

Preston-Shoot, M. (2007) 'Engaging with Continuing Professional Development: with or without qualification', in W. Tovey (ed) *The Post-Qualifying Handbook for Social Workers*, London: Jessica Kingsley, pp 18–27.

Quality Assurance Agency for UK Higher Education (2019) *Subject Benchmark Statement for Social Work*. https://www.qaa.ac.uk/docs/qaa/subject-benchmark-statements/subject-benchmark-statement-social-work.pdf?%20sfvrsn=5c35c881_6

Redcliffe, J. (2021) 'Adult social services', in H. Gwilym and C. Williams (eds) *Social Policy for Welfare Practice in Wales* (3rd edn), Bristol: Policy Press, pp 193–205.

Rees, J., de Villiers, T., Livingston, W., Maegusuku-Hewett, T. and Prysor, G. (2018) 'A new distance learning national framework for social work continuing education: critical reflections on the first phases of implementation', *Social Work Education*, 37(6): 761–774.

Roulstone, A. (2012) 'Stuck in the middle with you': towards enabling social work with disabled people', *Social Work Education*, 31(2): 142–154.

Short, M., Halton, C., Morris, B., Rose, J., Whitaker, L., Russ, E., et al (2022) 'Enablers, markers, and aspects of quality innovative placements across distance: insights from a co-operative inquiry', *Social Work Education*. https://doi.org/10.1080/02615479.2022.2060959

Skoura-Kirk, E., Brown, S. and Mikelyte, R. (2021) 'Playing its part: an evaluation of professional skill development through service user-led role-plays for social work students', *Social Work Education*, 40(8): 977–993.

Social Care Wales (2011) *National Occupational Standards for Social Work*. Cardiff: Social Care Wales.

Social Care Wales (2015) *The Code of Professional Practice for Social Care*. Cardiff: Social Care Wales.

Social Care Wales (2017) *The Code of Professional Practice for Social Care*. Cardiff: Social Care Wales.

Social Care Wales and Health Education and Improvement Wales (2020) *A Healthier Wales: Our Workforce Strategy for Health and Social Care*. https://socialcare.wales/cms-assets/documents/Workforce-strategy-ENG-March-2021.pdf

Social Work Task Force (2009) *Building a Safe, Confident Future: The Final Report of the Social Work Task Force.* https://dera.ioe.ac.uk/10625/

Soldatic, K. and Meekosha, H. (2012) 'Moving the boundaries of feminist social work education with disabled people in the neoliberal era', *Social Work Education,* 31(2): 246–252.

Taylor, I. and Bogo, M. (2014) 'Perfect opportunity-perfect storm? Raising the standards of social work education in England', *The British Journal of Social Work,* 44(6): 1402–1418.

Taylor-Beswick, A. (2022) 'Digitalizing social work education: preparing students to engage with twenty-first century practice need', *Social Work Education.* https://doi.org/10.1080/02615479.2022.2049225

Wallengren Lynch, M., Dominelli, L. and Cuadra, C. (2022) 'Information communication technology during Covid-19', *Social Work Education.* https://doi.org/10.1080/02615479.2022.2040977

Wang, W., Wang, H., Ortiz, J., Alidaee, B. and Bowen, S. (2021) 'The role of economic development on the effectiveness of industrial pollution reduction policy in Chinese cities', *Journal of Cleaner Production,* 339, Article 130709.

Wilson, G. and Campbell, A. (2012) 'Developing social work education: academic perspectives', *British Journal of Social Work,* 43(5): 1005–1023.

Wilson, G. and Kelly, B. (2010) 'Evaluating the effectiveness of social work education', *British Journal of Social Work,* 40: 2431–2449.

6

Coproduction and service user involvement

Sarah-Jane Waters

Chapter objectives

- To understand why social work and wider public services in Wales involve those who use services.

- To appreciate the importance of service user voice and how barriers between people occur.

- To give a snapshot of the current position of this work and what could be improved.

Introduction

This chapter is not written by a social worker. It is not written by a health care or social care professional. It is a view from a person who uses a variety of public services after being diagnosed with a life-changing, multi-systemic, general pain in the backside genetic disorder. However, thanks to this and the progressive Welsh legislation discussed here, the scrap heap can wait. There is much work to be done in partnership with those who provide education, delivery and evaluation of those services I, along with many others, must use. The subject matter is extensive, this discussion will explore briefly why user participation is undertaken, a little about how, and some current limitations of this flavour of coproduction from the perspective of Welsh users of services.

Consider living in a world of disarray, of perpetual struggle with ever-changing financial challenges governed by an archaic structure with rules not now fit for purpose. Now, imagine living in a society where your voice is heard, you can help update processes, your needs are met and all can thrive in an equitable manner. That is what we should want, to give all and future generations a chance to reach potential. We need to disrupt the system, find novel solutions to problems caused by inflexibility, austerity and pandemics. There needs to be service resilience from Brexit, centralised non-local power and all other agenda-driven twists challenged within public services.

Disruption of public service organisation is possible because we live in a devolved nation: Wales. With the implementation of the Social Services and Well-being (Wales) Act 2014 (SSWWA), service users were legislatively given their voice and

71

control back by becoming equal decision makers with respect to public services. The Co-production Network of Wales (2021) discusses 'doing with' not 'doing to' and this is the very essence of partnership working. This legislation is young and in order to make it robust and fit for purpose, we all have a steep, often frustrating, evolution ahead. Part of this process, in my opinion, is transparency, reflective practice and honestly learning from those less than ideal outcomes. I can see much positive change, especially when in comparison with services others I know receive over the bridge and border. I still would like to see more equitable, considered and consistent collaboration with service users, particularly within Welsh health services and between different council and health areas in Wales.

We all use services, every single one of us, so all are service users. For example, when you go to see a medic or arrange something for a family member, think about how that feels. What emotional response do you have when you realise you are not being listened to, your concerns are being diminished and what you need has been dismissed? That is a power imbalance and we have all felt it or seen it play out at some point. Consider how much easier this becomes when there is respectful engagement, when you feel like an equal. If there is transparency and mutual regard it just makes life easier. It can help when the conversation is directed to outcomes you do not consider favourable; it assists when there can be negotiation. Instead of services being organised and delivered top to bottom, this legislation gives Wales a chance to use its assets (that is us, all of us) to redesign from the user up. The core economy, as described by Cahn (2014) consists of those assets who give so much of their time, often unrecognised and unrewarded. They have an inestimable wealth of experience, knowledge and insight to shape society and develop Welsh services.

What is the common noun for people who use services? The use of language to describe a person who uses services is difficult; many terms are used but no expression is universally liked or formally recognised. Lived experience, expert by experience, service user, citizen, stakeholder, asset, power sharer and member of change team are all terms I have heard. It is likely there will be local variations and that more suitable, mutually agreed terms will evolve over time. In this chapter, service user is the term employed.

In our current political climate and public financial situation, I would argue that coproduction and service user involvement are integral to keeping our services afloat and our identity separate from the other British nations. There is little we can do to generate hard cash from the Westminster central purse, but we can change the way we work or our approach to services. I have been struck, over the past few years, by how silently the United Kingdom (UK) is sleepwalking back in time, to a place of imperial deference and a collective belief that those in power know better. When I hear of punitive measures applied by the umbrella UK Government to those who are dependent on their services and funding, with no vigorous tested rationale, I wonder if populist appeasement of the party faithful, donors and client media organisations are the predominant motivators. There is certainly no coproduction as we understand it, or published meaningful evidence fully exploring short-, medium- and long-term consequences of change. It is disturbing to hear of scrutiny being hindered or flatly rejected by Westminster as it was when Philip Alston, the UN Special Rapporteur reported on poverty inequality in the UK (Alston, 2022) and the disastrous effect of ideological cuts on public money. Here, our Well-being and Future Generations (Wales) Act 2015 and SSWWA allow Wales to uniquely be able to halt this, should it be able and allowed by the UK Government to use legislation forcefully and be creative.

Looking to the past, the *Tuesday Documentary – The Block* (British Broadcasting Company, 1972) which followed the lives of residents in a temporary housing block in Southwark, London in the early 1970s, feels significant in the UK today. It portrayed the dire poverty the residents faced, the dehumanising value judgements made about them by civil servants and the effect these outrageous attitudes had on their lives and outcomes. It is bleak. I desperately do not want to live in a society like that. If you do not either, when you apply your practice, please consider the service user, the human beyond the problem. Remember that you are also a user of public services.

Embedding service users and carers in social work education

The Masters in Social Work programme (MASW) at Cardiff University has engaged service users, for over two decades, long before any mandatory statutory requirement. Over the years, activities for the service user/carer group have evolved, there is now more coproduction. The group is administered to fulfil a remit, namely to support the academic programme. It works in partnership with academic staff, students and placement hosting organisations. Having a clear purpose when embedding service users is critical to success. The programme's calendar details activity from interviews of applicants to final exam board.

In terms of coproducing, how can the group have a voice or give meaningful input into the course? Despite the course having to uphold standards and processes defined by regulatory bodies and the university, the programme is keen to make sure the group shares research ideas for dissertations, contributes to student research, gives feedback on course content and comments on student portfolios. Some members like to help with programme meetings, others only want to interview. Service users live lives which are often difficult, and plans change quickly. People can be unreliable through no fault of their own. Flexibility is important for retention of members. Other service user involvement groups may struggle to keep momentum, purpose and members, projects end, providers change but while social workers are being trained, the MASW group is needed and embraced.

Members have contributed to other research projects and academic study across the UK (McLaughlin et al, 2021). Conferences have been attended and hosted. Group membership is predominantly those with direct experience of services/carers/those who care informally. Other members are nominated academic members of staff and, due to safeguarding, representatives of partner organisations delivering relevant service contracts. Those organisations have users who can contribute their help.

Some of our members help with lectures; feedback from students is that this is a powerful experience and allows them to gain a fuller understanding of the area under study by engaging with first-hand testament. I think most of us can relate to this concept. I have been re-reading a book recently which is a series of accounts from people who lived under the Soviet regime post-1917 until its downfall (Figes, 2008). I have never read it in a timely manner. I dip in and out. When it is finished, it is put on the shelf. It is absorbing and I am drawn into the narrative. I think about how my family would have behaved living under a similar unstable regime. Would I have been the child who accidentally said something which sent my parents to the gulag? Probably yes. Without the individual, harrowing testaments in the book, it is doubtful it would have been read. I would have struggled to engage in the same way and likely given up. It is the personal reflections and explanations which provide enduring impact.

What are the benefits of involvement?

It is easy, when in an echo chamber, bubble of work, home and play, to lose perspective. We form opinions from our experiences and background. Unconscious biases, belief and practice based around a point in time or events can lead to an inability to connect with reality, the here and now. Power imbalances can happen between people when one party is dependent on the input of another. Coproduction/involvement of people who will ultimately use or benefit from services can not only improve the success of a project or service, but enhance, inform and empower all involved (England, 2019). In the book *They* (Manzoor, 2021), the author questions tensions arising in relationships between Muslim and non-Muslim communities. He says that he began his research believing the problem lay within his own Muslim community, but by visiting and talking to all his opinion changed. He needed to engage with real people and this engagement was revealing.

Truly coproduced projects such as community groups (subtly different from the work of the MASW group), can save money. Typically, the Co-production Network of Wales (2021) estimates for every £1 spent on establishing and running projects, £7 is saved of public money, based on the Australian Centre for Public Impact (2016). How? When people feel listened to, can contribute, feel a sense of belonging and take ownership, they use public services less. The TR14ers are a community dance group set up by the police, Exeter University Health Professionals' Connecting Communities project (C2) and young people in 2005. The project detailed less truancy, less petty crime, less social service engagement (TR14ers, 2021) and the police involvement ultimately dropped off. Research proposals by Exeter University to look at sustainable change and health outcomes have been submitted to the National Institute of Health Research by Wyatt (nd). When councils across the country are struggling to fund services, demonstrable cost benefits must be attractive.

Similarly in groups, service users who contribute to service improvement facilitate the removal of barriers when purposeful conversation happens. Better, more resilient services are created when there is more transparency between the parent organisations and end user; it is empowering to feel respected, considered and an equal. *Seeing is Believing* from the Co-production Network of Wales details this (Dineen, 2015). Reciprocal respect can be created. Members of the MASW group say that they feel that they can give something back, have a different sense of purpose and it can be a chance to help mould social workers of the future. The group does not hold back when describing adverse events and poor practice they have observed or been subjected to. Importantly, they also highlight what was helpful and what they consider success.

What needs improvement?

Sounds like Utopia? Overall clearly not, as services, providers and users alike still experience less than ideal situations and pressure (Welsh Government, 2022). Optimum conditions for involvement have not yet been reached.

Getting people involved with this work is difficult. Often professionals have service user involvement pushed on them without adequate resource or information provision. If there is no appetite, work-time or understanding/ training about how involvement enhances services, it is unlikely that the output will be anything but tokenistic; something to satisfy a regulatory body or auditor. Professor Peter Beresford is both an academic and service user who is a co-chair for Shaping Our Lives. In a recent report (Batty et al, 2022) he supported the findings that involvement organisations are not equipped to involve disabled people meaningfully.

Tokenism is problematic, as is recruitment and retention. In Arnstein's ladder of citizen participation (Arnstein, 1969) there is a scale of pure coproduction. Arnstein described degrees of citizen power where real power is attained (doing with), degrees of tokensim where power is spurious, falling to non-participation where there is no power (doing to). At worst there is manipulation. However, it is not practical or appropriate to involve the ultimate user in every aspect of public service, nor is it reasonable to expect current working practice to change overnight. It is a non-linear process. As discussed previously, service users cannot be expected to participate at all times as the paid/salaried professionals would.

Currently, many people can only access services when they are at disaster point, which then causes other chaos in their lives and more problems needing services. In many ways, it is this experience that would be most valuable but they are understandably unable to contribute. Much involvement of users is undertaken by familiar faces as they can offer the time, they are retired or are supported financially. Is this giving a voice to the whole community and improving the services? It is doubtful. People in receipt of benefits are particularly vulnerable and benefits are centrally managed by the UK Government, so not devolved. There is much conflicting information, some professionals believe that involvement is fine, time credits or vouchers are allowed, others say not. At the time of writing, if there is a formal contract, an agreement to do some work with the Department for Work and Pensions (DWP), some payment is allowed. Anything else technically breaches this. True equality will not occur until payment, in pounds, is given and service users can ring-fence involvement payment and time. I would urge anyone dealing with the DWP as it stands now, to always ring and check, then ring and check again as rules change often, staff are not always up to date and service users do not want to incur the wrath of regulatory investigation. There are numerous benefits and the supporting legislation is complex and not found in one document. I would like organisations like Social Care Wales, Welsh Government to challenge this while being mindful of Arnstein's Ladder of Participation (greater discussion of the ladder can be found in later chapters).

Minority voices are also currently poorly represented, certainly within involvement I have seen. It is difficult for people to get involved when organisations appear impenetrable, service providers change regularly with turnover and continuity of staff is poor. In my opinion, delivery models which mimic private business, pseudo-privatisation of public services and silo working, are hugely detrimental to coproducing and the quality of delivery. Longer contracts for organisations would help, along with centralisation of some services; merging the Welsh National Health Service and Social Care could minimise silo working and excess bureaucracy.

To conclude, I think of some well-worn expressions I have heard, namely that none of us will ultimately get off this planet alive and a reminder that we all bleed red. We have started our Welsh process of change and, as anyone faced with a daunting piece of work will tell you, that is the difficult part. Endeavouring to humanise situations is a good place to continue building from; be creative but always accountable in your practice.

Further resources
1. Co-Production Network for Wales. https://copronet.wales/
2. Blanluet, N. (2021) 'Why Welsh government should be involving us (citizens) more'. Building Communities Trust. https://www.bct.wales/blog/why-welsh-government-should-be-involving-us-citizens-more?locale=en
3. McLaughlin, H., Beresford, P., Cameron, C., Casey, H. and Duffy, J. (2021) *The Routledge Handbook of Service User Involvement in Human Services Research and Education*, Abingdon: Routledge.

References
Alston, A. (2022) *Statement on Visit to the United Kingdom, by Professor Philip Alston, United Nations Special Rapporteur on extreme poverty and human rights*. https://www.ohchr.org/sites/default/files/Documents/Issues/Poverty/EOM_GB_16Nov2018.pdf

Arnstein, S. (1969) 'A ladder of citizen participation', *Journal of the American Institute of Planners*, 35(4): 216–224.

Batty, G., Humphrey, G. and Meakin, B. (2022) *Tickboxes and Tokenism? Service User Involvement Report 2022*. https://shapingourlives.org.uk/wp-content/uploads/2022/02/Tickboxes-and-Tokenism-Feb-2022.pdf

British Broadcasting Company (1972) *Tuesday Documentary – The Block*. https://www.bbc.co.uk/iplayer/episode/p055vzj1/tuesday-documentary-the-block

Cahn, E. (2014) *It's the Core Economy Stupid: An Open Letter to the Non-profit Community*. https://timebanks.org/wp-content/uploads/2014/01/CoreEconomyOp-Ed_001.pdf

Centre for Public Impact (2016) *The Australian Centre for Social Innovation: The Family by Family (FbF) Project*. The Australian Centre for Social Innovation. https://www.centreforpublicimpact.org/case-study/the-australian-centre-for-social-innovation/

Co-production Network for Wales (2021) *Manifesto – Elections 2021*. Co-production Network for Wales Knowledge Base. https://info.copronet.wales/manifesto-elections-2021/

Dineen, R. (2015) *Co-production Catalogue from Wales (Seeing is Believing)*. Co-production Network for Wales Knowledge Base. https://info.copronet.wales/co-production-catalogue-from-wales-seeing-is-believing/

England, L. (2019) *Creating Empowered and Resilient Communities*. Co-production Network for Wales Knowledge Base. https://info.copronet.wales/empowering-communities/

Figes, O. (2008) *The Whisperers: Private Life in Stalin's Russia*, London: Penguin Books.

Manzoor, S. (2021) *They*, London: Headline Publishing Group.

McLaughlin, H., Beresford, P., Cameron, C., Casey, H. and Duffy, J. (2020) *The Routledge Handbook of Service User Involvement in Human Services Research and Education*, Abingdon: Routledge.

The Future Generations Commissioner for Wales (2022) *Acting Today for a Better Tomorrow*. https://www.futuregenerations.wales/

TR14ers (2021) *About TR14ers*. https://www.tr14ers.org.uk/

Welsh Government (2022) *"Expectations and Experiences Service User and Carer Perspectives on the Social Services and Well-being (Wales) Act 2014*. https://gov.wales/sites/default/files/statistics-and-research/2022–03/expectations-and-experiences-service-user-and-carer-perspectives-on-the-social-services-and-well-being-wales-act.pdf

Wyatt, K. (nd) *TR14ers: Understanding How the Sustainable Processes Are Created to Support Engagement in a Self-organising, Peer-led Dance Group in West Cornwall*. https://medicine.exeter.ac.uk/research/healthresearch/relationalhealth/tr14ers/

7

Applying the principles of coproduction

Liz Lefroy

Chapter objectives

- To explore definitions of coproduction in relation to participation, involvement and expertise through experience.
- To consider coproduction as it relates to social work practice and education in Wales.
- To demonstrate how coproduction principles are enacted within a university social work degree.

Coproduction in Wales

Coproduction is a legislatively driven and evolving approach used across communities in Wales. It was identified by individuals and carers in a 2022 evaluation of the Social Services and Well-being (Wales) Act (2014) (SSWWA) as a key mechanism to achieve voice and control, while at the same time, the report recognised 'the ways in which potential benefits associated with coproduction had not yet been realised' (Welsh Government, 2022: 15). Coproduction is not unique to social work and social care contexts. *Have Your Say*, for example, is the 'consultation and engagement portal for Powys' (One Powys, 2022): a joint partnership between Powys Council, the National Health Service (NHS) and the voluntary sector. In this chapter, coproduction is considered as it relates to social work practice and education with citizens who can be both 'individual(s) – the person accessing care; whether a child, young person or adult', and 'carer(s) – a carer provides unpaid care and/or support and could include family members, partners, neighbours or friends' (Social Care Wales (SCW), 2017: 6).

Although not specifically mentioned in the text of the SSWWA, social work practitioners and educators, seeking a first point definition of coproduction, may consult the Code of Practice for the implementation of the Act to further their understanding. As part of a fuller definition, Part 2 Code of Practice (General Functions) presents a summary phrase within an explanatory diagram: 'Coproduction – Citizens & professionals valued equally' (Welsh Government, 2015: 53, para 241). The key thought is of *equal value*: of finding 'a way of working whereby practitioners and people work together as equal partners to plan and deliver care and support ... to find appropriate solutions' at 'individual, and at organisational and strategic levels' (Welsh Government, 2015: paras 12 and 135). What is more, local authorities '*must* involve people in the coproduction of the design and operation of services' (para 108).

Coproduction: contested definitions

Thus far, what coproduction is seems clear: in the context of developing and delivering care and support, professionals and citizens are to be regarded as equally influential. It does not take long to realise, however, that coproduction is not the only label being used to describe such power sharing. 'Quietly, almost unnoticed, a fundamental change has been taking place in human and helping services in recent decades' state Beresford and McLaughlin (2021: 1). Perhaps it is this 'unnoticed' nature that means commentators are still working towards a shared understanding of what to call the change. McLaughlin et al's landmark 2021 text is titled: *The Routledge Handbook of Service User Involvement in Human Services Research and Education.* Involvement is a term linked to other concepts such as knowledge, expertise through lived experience, participation and partnership, as well as coproduction. Involvement is the term preferred by McLaughlin et al (2021), and also, in the Welsh context, SCW documentation refers to involvement of individuals and carers in the social work degrees in Wales (Care Council for Wales, 2005; the Care Council for Wales was superseded by Social Care Wales in 2017). Elsewhere, Patient and Public Engagement (PPE) and Patient and Public Involvement (PPI) are phrases used in health education settings (Serrant et al, 2021). It is a complex picture, but it is clear that these different terms are, at their core, part of the movement for change.

In their analysis of this situation, Beresford and McLaughlin (2021) argue that what the terms have in common is a questioning of the power relationships experienced in professional services. They are at their 'heart concerned with challenging traditional exclusionary roles, breaking down traditional barriers and assumptions and, at (their) best, enabling real co-production at both a personal and a policy level' (p 2). So a key characteristic of coproduction (along with participation, involvement, and so on) is that it is inclusive of those often excluded from making decisions about their lives, and, as such, the activities challenge a status quo which has exclusively seen professionals as the experts.

In Wales, fluidity in use of terminology is also evident: the Well-being of Future Generations (Wales) Act (2015) uses a vocabulary of involvement and partnership rather than coproduction. Although the way in which these words are used seemingly interchangeably is now a familiar situation, there are also those who argue for more precise usage, for whom coproduction represents a gold standard in terms of power-sharing. Burke and Newman (2021), for example, state that this difference in vocabulary is an articulation of the extent, or depth, of involvement: 'discourses regarding the level of service user involvement have shifted in focus over the years'. They relate this to changes in vocabulary 'developing from an earlier emphasis on collaboration and consultation of service users to that of partnership and latterly coproduction with service users' (p 55).

Despite Burke and Newman's (2021) assertion, a move towards greater degrees of power-sharing has not resulted in a trajectory in which the term coproduction has replaced all other words. This leaves Casey, Vale and Zonouzi (2021) observing that even if one term were to be settled upon, coproduction itself lacks a singular definition and, in consequence, 'the theoretical differences behind the concept of co-production' are not clear, 'which means there is an absence of methodological framework for its practice' (p 207).

Given this lack of consistency regarding vocabulary used, and the absence of a precise definition of coproduction, how can social work students and professionals, individuals and carers, know what to expect when asked to coproduce? Do they expect the same, or something different, when they are asked to participate, work in partnership or be involved? Welford, Milford and Moreton (2022) argue that yes, coproduction is different from these other activities, being the ideal with which other methods compare poorly: 'genuine coproduction goes beyond consultation and service user involvement' (p 5). According to this stance, coproduction incorporates greater potential for power-sharing, with its emphasis on the meaningful presence of people using services from the start to the finish of any project or development, in contrast to participation or involvement when individuals' perspectives are incorporated into existing structures.

The idea of progression, or a scale against which coproduction can be judged is, in some ways, very useful, providing an appearance, at least, of greater clarity. This scale has been represented many times as a ladder, ever since Arnstein (1969) published her 'Ladder of Participation' (see Figure 7.1). A contemporary version of this metaphor, a coproduction ladder, presents a rationale for the changes of the past 50 years. On their website, Think Local Act Personal (TLAP, 2022) pay tribute to Arnstein and describe the 'Ladder of Coproduction' as representing 'a series of steps towards co-production', with consultation and other terms regarded as pre-steps. Activities such as engagement are, in this visual metaphor, less valuable than coproduction on the top rung: to be top of the ladder is to be of *equal value*. To be at the bottom is to be a 'passive recipient of services' whose views are 'not taken into account' (TLAP, 2022). Commentators speaking in the Social Care Institute for Excellence's video resource *What Makes Coproduction Different from Participation?* (SCIE, 2014) would agree that the model is intentionally hierarchical, stating that coproduction is about 'joint power ... respecting each other's areas of expertise'. Participation, in contrast, is readily dismissed as amounting to listening to what people say, not necessarily acting on viewpoints or sharing power.

This idea of progression up a ladder towards an ideal can be helpful as a way of highlighting ways of improving practice (TLAP, 2022). That it can also be misleading to think of a linear hierarchy of improvement in the way power is shared is a paradox rooted in the ideologies in which coproduction originates. On the one hand, coproduction is a rights-based, emancipatory, radical approach to practice in which individuals are identified as citizens. On the other hand, the basis is consumerist and neoliberal (Beresford, 2020). Both approaches are, Barnes and Cotterell (2012) argue, written into the NHS and Community Care Act (1990):

Figure 7.1 The ladders of participation and coproduction

The ladder of participation (Arnstein,1969)	The ladder of coproduction (TLAP, 2022)
Citizen control Delegated power — Citizen power Partnership Placation Consultation — Tokenism Informing Therapy — Non-participation Manipulation	**Coproduction** – An equal relationship between individuals and people responsible for services **Codesign** – Genuine, but incomplete, influence **Engagement** – Individuals have some influence **Consultation** – Individuals have involvement such as filling in surveys or attending meetings **Informing** – The people responsible for services share information about services **Educating** – Services and their design are explained to individuals **Coercion** – Although in attendance at events, the views of individuals are not influential

UK-wide legislation which separated purchasers from providers 'in order to increase patient and user choice' (p xv) making individuals customers within the marketplace of services. The Community Care Act (1990) also supported person-centred care, encouraging 'user involvement' (p xvi). These ways of considering coproduction, neoliberal and emancipatory, compete for territory, as can be seen in the Social Services and Well-being (Wales) Act (2014) Code of Practice (Welsh Government, 2015). In this, the first principle of coproduction defines people who use services as 'assets' (para 252), terminology which linguistically commodifies individuals, seeing service provision as transactional rather than relational. Elsewhere, coproduction 'empowers people to take responsibility for, and contribute to, their own well-being' (Welsh Government, 2015: para 237). Empowerment, a value recognisable to students as one of those identified as radical by Thompson (2020), 'often involves the empowered developing confidence in their own capacities' (Bhatt, 2010: 1).

The tensions inherent in coproduction were identified by Martin (2012), writing about opportunities and challenges for third sector organisations. The process of bringing the voices of individuals and carers from 'margin to mainstream' (Barnes and Cotterell, 2012: xv), has, he argues, the potential to subsume the very voices being heard to 'managerial, professional and academic ways of thinking' (Martin, 2012: 50). Is this movement to embed the viewpoints of individuals and communities in the development and functioning of services, he asks, 'a noble compromise or Faustian pact?' (p 51). Coproduction is a 'trade-off' (p 51), and maybe Arnstein would agree, because professionals are not displaced from their traditional positions of power entirely in the coproduction model, as they are in her model of participation in which citizen control is the bold top rung.

Bahooshy (2020), urging members of the British Association of Social Workers not to lose sight of coproduction during the 2020 lockdowns, offers an understanding of coproduction as a process which incorporates participation, involvement, and so on, as elements which can contribute towards the aim of coproduction, for which there is 'no one model' (np). In *That Coproduction Podcast* (National Institute for Health and Care Research, 2021a), Williams offers a similarly pragmatic viewpoint, suggesting that to see coproduction as a 'gold standard' (np) is unhelpful. Coproduction, participation, involvement, consultation, co-creation, engagement: these are different activities, not competitors within a hierarchy, but useful methodologies for power-sharing at the personal and service levels. He advocates that in order to try to equalise power relations, practitioners should be explicit about what method is being used. This can be as practical as ensuring individuals have prior knowledge, for example, about levels of payment, and the intended outcomes of a project. All these activities have the potential to acknowledge the rights and strengths of those traditionally marginalised, 'those perceived as lacking desirable traits … (who) tend to be excluded by wider society' (Bhatt, 2010: 1) and absent from knowledge creation, service development, practitioner education, and even from determining their own care and support.

The Welsh way

Outside In, the focus group of individuals and carers involved, participating and coproducing within the Faculty of Social and Life Sciences at Wrexham Glyndŵr University (WGU) can be seen as existing as a direct result of the Welsh way of implementing the requirements of the Care Standards Act (2000). This Act made provision for 'the involvement of service users and carers in all aspects of the curriculum, course management and delivery' (Casey et al, 2021). Current requirements for involvement are set out in the *Framework for the Degree in Social Work in Wales*:

(b) The institution must involve people with care and support needs and carers, and representatives of employers of social workers in all stages of the development, management and delivery of the degree programme (including the selection and assessment of students). (SCW, 2021: 26)

This involvement is judged annually against a set of *Standards for Involving Service Users and Carers in the Degree in Social Work in Wales* (CCW, 2005). There is overlap between these standards and coproduction, and emphasis is focused on best practice principles of supporting individuals to avoid 'experience of poor and unpleasant involvement … we need to be offered a sympathetic setting and good conditions for our involvement, without hidden and unmet personal or financial costs' (Duffy and Beresford, 2021: 14). The Welsh Standard 5 can be read in this light – there must be 'clear and understandable contracts/formal agreements negotiated with service users and carers covering responsibilities, expectations and arrangements for payment' (CCW, 2005).

CCW's, now SCW's, *People Using Services and their Carers* scheme is available to all universities in Wales and is in place to provide a practical means of enabling Standard 5 (CCW, 2005). The scheme allocates an annual grant to universities, ensuring ring-fenced resources are in place to support participation and coproduction from the start of a student's journey to becoming professionally qualified.

In 2020, Outside In won a Social Care Accolade for *Developing and inspiring the workforce of tomorrow* (SCW, 2020).

Stories of coproduction (see Further resources, and examples in Chapters 10 and 12) demonstrate that the sharing or relinquishing of power is rarely a linear or complete process. They illustrate the ways a variety of organisations have managed the complexities of subscribing to *equal value*. The image summonsed by coproduction in practice can often seem more like a patchwork quilt than a ladder, or according to one expert by experience, it is like a cake 'baked from different ingredients that make a common goal' (Welford et al, 2022: 10). For those in search of a metaphor to replace the ladder, the cake is one. Another is the jigsaw of coproduction (SCIE, 2022) which considers domains of Culture, Structure, Practice and Review. These metaphors sit comfortably with a view of social work as art (England, 1986) and of coproduction as both an important and complicated activity, one which is compelled to address scenarios such as this: 'Local authorities must find an appropriate balance between involving a child in the design and delivery of a service through giving them the opportunity to express their views, wishes and feelings, whilst ensuring that the best interests of that child are met' (Welsh Government, 2015: para 249).

The application of coproduction principles

So, among the contested definitions and competing ideologies, is it possible to agree on the principles of coproduction? The Welsh Government provides a list as follows (2015: para 252). Coproduction is:

- Seeing people as assets
- Building on capabilities
- Developing mutuality and reciprocity
- Investing in networks to share information
- Blurring distinctions between providers and people who need care and support and carers who need support
- Facilitating rather than delivering services

The Coproduction Network for Wales (2022: np) lists five coproduction principles, expressed in accessible and inclusive language:

- We build up our strengths: everyone has something to offer
- We link up with others, because together we are better
- We focus on what matters to us (not what matters to the system)
- We build trust between us and share power equally
- We can create change and organisations help us to do this

These lists are similar, but not the same and not exclusive, and the remainder of this chapter considers how principles of coproduction have been applied in a specific context, the BA (Hons) Social Work at WGU, and in particular its 'focus group that uses innovative ways to educate future social workers' (SCW, 2020). As a result of this Outside In project, individuals and carers whom Allegri (2022) describes as 'otherwise experts' (p 138) have been integrated into the degree, in recognition of the fact that it is an SCW requirement for approval to do so, but also because Outside In 'brings with it a particular type of knowledge' not least 'their experience of being on the receiving end of social policies' (Duffy and Beresford, 2021: 11).

A strengths-based approach

Recognition of phenomenology, the validity of lived experience as a source of knowledge, is an important feature of the involvement of Outside In. It is an approach which 'does not subscribe to ideas of "universal" knowledge' (Duffy and Beresford, 2021: 14), and it is sometimes termed *Service User Standpoint Theory* (McLaughlin, 2009). The individual is an expert with valid, personally held knowledge. The range of expertise within Outside In is vast, and it includes many of the labels used to identify social work services: experience of learning disability, sensory impairment, degenerative neurological conditions; of adult and children's safeguarding, enduring mental ill-health, neurological diversity; of seeking asylum; of domestic violence, substance use, recovery, rehabilitation; of the looked after system, the criminal justice system, being a young carer, an older person, a carer. It extends far beyond these labels to include experience as engineers, community workers, cooks, artists, physiotherapists, nurses, radiographers; as members of families experiencing the ever-changing lifespan, the light and shade of human existence. Elsewhere this group might be termed a human library (Driessens and Lylseens-Danneboom, 2022).

As with other sources of knowledge, expertise through experience is shared within the social work programme in a variety of ways: lectures, workshops, discussion, role play. What is important is that Outside In representatives are additionally able to tell narratives in their chosen way, since elsewhere, 'service users' current stories may have been largely scripted by other people such as family, friends and professionals' (Doel and Best, 2008: 121). As such, coproduction principles indicate that individuals must be enabled to bring their knowledge to the social work degree in a way that fits with their strengths.

Sharing power through building equal relationships

Creative ways of working have been shown to have relevance to social work practice – see for example the use of poetry (Lefroy, 2018), zine-making (Desyllas and Sinclair, 2014) and animation (Morris et al, 2013). Using creative methods in the classroom represents a departure from traditional approaches. Martin's concerns (2012) about coproduction becoming mainstream, colluding with existing structures, are relevant here. Devising curricula based around expertise and knowledge that Outside In members hold challenges this tendency. Creative approaches might, according to the expert through experience's preference, mean using an art studio rather than a classroom as the context for learning, working with messy materials such as paint and glue. One such example is the experience of an animation workshop at WGU, in which an Outside In representative was the director of a film telling her narrative of experience, with students supporting the production, using animation techniques for the first time. Evaluating the experience, a social work student commented: "I was quite nervous ... I could feel a shift in the balance of power from being trained as a professional with the 'gaze' that objectifies the service user/carer as someone in need of expert help and services to suddenly becoming the unknowing student" (Morris et al, 2013: 25). Morris outlines his own phenomenological take on this: 'We had learned ... about the "Exchange Model" (Smale & Tuson, 1995) ... but this was the first time that I really *saw* and understood it' (p 26).

Learning together

The learning together coproduction principle is enacted in the modules validated as core to the BA (Hons) Social Work at WGU that are also available to Outside In to study as standalone modules. For these modules, classroom activities need to be relevant to the requirements of the programme, as well as accessible to a group with varied learning styles and experiences. In one session, for example, a group poem *The Desk* was co-created. Social work and Outside In students (about 30 people from the Class of 2022) were introduced by the author/lecturer to a poem by Edip Cansever, translated from the Turkish: *The Table*. This served as a prompt (Clanchy, 2020), showing that a poem can be a list, and a wild one at that. The group chose a familiar piece of furniture, a desk, as a starting point, and soon were expressing their feelings about social work and study. The class spoke out, line by line, what they would like to put on the imaginary desk, the author/lecturer acting as scribe, the poem growing longer and longer on the display screen. Here is the beginning of the poem:

The Desk
(after Edip Cansever)

Students filled with a sense of injustice
put their laptops on the desk,
set their coffees down next to them.
They laid their experiences in a pile on the desk,
along with their eggs, bacon, sausages, beans
(and brown sauce in a squeezy bottle).
They put their frustration and anger on the desk.
They put clowns on the desk.
The sound of despair, the imbalance of scales,
the song of the birds, their laughter, their tears,
reflection – they put them all on the desk.

The poem continues: line after line of literal, surreal and metaphorical ideas together adding up to an expression of many of the emotions felt in the collective social work experience. It was a poem no individual could have written, and it is not obvious, reading the poem months later, who imagined or spoke each line. It is an example of 'blurring distinctions between providers and people who need care and support' (Welsh Government, 2015: para 252). This blurring took place, co-imagined, safely, but with spark.

Valuing diverse roles and identities

In coproduction, individuals and carers are involved from start to finish of a project. WGU has clearly defined processes in place for recruitment of students to the BA (Hons) Social Work, and this could seem, therefore, to be a part of the programme in which coproduction is not possible. Nevertheless, Standard 7 (CCW, 2005: 10) requires that 'people using services and Carers are involved in developing and implementing the arrangements for selecting students on to the degree programme'. All candidates for the social work programme will be interviewed by an Outside In representative, alongside a social work practitioner and a lecturer.

The panel members have different roles and diverse identities – the power of decision-making is shared. In a letter to the *International Journal of Mental Health Nursing*, Browne et al (2015: 281) make the following observation: 'Having service users on local interview panels ... serves to moderate and soften the conversation, so that it is more respectful and ultimately impacts positively on the culture of the workplace.' In terms of roles, the lecturer has specialist knowledge of the university requirements, the registered social worker can anticipate how the candidate will perform in the practice learning opportunities, the Outside In representative will make a judgement about whether the candidate has appropriate skills of engagement and demonstrates values in line with the *Code of Professional Practice for Social Care* (SCW, 2017). Each perspective is necessary and given equal value in the way final decisions are reached.

Messages for practice

- The application of coproduction principles illustrated here has been arrived at via two decades of experience, learning and reflection. Coproduction is a way of *being* in practice and education, as much as a way of *doing*.
- When approached with flexibility and imagination, coproduction becomes more possible and enjoyable.
- Whatever the activities of coproduction – meetings, lectures, interview panels, programme management – the over-riding principle of *equal value* stands firm.

Conclusion

In an episode of *That Coproduction Podcast* (National Institute for Health and Care Research, 2021b), host Nicola Hutchinson-Pascal asks a final question of the panel: "If there is one thing you could wish for in relation to coproduction, what would it be?" The panel's wishes were:

1. for a national, coproduced payments policy for individuals;
2. for a change in the way universities operate and are funded, particularly reducing the emphasis on the Research Excellence Framework;
3. for more time – coproduction takes longer.

These three wishes are notable in that they all focus on resources, and the way a lack of resources impacts the ability of any group of people to coproduce. More than 50 years after Arnstein's (1969) ladder provided a way of evaluating the quality of participation, the bottom rungs of the participation and coproduction ladders, manipulation and coercion, remain a potential trap when adequate resources of time and money are not allocated to taking a strengths-based approach, sharing power through building equal relationships, learning together and valuing diverse roles and identities.

Further resources

1. McLaughlin, H., Beresford, P., Cameron, C., Casey, H. and Duffy, J. (eds) (2021) *The Routledge Handbook of Service User Involvement in Human Services Research and Education*, Abingdon: Routledge.

2. Website for the Co-production Network for Wales – particularly the Knowledge Base section info.copronet.wales
3. Website for the Co-production Collective – particularly the Co-Pro Stories section coproductioncollective.co.uk

References

Allegri, E. (2022) 'Service users' involvement in social work education: lessons from an innovative experience', *Italian Journal of Sociology of Education*, 14(1): 133–150.

Arnstein, S.R. (1969) 'A ladder of citizen participation', *Journal of the American Institute of Planners*, 35(4): 216–224.

Bahooshy, S. (2020) 'Despite social distancing, we must not lose focus on coproduction'. *Professional Social Work Magazine*. https://basw.co.uk/resources/psw-magazine/psw-online/despite-social-distancing-we-must-not-lose-focus-co-production

Barnes, M. and Cotterell, P. (2012) 'From margin to mainstream', in M. Barnes and P. Cotterell (eds) *Critical Perspectives on User Involvement*, Bristol: Policy Press, pp xv–xxvi.

Beresford, P. (2020) 'PPI or user involvement: taking stock from a service user perspective in the twenty-first century', *Research Involvement and Engagement*, 6(36): 1–5.

Beresford, P. and McLaughlin, H. (2021) 'Introduction to the book', in H. McLaughlin, P. Beresford, C. Cameron, H. Casey and J. Duffy (eds) *The Routledge Handbook of Service User Involvement in Human Services Research and Education*, Abingdon: Routledge, pp 1–5.

Bhatt, S. (2010) *Empowerment and Social Work Participation*, New Delhi: Adhyayan Publishers.

Browne, G., Lakeman, R., O'Brien, A.P. and Chan, S. (2015) 'Service users on interview panels in mental health', *International Journal of Mental Health Nursing*, 24(3): 281–282.

Burke, B. and Newman, A. (2021) 'Ethical involvement of service users', in H. McLaughlin, P. Beresford, C. Cameron, H. Casey and J. Duffy (eds) *The Routledge Handbook of Service User Involvement in Human Services Research and Education*, Abingdon: Routledge, pp 54–63.

Care Council for Wales (2005) *Standards for Involving Service Users and Carers in the Degree in Social Work in Wales*. Cardiff: CCW.

Casey, H., Vale, D. and Zonouzi, M. (2021) 'A case for radical co-production replacing worn out structures', in H. McLaughlin, P. Beresford, C. Cameron, H. Casey and J. Duffy (eds) *The Routledge Handbook of Service User Involvement in Human Services Research and Education*, Abingdon: Routledge, pp 206–217.

Clanchy, K. (2020) *How to Grow Your Own Poem*, London: Picador.

Co-production Network for Wales (2022) *Co-production: Definition and Principles* [resources]. https://info.copronet.wales/co-production-definition-and-principles

Cotterell, P. and Morris, C. (2012) 'The capacity, impact and challenge of service users' experiential knowledge', in M. Barnes and P. Cotterell (eds) *Critical Perspectives on User Involvement*, Bristol: Policy Press, pp 57–69.

Desyllas, M.C. and Sinclair, A. (2014) 'Zine-making as a pedagogical tool for transformative learning in social work education', *Social Work Education*, 33(3): 296–316.

Doel, M. and Best, L. (2008) *Experiencing Social Work*, London: Sage.

Driessens, K. and Lylseens-Danneboom, V. (2022) 'Involving service users in social work education and research: is this structural social work?', in K. Driessens and V. Lylseens-Danneboom, *Involving Service Users in Social Work Education, Research and Policy: A Comparative European Analysis*, Bristol: Policy Press, pp 224–237.

Duffy, J. and Beresford, P. (2021) 'Critical issues in the development of service user involvement', in H. McLaughlin, P. Beresford, C. Cameron, H. Casey and J. Duffy (eds) *The Routledge Handbook of Service User Involvement in Human Services Research and Education*, Abingdon: Routledge, pp 9–16.

England, H. (1986) *Social Work as Art*, London: Allen and Unwin.

Lefroy, L. (2018) 'I'm afraid I don't know: poetry and social work', *Writing in Education*, 75: 14–19.

Levin, E. (2004) *Involving Service Users and Carers in Social Work Education*, Egham: SCIE.

Martin, G.P. (2012) 'Service users and the third sector: opportunities, challenges and potentials in influencing the governance of public services', in M. Barnes and P. Cotterell (eds) *Critical Perspectives on User Involvement*, Bristol: Policy Press, pp 47–55.

McLaughlin, H. (2009) 'What's in a name: "client", "patient", "customer", "consumer", "expert by experience", "service user" – what's next?', *British Journal of Social Work*, 39(6): 1001–1117.

McLaughlin, H., Beresford, P., Cameron, C., Casey, H. and Duffy, J. (eds) (2021) *The Routledge Handbook of Service User Involvement in Human Services Research and Education*, Abingdon: Routledge.

Morris, G., Prankard, S. and Lefroy, L. (2013) 'Animating experience: bringing student learning to life through animation and service user and carer experience', *Journal of Practice Teaching & Learning*, 12(1): 22–33.

National Institute for Health and Care Research (2021a) 'What's the difference between coproduction and public involvement in research?', *That Coproduction Podcast*. https://rds-se.nihr.ac.uk/podcasts/that-co-production-podcast

National Institute for Health and Care Research (2021b) 'Co-production in a research design service', *That Coproduction Podcast*. https://rds-se.nihr.ac.uk/podcasts/that-co-production-podcast

One Powys (2022) 'Have your say'. https://www.haveyoursaypowys.wales/

Serrant, L., Janes, G. and Odejimi, O. (2021) 'Service user involvement in nurse education', in H. McLaughlin, P. Beresford, C. Cameron, H. Casey and J. Duffy (eds) *The Routledge Handbook of Service User Involvement in Human Services Research and Education*, Abingdon: Routledge, pp 260–273.

Smale, G. and Tuson, G., with Biehal, N. and Marsh, P. (1995) *Empowerment, Assessment, Care Management and the Skilled Worker*, London: HMSO.

Social Care Institute for Excellence (2014) 'What makes coproduction different from participation?' [video]. https://www.youtube.com/watch?v=iJjmFYSB_qo

Social Care Institute for Excellence (2022) 'Co-production: what it is and how to do it' [guide]. https://www.scie.org.uk/co-production/what-how

Social Care Wales (2011) *National Occupational Standards for Social Work*. Cardiff: SCW.

Social Care Wales (2017) *Code of Professional Practice for Social Care*. Cardiff: SCW.

Social Care Wales (2020) 'Social care accolades, award ceremony, winners and finalists' [news article]. https://socialcare.wales/2020-accolades-awards-cerem ony-winners-and-finalists

Social Care Wales (2021) *Framework for the Degree in Social Work in Wales*. Cardiff: SCW.

Think Local Act Personal (2022) 'The ladder of co-production – where are you on the ladder towards co-production?' [resource]. https://www.thinklocalactperso nal.org.uk/_assets/TLAP-Ladder-of-Coproduction-Landscape-Poster-A3.pdf

Thompson, N. (2020) *Understanding Social Work* (5th edn), London: Red Globe Press.

Welford, J., Milner, C. and Moreton, R. (2022) *Coproduction: Principles into Practice, Evidence from the Fulfilling Lives Programme: Supporting people experiencing multiple disadvantage*. CFE Research/University of Sheffield.

Welsh Government (2014) *Social Services and Well-being (Wales) Act 2014*. Cardiff: Welsh Government.

Welsh Government (2015) *Social Services and Well-being (Wales) Act 2014 – Part 2 Code of Practice – General Functions*. Cardiff: Welsh Government.

Welsh Government (2022) *Expectations and Experiences: Service User and Carer Perspectives on the Social Services and Well-being (Wales) Act (Summary)*. Cardiff: Welsh Government.

PART II

Practice examples

8

Child and family social work in Wales

David Wilkins

Chapter objectives

- To highlight what is distinctive about the national and legal context for child and family social work practice in Wales.

- To reflect on what we know about the nature of social work practice with children and families in Wales.

- To make suggestions about what (more) may be required to close the gap between (legal) aspiration and (practical) reality.

Introduction

Despite having one Welsh grandparent, supporting Wales in the Six Nations rugby tournament, and having a Welsh dragon tattoo on my left shoulder, I am still more English than I am Welsh. I was born, went to school and university, completed my social work education, and spent my practice career in England. I do now live in Wales, having moved in 2018, along with my family, to take up a social work lectureship at Cardiff University.

The aim of this chapter is to provide my perspective on the nature and distinctiveness of child and family social work practice in Wales. I do so explicitly from the position of an 'outsider'. While this brings with it some obvious limitations (I have never been employed as a practising social worker within Wales), it also brings with it some potential advantages. For example, some things that are taken-for-granted by readers immersed in the Welsh context may strike me as being distinctive, particularly in comparison with England. The chapter is divided into three main sections – starting with the national context, then considering local means and outcomes, and finishing with possible future developments.

The national context

As countries go, Wales is relatively small, with a population of just over three million (around 4.8 per cent of the UK total), and a total land area of 8,023 square miles. This represents a challenge, and an opportunity. A challenge, not least because the UK Government often stands accused of ignoring and overlooking the place and its people (see for example, Henry, 2013; Burton, 2019; Howell,

2020). Yet, an opportunity, as it allows for the creation of a distinctive national approach in devolved competencies such as child and family social work. From my perspective, this opportunity is reflected in two key ways.

First, the relationship between the Welsh National Government and the 22 Welsh local authorities is distinctive because of its closeness, potential and actual. The Welsh Government can be relatively well informed about the nature and challenges of social work practice in each authority and take a day-to-day interest in each one. This is different from the situation in England. Having 152 local authorities inevitably means that the Department for Education in London is not able to have a meaningful working relationship with each one, partly because of the sheer number and partly because of geographical distance. They must instead rely on other means to gain insights into the nature of practice, and the opportunities and challenges faced in each local area. Perhaps this explains the English reliance on Ofsted, the social care inspectorate, to monitor local performance, and central government's willingness to intervene more directly and more often in the work of local authorities. Such intervention in England has included the direct imposition of government commissioners to oversee local services and the outsourcing of provision away from local authorities and into the hands of independent children's trusts (Blewett, 2016). In Wales, while there has been some use of commissioners and other forms of direct intervention (for example, in Powys and Ynys Mon), it is less common, and no councils have been made to outsource their services to other organisations. And indeed, there is no prospect of this, unlike in England where authorities are regularly reminded (or threatened) with this eventuality. Likewise, relationships *between* local authorities in Wales can be closer for similar reasons, and there is greater potential for inter-authority learning and development. While local governments in larger countries can work together effectively at a regional level, it is only in smaller countries such as Wales that genuine national working relationships may exist.

Second, this creates the potential for legislation to be developed at the national level, yet remain relevant for local circumstances, and for national principles of practice to apply across the country. A good example of this is the Social Services and Well-being (Wales) Act 2014 (SSWWA). The principles of the Act – voice and control, prevention and early intervention, well-being, and coproduction (see Chapter 1) – apply equally to working with adults, as they do for working with children and families, and suggest the possibility of a 'whole family' way of working. The national orientation in Wales also represents a more explicitly rights-based conception of practice (see Chapter 2), and of childhood, certainly compared with England, and a clearer focus on family support and early help (Lyttleton-Smith, 2021). Similarly, the use of an outcomes-focused approach in Wales is also distinctive, aiming to understand what matters to people and to develop a set of personal outcomes (Social Care Wales, 2021). A tangible example is the use of 'what matters' conversations and assessments in Wales, with a clear focus on coproduction between practitioners and people using services (Social Care Wales, 2019). These developments have even been said to indicate a return to 'real social work practice' (Hardy, 2016: 2).

This legal framework creates the conditions for, but does not determine, a more unified set of social work practices, even though adults' and children's departments continue to operate largely on a separate organisational basis. This unified approach in primary legislation sets the context for numerous different activities. For example, inspections of children's services, undertaken by the Care Inspectorate Wales, can apply these principles when evaluating the performance of individual councils, while the national safeguarding procedures refer to both adults *and* children and young people at risk (Welsh Government, 2013). In England, safeguarding procedures for children (HM Government, 2018) and adults (Office of the Public Guardian, 2015) are separate, while inspections of services undertaken by Ofsted are not explicitly founded on any shared set of principles. Wales also has a National Outcomes Framework for everyone in need of services (Welsh Government, 2022), whereas England's outcomes framework only considers adults (Department of Health and Social Care, 2018). Finally, it is easier and more feasible in Wales to introduce specific yet national ways of working, such as intensive family support services (Forrester et al, 2008a).

Local means and outcomes

It is one thing to articulate a national context in principle, via legislation and statutory guidance, and quite another for this to make a difference for local practice and outcomes.

Wales has the highest proportion of children in state care in the UK, and probably one of the highest rates in the world (Hodges and Bristow, 2019). The country has also experienced several high-profile child deaths, in which social workers and others have been criticised for not identifying signs of abuse, for not sharing information between professionals, and for not intervening quickly and effectively enough to keep children safe (BBC, 2022; Morris, 2022). This despite the apparent long-term reduction in the annual incidence of child maltreatment (Pritchard and Williams, 2010; Degli Esposti et al, 2019). Many social workers in Wales do think there are too many children in care, and some have suggested that decision-making is too risk averse (Forrester et al, 2022). There is also some significant variation between authorities, so that for example a child living 'in Torfaen is five times more likely to be in care than one in Carmarthenshire' (Forrester et al, 2022: 8). Others have argued that having more children in care is a positive thing for Wales, indicating that 'local authorities here take child protection seriously' (Mair Edwards, child psychologist, quoted in Loader, 2021). The implication is, of course, that local authorities elsewhere do not take it so seriously, or at least not to the same extent. This strikes me as a questionable suggestion, given the growing use of child protection investigations in England, for example (Bilson and Martin, 2017).

Looking at the socioeconomic context, around one-third of children in Wales are living in poverty, which is the highest percentage of any UK nation (BBC, 2021). This may help partly to explain the high rates of care in the country, because as income inequality increases, so does the use of state care, albeit poverty and inequality are not the same thing (Bywaters et al, 2020; Webb et al, 2021). Many local authorities in Wales, as elsewhere in the UK, continue to suffer from central government-imposed austerity measures, especially in more deprived areas, with detrimental effects on services and for children and families (Drakeford, 2012; Tickle, 2018). However, it is also true to say that variations in care rates between local authorities in Wales cannot be explained solely by differences in rates of deprivation or poverty (Forrester et al, 2022).

The evidence we have about the nature of social work practice in Wales is limited, as for the rest of the UK. A study worth noting – and celebrating – is one which started from the (surprise?) finding that social workers in Wales were the 'happiest' in the whole of the UK (Pithouse et al, 2019). Despite living in a country with lower average levels of prosperity, and marked social disadvantages, social workers in Wales were nonetheless found to report higher levels of job satisfaction than their colleagues in England, Northern Ireland or Scotland. To understand why, Pithouse, Brookfield and Rees (2019) undertook a follow-up survey of 995 social workers in Wales. They found that the workforce was relatively mature and experienced (p 1997), with most feeling able to exercise their professional judgement to a 'large' or 'very large' degree (64 per cent) (p 1998). Nearly half (44 per cent) said they looked forward to work to a 'large' or 'very large' degree (p 1999). Similar proportions said they were satisfied with the quality of their own work (p 2000). Many expressed relatively positive views about their social work managers. As the authors note, so much for a view of (Welsh) social work in which managers are heavy-handed, and practitioners dissatisfied because of spending all their time desk-bound and on screens.

Some of the other evidence we have, not based on self-report, is less positive. While not specific to Wales, a recent survey asked 500 parents from across the UK what they thought about their experience of contact with social services (Wilkins and Forrester, 2021). Overall, parents had low levels of satisfaction – lower than for any other type of comparable public service – and this was irrespective of the type of intervention (for example, family support or child protection). Parents from lower socioeconomic groups and parents of adolescents reported even lower levels of satisfaction. The feedback provided by parents in Wales (who made up just under 5 per cent of the sample, in line with the UK population) was no different from that of the whole-group sample, albeit based on relatively small numbers.

Observations of social work practice (from England) have suggested, among other things, that child protection social workers '[tend] to use a very confrontational … communication style' (Forrester et al, 2008b). When speaking with parents, they ask 'many closed questions and often [raise] concerns [while using] few reflections and rarely identifying positives' (Forrester et al, 2008b). More recently, a review of children's social care in England has suggested that 'process continues to dominate over direct work with families' and when families ask for help, the involvement of social services ends up '[adding] stress to an already difficult situation without meaningful support being offered' (Independent Review of Children's Social Care, 2021a). The question is, do we have good reason to think things might be different in Wales?

While we have much less direct evidence about the nature of social work practice in the country, that which we have does not suggest a radically different picture – which is not a criticism of the very many dedicated professionals who work in the field. Given how widespread these difficulties are, it is more appropriate, and useful, to ask questions about the wider system conditions, and not 'point the finger' at individuals. In terms of what we do know about practice in Wales, Treby (2022) found that home visits to see families were organised primarily to fulfil statutory obligations and took place without a clear purpose or shared agenda. Many workers made 'no observable preparation to speak or interact with children' (p 69). On the other hand, Treby noted that social workers are tasked with undertaking difficult and complicated activities, that they must respond to the unexpected, manage competing priorities, and hold sensitive conversations within the context of complicated lives and busy family homes. Sheehan (2022) has similarly observed child protection social work practice in Wales and identified how the focus is often on highly individualised behaviour-change work with parents. Sheehan asks whether this is 'how society wants social work to be?' (p 182). I suspect unfortunately that this might be *exactly* what many people in society do expect from child protection social work, but whether this is an acceptable or progressive vision for the Welsh profession is another question.

Overall, the limited evidence we have about social work practice with children and families in Wales, and the views of parents about those services, is not so different from the larger volume of data we have from England. Perhaps this should not be surprising, given the social, cultural, economic and legal similarities between the two countries, as well as their relative geographies. It highlights *either* how long it takes for national legislation and practice frameworks to have an impact on practice *or* suggests a need to manage our expectations about the likely impact of these things. It also suggests the need for more Welsh-based research on this very important topic.

The Welsh way

The Welsh way includes a clear (legal and policy) aspiration to create a more person-centred social work service for children and families, and a commitment to children's rights. Current and recent practices have also resulted in Wales having the highest rate of children in public care in the UK, and probably one of the highest rates in the world. This represents a clear juxtaposition between genuinely held values and principles and the reality of how difficult life is for far too many children and families in Wales.

However, there are reasons to be optimistic. The Welsh way of a more aspirational legislative framework is increasingly well established, including a shift towards more joined-up working around families, an emphasis on well-being and on future generations. From here the difficult task of investing in different forms of preventative and coproduced practice and a reshaping of resources is tentatively afoot – including moves to end profit-making from the care of looked after children, and greater use of more inclusive services, such as family group conferences, and parental advocacy (see Chapter 22).

Closing the gap further between aspiration and reality

If one accepts this picture of child and family social work in Wales – of a good national foundation based on key social work principles, and potential to develop local services which can put these principles into practice – what more might be done to close the gap between aspiration and reality?

When thinking about this question, it is hard not to start with the obvious. The UK Government needs to reverse spending cuts made in the name of austerity and invest properly in family services. Doing so makes not only moral sense, but economic sense too, saving money in the longer term (Independent Review of Children's Social Care, 2021b). Policymaking in Westminster would benefit from being more child-focused, which could be helped along by making the United Nations Convention on the Rights of the Child part of UK law, as it is in Wales and Scotland. More locally, the Welsh Government needs to do more to make social work an attractive career choice, for undergraduates and post-graduates alike, and ensure parity of financial support for students studying towards NHS and social work-related qualifications (British Association of Social Workers, 2022). At the time of writing, there have also been calls for an independent review of children's services in Wales, as there have been in England, Northern Ireland and Scotland (Pollock, 2022). While the Welsh Government already has a policy priority to reduce the need for children to come into care, it is clear (to me and others) that things are not working well enough for children and families, let alone for practitioners, as currently organised.

Yet even without a review, there are things that can be done. The development of parental advocacy services in Wales should be accelerated and expanded, so that it can be available everywhere, and for every parent who wants it. Such efforts are in accordance with the principles of the SSWWA and have been shown to help safely reduce the need for children to be in care (Tobis, 2013; Diaz et al, 2021). Ditto a national service for child advocacy, although one can argue that such services are only necessary because social workers are too often unable to be the genuine advocates for parents and children that they might want to be and should be.

Finally, given the association between self-reported use of an outcomes-focused approach and lower rates of care in Wales (Forrester et al, 2022), more should be done to help local authorities embed such a focus in practice. For example, by considering how supervision can be used to help focus practice on child- and parent-defined ideas of help and successful outcomes (Wilkins et al, 2020, 2022).

Messages for practice

- Child and family practice in Wales is based upon a solid legal foundation inspired by some important social work principles. The challenge for practitioners is to ensure these principles are meaningful for every child and family using services.
- Wales has the highest rate of children in care in the UK, and one of the highest rates in the world. While the reasons for this are obviously complicated, part of the explanation can be found in our organisational and personal values. It is thus important to reflect on our views and beliefs about parents and childhood, about the effectiveness of public care, about the stereotypes we hold in relation to different people, groups and communities, about how we assign responsibility for problems such as substance use and poor parenting, and about our thresholds for intervention and levels of risk-aversion.
- When organisations, and practitioners, share more positive views about birth families, are confident in their practice, prefer to keep children at home where possible, and report using an outcomes-focused approach, there are likely to be proportionally fewer children in care. For individual practitioners, this means having regular 'what matters' conversations and using existing activities such as supervision to talk explicitly about outcomes and review whether and to what extent we are helping (or not) children and families using services.

Further resources

1. Elliot, M. and Scourfield, J. (2017) 'Identifying and understanding inequalities in child welfare intervention rates: comparative studies in four UK countries. Single country quantitative study report: Wales', Nuffield Foundation [Research report]. https://www.exchangewales.org/wp-content/uploads/sites/14/2020/04/Wales-Country-Report-Final.pdf
2. Forrester, D., Wood, S., Waits, C., Jones, R., Bristow, D. and Taylor-Collins, E. (2022) 'Children's social services and care rates in Wales: a survey of the sector', CASCADE Centre for Children's Social Care and Wales Centre for Public Policy, Cardiff University [Research report]. https://www.wcpp.org.uk/wp-content/uploads/2022/03/220216-Childrens-social-services_en_final.pdf
3. Treby, L. (2022) 'What is the relationship between supervision and practice in child and family social work? An analysis of 12 case studies' [thesis for a professional doctorate]. Cardiff University. https://orca.cardiff.ac.uk/id/eprint/149545/2/1470101%20Lucy%20Treby%20DSW%20thesis%20FINAL%20April%202022.pdf

References

Bilson, A. and Martin, K. (2017) 'Referrals and child protection in England: one in five children referred to children's services and one in nineteen investigated before the age of five', *British Journal of Social Work*, 47(3): 793–811.

Blewett, J. (2016) 'Are independent children's trusts really the answer to struggling services?' https://www.communitycare.co.uk/2016/06/08/independent-childrens-trusts-really-answer/

British Association of Social Workers (2022) *SWU Campaign Fund Update: Welsh Government pledges action on bursaries following student campaign.* https://www.basw.co.uk/media/news/2022/feb/swu-campaign-fund-update-welsh-government-pledges-action-bursaries-following

British Broadcasting Corporation (2021) 'Wales "has highest child poverty rates in the UK" says Save the Children'. https://www.bbc.co.uk/news/uk-wales-57157436

British Broadcasting Corporation (2022) 'Logan Mwangi murder: Mum, stepdad and teen found guilty'. https://www.bbc.co.uk/news/uk-wales-60953867

Burton, M. (2019) 'Scotland and Wales "ignored by Westminster"'. https://www.themj.co.uk/Scotland-and-Wales-ignored-by-Westminster/213237

Bywaters, P., Scoufield, J., Jones, C., Sparks, T., Elliot, M., Hooper, J., et al (2020) 'Child welfare inequalities in the four nations of the UK'. *Journal of Social Work*, 20(2): 193–215.

Degli Esposti, M., Humphreys, D.K., Jenkins, B.M., Gasparrini, A., Pooley, S., Eisner, M. and Bowes, L. (2019) 'Long-term trends in child maltreatment in England and Wales, 1858–2016: an observational, time-series analysis'. *The Lancet Public Health*, 4: e148–e158.

Department of Health and Social Care (2018) *The Adult Social Care Outcomes Framework 2018/19.* https://assets.publishing.service.gov.uk/government/uploads/system/uploads/attachment_data/file/687208/Final_ASCOF_handbook_of_definitions_2018–19_2.pdf

Diaz, C., Westlake, D. and Evans, L. (2021) *The Perceived Impact of Peer Parental Advocacy on Child Protection Practice: A Pilot Evaluation.* Research protocol. https://orca.cardiff.ac.uk/id/eprint/145562/

Drakeford, M. (2012) 'Wales in the age of austerity', *Critical Social Policy*, 32(3): 454–466.

Forrester, D., Copello, A., Waissbein, C. and Pokhrel, S. (2008a) 'Evaluation of an intensive family preservation service for families affected by parental substance misuse'. *Child Abuse Review: Journal of the British Association for the Study and Prevention of Child Abuse and Neglect*, 17(6): 410–426.

Forrester, D., Kershaw, S., Moss, H. and Hughes, L. (2008b) 'Communication skills in child protection: how do social workers talk to parents?', *Child and Family Social Work*, 13(1): 41–51.

Forrester, D., Wood, S., Waits, C., Jones, R., Bristow, D. and Taylor-Collins, E. (2022) *Children's Social Services and Care Rates in Wales: A Survey of the Sector.* CASCADE Centre for Children's Social Care and Wales Centre for Public Policy, Cardiff University [Research report]. https://www.wcpp.org.uk/wp-content/uploads/2022/03/220216-Childrens-social-services_en_final.pdf

Hardy, R. (2016) 'Welsh social workers warned about impact of impending cuts'. https://www.theguardian.com/social-care-network/2016/jan/15/welsh-soc ial-workers-warned-impact-cuts

Henry, G. (2013) 'Wales ignored in the debate on Scottish independence, says academic'. https://www.walesonline.co.uk/news/wales-news/wales-ignored-debate-scottish-independence-6407204

HM Government (2018) 'Working together to safeguard children. a guide to inter-agency working to safeguard and promote the welfare of children'. https://assets. publishing.service.gov.uk/government/uploads/system/uploads/attachment_data/ file/942454/Working_together_to_safeguard_children_inter_agency_guidance.pdf

Hodges, H.R. and Bristow, D. (2019) 'Analysis of the factors contributing to the high rates of care in Wales'. https://www.wcpp.org.uk/publication/analy sis-of-the-factors-contributing-to-the-high-rates-of-care-in-wales/

Howell, J. (2020) 'Wales "ignored" by UK Government over English student cap'. https://jordn.co/articles/2020/6/5/wales-ignored-by-uk-government-over-english-student-cap

Independent Review of Children's Social Care (2021a) 'The case for change'. https://childrenssocialcare.independent-review.uk/wp-content/uploads/2021/ 06/case-for-change.pdf

Independent Review of Children's Social Care (2021b) 'Paying the price: the social and financial costs of children's social care.' https://childrenssocialcare. independent-review.uk/wp-content/uploads/2021/11/Paying-the-Price.pdf

Loader, G. (2021) 'Alarm over growing numbers of children in care in Wales'. https://www.bbc.co.uk/news/uk-wales-57388802

Lyttleton-Smith, J. (2021) 'Child and family services: Welsh policy developments 2010–2020', in H. Gwilym and C. Williams (eds) *Social Policy for Social Welfare Practice in a Devolved Wales* (3rd edn), Birmingham: Venture Press, pp 108–130.

Morris, S. (2022) 'Logan Mwangi: vibrant child murdered after months of terror'. https://www.theguardian.com/uk-news/2022/apr/21/logan-mwangi-vibrant-child-murdered-after-months-of-terror

Office of the Public Guardian (2015) *Safeguarding Policy*. https://assets.publishing. service.gov.uk/government/uploads/system/uploads/attachment_data/file/934 858/SD8-Office_of-the-Public-Guardian-safeguarding-policy.pdf

Pithouse, A., Brookfield, C. and Rees, A. (2019) 'Why are social workers in Wales the "happiest"? A conundrum explored', *The British Journal of Social Work*, 49(7): 1987–2006.

Pollock, I. (2022) 'Logan Mwangi: independent review needed of Wales' social services'. https://www.bbc.co.uk/news/uk-wales-61240335?at_medium= RSS&at_campaign=KARANGA

Pritchard, C. and Williams, R. (2010) 'Comparing possible "child-abuse-related-deaths" in England and Wales with the major developed countries 1974–2006: signs of progress?', *British Journal of Social Work*, 40(6): 1700–1718.

Sheehan, L. (2022) *Fixing Change – An Ethnographic Study of Child Protection Practice*. https://orca.cardiff.ac.uk/id/eprint/149419/1/PHD%20ed%20Final.pdf

Social Care Wales (2019) *What Matters Conversations and Assessments.* https://soc
ialcare.wales/service-improvement/what-matters-conversations-and-assessment

Social Care Wales (2021) *Understanding an Outcomes Approach.* https://socialcare.
wales/service-improvement/understanding-an-outcomes-approach

Tickle, S.J. (2018) *The Impact of Austerity on Children and Young People's Health
and Well-being in England and Wales.* Liverpool: Centre for the Study of Crime,
Criminalisation and Social Exclusion.

Tobis, D. (2013) *From Pariahs to Partners: How Parents and their Allies Changed
New York City's Child Welfare System,* New York: Oxford University Press.

Treby, L. (2022) 'What is the relationship between supervision and practice
in child and family social work? An analysis of 12 case studies' [thesis for a
professional doctorate], Cardiff University. https://orca.cardiff.ac.uk/id/epr
int/149545/2/1470101%20Lucy%20Treby%20DSW%20thesis%20FINAL%20
April%202022.pdf

Webb, C.J.R., Bywaters, P., Elliot, M. and Scourfield, J. (2021) 'Income inequality
and child welfare interventions in England and Wales', *Journal of Epidemiology
Community Health,* 75(3): 251–257.

Welsh Government (2013) *Social Services and Well-being (Wales) Act 2014. Working
Together to Safeguard People Volume 1 – Introduction and Overview.* https://gov.
wales/sites/default/files/publications/2019–05/working-together-to-safegu
ard-people-volume-i-introduction-and-overview.pdf

Welsh Government (2022) *Measuring National Well-being: A Report on the National
Outcomes Framework for People Who Need Care and Support and for Carers Who
Need Support, 2020–2021.* https://gov.wales/sites/default/files/publications/
2022–04/a-report-on-the-national-outcomes-framework-for-people-who-
need-care-and-support-and-for-carers-who-need-support-2020–2021.pdf

Wilkins, D. and Forrester, D. (2021) 'What do parents think about statutory
child and family social work services in the UK?', *British Journal of Social Work,*
51(6): 2210–2227.

Wilkins, D., Warner, N., Addis, S., El-Banna, A., Pitt, C., Mayhew-Manistre,
et al (2020) *Outcomes-focused Supervision: A Pilot and Feasibility Study.* https://
whatworks-csc.org.uk/wp-content/uploads/WWCSC_Outcomes-Focused-
Supervision_full-report.pdf

Wilkins, D., Pitt, C. and Addis, S. (2022) 'What do child protection social workers
talk about when they talk about helping children and families? An observational
study of supervision', *Practice* [online]: 1–19. https://doi.org/10.1080/09503
153.2022.2034777

9

A joint children and adult approach to safeguarding

Hayley Douglas and Helena Barlow

Chapter objectives

- To explore the issues around the child/adult binary in safeguarding practice.

- To identify how the Social Services and Well-being (Wales) Act (2014) seeks to promote a joint child and adult approach to safeguarding.

- Outline the implications of a joint approach for social work and social care professionals, and those working in the helping professions.

- Critically analyse the joint approach and changes in discourse around safeguarding.

Introduction

For many, the transition from childhood to adulthood is not a smooth one (Chisnell and Kelly, 2019), with those in the transition stage deemed most at risk (Keeling and Goosey, 2021). The problems and issues that require safeguarding support as a 17-year-old do not suddenly disappear on the young person's 18th birthday. Some professions, such as Youth Work in Wales, support young people through this transition; working with young people aged 11–25 years. Specific groups of young people, such as those who are young carers, care leavers, young people in the criminal justice system, and young people with disabilities, may require ongoing support. Some children and young people find themselves in need of safeguarding intervention as a result of adult behaviours that require support for parents, guardians and carers to reduce the risk of harm. Examples here may include where there is domestic violence in the home or parental substance use (Coates, 2017). Therefore, successful safeguarding requires a different approach that advocates an integrated paradigm between children and adult services (Cocker et al, 2021). However, often there remains a disjuncture between child and adult safeguarding services (Webber et al, 2013). The transition between these can be disjointed and cumbersome, resulting in services and support being removed, and young people and adults subject to increasing vulnerability and safeguarding concerns (Bowes and Daniel, 2010).

The child/adult binary in safeguarding

Bowes and Daniel (2010) identified that there has been limited cross-over in the dissemination of theory and learning from practice between safeguarding teams involved in safeguarding of children, young people and adults. They argue that evolving legislative protective responses for adults are often an extension of those already in place for children. Keeling and Goosey (2021) echo this, stating that traditionally the organisation of children's safeguarding services has been more elaborate than adults' due to political potency and media attention focused on serious child case reviews, for example in respect of the Victoria Climbié Inquiry (Department for Health and Home Office, 2003).

However, 'safeguarding children is everyone's responsibility; including professionals working with adults' (Webber et al, 2013: 149). This is especially the case where adults themselves are at risk due to mental health, or substance use, which impact on all members of the family (Webber et al, 2013). A number of different social workers and other professionals may be separately supporting either the adult or child; each in accordance with their own legislation and agency policy regarding risk management. Thus, the child or adult's voice can become lost in the confusing and arduous process through the different stages of their life (Peckover and Goulding, 2017). Therefore the child/adult binary does not just exist for young people's transition to adulthood, but across the lifespan and into older age.

Cocker et al (2021) argue that safeguarding often operates within a binary of either child or adult services; viewing young people as fitting into either one of these categories, and ignoring the adolescent transition in the middle, with neither system meeting the needs of the young person. Instead, the needs of the safeguarding organisation are served, rather than the individual (Chisnell and Kelly, 2019). Connolly, Hothersall and Maas-Lowit (2020) surmise that safeguarding, therefore, needs to move away from the separatist view. In order to support children, young people and adults effectively, a joint approach to safeguarding is needed.

Safeguarding within The Social Services and Well-being (Wales) Act (2014)

In 1997 the devolved Welsh Government was empowered to implement new legislation, policy and processes in respect of a number of key areas including social services. Publishing the paper *Sustainable Social Services for Wales – a Framework for Action* (Welsh Assembly Government, 2011), the Welsh Government highlighted a number of challenges facing health and social care, including a lack of resources amid an ageing population, and unrealistic thresholds for services in place for children, young people and adults. Some individuals would ultimately not receive much-needed support in the future.

Previously there was no separate legislative structure for Wales, and separate legislature for the safeguarding of adults and children. In terms of safeguarding adults, Welsh local authorities discharged their duties in relation to the *In Safe Hands* guidance (Welsh Assembly Government, 2000), while *No Secrets* (Department of Health, 2000) was the respective guidance for England. These mirrored the previous Care Act (1990) which applied to both England and Wales (Chisnell and Kelly, 2019). This often meant that adults at risk, requiring preventative support, did not meet a threshold for intervention until they hit crisis point; impacting adversely on the individuals and their families. In England, an updated Care Act (2014) was enacted and this continues to apply only to adults (Community Care Inform, 2021); hence a lack of unified approach for children, young people and adults.

Within the Children Act (1989), children and young people had very little voice within the Assessment Framework. Their views and what mattered to them were often missing; with key decisions remaining solely in the hands of social services. Although it is appreciated that S47 child protection procedures are still prioritised in respect of the Children Act (1989), a different ethos was developing in Wales, where through all stages of a person's life journey, and the social care services they access, a child's views, wishes and feelings are just as central to any intervention as adults' (Welsh Government, 2015).

In 2014, Wales chose to take a different approach through its creation of one piece of legislation for safeguarding both adults and children; encouraging a smoother transition in provision for children and young people, especially care leavers. The Social Services and Well-being (Wales) Act (2014) (SSWWA) came into effect in 2016, and revolutionised how both adult and children's health and social care needs are to be met in Wales. The first piece of legislation of its nature, it placed a duty on all professionals working within the areas of health, social services and social care to support, empower and work in partnership with individuals, their family or carers to safeguard children and vulnerable adults, with an emphasis on the voice of the individual (Welsh Government, 2015; Public Health Wales, 2021). In summary, the SSWWA brought together in one Act a strengthened voice for both adults and children at risk, established a duty of well-being, as well as the responsibility of local partners to report safeguarding concerns for both adults and children. For the first time, and in a major divergence from the English legislature, arrangements for the safeguarding of adults and children were brought together in one Act (Keeling and Goosey, 2021).

Analysing the discourse

Both Chisnell and Kelly (2019) and Keeling and Goosey (2021) highlight the importance of analysing discourse in terms of safeguarding, as the language used within legal frameworks reflects wider societal views, values and norms about risk, safeguarding, childhood, adolescence and adulthood. Language is important here, as discourse can be regarded as established ways of talking that people adopt at certain points of time that help to inform their understanding of the world, and how they should act within it (Douglas, 2022). The SSWWA reinforced new language which moved from 'protection' of adults and children to 'safeguarding'. Safeguarding under the remit of the Act, is the protection from harm or abuse of children and adults who otherwise would be unable to keep themselves safe. Abuse is categorised into key areas, which apply to both children and adults, these being: physical, sexual, emotional/psychological and neglect. There is an additional category of financial abuse which applies to adults. Particularly within adult safeguarding, the focus was revised to concentrate on what the person is able to do for themselves and on state intervention only where the three-stage criteria are met (Welsh Government, 2018b). These criteria are that the individual is at risk of harm or abuse, has care and support needs and, due to these, is unable to protect themselves. Thus, changes in the language of safeguarding shifted the discourse away from an individual or pathological focus of blame and protection, to a better focus on strengths-based rather than deficit-based practice approaches to safeguarding (Pritchard-Jones, 2018).

Through the SSWWA, terminology within adult and children's services became aligned to include a focus on well-being, coproduction and multi-agency working; and in most cases a reference to 'people' as opposed to definition based on life stage. The discourse of 'safeguarding as everyone's responsibility' was re-emphasised through the legislation applying to health, social care and social services, thus encouraging more joint working across these services through the use of the same assessment document entitled *What Matters* (Social Care Wales, 2019). This utilises a person-centred approach which ensures that the individual's voice is heard throughout all stages of practice.

Further changes to language brought about by the Act relate to the 'Protection of Vulnerable Adults' and the term 'child in need' with both terms having now been replaced. The term 'vulnerable' had been heavily criticised in respect of adult safeguarding previously as it appeared to infer that, due to an individual experiencing an impairment of body or mind, they were in need of protection, deemed to be to blame for their situation and unable to protect themselves from harm. Instead, a welcomed move to introduce the term 'Adult at Risk' was implemented in both Wales and England (Phillips, 2016; Williams, 2017; Pritchard-Jones, 2018). In Wales the emphasis is now on services only becoming involved if it is deemed that an individual is not able to 'protect themselves', hence an adult can be vulnerable due to experiencing domestic abuse or stalking for example, but if the individual has capacity, no care and support needs and is able to seek assistance for themselves, they may not be an 'Adult at Risk' in terms of the legal definition (Barlow, 2022). Thus the SSWWA brought with it not only new legislation, but new discourse that frames practitioners' views of the concept of safeguarding in relation to all people, and subsequently their role and responsibilities within this.

Even prior to the SSWWA, the Welsh Government had outlined their long-term vision of a joint approach to safeguarding adult and children in respect of tackling child poverty. The whole family ethos was initially highlighted within the Children and Family (Wales) Measure (2010), where one of the outcomes was the development of 'Integrated Family Support Service' (IFSS) teams. The criterion for the service is a family in crisis due to parental alcohol or substance use, whereby the children are at significant risk of harm and likely to be on the child protection register, with the prospect of court proceedings should the situation not improve rapidly. The aim is to enable the child to remain in the family home. Importantly, the focus of IFSS is to allocate one IFSS worker who intensively works with the whole family over a period of six weeks initially. Feedback has been positive from families who have benefitted from the IFSS, and it was also welcomed by local authority child protection teams who were already resource stretched and unable to provide the level of intensive support that the families needed. However, there was concern regarding how the service would be funded long term (Welsh Government, 2012, 2014; Wales Centre for Public Policy, 2021).

Messages for practice

- Within Children's Services, from 2016, Part 3 (Children in Need) of the Children Act (1989) no longer applied in Wales, replaced by the SSWWA s21 and s37, which places a duty on Welsh local authorities to assess a child's need for care and support. However, safeguarding enquiries in respect of children are still undertaken in accordance with s47 of the Children Act (1989), with reference to volume 5 (SSWWA).
- Within Adult Safeguarding, s126 (safeguarding) enquiries are conducted in relation to volume 6 (Part 7 SSWWA).
- In practice, these policy changes have led to joint terminology and processes being used for children, young people and adults who require input from health and social care.

The *What Matters* (Social Care Wales, 2019) assessment document is transferred between child and adult services, and also from health to social care departments, hence the individual does not have to share the same information over and over again and delays in the person accessing essential services are reduced (Welsh Government, 2015).

A National Independent Safeguarding Board has been set up, as well as Local Safeguarding Boards for adults in addition to the already established children's board, thus attributing adult safeguarding the same level of importance as children's. The SSWWA (s135) also provides the opportunity for child and adult safeguarding boards to form a joint board. These boards have close working links between them, for instance, the North Wales Safeguarding Board (which links the six neighbouring local authorities) has a joint adults' and children's workforce development sector, thus reinforcing the Welsh approach (North Wales Safeguarding Board, 2022). Throughout North Wales, the board has ratified the use of the same referral documentation for all of their local authorities, thus further demonstrating the cross-country multi-agency working. The safeguarding boards' members include for example, police, health, secretary of state, the local authority and the probation service. In terms of preventative services there has also been a move from 'Team Around the Child' to 'Team Around the Family' and more recently to 'Together Achieving Change' services, that recognise the importance of support for children, young people and adults in families to promote well-being and prevent safeguarding incidents.

Statutory guidance was published in respect of the individual parts of the SSWWA. Part seven of the statutory guidance in relation to safeguarding is entitled *Working Together to Safeguard People* (Welsh Government, 2018a). *The Wales Safeguarding Procedures* (Welsh Government, 2019) are now available digitally and via a downloadable application to support practitioners. Their aim was to further enhance the statutory guidance contained within the *Working Together to Safeguard People* volumes; replacing also the *All Wales Child Protection Procedures* (Welsh Assembly Government, 2008) and incorporating Adult at Risk guidance. The procedures provide a clear outline of actions expected to be taken by all practitioners who work with children and/or adults in Wales. Although there are separate sections which apply to adults or children, the guidance further highlights the similarity in approach to safeguarding within the child and adult arena, with common themes and language throughout (Community Care Inform, 2018; Welsh Government, 2022).

Critique of a joint approach

Although the previous examples outline what should happen in practice, the application of the SSWWA is not without its limitations. For Williams (2017), the SSWWA provided an opportunity to rethink the approach to safeguarding; providing a 'people approach' to safeguarding rather than a binary child/adult approach that failed to respond to family dynamics, and support transition between services. However, in terms of adult safeguarding, the Act is still limited in relation to its power for intervention with adults at risk, with limited use and implementation of Adult Protection and Support Orders (Williams, 2017).

McManus and Boulton (2020) conducted an evaluation of the integrated multi-agency operational safeguarding arrangements in Wales. They concluded that while the language and vision of the SSWWA had been adopted in terms of ensuring a 'person-centred' approach to safeguarding, children and adult services were still often seen as separate. Examples included where local authority safeguarding leads still had responsibility for either child *or* adult services, difficulties in information sharing, and a lack of co-location of teams (McManus and Boulton, 2020). As Webber et al (2013) assert, inter-service collaboration cannot be fostered by policy or guidance alone; positive experience of working

Case study 1

Gemma is a care leaver approaching her 18th birthday. She has limited contact with family or friends. She has moderate learning disabilities and has recently disclosed that her now ex-boyfriend was abusive towards her during their relationship. He continues to stalk and harass Gemma, leaving her upset and afraid. She has never reported these incidents before and is unsure of what to do to keep herself safe.

- Does Gemma meet the criteria of Child or Adult at Risk?
- What duties can her social worker exercise under the SSWWA?
- What would be the responsibility of other professionals working with Gemma, such as her youth worker, care home staff, college tutor and so on?
- Utilising the Welsh way, what steps should the social worker take?

Comments

In accordance with the Act, Gemma would meet the definition of Child at Risk until her 18th birthday, at which point a referral could be made into the local authority Adult Safeguarding Team. The social worker would consider Gemma's capacity (in accordance with the Mental Capacity Act, 2005) and level of understanding around the risks of experiencing stalking and domestic abuse, and this would determine if her consent was required prior to being submitted to an Adult at Risk referral. Regardless of capacity, Gemma would be fully involved in this process and her views and wishes and feelings gained throughout via *What Matters* (Social Care Wales, 2019) assessment. As the criteria in Wales utilises similar terminology and specification for both adult and children safeguarding, she would likely meet the criteria of Adult at Risk. Gemma would be considered to be at risk of harm or abuse from her ex-partner, she has care and support needs due to learning disabilities and, being an open case to statutory services, thus requires support from services to keep safe. This would lead to s126 (safeguarding) enquiries being undertaken by the social work department which would involve multi-agency working and sharing of information between leaving care, adult safeguarding, and the police (also considering the Protection of Freedoms Act (2012) in respect of stalking) to develop a protection plan in partnership with Gemma, to reduce any risks to her safety.

The Welsh way aims to provide a more seamless transition from child to adult safeguarding services. However, in practice, with the considerations of capacity and consent to refer within adult services there are, on occasion, complexities with regard to whether the criteria of Adult at Risk are met especially within domestic abuse situation where there may be other factors at play such as coercive control.

together and collaboration are needed. The SSWWA and subsequent guidance can only be effective when, and if, practitioners become comfortable stepping outside of their professional and organisational boundaries. The evaluation outlined previously by McManus and Boulton (2020) indicates that safeguarding services in Wales may not be there yet.

Case study 2

David is a single father of James, his five-year-old son. They live with David's mother Rosemary who is 91 years old, has physical disabilities and is a wheelchair user. David is also Rosemary's full-time carer. Over the last six months, James has been missing several days at school with no explanation, and has started looking unkempt, withdrawn and tired at school. He is always hungry and has been seen trying to place extra food in his school bag from the canteen at lunch time. School had submitted a safeguarding referral a few months back into Children's Social Services and James has an allocated social worker. Due to significant concerns around David's alcohol use, the conditions of the home and general neglect of James, a Child Protection conference has been arranged and the social worker has referred the case to the IFSS with David's consent. Rosemary has also confirmed that she would like to access additional support.

- What actions could the IFSS take to provide a holistic approach to supporting David, Rosemary and James? How is this approach beneficial?
- How does this meet the aims and objectives of the SSWWA and the Welsh way?

Comments

The IFSS approach is now further embedded within SSWWA and policy, moves away from the discourse of blame and protection, and applies a strengths-based approach. For instance, the 'miracle' question is used, whereby David, Rosemary and James would be asked individually to draw, or write or talk about what their perfect day would look like and then what small steps they would like to take to reach these goals (Welsh Government, 2014). In accordance with the aims of SSWWA, the focus is on David, Rosemary and James being at the centre of what matters to them, and then working together as a family to achieve these aims. The family are allocated one IFSS worker who intensively works with them over a period of six weeks initially. The family are seen either together or separately, and sessions may involve supporting each of their individual needs, such as accessing support services for substance use for David, access to carer's support and care interventions (for Rosemary), and referrals to children's support activities and services for James). This approach encourages David, Rosemary and James to build a rapport with one worker as the main point of contact through the intensive phase, as opposed to many different social workers or support workers being involved. It allows for consistency and a trusting relationship to be built over time and reduces the need for David, Rosemary and James to tell their story to many different people (Pithouse and Crowley, 2016).

Keeling and Goosey (2021) indicate that for this to be effective it requires the challenging of disciplinary and professional perspectives, assumptions, values and principles; even concepts of risk that exist due to years of separation of child and adult safeguarding services. This starts with the challenging of dominant discourse about the way that management of risk in both child and adult safeguarding services is thought about (Keeling and Goosey, 2021), but also challenging practitioner resistance to joint approaches brought about by the discourse of neoliberalism and austerity (Chisnell and Kelly, 2019). Changing the language used is the first step to changing the discourse as demonstrated in the SSWWA, which will take time to implement in practice through training and education of existing and new practitioners, and reinforced positive practice experiences.

Using the previous example case studies, the SSWWA advocates a joint approach. However, as outlined this may not be the reality. One alternative may be a lifespan approach to safeguarding as advocated by Bowes and Daniel (2010), Chisnell and Kelly (2019), Connolly et al (2020) and Keeling and Goosey (2021). A lifespan approach to safeguarding involves health, social care and social work practitioners (and others), developing universal skills and knowledge in safeguarding that are not age specific, and are transferable between children, young people and adults (Chisnell and Kelly, 2019). After all, a person's fundamental needs are not always dependent on age (Connolly et al, 2020).

The Welsh way

- People can be at risk of harm at any age or point in their lifespan. There is not a clear distinction between child and adult as young people transition into adulthood.

- The SSWWA brings together arrangements for safeguarding both children and adults in Wales to promote a joint approach to safeguarding.

- The legislation has placed a focus on well-being, strengthened the voice of both children and adults, and provided a legislative footing for supporting adults at risk on a par with children; aiding the transition between services for young people.

- This has led to clear statutory guidance for professionals with responsibility for social work, social care and the helping professions, the creation of Regional Safeguarding Boards, and an online application to support practitioners.

- However, while the discourse and language of the Act has been adopted strategically in both children and adult safeguarding services, there is still much work to be done to ensure collaboration and a joined-up approach at a practice level.

Conclusion

Both the Care Act (2014) in England and SSWWA in Wales have similar terminology in respect of adult safeguarding, however clear differentiations can be made between the approach in terms of the SSWWA imposing legislation that incorporates adult and child safeguarding, and encourages a joint approach and increased multi-agency working across the adults' and children's sector. The Welsh way places adult safeguarding on the same footing as children's, which is an encouraging move forward for adults at risk, and young people transitioning to adult services. The emphasis on working across health, social care and the associated people professions is also a positive move which will ultimately benefit the individual involved with safeguarding services. However, as McManus and Boulton (2020) contend, while Wales may be leading the way in some aspects, there is a danger that this is being lost at the expense of an overwhelming application of new policy. As this chapter has demonstrated, while the discourse of safeguarding has changed at the policy and strategy level, there are limitations to this being implemented in practice, with barriers still existing for a joint approach; including practitioners themselves still engaged in silo-ways of thinking and practising (Coates, 2017). It is therefore hoped that this will change with time through professional education, training and positive experience of collaboration. What remains to be seen, however, is whether Wales will move beyond a joint child and adult safeguarding approach to a more pragmatic lifespan approach.

Further resources
1. Chisnell, C. and Kelly, C. (2019) *Safeguarding in Social Work Practice: A Lifespan Approach* (2nd edn), London: Sage Publications.
2. Keeling, J. and Goosey, D. (2021) *Safeguarding Across the Life Span*, London: Sage.
3. Pithouse, A. and Crowley, A. (2016) 'Tackling child neglect: key developments in Wales', *Research, Policy and Planning*, 32(1): 25–37.

References
Barlow, H. (2022) 'Women's experiences of stalking and their interaction with the criminal justice service, local authority and third sector agencies' [PhD thesis-ongoing]. Wrexham: Glyndŵr University.

Bowes, A. and Daniel, B. (2010) 'Introduction: interrogating harm and abuse: a lifespan approach', *Social Policy & Society*, 9(2): 221–229.

Chisnell, C. and Kelly, C. (2019) *Safeguarding in Social Work Practice: A Lifespan Approach* (2nd edn), London: Sage Publications.

Coates, D. (2017) 'Working with families with parental mental health and/or drugs and alcohol issues where there are child protection concerns: inter-agency collaboration', *Child & Family Social Work*, 22: 1–10.

Cocker, C., Cooper, A., Holmes, D. and Bateman, F. (2021) 'Transitional safeguarding: presenting the case for developing Making Safeguarding Personal for young people in England', *The Journal of Adult Protection*, 23(3): 114–157.

Community Care Inform (2018) *Adult Safeguarding and Social Services Well-Being Wales Act 2014.* https://adults.ccinform.co.uk/practice-guidance/adult-safeg uarding-and-the-social-services-and-well-being-wales-act-2014/

Community Care Inform (2021) *Adult Safeguarding and the Care Act 2014.* https:// adults.ccinform.co.uk/practice-guidance/care-act-2014-adult-safeguarding/

Connolly, S., Hothersall, S.J. and Maas-Lowit, M. (2020) 'Protecting people across the lifespan', in S.J. Hothersall and J. Bolger (eds) *Social Policy for Social Work, Social Care and the Caring Professions* (2nd edn), London: Routledge, chapter 17.

Department of Health (2000) *No Secrets: Guidance on Developing and Implementing Multiagency Policies and Procedures to Protect Vulnerable Adults from Abuse.* London: Department of Health.

Department for Health and Home Office (2003) *The Victoria Climbié Inquiry: Report of an Inquiry by Lord Laming.* https://assets.publishing.service.gov.uk/governm ent/uploads/system/uploads/attachment_data/file/273183/5730.pdf

Douglas, H. (2022) 'Discovering discourse analysis: uncovering the "hidden" in youth work research', Methodological Approaches to Research in Youth Work: Changing the Paradigm, Special issue of *Youth Voice Journal*, pp 8–21. https://www.rj4allpublications.com/product/discovering-discourse-analysis/

Keeling, J. and Goosey, D. (2021) *Safeguarding Across the Life Span*, London: Sage.

McManus, M. and Boulton, L. (2020) *Evaluation of Integrated Multi-Agency Operational Safeguarding Arrangements in Wales.* National Independent Safeguarding Board Wales/Welsh Government. https://researchonline.ljmu.ac.uk/id/epr int/13717/1/Evaluation%20of%20Integrated%20Multi-Agency%20Operatio nal%20Safeguarding%20Arrangements%20in%20Wales.pdf

North Wales Safeguarding Board (2022) *Strategic plan 2022–2023.* https://www. northwalessafeguardingboard.wales/wp-content/uploads/2022/03/NWSB-Annual-Plan-2022–23-Final-Mar-22.pdf

Peckover, S. and Golding, B. (2017) 'Domestic abuse and safeguarding children: critical issues for multi-agency working', *Child Abuse Review*, 26: 40–50.

Phillips, C. (2016) 'Wales' safeguarding policy and practice: a critical analysis', *Journal of Adult Protection*, 18(1): 14–27.

Pithouse, A. and Crowley, A. (2016) 'Tackling child neglect: key developments in Wales', Research, Policy and Planning, 32(1): 25–37.

Pritchard-Jones, L. (2018) 'Adults at risk: vulnerability by any other name', *The Journal of Adult Protection*, 20(1): 47–58.

Public Health Wales (2021) *Safeguarding Policy.* https://phw.nhs.wales/about-us/ policies-and-procedures/policies-and-procedures-documents/safeguarding-vul nerable-children-and-adults-policies/safeguarding-policy/

Social Care Wales (2019) *What Matters Conversations and Assessment.* https://soc ialcare.wales/service-improvement/what-matters-conversations-and-assessment

Wales Centre for Public Policy (2021) *Multi Agency Working for Children Looked After: A Policy Timeline.* https://www.wcpp.org.uk/wp-content/uploads/2021/ 09/Multi-agency-working-for-children-looked-after-A-policy-timeline.pdf

Webber, M., McCree, C. and Angeli, P. (2013) 'Inter-agency joint protocols for safeguarding children in social care and adult mental-health agencies: a cross-sectional survey of practitioner experiences', *Child & Family Social Work*, 18: 149–158.

Welsh Assembly Government (2000) *In Safe Hands: Implementing Adult Protection Procedures in Wales*. Cardiff: Welsh Assembly Government.

Welsh Assembly Government (2008) *All Wales Child Protection Procedures*. Cardiff: Welsh Assembly Government.

Welsh Assembly Government (2010) *Children and Families (Wales) Measure 2010*. Cardiff: Welsh Assembly Government.

Welsh Assembly Government (2011) *Sustainable Social Services: A Framework for Action*. http://www.wales.nhs.uk/sitesplus/documents/829/WAG%20-%20Sust ainable%20Social%20Services%20for%20Wales%202011.pdf

Welsh Government (2012) *Evaluation of the Integrated Family Support Service: First Interim Report, Executive Summary*. https://gov.wales/sites/default/files/statist ics-and-research/2019–07/120914integratedfamilysummaryen.pdf

Welsh Government (2014) *Evaluation of the Integrated Family Support Service: Final Year 3 Report*. https://gov.wales/sites/default/files/statistics-and-research/ 2019–07/140328-evaluation-integrated-family-support-service-year-3-en.pdf

Welsh Government (2015) *Social Services Well-being (Wales) Act 2014: The Essentials*. https://gov.wales/sites/default/files/publications/2019–05/social-services-and-well-being-wales-act-2014-the-essentials.pdf

Welsh Government (2018a) *Social Services Well-being (Wales) Act 2014: Working Together to Safeguard people, Volume 1: Introduction and Overview*. https://gov. wales/sites/default/files/publications/2019–05/working-together-to-safegu ard-people-volume-i-introduction-and-overview.pdf

Welsh Government (2018b) *Social Services Well-being (Wales) Act: Working Together to Safeguard People, Volume 6: Handling Individual Cases to Protect Adults at Risk*. https://gov.wales/sites/default/files/publications/2019–06/volume-6-handl ing-individual-cases-to-protect-adults-at-risk.pdf

Welsh Government (2019) *Wales Safeguarding Procedures*. https://safeguarding. wales/

Welsh Government (2022) *Social Services Well-being (Wales) Act 2014: Working Together to Safeguard People: Codes of Safeguarding Practice*. https://gov.wales/ sites/default/files/publications/2022–01/working-together-to-safeguard-peo ple--code-of-safeguarding-practice.pdf

Williams, J. (2017) 'Adult safeguarding in Wales: one step in the right direction', *Journal of Adult Protection*, 19(4): 175–186.

10

Experiences of social care and social work education: completing the circle

Sarah Buckley, Graham Attenborough, Hope Lawrence,
Tim Wynn, Jenny Burgess, Eluned Plack, Anna-Louise Edwards,
Rhiana Povey and Sandra Williams, with Liz Lefroy

This chapter is dedicated to the memories of Outside In representatives
Emmett Roberts, Harry Prankard, April Harper, Graham Attenborough
and Brian Stapley, and to all those many individuals who have made a
contribution to Outside In, past and present.

Chapter objectives

- To ensure that voices of individuals and carers are at the heart of social
  work literature.

- To demonstrate the variety of ways in which our voices can be heard.

- To emphasise our interconnectedness in communities of learning, as we all
  carry with us expertise through experience which can be beneficial to others.

Outside In: context

It was founding Outside In representative, Sandra Williams, who came up with
the phrase 'completing the circle' in relation to the purpose of the involvement
of individuals with lived experience of health and social care services in the BA
(Hons) Social Work at Wrexham Glyndŵr University (WGU). It is a phrase that
has stuck: the group's purpose and approach to coproduction distilled in three
words. In order to complete the circle, this chapter takes a different format; readers
will notice an informal tone, and little reference made to other texts. These
factors in themselves are points for learning. The material has been coproduced
and the starting point is experience, not the requirements of publication. It is
written and drawn in individuals' own voices, and the editing process, undertaken
collaboratively, has aimed to maintain the authenticity of contributors' voices.
Readers are advised to experience the chapter with an open ear and eye. Read
the poetry aloud alone or to each other; spend a few minutes focusing on the
visual art; browse the links given in the Further resources section. The chapter
is crafted from expertise through experience – set aside your assumptions about

what expertise constitutes, engage your lived experience to become part of the community of learning demonstrated here.

From the outside, in

Two stills have been selected from the animated film *What Is Social Work?* (see Further resources) coproduced remotely by Outside In and social work students during the lockdown restrictions of 2020–21. The first picture (Figure 10.1) refers to the time before Outside In existed. It was in 2006 that one of the original representatives, Sylvia Prankard, came up with the name for the participation group that was already active, interviewing candidates for the social work programme. Two groups are depicted: students in a classroom inside the university, and individuals and carers, from North Wales and beyond, outside. The groups are cut off from each other by a window. Those outside are looking in, wanting to be part of the university community, to experience *equal value* in a context from which they have often been excluded.

In the second picture (Figure 10.2), the circle of learning is completed. The community of stakeholders in the BA Social Work is working to develop and improve the education of future social workers and, additionally, to enrich the lives of Outside In representatives themselves, giving opportunities that might otherwise not be experienced. It does not matter what disadvantage the individual has gone, or is going, through: the community (students, individuals,

Figure 10.1 *Looking in from the Outside*, Sarah Buckley

Figure 10.2 *Coming Together*, Sarah Buckley

carers and tutors) overcomes barriers together. This learning community is for everyone, and it brings out the humanity in education, not just of social workers, but also (as the scope of Outside In has grown) nurses, occupational therapists, physiotherapists and other future health and social care professionals studying at WGU. People are just being people, with one goal in mind: better health and social care services.

Having explained the context and origins of Outside In through Sarah's drawings, a way to develop understanding further is to get to know the stories of other individuals involved. Graham Attenborough, Hope Lawrence, Tim Wynn, Jenny Burgess, Eluned Plack and Anna-Louise Edwards, whose stories follow, are Outside In representatives who, along with many others, have participated in a number of ways at WGU. One of these is that they have enrolled as students alongside social work students. The module, *Learning Together*, is at level 4, and core to the social work degree, as are *Conflicts and Dilemmas* (level 5) and *The Creative Practitioner* (level 6). Outside In representatives study these as standalone modules, attending the scheduled sessions. This week-by-week involvement has had a profound effect on the way social work students and Outside In get to know each other. The module learning continued through lockdown restrictions via video-call. As part of *The Creative Practitioner*, different methods of working are explored together, including poetry, painting, animation and dance. Examples of these methods are demonstrated throughout this chapter and also in the Further resources section.

The first story comes from Graham Attenborough. Sadly, Graham died in September 2021, but he has left a wealth of material: poetry, lectures, films.

The inclusion of his story here is representative of the rich legacy of those from Outside In whose influence on social work education continues beyond their lifetimes.

The perfect social worker – *Graham Attenborough*

As a member of Outside In, I like to think that my participation in the Social Work degree is twofold. First, I bring an historical dimension that stems from my experience as a heroin addict during the 1980s. My drug use began in the late 1970s and became increasingly problematic when I moved into a squat in Bristol in 1982. By 1989 I was a serious addict, using perhaps £100-worth of illegal drugs a day which I acquired mainly through dealing. I'd spent time in prison for fraud and deception and had been arrested several times for petty offences.

My partner and I had two children, both of whom were on the 'at risk' register, with dedicated social workers monitoring our household. Furthermore, I was on a two-year probation order. It was my long-suffering social worker Andrew (employed as a probation officer) who finally persuaded me to go into rehabilitation. I summarised what made him such a good social worker in my poem *Andrew*, and in 2019 this was used as the soundtrack to a film by social work students (see Further resources for links). My subsequent experiences of rehab and separation from my partner and children are useful, if difficult, subjects to share with students.

This brings me to the second area of participation in the social work degree. I spent over a year at the residential rehab centre, Alpha House, in Hampshire and lived in the city of Portsmouth for the following 22 years. During that time I worked as a driver and cleaner, but was also studying history, art and literature, eventually enrolling on an access course in humanities and becoming an undergraduate student at Portsmouth University, studying history.

After graduating, I continued my studies and was awarded two masters degrees in history and creative writing, and was given an hourly-paid teaching job. Five years later, I took up a permanent teaching post in the history department. I left that post in 2013, moving back to my home town of Shrewsbury to care for my elderly father and devote time to writing and performing poetry. This second stage of my story encourages students to challenge preconceived notions that individuals who've committed criminal acts will always return to their deviant behaviour. I'm living proof that change is certainly possible and that education is a key driver in this process.

The real value of student engagement with Outside In is a practical involvement with people who bring diverse life experience into the classroom. This approach works particularly well with a vocational degree subject. Of course, theoretical analysis of social issues is invaluable to any student, but meeting and engaging with 'outsiders' who use, or have used, social services provides students with a rich resource: the experience of being able to meet, listen and talk with the very people they are likely to be working with in their future careers.

I've changed my mind about social workers – *Hope Lawrence*

I have been a representative of Outside In and participated in the social work degree for three years, and I have enjoyed it and learned so much. When I was first asked, I wasn't sure. The social work profession often has a bad reputation – it is sometimes seen as a way of separating or splitting up families for no real reason. Someone once said to me that social workers are hard and difficult people to deal with: now I see it in a very different way. Since I enrolled on the *Learning Together* module at WGU and started the classes with social work students, I have come to know how much impact social workers have in Wales today, and their passion and willingness to work with people.

This experience has been my first time at a university in the UK – I was a bit naive and didn't have a clue what studying in the UK looks or feels like. One way to learn from, and experience, other people's behaviour is to work with them. On only my second day in class, I was fortunate to be among the group working on a project focused on a story about our strengths. This project lasted for about two weeks before we had to make a presentation to the rest of the class. During the planning of this presentation, we had time to talk about what makes us stronger, how we deal with difficult experiences, and how we felt during the pain and struggling. Talking about what we had been through in the past set the picture of what we were going to work on, and this showed the strength of every individual. It also enabled me to think a lot about social work, and not just the title 'Social Science'.

When talking about strengths, one of the group members came up with a name for our project from a Japanese word – *Kintsugi* – meaning a broken vase: a vase that was broken or neglected but was later fixed and made beautiful with gold, making it stronger than ever! This idea fitted with the stories some of us had shared.

The presentation went well as far as I am concerned. I really did enjoy every bit of the session, both our presentation and the other groups' presentations, because every person played a part in their own way, and this demonstrated different aspects of individual strengths. Without presentations like this, it would be difficult to know what someone has been through and what has made them stronger.

On the day of the presentation, some people made their presentations in Welsh, which I found so interesting – it is their first language or mother-tongue. In our group, one student was able to translate parts of our presentation into Welsh, which I loved, even though someone in the group was against this idea! Still, the Welsh-speaking student insisted on translating aspects of the presentation into Welsh, so that the Welsh speakers in the class would see our story and be able to follow it. This made me also see and understand the importance of using one's own language. I myself didn't know much about Welsh before I came to Wales, until I was told by a doctor about the Welsh language. I wish to learn Welsh someday so that it isn't strange to me. It's been a fight to get the right to speak Welsh in public and I totally agree with this and want to support its use.

Not all students understand the role of Outside In in the same way. Most have been supportive, but not all understand the equality of Outside In students. I think it's new for them, to have Outside In in the classroom on an equal footing, and it's a challenge to their power. If any student has a bias towards an Outside In member, or feels superior for whatever reason, the experience of learning together will humble the person so that they understand the other's point of view. When a situation like this occurs, with the lecturer's intervention, and gaining strength by thinking of myself as a role model to my young daughter, I've carried on and challenged this viewpoint. I completed the module to a very high standard, gaining a twenty credit certificate from WGU.

Graham's story about Andrew, is, in my view, a picture of a perfect social worker who chose not to judge a person by his lifestyle, but to help the person who got lost in the wrong direction in life. I hope a lot of the students, when qualified, whether working with children, teens, adults or families, will emulate Andrew.

I now have the courage to defend anyone trying to mislead people about what social work is, or speaking against social workers. The presentation activity stays with me, lingering in my thoughts, showing me a different picture of social workers and contradicting the stories I had heard. The purpose of social work is to make those who are not free in themselves for some reason to come out of their shells and become who they really are. In life, everyone has potential – but we need support and not to be downgraded by one another.

From my point of view – *Tim Wynn*

I wrote the poem *Freedom* during the first lockdown in 2020. As a result of a degenerative neurological condition I have become physically less able. Many aspects of my life that I used to enjoy, but also took for granted, I can no longer experience. Therefore, I often find myself reminiscing and longing to return to a time when I was spontaneous and independent.

I noticed during this period of lockdown, through the media outlets, what appeared to be able-bodied people bemoaning the restrictions preventing them from being allowed to live their lives in whatever manner they saw fit. It occurred to me that I and a vast number of disabled people are always living in a type of lockdown due to personal limitations. Through the poem I wanted to highlight this situation and, at the same time, show that even though people's liberties had been restricted, a positive mental attitude is an attribute that can help overcome any situation.

[Trigger warning – the following poem includes mention of suicidal thoughts.]

Freedom
I let my mind go free,
no lockdown or restrictions on my liberty.
A great deal of nothing has changed for me,
and why, you might ask, how can this be?

So, my body's been in its own kinda lockdown for years,
because of my wretched, f*cking disability.
So, to try and retain what's left of the real old me
there's one way to achieve this … I let my mind go free.

I'd love to still go walking through the woods or along the shore,
I'd love to go out dancing and moonwalk just once more,
but I know if I tried it today, I'd end up a heap upon the floor.
I often think of suicide: it's true I really do,
I'm afraid I'm not that brave, there's only one thing left to do.
Ha! Yes, I s'pose you've guessed it, the alternative for me?
It really is quite simple: I can let my mind go free.

It's 3.43am: awake when I shouldn't be.
That's okay 'cause there's no restrictions you see.
And off I go … there'll be wonders for me,
that's what happens, when I let my mind go free.

Bond, James Bond … phaff! He's got nothing on me.
I kill off the baddies with such style and panache,
then make love to a beautiful woman in some long dewy grass …
… and speaking of grass, here I go once more:
with a flash of my left boot the ball will soar
to the back of the net: the crowd will roar.
Yes!
I'm a winner for sure.

Now, how can this be? I'm alone in my bed
with the weight of the darkness crushing my head.

So, all you able-bodied people, don't moan and complain
'cause you can't go here or there, can't get on a plane,
and you can't do this, and you can't do that.
The restrictions will be lifted soon, you can be sure of that.

Until they do, make a big mug of tea, sit down, relax …
let YOUR mind go free.

The way I share my expertise through experience with students varies enormously. Sometimes it's conversation in class, sometimes it's giving presentations. As well as the more traditional methods, I've been part of several creative projects. One of these was making the animated film, *What Is Social Work?* I participated with a group of social work students to create a section of the film which highlights my experience of working with a social worker and a multidisciplinary team to prepare for discharge from Walton hospital. It's chapter 6 – 'A True Story' – of the film *What Is Social Work?* The link to this is in the Further resources section at the end of the chapter.

Dancing my way to identity – *Jenny Burgess*

For me dance is everything, the dancefloor is the canvas where I create my art, an art that's forever moving and changing. When I leave the floor there's no physical creation left: that floor is unmarked from my presence, but that creation is not lost, it remains in my heart and soul forever.

Since my early childhood, I've loved music and moving to the rhythm, but it wasn't until the early 1960s, while at senior school, that I had my introduction to a more structured form of dance when our headmaster would take us once a week for country dancing. The girls lined up on one side of the hall, the boys on the other, then the headmaster would instruct the boys to ask a girl to partner them. The majority of boys did this grudgingly. I loved it, and this session was a highlight of my school week (please remember I'm transgender, and back then I identified as male: my transition was not to happen for many a year).

After leaving school for the wide world of employment, my dancing was confined to weekly visits to our local dance hall where we would jive, disco and smooch the night away. It was 1980, and a work colleague, also a friend, had just started ballroom classes and was loving it. He asked me if my wife and I would like to give it a try. It took one class and we were hooked. We danced ballroom and Latin for years, until our daughter took seriously ill in 1992 and our dancing ground to a halt. Lucy sadly passed away in 1994, and for several years after neither of us functioned properly. This situation had been made even worse for my wife as a month before my daughter's diagnosis, I'd come out to her about my gender identity issue, and that I was trans. So my wife was having to deal with coming to terms with me being transgender and our daughter's illness and subsequent death.

As time went on, life slowly started to return to normal; the grief was still there. Even today, many years later, it's still there. We started to talk a lot about my gender issue and came to a compromise that would work for many years.

Now, feeling better in ourselves, we went back to dancing, but ballroom had lost its appeal. We started to explore other dance genres and got taken by salsa and club Latino, which is a much more relaxed form of dance, although you wouldn't think so considering the intricate moves you have to do. Salsa and associated dances are more about personal expression than your ability to hold a pose. A plus for salsa and the Latino dance is that the music is fantastic. Not satisfied with just salsa, we even tried our hand (or should I say feet) at modern jive and absolutely loved it. This continued for several years until, sadly, due to my need to be true to myself and the need to transition, we parted.

It was a very difficult time for both of us, and our dancing lives suffered. Eventually, I returned to salsa. As a male, I thought myself a competent dancer and lead, but being a female, being led and in high heels, dancing backward, is quite a culture shock; but with perseverance I got there, although I still tended to lead at times much to the guy's annoyance. It was at this time I also realised that life wasn't going to be easy as a lot of the guys were reluctant to ask a transgender female to dance, so my visits to the club got fewer and fewer.

Then by chance I got involved with a local line dance class, and I've not looked back since. No partner needed, just a dance floor, music and I'm in heaven. No matter how low I feel when I start, I know, by the time the music stops, all my worries will have vanished and I'll be eager for the next dance.

I've recently gone full circle and returned to my ballroom roots at the request of friends at Chester Pride, who are promoting well-being among the LGBT+ community, so I've partnered up with this wonderful guy who, like me, hasn't danced ballroom for many years. Our aim is to put on a passable demo: wish us luck.

It's not just about the making of hedgehogs – *Eluned Plack*

My social worker at this time was absolutely brilliant. She suggested I go to the KIM project (kim-inspire.org.uk) for a Tuesday afternoon group. This was the day they accepted new members and did craft sessions. The idea was frightening, but she arranged for a care worker to come with me for the first few sessions. My care worker reassured me that the venue was fully accessible and the toilets were suitable for me. I was suffering from depression brought on by a number of things that were occurring at that time in my life: losing my career and suddenly, without warning, becoming a person with a severe and painful disability.

The depression resulted in me becoming isolated from everyone and everything. I could not concentrate or keep hold of any information. I showed no emotion, held no conversations. This behaviour was my safety-net, a means of self-preservation. 'Detached personality disorder', 'depressed' and 'socially awkward' were the ways the medical model had described me.

I had an initial meeting with the KIM worker and was pleased to know she would be at every meeting. We had numerous test runs, involving me and my care worker. These were just to get me used to going out of the door, then to Wrexham. Then we attempted to go to one of the meetings. I remember the third attempt at going to this meeting. Why the third? Because this was the time I actually went in. I did not know what we would be doing, but no one in the group knew this. I think that was a good thing: it was the start of going into the unknown. I remember the lack of fuss that was made. It was just, 'Hi everyone, this is a new member. Make room!' I was introduced to those who sat next to me. I wouldn't have remembered names and it again meant lack of fuss and attention on me. I didn't make eye-contact with anyone, and I was sweating really badly.

In one session, I was given a pre-loved paperback and we were shown how to fold the pages. It was the perfect task: no need to talk, no need to concentrate. The group chatted among themselves. I made a hedgehog out of the book as instructed, and went home. I had something to smile about when the hedgehog

Figure 10.3 *Hedgehogs*, Eluned Plack

took its place on the mantelpiece: I was actually proud of it. That feeling was new for me. But that's not the end of the hedgehog story. I showed my grandchild how to make hedgehogs. That was the start of interacting with the family, having fun and planning. I used to make sure I had books and decorations in stock: this gave me a purpose for leaving the house.

I carried on attending KIM. Each time was easier. I began to smile at everyone and show my unique humour. I realised I was a member of something and felt a sense of belonging and built up friendships and trust. As I gained confidence, I became the one sitting next to newcomers and helping them. I had a feeling that I had something to give. I've sold some folded books, and recently raised £218 for Women's Aid. I learned from the group what was going on in Wrexham and went to a few events, so I brushed my hair and put on clean blouses. Among other activities, I heard about Outside In and joined the group.

As part of my involvement with Outside In, I've led painting sessions with students, and then in 2021 I taught them how to make hedgehogs as part of *The Creative Practitioner* module (see Figure 10.3). I could see they were doubtful at first, but then they were proud of the end results. I hope that they, in turn, will be able to use this skill in their future practice whether it's for their own self-care, or in working with others who need, like I did, to engage in a way which is low-key, fun and rewarding.

Experts through experience – *Anna-Louise Edwards*

One way to identify good coproduction is when there is an inability to identify who holds the power. Looking at Outside In, there are three groups within our community: members of Outside In, students and tutors. In many circumstances, these are three very different groups that have their own individual roles to play and do not shift into each other. However, at WGU, lines between the groups are much more blurred. Members of Outside In are not only service users. We are also students when we sit and learn alongside fellow students, and also teachers when we share the knowledge we have acquired as individuals or a collective. Students become teachers, able to share information with us that may help in our lives, with being involved with health and social care services and what we can do. Sometimes they just teach us how to do academic writing: for some, this is a skill we've never acquired. And tutors become students when they learn something new from students or Outside In. There is an amazing amount of shared learning between the groups. This allows our learning community at WGU to grow strong.

The lines are blurred with some people more than others, as we do have members of Outside In who are students at WGU on programmes other than the BA (Hons) Social Work, and also tutors who have experienced social care and social work practices, both from professional and personal viewpoints.

When I first started Outside In with Year 2 students, I personally had a very good knowledge of social care services and their practices, and when joining in the classes I came up with some very interesting answers and had the confidence to raise my hand and to say what I thought. I still have youth on my side and no visible indications to say that I might be part of Outside In – I don't use a wheelchair, for example. For several months, students within the class had no idea that I was an Outside In representative, and many of them believed me to be a social work student.

I questioned very much why the students thought this, and after conversations with the tutor there were many theories we came up with as to why this was. One of them was that my knowledge and ability to present knowledge about social work practice threw them off: surely, I must be a professional? Others assumed I was a social work student because I was not the average demographic within Outside In. Instead, I was stereotyped to be a student. It was very interesting once students found out that I was not a social work student: they were in shock and awe and felt bad that they had made assumptions about my role.

A final thought: assumptions make an arse of you and me!

A question of identity – *Rhiana Povey*

As Anna-Louise has written, students and tutors can also have experiences of services. This poem was written when I was a third year student on the BA (Hons) Social Work, and it asks those questions about assumed identities.

So ... Who's Mum?
I did not carry you,
I didn't give birth ...
but you still were my child
who I gave the earth.

We did not have the same eye colour,
neither did we share the same blood,
but I loved you more
than a mother possibly could.

We'd laugh and joke,
we had so much in common,
there will never be a day
that you are forgotten.

The countless times,
we were asked 'Who is mum?'
made me uneasy and hurt
by a careless tongue.

I'd be disappointed and wounded, with the professionals,
explaining ourselves like confessionals.
Is it so hard to accept in this day and age
that a child can have two mums without it being strange?

So please think before you ask that question,
take a moment to ponder – may I make a suggestion?
Open your mind and don't take offence,
words can wound, make a situation tense.

Embrace life changes, love is love after all.
Let's build bridges, not create a wall.
I am mum, and so is my wife,
our daughter is our daughter, to whom we both give life.

Full circle

Having heard the accounts from individuals, the last word in the chapter goes to Sandra Williams, founder of what came to be known as Outside In:

To end where we began – for me, it's about the fact that nothing is complete until all the partners are equal. For Outside In, it has taken a while, but I now feel equal when I participate in the education of social workers at WGU. We make a difference, and we are valued for our contributions, whatever shape or form they take: interviewing, lecturing, assessment of presentations, validation consultations, programme management, creative work which results from the modules we study together. It's true too that other people's values can have an effect on both mental and physical states, and the *equal value* we feel increases our feelings of well-being. For me, this feeling of well-being is what tells me coproduction is happening, that the circle is being completed.

Acknowledgements

Thanks to Jeff Dale, Rob Poustie and Dawn Jones for reviewing this chapter.

Further resources

Animated films:
1. *Anorexia, A History: Abridged Version* (2013) directed by Ian Lee from a poem by Imogen Belcher. https://www.youtube.com/watch?v=7oGAIxzeiYo&t=3s
2. *Andrew* directed by Darren Mason, from a poem by Graham Attenborough. https://www.youtube.com/watch?v=gs1-eOuJgew https://www.youtube.com/watch?v=2verB2KdoyU&t=1s (Cymraeg)
3. *What Is Social Work?* (2021) directed by Darren Mason, coproduced by Outside In and Year 1 social work students. https://www.youtube.com/watch?v=OJ_ _4paqzRE

Further reading

Morris, G., Prankard, S. and Lefroy, L. (2013) 'Animating experience: bringing student learning to life through animation and service user and carer experience', *Journal of Practice Teaching & Learning*, 12(1): 22–33.

Pescod, J. (2020) 'We are not cases that can be closed: Why I help educate the social workers of the future', Community Care Inform. https://communityc are.co.uk/2020/08/05/participation-expert-by-experience-social-work/

Simpson, C. (2021) *Transplants and Fears*, Wrexham: WGU. Available from Kidney Wales.

11

Unpaid carers

Daniel Burrows and Jen Lyttleton-Smith

Chapter objectives

- To articulate the challenges unpaid carers face in contemporary Wales.

- To explore the implications of Welsh legislation and policy for unpaid carers.

- To suggest a way forward for social workers in Wales to develop practice in support of unpaid carers.

Introduction

Under the Social Services and Well-being (Wales) Act 2014 (SSWWA), an unpaid carer is understood as an adult or child who provides care or support to another person who would not be able to cope without that support, due to a variety of issues including physical or mental illness, physical or learning disability, or addiction. In many wealthy countries throughout the world, the needs of unpaid carers are receiving new attention from both welfare policy makers and practitioners due to the rise in numbers of people in need of care and the challenges that arise from providing unpaid care (Bourgault and Robinson, 2020). Throughout the UK, unpaid carers make an enormous, and often unacknowledged, contribution to the health and social care systems. Indeed, Carers UK (2021) argue that if the support provided by financial carers to those in need were assessed in purely monetary terms, its value would exceed that of the budget of the entire NHS.

The unique demographic, social and cultural context of Wales gives rise to distinct challenges for unpaid carers, yet alongside these challenges is the opportunity to develop innovative ways of supporting carers. Welsh policy and legislation offer fertile ground for the development of new models of social work practice, which can help to make caring for another person a sustainable and fulfilling part of life.

Unpaid caring in context

In Wales, even before the advent of the COVID-19 pandemic, mounting pressure on unpaid carers had been driven by a simultaneous rise in the number of people needing care and support in their daily lives and a tightening of funding available for the provision of social care. Increases in demand for care are being driven by changes in the age profile of the Welsh population, with the overall proportion aged over 65 rising due to increased life expectancy, reduced immigration and lower birth rates (Welsh Government, 2020). As people age, they become more likely to depend on support and assistance from others in their daily lives due to the development of complex chronic health conditions (Age UK, 2017), with dementia, in particular, a growing concern (Prince et al, 2014). The overall trend is that increasing numbers of people need care from a decreasing pool of people who are in the position to be able to provide care unpaid. Meanwhile, austerity policies pursued by the UK Government since 2010 have led to significant reductions in the amount of spending on services by Welsh local authorities (Gray and Barford, 2018), with the result that unpaid carers are required to fill the gap.

Providing care and being cared for are fundamental, universal human experiences (Engster, 2019), yet both our needs for care and our needs as carers often appear to be incompatible with the sociopolitical and cultural currents of contemporary life in Wales. The dominance of neoliberal ideology in UK Government welfare reform since 1979 has produced a marketisation of social care (Penna and O'Brien, 2013) and, concurrently, a reformulation of universal provision as individuals and families are increasingly expected to shoulder the financial and practical burden of their own care. This remains the prevalent model in Wales, despite the ascendancy of the Labour Party, with its more statist inclinations, within Welsh Government policy since devolution.

Ironically, the same economic model which demands that state care service provision is kept to a minimum also makes it more difficult for family members to provide care. Within advanced capitalist economies, people of working age are expected to be highly flexible in meeting the needs of their employers – relocating where necessary and working additional hours when required (Harvey, 2005). This means that it can be difficult for employed people with caring responsibilities to juggle the demands of their job with their caring role. This has the effect of forcing a choice between providing one's family members with care, and improved career prospects for oneself. Opportunities to be physically present to provide care for loved ones are curtailed for many not only by the demands of the economy, but also the lifestyle expectations that arise from capitalist and neoliberal ideology. Bauman (2000) has argued that the contemporary period in Western countries is dominated by a rampant individualism that places emphasis on personal agency and living life purely according to personal wishes and inclinations – for which he coined the term, 'liquid modernity'. Becoming a person's carer may therefore come as a profound psychological and social shock, since it reduces the flexibility and freedom required to thrive in a fast-paced, ever changing social and economic landscape. This shock is compounded for many carers in Wales by the fragmented and incomplete nature of social care services.

The neoliberal economic model and the highly individualised lifestyles of liquid modernity result in a society in which unpaid carers will be increasingly needed, since the management of threats to our well-being and, indeed, of misfortunes, is left to the 'care, ingenuity and cunning of individuals' (Bauman, 2007: 68). This is epitomised by the discourse of 'self-care', where responsibility for well-being in the face of external stress and anxiety is increasingly placed upon the individual, with no regard for the impact of socioeconomic inequalities. Our reliance on unpaid carers therefore creates a political challenge, since it is apparent that unpaid carers experience considerable inequalities both prior to and due to their caring role.

International evidence suggests that both the mental and physical health of unpaid carers are poorer than the general population and that they score lower in measures related to quality of life (Robison et al, 2009; Moriarty et al, 2015; Verbakel et al, 2017; Vasileiou et al, 2017). In Wales, a survey carried out by Carers Wales (2019) found that unpaid carers report considerably lower levels of satisfaction with life and levels of anxiety twice as high as the general population. Further, in a qualitative study exploring unpaid carers' experiences before and during the COVID-19 pandemic in Wales, Burrows et al (2021) found that, even before the pandemic, loneliness and social isolation were common experiences for unpaid carers, who also experience considerable stress as a result of their caring responsibilities. This study also highlighted how many unpaid carers face conditions that breach their human rights, sometimes because caring can pose physical danger, whether due to manual handling with inadequate support, or to the violent behaviour of the person cared-for, and sometimes in terms of the hours a week they devote to caring, which would breach employment laws were they providing care as paid work. One participant in the study is quoted as saying, 'Carers knew what lockdown was before lockdown was a thing' (Burrows et al, 2021: 34). Having caring responsibilities can often increase stress in a person's life, and simultaneously may reduce avenues through which stress can be managed, such as spending time in leisure activities and with supportive friends. Other disadvantages and challenges experienced across the life course are therefore likely to be amplified by becoming an unpaid carer.

In addition to adverse impacts on their physical and mental health, many unpaid carers experience economic disadvantages as a result of their caring responsibilities: 38 per cent of unpaid carers report giving up work altogether in order to be able to meet their caring responsibilities (Carers UK, 2019). Those who remain in work may reduce the hours they work, may avoid seeking promotion or more senior jobs and may find that their performance in work is negatively affected. Economic disadvantages arising from caring affect women disproportionately, because women tend to become carers at earlier ages than men. Overall, according to the 2011 UK Census, 57.7 per cent of carers were female, compared to 42.3 per cent male, suggesting that stereotypes around women as the more caring gender continue to be influential in the realities of family life. One in four women aged 50–64 are carers, compared to one in six men (Carers UK, 2019). This means that women are more likely to experience economic disadvantage because of the impact of caring on their working life – a conclusion that is supported by the fact that 73 per cent of claimants for Carers Allowance are female (Fry et al, 2011).

Carers from minoritised ethnic groups in Wales are likely to experience further disadvantages. There is some evidence to suggest that such carers are more likely both to be struggling financially and to do more hours of caring per week (NHS Information Centre, 2010). Further, carers from minoritised ethnic groups access services less frequently, despite these additional challenges (Greenwood, 2018). Cultural misunderstandings, stereotyping and language barriers may all contribute to barriers to accessing services (Greenwood et al, 2015). Where people from minoritised ethnic groups do access services, they appear to express lower satisfaction than white carers (Health and Social Care Information Centre, 2013). Ensuring equitable access to support must therefore be a key area for the development of policy and practice with unpaid carers in Wales.

Welsh policy and unpaid carers

The Welsh Government's *Strategy for Older People in Wales 2013–2023*, and the 2018 *Healthier Wales* strategy are both predicated upon the availability of unpaid carers to provide care and support to enable individuals with care needs to live independently. This reliance on unpaid carers is acknowledged through the Welsh Government's *Strategy for Unpaid Carers* (Welsh Government, 2021a), which sets out four key priorities, discussed next. As Burrows et al (2021) discovered, there is much work to be done in each of these key areas. From their findings, some issues for each priority area are as follows:

1. Identifying and valuing unpaid carers

Unpaid carers often find it difficult to identify with the term 'carer' – many people see their caring role as simply part of the relationship they have with the person cared-for, for example, the obligation of an adult child towards their parent (Øydgard, 2017). This issue may be particularly acute for people from minoritised ethnic communities, whose first language is not English, since some languages, including Bengali, Gujarati, Punjabi and Urdu, do not even have a direct translation for the term 'carer' (Williams and Johnson, 2010). It is important that people with caring responsibilities are recognised at the earliest possible time, which means that services and professionals who may have first contact with unpaid carers need to be cautious about even using the term 'carer'. Inclusive language that describes the roles carers fulfil without relying upon the term 'carer' is likely to help people with caring responsibilities to recognise that they have rights to services.

2. Providing information, advice and support

The services available to carers vary depending on the local authority area in which the carer lives. While the Welsh Government has consistently worked towards a citizenship rights approach since the beginning of devolution (Guarneros-Meza et al, 2014), the fragmentation of social care services initiated in the 1990s has not been reversed. While the SSWWA gives all carers the right to an assessment, even prior to the pandemic, only around 15 per cent of unpaid carers said that they had received one (Carers Wales, 2020). Where such assessments are completed, the impact of the UK Government's austerity policies (Glasby et al, 2021) and staff shortages in social care services (Welsh Government, 2021b) mean that the resources available to carers are highly limited.

3. Supporting unpaid carers' lives alongside caring

A key aspect of ensuring that caring is sustainable for unpaid carers is that they should have access to short breaks from their responsibilities, to pursue their own leisure activities and to draw upon social supports from their own networks of friends and family members. Burrows et al (2021) found that many unpaid carers were feeling isolated and lonely even before the pandemic, meaning that the provisions carers needed were already falling short. Since the pandemic began, local authorities' budgets have become even more stretched and domiciliary care providers have struggled to recruit and retain staff (Delahunty, 2021), meaning that local authorities are obliged to direct their limited services to those with the most acute need. The likely result of a chronic inability to provide effective support for unpaid carers is that situations in which unpaid carers may have been able to cope with minimal support are more likely to become crisis situations requiring higher levels of support and resources.

4. Supporting unpaid carers in work and education

An unexpected benefit of the pandemic for some unpaid carers was that a new level of flexibility was established in many jobs, with the increase in working from home. Burrows et al (2021) found that some carers appreciated the ability to stay at home near to the person cared-for and found that the reduced time spent on commuting made it easier to balance care with work. For others, however, especially younger carers in education, working at home was difficult due to the added distraction from work brought about by being physically available to provide care at all times. While home working can ease the pressure on carers caused by needing to be in two places at once, it is possible that losing out on having a workplace away from caring responsibilities might lead to loss of some of the social supports that unpaid carers derive from work and a space in which the carer can focus on another aspect of their identity. Another consideration as policies around the workplace develop must be that access to flexible working will not be available to all, since jobs involving manual labour tend to require physical presence in the workplace, producing further socioeconomic inequalities around caring.

Future developments in Welsh policy for unpaid carers are likely to include a charter setting out the rights of unpaid carers and the levels of service they should receive (Welsh Government, 2021a). The Welsh Government's ambition is to develop a society that 'recognises, values and supports unpaid carers of all ages and backgrounds to live well and achieve their own well-being outcomes' (Welsh Government, 2021a). Central to this is the role of local authorities in assessing and providing support for carers, a duty that is fully acknowledged in the SSWWA. We therefore now turn to explore social work with unpaid carers under this Act, to explore the possibilities implicit within it for a distinctive 'Welsh way' of practice aimed at ensuring that caring is a sustainable part of individuals' lives.

The Welsh way

The legislation and policy context of Wales lends itself to an approach in which the voices of carers must be heard and have genuine influence on the design and delivery of personalised care and support. However, early evidence suggests that the practice mechanisms supported by this policy (such as 'what matters' conversations and person–centred carer assessments) are falling short of their potential to improve prospects for this vulnerable population due to a lack of resources and low prioritisation of carers by local authorities – challenges which have been exacerbated by the COVID-19 pandemic. Social work in Wales should increasingly step forward and embrace the opportunity to engage in meaningful practice with unpaid carers that focuses on understanding and optimising their social systems. The Welsh policy context offers social workers the exciting prospect of developing practice rooted in relational work and human rights advocacy to advance the well-being of unpaid carers.

The Social Services and Well-being (Wales) Act 2014

Section 24 of the SSWWA obliges local authorities to offer an assessment to any unpaid carer who may have needs for care and support, regardless of whether the person cared-for wishes to have an assessment or to receive services. The assessment must be focused on the outcomes the carer wants to achieve – in other words, what they want their life to be like, not just what help they need with caring – and the resources they already have available. Social workers need to engage with carers not only to draw on their expertise to establish how the person cared-for can be supported, but also to think about how they will live with their ongoing caring role. Clearly, if services are provided for the person cared-for, these often bring benefit to their carer as well. For example, if the local authority arranges for paid domiciliary carers to call each morning to help an individual with their morning routine, this relieves the unpaid carer of some of their duties. The implication of the duty to assess carers under the Act, however, is that a more holistic approach needs to be taken, that goes beyond care planning for the individual, to ensure that the unpaid carer's role is as sustainable as possible.

At the heart of all assessments under the Act is the 'what matters' conversation, which represents an opportunity for the individual concerned to have their voice and views heard, and to contribute to the design of the services they are to receive. At present, the reality is not always matching the rhetoric. For example, Burrows et al (2021) found that some carers perceived that assessments of their needs, including the 'what matters' conversation, only went as far as examining the extent to which they were fit and capable to provide care, rather than exploring what they needed to live well in their caring role. With the strain facing many local authorities following years of austerity measures and the ongoing impact of the pandemic, it is not surprising that practice around assessing and supporting unpaid carers has been underdeveloped, since social workers so regularly find themselves with only the time and resources to address the most acute crises. Failure to address this concern in the short-to-medium term is not an option, however, because the importance of unpaid carers is bound to increase due to the demographic shifts described earlier. Under the Act, making caring sustainable for unpaid carers must be a key priority for social workers in Wales in the coming years.

Messages for practice

- Unpaid carers need and deserve social workers who follow a holistic approach to understanding how they want to live their lives and who will take meaningful action to help make their caring roles sustainable.
- 'What matters' conversations provide an excellent framework for developing social work practice with unpaid carers that can make a tangible difference in their lives. They enable practitioners to explore with the carer how they want to live, what is preventing those aspirations and what support might help to make those aspirations a reality (Social Care Wales, 2019). This needs to be part of a process that goes beyond the old model of the social worker as a broker of services, however.

An approach drawing upon Bronfenbrenner's (1979) ecological systems theory offers the opportunity for the carer's encounter with the social worker to be a transformative event in which their social systems can be optimised to support them in integrating their caring responsibilities. At each level of the ecological system, social workers have a role to play.

- Microsystem of carer/person cared-for: Caring is not simply a transaction of services from one person to another but, for most unpaid carers, an act of love and duty towards the person cared-for. It is vital, therefore, that this relationship is supported, including by ensuring as far as possible that the carer and the person cared-for have the opportunity to spend meaningful leisure time together doing things for enjoyment. Social workers can help by exploring the dynamics of this relationship and considering how opportunities for leisure together can be developed.

- Carer's mesosystem: The carer's mesosystem is the network of all the microsystems in which they are engaged (for example, work, wider family, social groups, religious groups, and so on). A properly coproduced carer's assessment can help the carer to identify sources of stress and support, and to manage these to help them achieve the life they want to live. Social workers will also need to continue to secure resources to provide unpaid carers with short breaks and practical support for their caring responsibilities, so that carers can have time to access parts of their mesosystem from which they derive support and relief.
- Carer's exosystem: Social workers have a role to play in advocating directly for individual carers, for example with employers or benefits agencies, to ensure that their needs are understood and their rights are upheld.
- Carer's macrosystem and chronosystem: Social work gains unique insights into the ways people live their lives and the challenges they face. In a small country such as Wales, social work needs to use its voice to continue to influence national policy to articulate the needs of both carers and people receiving services and, wherever possible, to 'pass the microphone' so that those voices are heard directly.

Conclusion

In the years to come, unpaid carers, whose contribution to the health and social care system in Wales is already considerable, will become ever more important. Caring is a normal part of human life and the rights of those who look after others need recognition and protection, especially amid the excitement and chaos of liquid modernity. Under the pressures imposed by the UK-wide neoliberal model of social care, unpaid carers in Wales suffer economic, social and well-being detriments similar to their peers across the four nations. The Welsh Government is seeking to address the ongoing crisis in carer well-being through the development of a new strategy for unpaid carers in Wales informed by contemporary research. Welsh policy, through the SSWWA, has focused practice on incorporating carer views into care planning to produce positive outcomes for both the person cared-for and their unpaid carer. Social workers have a vital part to play in delivering these outcomes.

Further resources
1. Tronto, J. (2005) 'Care as the work of citizens: a modest proposal', in M. Friedman (ed) *Women and Citizenship*, Oxford: Oxford University Press, pp 130–145.
2. Carers UK (2021) *State of Caring 2021 Report*. https://www.carersuk.org/for-professionals/policy/policy-library/state-of-caring-2021-report

3. Burrows, D., Lyttleton-Smith, J., Sheehan, L. and Jones, D. (2021) *Voices of Carers during the COVID-19 Pandemic: Messages for the Future of Unpaid Caring in Wales*. Cardiff University. https://phw.nhs.wales/publications/publicatio ns1/voices-of-carers-during-the-covid-19-pandemic-messages-for-the-fut ure-of-unpaid-caring-in-wales/

References

Age UK (2017) *Briefing: Health and Care of Older People in England 2017*. http:// www.ageuk.org.uk/Documents/EN-GB/For-professionals/Research/The_ Health_and_Care_of_Older_People_in_England_2016.pdf?dtrk=true

Bauman, Z. (2000) *Liquid Modernity*, Cambridge: Polity.

Bauman, Z. (2007) *Liquid Times: Living in an Age of Uncertainty*, Cambridge: Polity.

Bourgault, S. and Robinson, F. (2020) 'Care ethics thinks the political', *International Journal of Care and Caring*, 4(1): 3–9.

Bronfenbrenner, U. (1979) *The Ecology of Human Development: Experiments by Nature and Design*, London: Harvard University Press.

Burrows, D., Lyttleton-Smith, J., Sheehan, L. and Jones, D. (2021) *Voices of Carers during the COVID-19 Pandemic: Messages for the Future of Unpaid Caring in Wales*. Cardiff University. https://phw.nhs.wales/publications/publications1/voi ces-of-carers-during-the-covid-19-pandemic-messages-for-the-future-of-unp aid-caring-in-wales/

Carers UK (2019) *State of Caring Report 2019*. https://www.carersuk.org/ima ges/News__campaigns/CUK_State_of_Caring_2019_Report.pdf

Carers UK (2021) *State of Caring 2021 Report*. https://www.carersuk.org/for-professionals/policy/policy-library/state-of-caring-2021-report

Carers Wales (2019) *Press Release: Wales' Unpaid Carers Suffering Anxiety and Stress*. https://www.carersuk.org/news/press-release-wales-unpaid-carers-suffer ing-anxiety-and-stress/

Carers Wales (2020) *Track the Act: Briefing 5*. https://www.carersuk.org/files/sect ion/6609/carers-wales-track-the-act-briefing-final-version-eng.pdf

Delahunty, S. (2021) 'Care sector facing "most acute recruitment and retention crisis" in its history, not-for-profit organisations warn', *Third Sector*, 23 September 2021. https:// www.thirdsector.co.uk/care-sector-facing-most-acute-recruitment-retention-crisis-its-history-not-for-profit-organisations-warn/management/article/1728476

Engster, D. (2019) 'Care ethics, dependency, and vulnerability', *Ethics and Social Welfare*, 13(2): 100–114.

Fry, G., Singleton, B., Yeandle, S. and Buckner, L. (2011) *Developing a Clearer Understanding of the Carer's Allowance Claimant Group*. Department for Work and Pensions-Research Report (739).

Glasby, J., Zhang, Y., Bennett, M. and Hall, P. (2021) 'A lost decade? A renewed case for adult social care reform in England', *Journal of Social Policy*, 50(2): 406–437.

Gray, M. and Barford, A. (2018) 'The depths of the cuts: the uneven geography of local government austerity', *Cambridge Journal of Regions, Economy and Society*, 11(3): 541–563.

Greenwood, N. (2018) *Supporting Black and Minority Ethnic Carers*. https://www.raceequalityfoundation.org.uk/wp-content/uploads/2018/10/REF-Better-Health-484.pdf

Greenwood, N., Habibi, R., Smith, R. and Manthorpe, J. (2015) 'Barriers to access and minority ethnic carers' satisfaction with social care services in the community: a systematic review of qualitative and quantitative literature', *Health & Social Care in the Community*, 23(11): 64–78.

Guarneros-Meza, V., Downe, J., Entwistle, T. and Martin, S.J. (2014) 'Putting the citizen at the centre? Assembling local government policy in Wales', *Local Government Studies*, 40(1): 65–82.

Haberkern, K., Schmid, T. and Szydlik, M. (2015) 'Gender differences in intergenerational care in European welfare states', *Ageing & Society*, 35(2): 298–320.

Harvey, D. (2005) *A Brief History of Neoliberalism*, Oxford: Oxford University Press.

Health and Social Care Information Centre (2013) *Personal Social Services Survey of Adult Carers in England: Provisional Report England 2012–13*. https://files.digital.nhs.uk/publicationimport/pub10xxx/pub10963/per-soc-ser-sur-adu-car-eng-2012–13-prv-rep.pdf

Moriarty, J., Maguire, A., O'Reilly, D. and McCann, M. (2015) 'Bereavement after informal caregiving: assessing mental health burden using linked population data', *American Journal of Public Health*, 105(8): 1630–1637.

NHS Information Centre (2010) *Survey of Carers in Households – England, 2009–10*. https://digital.nhs.uk/data-and-information/publications/statistical/personal-social-services-survey-of-adult-carers/survey-of-carers-in-households-england-2009–10

Øydgard, G.W. (2017) 'The influence of institutional discourses on the work of informal carers: an institutional ethnography from the perspective of informal carers', *BMC Health Services Research*, 17(1): 1–12.

Penna, S. and O'Brien, M. (2013) 'Neoliberalism', in M. Gray, and S.A. Webb (eds) *Social Work Theories and Methods* (2nd edn), London: Sage, pp 137–146.

Prince, M., Knapp, M., Guerchet, M., McCrone, P., Prina, M., Comas-Herrera, A., et al (2014) 'Dementia UK: update' [PhD dissertation], King's College London.

Robison, J., Fortinsky, R., Kleppinger, A., Shugrue, N. and Porter, M. (2009) 'A broader view of family caregiving: effects of caregiving and caregiver conditions on depressive symptoms, health, work, and social isolation', *Journals of Gerontology Series B: Psychological Sciences and Social Sciences*, 64(6): 788–798.

Social Care Wales (2019) *What Matters Conversations and Assessment*. https://socialcare.wales/service-improvement/what-matters-conversations-and-assessment

Vasileiou, K., Barnett, J., Barreto, M., Vines, J., Atkinson, M., Lawson, S. and Wilson, M. (2017) 'Experiences of loneliness associated with being an informal caregiver: a qualitative investigation', *Frontiers in Psychology*, 8: 585.

Verbakel, E., Tamlagsrønning, S., Winstone, L., Fjær, E.L. and Eikemo, T.A. (2017) 'Informal care in Europe: findings from the European Social Survey (2014) special module on the social determinants of health', *The European Journal of Public Health*, 27(suppl. 1): 90–95.

Welsh Government (2013) *The Strategy for Older People in Wales 2013–2023*. https://www.gov.wales/sites/default/files/publications/2019-06/the-strategy-for-older-people-in-wales-2013-2023.pdf

Welsh Government (2018) *A Healthier Wales: Our Plan for Health and Social Care*. https://www.gov.wales/sites/default/files/publications/2021-09/a-healthier-wales-our-plan-for-health-and-social-care.pdf

Welsh Government (2020) *Summary Statistics for Wales, by Region: 2020*. https://gov.wales/summary-statistics-regions-wales-2020

Welsh Government (2021a) *Strategy for Unpaid Carers*. https://gov.wales/strategy-unpaid-carers-html

Welsh Government (2021b) *Consultation – Summary of Response: Rebalancing Care and Support*. https://gov.wales/sites/default/files/consultations/2021–06/summary-of-responses_2.pdf

Williams, C. and Johnson, M.R.D. (2010) *Race and Ethnicity in a Welfare Society*, Maidenhead: Open University Press.

12

Peer-led alcohol and drug services

Tim Versey, Sarah Vaile, James Deakin and Wulf Livingston

Chapter objectives

- To provide an understanding of recovery and peer-led provision within a Welsh context.

- To explore two exemplars: North Wales Recovery Community and Recovery Cymru.

- To analyse some of the core considerations of inclusion, identity, (non) commissioning, community and power.

- To understand the role that Welsh social workers can play in facilitating, promoting and supporting peer-led provision and recovery.

Introduction

Between us, we, the authors of this chapter, have more than 120 years of direct experience with alcohol and other drugs. For each of us this has included substantive personal formative experiences, before then journeying into providing support and services with others. This chapter encapsulates some of the key learning from these collective journeys. It focuses on Wales and recovery. Wales is where each of us currently practises within alcohol and drug provision and research. In particular we explore two examples of recovery organisations, one in the north and the other in the south, which illustrate the unique potential of peer-led organisations to go beyond mainstream provision in the way they offer support with sustained and meaningful lifestyle change. This focus on recovery reflects our shared exposure to hearing from others that the 'staying off' alcohol and drugs is often much harder than the 'getting off'. The account is framed by some brief discussion of the policy context and the messages that can be drawn to inform social work practice. Given the starting points and personal investment, what we offer are specific and illustrative recovery focused messages rather than any comprehensive guide to all potential social work considerations for working in the alcohol and drug arena (for this see Galvani, 2012; British Association of Social Workers, 2022).

The context for recovery

Those who end up in sustained patterns of alcohol or other drug use are frequently stigmatised and discriminated against (Rwatschew et al, 2019). They are further encouraged to engage in treatment that can be insisted on by the criminal justice system, health and social services, and even their own families (Stothard, 2021). While acute treatment interventions help stabilise individuals' use of substances, they pay less attention to well-being and long-term life goals (Mayock and Butler, 2020). Most models of recovery within statutory substance use services focus on decreasing anti-social behaviour associated with alcohol and illicit drug use (Her Majesty's Government, 2021). Supporting the use of prescribed medication is often the treatment most used by practitioners and clinicians, with the end goal being total abstinence (Klingemann, 2020). Addiction and recovery treatment is frequently medicalised and defined as an illness in which medication can be the cure all (Klingemann, 2020).

Recovery is, however, much more than this for many people. It sits within a multiplicity of definitions, discourses and debates (Livingston, 2022). A plausible argument is that recovery from substance use has a much broader, socially constructed definition, one taken from the personalised narratives of those actively using substances, and those in recovery (Kougiali et al, 2017). The simple answer to the question of how best to define recovery may be that recovery is whatever it is required to be. It encompasses the personal, social and health outcomes of those seeking a way out of their substance use experiences, rather than perhaps just focusing on the outcomes for policy makers and service monitoring.

Recovery discourse has its roots in Victorian England's temperance movement, whereby organised mutual support for those seeking abstinence from alcohol became the foundations of Alcoholics Anonymous (White, 2008). Peer-led group provision has since evolved to become an integral approach to recovery from alcohol and other drug use, where social identity and community validation as part of recovery group membership are valued (Galvani et al, 2022). Substance use recovery organisations have more recently been informed by the advocacy and discourse movements within mental health, and the direct challenges to a medicalised model of provision and the discrimination and stigma associated with mental ill health (Beresford, 2020).

The recovery movement and policy shifts

The latter part of the 20th century saw the emergence of some distinct 'addiction' recovery movements across the globe. These advocacy efforts created a paradigmatic shift in the United States and the United Kingdom (UK) towards addressing substance use, beyond harm reduction, and with the emphasis on recovery as the leading framework (Best and Hamer, 2021). In the UK, between 2005 and 2010 the recovery movement gained political momentum, resulting in it being the focus of both the UK and Scottish governments' strategies (Scottish Government, 2008;

Her Majesty's Government, 2010). Many have argued that since then recovery has been hijacked to serve political agendas and utilise a cheap workforce within core treatment provision (Kalk et al, 2017). Some of these broader trends are visible within recent Welsh policy developments and are examined next.

The Welsh context

While the move to support recovery and peer-oriented provision is neither unique to alcohol and other drugs nor to Wales, it is possible to argue that it is particularly well situated within current Welsh policy contexts.

Over the last decade, the Welsh way has been ambitious within its move towards endorsing coproduction and inclusive participation as essential factors in improving the health, well-being and sustainability of its population (see Chapter 7). Recent Welsh policy and legislation has placed an increasing emphasis on long-term sustainability, including supporting the United Nations Sustainable Goals agenda for transforming the world for people, planet and prosperity (Welsh Assembly Government, 2011; Welsh Government, 2019). Peer-led community provision sits comfortably within this context.

Furthermore, the Social Services and Well-being (Wales) Act 2014 (SSWWA), sets out a legal framework for improving the well-being of those who require care and support, carers who need support, and for transforming social services, and includes the fundamental principles of voice and control, and coproduction (see Chapters 1 and 2). Building recovery within communities became a key theme in tackling drugs and addressing alcohol dependence when the UK Government published its roadmap for building a new treatment system guided by the principles of well-being, citizenship and freedom from dependence (Her Majesty's Government, 2012). Today, this focus on community recovery finds itself at the forefront of the devolved government of Wales' strategic delivery plan for improving the lives of those affected by substance use (Welsh Government, 2021).

The Welsh way

The Welsh framework provided by the SSWWA and The Future Generations (Wales) Act 2016, mainstreams regard for inclusive participation (coproduction) and long-term sustainable lifestyles. A commitment to peer involvement, peer-led provision and recovery is integral to these considerations. Wales is a nation of communities, with a long history of collective giving and self help in response to adversities, and by consequence it has many projects rooted in the traditions of peer-to-peer support (Redcliffe, 2021). More specifically Welsh Government substance use policy requires active regard for individual involvement and participative approach including the explicit development of peer-led services. Wales has some interesting examples of how inclusive recovery projects can evolve.

For us, this sense of Welsh-oriented recovery approaches is best encapsulated through the following two exemplars.

North Wales Recovery Community

North Wales Recovery Community (NWRC) is a registered charity, established in 2015, that provides abstinence-based housing, access to mutual aid and community projects for individuals seeking recovery from long-term alcohol and other drug use. It was founded by James Deakin (the author of this section), who identifies as being in long-term recovery from poly drug use and is building a 'straight life' in Bangor. James believed that there had to be others with similar backgrounds who wanted to change, and that sharing his story could inspire them. While this now sounds incredible and egotistical, it nevertheless encapsulates what recovery is about: using the power of one's strength, hopes and experiences to help somebody else, and turning horrendous personal stories into symbols of hope for those most in need of hearing them.

The idea behind NWRC thus became to build upon the initial work done by the active but dispersed Anglesey and Gwynedd Recovery Organisation and to concentrate all the available recovery assets under one roof. This would create a self-sufficient 'hub' where individuals who were actively seeking recovery could access a wide variety of mutual aid groups and diversionary activities. We had learned that quite often the options for recovery were fairly narrow, especially those of residential settings, and were often confined to singular 12-step or cognitive behavioural models. This meant that individuals who were unable to identify and 'buy in' to the dominant model from an early stage quite often perceived themselves in failure, which further reinforced the sense of hopelessness and futility that had come with years of damaging use. Rarely did a multiplicity of recovery choices exist in the same space.

NWRC works through peer-to-peer processes. All staff, volunteers, residents and community members have shared formative alcohol and drug use experiences. It provides a combination of residential support, recovery programmes, community projects, lifestyle skills building and social activities. The community strengthens as the initial ripple continues to get bigger and adds additional layers. The latest element of this is Bwyd Da, a high street-based social enterprise café that, in addition to offering great food and a food club, supports work and training opportunities, challenges stigmas, promotes local produce and provides a positive public profile about the possibilities of recovery.

Successful recovery communities are a strong example of social contagion. This was once explained quite simply by a community member who stated: "If I spend my time with people who drink and take drugs then I'll drink and take drugs whereas if I choose to spend my life with people who are clean and sober then I'll stay clean and sober."

Inherent in the contagion model is the key concept of the 'recovery carrier' (White, 2012). A recovery carrier is an individual who has a disproportionate effect within their social circles. These individuals, by the strength of their own personality, can make recovery seem far more attractive and achievable and can help foster early recovery both in individuals and communities. Using their own strong experiences of recovery, they then start to transfer that disproportionate social effect into a force for good, encouraging others to strive for recovery and acting as a focal point or leader within their now positive social grouping. Best and Ivers (2021) suggest that these types of individuals are often found in Lived Experience Recovery Organisations such as NWRC.

NWRC has had several such identifiable recovery carriers, enabling the creation of a pool of employees who all believe passionately in their work. The targeting of 'carriers' also allows us to develop recovery in areas outside of our locality. Acting as 'beacons' within their own communities, they can make recovery seem more attractive and achievable and subsequently help to spread the growth of mutual aid in areas that are heavily affected by substance use but have little in the way of established recovery.

There are many aspects of NWRC that are unique and help us to be successful. We can but offer a snapshot here, rather than comprehensive detail. Despite the improbability of the concept to many outsiders, NWRC is an example demonstrating that altruistic societies can actually work. In our residential setting we actively encourage individuals to take on a leadership role. This helps develop their skill set alongside the natural strength of character and positivity that can help to support others onwards to recovery. This is exemplified through a cyclical model whereby community members who have successfully completed the programme of recovery are actively sought and employed. As such, the vast majority of our staff who have made the transition from peer to staff member were originally 'carriers' themselves. The sense of belief that staff have in their work is strengthened because they know that it directly helped them to get well.

We have found that individuals favour particular recovery pathways – for example, 12-step, physical activity or volunteering – and this leads to the need to ensure a diversity of such pathways are made available. Evidence from our research with the CSAR (Chester Spirituality and Addiction Research) group at Chester University suggests that quite often it is not necessarily the group itself that forms the initial attraction, rather the fact that individuals just like spending time with other individuals in recovery (CSAR, 2022).

NWRC is about raising the visibility of recovery and addressing the stigma that still surrounds addiction. This is particularly acute in September, world recovery month, when NWRC puts on an annual programme of highly visible events that serves the wider community and enables members to feel like they are paying something back. Visibility involves NWRC members regularly participating in a variety of community-based initiatives, ranging from straightforward community payback such as the removal of 'needle waste' from affected areas, to volunteering with mental health initiatives or providing long-term support to individuals affected by food poverty during the COVID-19 pandemic.

The core of our successful approach is that NWRC is built upon a flat hierarchy. Every community member, from the newcomer to the organisational lead, has input in the decision-making process. The concept of a flat hierarchy also seems to encourage individuals to take more of a lead in the delivery of mutual aid and other activities. When we first started out, we needed to ensure that there was a staff member in every group or activity initially to 'prop it up'; however, as the community has grown and developed this need has significantly reduced. While most traditional treatment services continue to discharge individuals when they achieve abstinence, NWRC views this practice as being indicative of a disconnect from the recovery process and instead believes that abstinence is simply a starting point on the recovery journey, not the end result (White, 2009).

NWRC's commitment to the power of peer-to-peer support, shared journeys and promoting the possibilities of change is typified in our annual big walk. This always involves a long-distance walking expedition such as the Anglesey Coast Path (Eternal Media, 2022) or the Hadrian's Wall National Trail. Externally this walk tackles the preconceptions held by wider society about the impossibility of recovery, and internally it fosters a team spirit and unity that is vital to recovery: "Only I can do this, but I can't do it alone." It also offers the participants a reference point in sobriety for any times that they may feel like they have nothing left to give but they still have to carry on putting one foot front in front of the other. It is recovery on the move (Livingston et al, 2011).

Recovery Cymru

Recovery Cymru (members of whom have contributed to this section) evolved from a single support group in Cardiff in 2008. At a time when aftercare following treatment was limited, peer support was largely confined to limited AA and Narcotics Anonymous (NA) fellowship meetings, with no alternatives or complements. The UK recovery movement was in its infancy and our aim was simple: meet, be yourself and support one another to make changes, progress through treatment and build a life in the community away from the problems caused by substance use.

Many people did not know others who had made and sustained change, so hope, inspiration and the giving of advice regarding practical ways to spend time were essential. A single group led to a local community movement, and Recovery Cymru as a recovery community organisation was founded in 2010. The basis of our growth has been our peer-led philosophy and community culture which make people feel welcomed, valued and that they are people with strengths. We adopt the notion of self-defined recovery, which means that there is no abstinence focus, people can choose what recovery looks like for them at different times in their lives. We are organised through a flat hierarchy whereby everyone has equal value regardless of position or achievements, and we focus on activity. This often means support groups, coproduced structured programmes, social activities, volunteering and community engagement, all of which are designed by and run by our community members. Our recovery centres act as hubs of support and, since 2020, we now also offer all our support at a distance, increasing access and options for those for whom the centres are not the best option. The concept is simple (even if the reality is not!).

With over a decade of experience, Recovery Cymru's peer community provides support, activity, hope and inspiration for people pre-, during and post-treatment, as well as offering alternatives for those for whom treatment is not the best option. Our First Steps to Recovery programme offers distance support to so-called 'change resistant substance misusers', people who are often seen in 'Bluelight' services such as Emergency Departments and are locked in a complex cycle of substance use (Alcohol Change, 2022). For our First Steppers, meeting a peer as an equal, building rapport and having a stable point of contact can be the first step in a longer journey of engaging with other support services and making changes. For some, believing and seeing change is possible is step one. Alongside supporting individuals we raise awareness of, and challenge, stigma and discrimination, often partnering with others such as education and employers to create environments for recovery. Stigma is damaging, it creates shame, perpetuates self-stigma, prevents or delays people from seeking help and makes it harder for people to sustain change. The visibility of lived experience in changing this is vital.

It is hard to describe the spirit of the peer recovery community; it is something you feel. Our members often tell us that it is not *what* we do but *how* we do it that makes all the difference. The culture of the 'Recovery Cymru Family' is the magic. The connection that comes from the shared values and experiences of peers means that there is no judgement, and this is critical. This culture is the foundation of our practical success. There are seemingly small but practical ways we continue this, and language matters (Livingston and Perkins, 2018). From day one we were clear that we are a community, not a service; our members are not service users and we refer to 'we' rather than 'them'. Staff, volunteers and members all have a collective and vested interest in what and why we do what we do. The flat hierarchy ensures people can 'turn up who and as they are' day in day out. We do not put on a front. This is often a culture shock for people, both for those used to being 'the service user who needs help' and for 'professionals who help others'. It can take some time to adjust!

Recovery, friendship and meaningful activity is about life. Life does not happen Monday–Friday 9–5pm. Our support is available 365 days per year, as and when people need it. For some this is seven days a week, others once per month or five years later during a tough time. As a community, we believe that engagement is not time limited. Long-term engagement can be seen as a positive, whereas 'retention in treatment' is often seen as a negative. We do not solely focus on substance use, our aim is to make people feel welcome, cared for and to inspire them to see what they are good at, as well as what they need to change. Often, the substance use is secondary and we help people to build a life that is rewarding and worth the effort of change. Some seemingly small actions can be profound. For example, every member receives a birthday card from us, and we have great stories of this making a real difference, from being the only acknowledgement someone might have of their birthday to being a reminder that we are thinking of them, which can prompt re-engagement in a time of need.

Working with others is essential for us. Our philosophy ensures we complement, not conflict with, all other treatment and recovery philosophies. We can support people as peers throughout engagement in other services. Critically we support people to (re)build their lives in the community, to live full and fulfilled lives thereafter. Examples include being core members of a transformational new alliance of providers to deliver local treatment services, working with the new local Family Drug and Alcohol Court with those most at risk of their children being taken into care, and partnerships with Substance Use Liaison Teams in hospitals.

A key component of the Recovery Cymru approach is the training, development and support of our peer workforce, paid staff and volunteers. Consideration and time are taken to build rapport, confidence, skills, knowledge and self-belief. Not only does this ensure the spirit of our approach and the sustainability of our model, it shows others (family members, people seeking recovery and professionals) the power of peer support. Our peers are highly skilled, committed and loyal. They undertake sensitive, emotionally difficult work to as high a standard as any professional and are valued throughout our local treatment system, combatting inherent discrimination and stigma. The impact of learning new skills, supporting others and feeling the positive benefits of meaningful activity are profound.

The power of our approach is best described by our members

> 'Thank you for believing in me, accepting me, having faith in me and just being there.'

> 'I'm doing so well and thanks to Recovery Cymru, I've got a tool bag that helps me manage my thoughts, feelings and emotions.'

> 'It is an organisation that treasures recovery and treats it like a valuable asset that enriches our lives and society.'

Recovery within social work practice

Social work is a diverse profession and social workers inhabit a variety of roles. Much of this involves direct contact with experiences of alcohol and drug use, and all social workers are well placed to provide a positive intervention (Galvani, 2015). From our account of recovery policy, movements and organisations it is clear that social workers should be expanding their understanding of recovery communities as possible supportive interventions and outcomes.

The origins of social work set out to challenge poverty and inequality and have a long-standing tradition of advocacy. Social work advocacy can provide interventions for short- and longer-term personal outcomes for individuals but can also make positive impacts on a macro level within communities and society itself. Being at the forefront of health and social care services, the social work emphasis on empowering others and creating positive change is perfectly suited to the issues faced by those experiencing difficulties with their or someone else's substance use. The policy shift towards coproduction and active participation now provides the role of social work in Wales with a lawful framework in which to practise these underpinning values and ethics. This is far more likely to happen in peer-led recovery and community contexts than individual statutory case management interventions. Such involvement also resonates with the inherent social justice orientation of the profession and many social work roles.

Messages for practice

- It is important for social workers to understand that meaningful and long-term sustained change for those with previous experience of alcohol and drug use is possible, that recovery is about more than substance abstinence, and often best supported in the context of peer-led provision. In doing so social workers must recognise they have a critical role in supporting individuals to access and engage with peer-led recovery organisations.

More specifically social workers might want to consider:

- Supporting individuals to engage in a peer group.
- Supporting individuals to begin to support themselves, start up peer groups.
- Groups that focus on support for specific groups of people – for example, women only, young people, and family members.
- The importance of peer support (or recovery groups), their capabilities and how they can offer important 'out of hours' support and motivation in times of need.
- The advantages and disadvantages of any peer support groups for each individual.
- Briefing individuals on what to expect from any group.

Social work has an active role to play in recovery groups; advocacy, challenging stigma, coproduction and social justice are all key social work aspirations.

Further resources
1. Best, D. (2012) *Addiction Recovery: A Movement for Social Change and Personal Growth in the UK*, Brighton: Pavilion Publishing.

2. Galvani, S., Roy, A. and Clayson, A. (2022) *Long-term Recovery from Substance Use: International Social Care Perspectives*, Bristol: Policy Press.
3. Roth, J. and Best, D. (eds) (2012) *Addiction and Recovery in the UK*, London: Routledge.

Links to Welsh recovery projects
https://northwalesrc.org/
https://www.eternalmedia.co.uk/
https://www.facebook.com/BwydDaBangor
http://www.recoverycymru.org.uk/

References

Alcohol Change (2022) *Blue Light Project*. https://alcoholchange.org.uk/help-and-support/training/for-practitioners/blue-light-training/the-blue-light-project

Beresford, P. (2020) 'PPI or user involvement: taking stock from a service user perspective in the twenty first century', *Research Involvement and Engagement*, 6(36): 1–5.

Best, D. and Hamer, R. (2021) 'Addiction recovery in services and policy: an international overview', in N. el-Guebaly, G. Carrà, M. Galanter and A.M. Baldacchino (eds) *Textbook of Addiction Treatment*, Cham: Springer. https://doi.org/10.1007/978-3-030-36391-8_50

Best, D. and Ivers, J.-H. (2021) 'Inkspots and ice cream cones: a model of recovery contagion and growth', *Addiction Research & Theory*, 30(3): 155–161.

British Association of Social Workers (2022) *Alcohol and Other Drugs SIG – Resources*. https://www.basw.co.uk/what-we-do/groups-and-networks/special-interest-groups/alcohol-and-other-drugs/resources

Chester Spirituality and Addiction Research Group (2022) *Home Page*. https://csarsg.org.uk/

Eternal Media (2022) *Trails of Recovery*. https://vimeo.com/eternalmedia/trailsofrecovery

Galvani, S. (2012) *Supporting People with Alcohol and Drug Problems: Making a Difference*, Bristol: Policy Press.

Galvani, S. (2015) *Alcohol and Other Drug Use: The Roles and Capabilities of Social Workers*, Manchester: Manchester Metropolitan University.

Galvani, S., Roy, A. and Clayson, A. (2022) *Long-term Recovery from Substance Use: International Social Care Perspectives*, Bristol: Policy Press.

Her Majesty's Government (2010) *Drug Strategy 2010: Reducing Demand, Restricting Supply, Building Recovery: Supporting People to Live a Drug Free Life*. London: Her Majesty's Government.

Her Majesty's Government (2012) *Putting Full Recovery First: The Recovery Roadmap*. London: Her Majesty's Government.

Her Majesty's Government (2021) *From Harm to Hope: A 10-year Drugs Plan to Cut Crime and Save Lives*. London: Her Majesty's Government.

Kalk, J.N., Robertson, R.J., Kidd, B., Day, E., Kelleher, J.M., Gilvarry, E. and Strang, J. (2017) 'Treatment and intervention for opiate dependence in the United Kingdom: lessons from triumph and failure', *European Journal on Criminal Policy and Research*, 24: 183–200.

Klingemann, H. (2020) 'Successes and failures in treatment of substance abuse: treatment services perspectives and lessons from the European continent', *Nordic Studies on Alcohol and Drugs*, 37(4): 323–337.

Kougiali, G., Fasulo, A., Needs, A. and Van Laar, D. (2017) 'Planting the seeds of change: directionality in the narrative construction of recovery from addiction', *Psychology and Health*, 32(6): 639–664.

Livingston, W. (2022) 'Is measuring long-term recovery desirable, necessary or even possible?', in S. Galvani, A. Roy and A. Clayson (eds) *Long-term Recovery from Substance Use: International Social Care Perspectives*, Policy Press: Bristol, pp 15–27.

Livingston, W. and Perkins, A. (2018) 'Participatory Action Research (PAR): Critical methodological considerations', *Drugs and Alcohol Today*, 18(1): 61–71.

Livingston, W., Baker, M., Atkins, B. and Jobber, S. (2011) 'A tale of the spontaneous emergence of a recovery group and the characteristics that are making it thrive: exploring the politics and knowledge of recovery', *The Journal of Groups in Addiction and Recovery*, 6(1): 176–196.

Mayock, P. and Butler, S. (2020) 'Pathways to "recovery" and social reintegration: the experiences of long-term clients of methadone maintenance treatment in an Irish drug treatment setting', *International Journal of Drug Policy*, 90: 103092.

Redcliffe, J. (2021) 'Adult social services', in H. Gwilym and C. Williams (eds) *Social Policy for Social Welfare Practice: New Directions* (3rd edn), Bristol: Policy Press, pp 193–205.

Rwatschew, F.L., Langan, K. and Dent, H. (2019) 'Embarking on recovery: when does stigma end? Investigating the experiences of discrimination and how these effect aspirations in recovery from substance misuse', *Journal of Humanistic Psychology*. https://doi.org/10.1177%2F0022167819853896

Scottish Government (2008) *The Road to Recovery: A New Approach to Tackling Scotland's Drug Problem*. Edinburgh: Scottish Government.

Stothard, B. (2021) 'Fifty years of the UK Misuse of Drugs Act 1971: the legislative contexts', *Drugs and Alcohol Today*, 21(4): 266–268.

Welsh Assembly Government (2011) *Sustainable Social Services for Wales: A Framework for Action*. Cardiff: Welsh Assembly Government.

Welsh Government (2019) *Wales and the Sustainable Development Goals*. Cardiff: Welsh Government.

Welsh Government (2021) *Substance Misuse Delivery Plan 2019–2022: Revised in Response to COVID-19*. Cardiff: Welsh Government. https://www.gov.wales/sites/default/files/publications/2021-01/substance-misuse-delivery-plan-2019-to-2022.pdf

White, W. (2009) 'The mobilization of community resources to support long-term addiction recovery', *Journal of Substance Abuse Treatment*, 36: 146–158.

White, W. (2012) *Recovery Is Contagious*. https://dbhids.org/wp-content/uplo ads/2015/07/2010-Possible-Resource-Papers-RecoveryIsContagious.pdf

White, W.L. (2008) *Recovery Management and Recovery Oriented Systems of Care* (vol 6), Chicago: Great Lakes Addiction Technology Transfer Center, Northeast Addiction Technology Transfer Center and Philadelphia Department of Behavioral Health and Mental Retardation Services.

13

Trauma-informed practice in the Welsh Youth Justice Service

Tegan Brierley-Sollis

Chapter objectives

- To examine the position and theoretical lens of trauma-informed practice within the Welsh Youth Justice Service landscape.

- To explore the emerging trauma-informed lens within the Welsh Youth Justice Service.

- To describe contemporary context in Wales regarding trauma-informed approaches within social policy.

Introduction

The association between trauma in childhood and offending in later life, as well as other unfavourable outcomes, has prompted services from an array of spheres, including criminal justice, to work with individuals via a trauma-informed lens. This chapter considers the theoretical context of trauma-informed practice within the criminal justice system (CJS) through child development, developmental criminology theories and contemporary trauma theory positioning in order to demonstrate a nuanced understanding of the influence trauma may have on life trajectories. Next, the chapter explores the commitment from the Youth Justice Service (YJS) in Wales to embed a multi-layered, trauma-informed approach to meet the statutory aim of preventing offending, and encouraging pro-social outcomes for children in Wales. This has included the Enhanced Case Management (ECM) roll-out across the Welsh YJS. Finally, this chapter addresses social policy, aligning with the YJS aim to embed trauma-informed approaches including the Social Services and Well-being (Wales) Act (2014) (SSWWA) and the Well-being of Future Generations (Wales) Act (2015) (WFGWA).

Theoretical context

Child development is understood as a developmental mosaic comprising cognitive, psychological and physical tesserae which encompass important transitionary periods and interpersonal relationships (Elder and Giele, 2009).

The developmental trajectory is influenced by the child's individual contexts as well as socioeconomic and historical circumstances (Elder and Giele, 2009). Disruptions to a child's life, including experiencing adversity and trauma, may lead to diversion from the developmental pathway (Almeida and Wong, 2009). This can be explained via contemporary trauma theory which acknowledges that developmental delays may stem from unresolved childhood trauma (Herman, 1992; van der Kolk, 2014).

Contemporary trauma theory appreciates the influence trauma may have on bio-psychosocial functioning (Goodman, 2017) and views individuals who have experienced trauma as requiring support to heal (van der Kolk, 2014). There are five central tenets to contemporary trauma theory, including dissociation, attachment, re-enactment, long-term influence in later life and emotional capacity impairment (van der Kolk, 2014; Goodman, 2017). If a child experiences trauma, displays elements of contemporary trauma theory and offends in adolescence, understanding may be gained via the developmental criminology paradigm.

Numerous theories attempt to understand adolescent offending and the multiple pathways which exist on the criminality trajectory (Casey, 2011). Developmental criminology is concerned with the onset of persistent offending while appreciating that human development is dynamic and influences behaviour both positively and negatively (Lussier et al, 2016). Akin to contemporary trauma theory, developmental criminology examines life event influences but departs from contemporary trauma theory (which focuses on the effects of trauma) through the exploration of offending. Therefore, trauma-informed practice within a YJS setting may be understood through the lenses of child development, developmental criminology and contemporary trauma theory which acknowledge the changing nature of life and the influence of individual, socioeconomic and historical factors on behaviour and development.

Trauma-informed youth justice in Wales

Despite being governed by Westminster, there are disparities in policy/practice which distinguish the Welsh YJS from England (Drakeford, 2010; Thomas, 2015) although policy divergence between Wales and England has recently narrowed and become more diluted (Brewster and Jones, 2019). Welsh Government has developed social policies for children which incorporate rights and child-based practice alongside the inclusion of 'child first' as the central guiding principle in the Youth Justice Board's (YJB) Strategic Plan for 2021–24 (YJB, 2021) which views children as partners in the youth justice (YJ) process, thus, enabling participation which spotlights the needs, rights and interests of the child (Case and Haines, 2015). The emphasis on children's rights has percolated YJ practice within Wales via the YJ Blueprint 2019, the All Wales Youth Offending Strategy (Welsh Assembly Government and YJB, 2004) and Children and Young People First (Welsh Government and YJB, 2014), suggesting that the centralisation of children's rights is considered a pillar of policy/practice in relation to YJ in

Wales. The YJ Blueprint 2019 sets out four key principles which include taking a trauma-informed approach throughout the various YJS stages, embedding trauma-informed approaches into community/custodial practice, a child-first approach, and the aligning of devolved/non-devolved services via shared values to create a whole system approach (Ministry of Justice and Welsh Government, 2019). The YJ Blueprint 2019 ambition is to aspire to a system that is rights-based and trauma-informed to enable services to deliver positive outcomes. However, changes at the strategic level have not been fully absorbed into YJS fabric, where an array of differing models of practice used by Youth Offending Teams, underpinned by distinct theories, exist (Smith and Gray, 2019).

Awareness of the association between trauma in childhood and criminal behaviour has grown, evidenced by the inclusion of trauma-informed approaches within the YJ Blueprint. A seminal study unearthed a relationship between childhood abuse and criminality (Widom, 1989). These findings have been replicated internationally and suggest a connection between childhood trauma and later offending behaviour (Baglivio et al, 2015; Malvaso et al, 2015). The Welsh Prisoner Adverse Childhood Experiences survey found that traumatic experiences, under the umbrella of adverse childhood experiences significantly increased the likelihood of youth incarceration (Ford et al, 2019). Indeed, there is overrepresentation within the CJS of children who have experienced trauma and adversity, however, the relationship remains complex and entangled with various other potential existing factors (Jung et al, 2014). Thus, the influence of trauma on criminality requires further exploration (Malvaso et al, 2015).

The YJB embarked on a study, involving children with 25 plus convictions and elevated reoffending rates, which indicated that trauma is prevalent in children who access the CJS (YJB, 2014). Thus, the YJS identified a requirement to work in a way which addresses underlying need prior to seeking to resolve offending behaviour (Evans et al, 2020). A call out was issued to the YJ sector in Wales and answered by the originators of the Trauma Recovery Model which weaves together psychological and criminological approaches (Skuse and Matthew, 2015). The Trauma Recovery Model is built upon a desistance-based assumption that children can reintegrate back to the community and are redeemable. Many individuals who offend are encouraged when others have high expectations of them (McNeil et al, 2005), referred to as the Pygmalion effect (Maruna and LeBel, 2010), thus, aligning to the positive influence optimism has on an individual's redeemability and motivation to transform their life (Maruna et al, 2009).

The Trauma Recovery Model was integrated into ECM which is more suited to community-based YJ and involves six elements including training in the Trauma Recovery Model and the underpinning theory, clinical psychologically led team case formulation meetings to map key events in children's lives, intervention (type and sequence) recommendations based on a clinical psychology formulation report, clinical supervision for practitioners, regular reviews/adjustments of formulation and guidance for management to help weave trauma-informed practice into the YJS fabric (Evans et al, 2020). The ECM scaffold encourages building positive relationships with children whilst understanding barriers which may prevent engagement with interventions (Skuse and Matthew, 2015). The ECM, which endeavours to align with 'child-first' rather than simply focusing on the offence (YJB, 2020), was piloted and rolled out across Wales and an initial evaluation recommended ongoing implementation with further evaluation (Cordis Bright, 2017). This was based on findings which suggested: support shown for the ECM from those involved in the study, a high degree of consistency with the approach and enhanced outcomes from children including in relation to their engagement and relationships within the YJS (Cordis Bright, 2017).

The Welsh way

Identified within the chapter are many policy examples in Wales with a trauma-informed flavour alongside one practice example of ECM which has been rolled out across the Welsh YJS. ECM evaluations have been largely positive, with benefits including enhanced relational progression and emotion regulation for children and freedom for staff to deliver developmentally informed interventions alongside improvements in multi-agency collaboration (Glendinning et al, 2021). However, further work is needed to embed trauma-informed approaches across the whole YJS which may be challenging if there is still a residue of existing and established practices, for example, risk-dominated practice.

Following the initial ECM evaluation, further research was conducted to assess the ECM implementation within Youth Offending Teams (YOTs) (Glendinning et al, 2021). The findings highlighted an array of benefits to ECM including practitioners gaining a more comprehensive view of the children, more opportunity to deliver developmentally appropriate interventions and effective multi-agency collaboration. Children involved in the ECM exhibited positive progression in their formal relationships (both internal and external to the YOT) and also demonstrated improvements in their emotional regulation (Glendinning et al, 2021) potentially due to the marked enhancements in the child–practitioner relationship if a secure attachment is formed (Shemmings and Shemmings, 2011), which is an important element for children with previous relational trauma. However, the evaluation also demonstrated that further work is needed to embed a trauma-informed and child-first lens into the YJS (Glendinning et al, 2021).

Despite growing internationally, trauma-informed practice does not have a universal definition, thus organisations/practitioners create individual definitions (Menchuner and Maul, 2016). Hopper, Bassuk and Olivet (2010: 82) combined principles from trauma-informed care settings to create the following definition: 'a strengths-based framework that is grounded in an understanding of and responsiveness to the impact of trauma, that emphasizes physical, psychological, and emotional safety for both providers and survivors, and that creates opportunities for survivors to rebuild a sense of control and empowerment.'

The Substance Abuse and Mental Health Services Administration (SAMHSA) have blended various concepts and models (for example, Harris and Fallot, 2001; Bloom and Farragher, 2011) to form six key principles of trauma-informed approaches, namely, 'safety, trustworthiness and transparency, peer support, collaboration and mutuality, empowerment, voice and choice and cultural, historical, and gender issues' (SAMHSA, 2014: 10). Although trauma-informed approaches appear suitable for many children within the CJS, the challenges lie in the practicality of embedding trauma-informed approaches into the processes/ systems such as police interviews, court systems and interventions, which may be primarily traumatising in their own right or re-traumatise children (Silvester, 2022), thus, contradictory to the trauma-informed 'Four R's' Framework which includes seeking 'to actively *resist re-traumatization*' (SAMHSA, 2014: 9). A systems-wide cultural change would support the YJS in their journey to becoming trauma-informed and may, simultaneously align with legislative aims.

Legislated understanding of the trauma-informed lens

There is a trauma-informed flavour to various social policies, which sit outside but potentially feed into the YJS, requiring services to positively influence the well-being of individuals, including children, and prevent offending in Wales. The SSWWA includes principles which speak in part to trauma-informed principles – namely, peer support and empowerment, voice and choice – which seek to ensure organisations are both person-centred and pursue service–individual collaboration (see Chapter 2). Despite services operating in accordance with the legislation, an SSWWA evaluation found that individuals felt obstructed in their ability to have their voices heard and influence decisions around their care (Llewellyn et al, 2022).

Another policy supportive of addressing trauma experienced in childhood is the WFGWA which provides a public services scaffold rooted in collaborative working practice to enhance well-being (Welsh Government, 2015). There are seven well-being goals included within the Act (see Welsh Government, 2015 and Chapter 1). In order to meet such goals, the policy framework relies on a childhood free of adverse childhood experiences, and societal understanding that trauma may also stem from environments which foster inequality (Bellis et al, 2015). The Future Generations Report (Future Generations Commissioner for Wales, 2020) outlined that, in order to be cohesive and prosperous, there should be acknowledgement that childhood experiences may shape life trajectories, thus, problem-solving skills, emotional literacy and fostering community connection are required to support individual healing. The report also calls for public services to be trauma-informed and relational at their core in order to break intergenerational cycles of adverse childhood experiences and trauma (Future Generations Commissioner for Wales, 2020), thereby, viewing trauma-informed approaches as a beacon to enhance relational practice while promoting healing and meeting individual needs. Healthy, positive, long-term relationships, advocated by the Future Generations Commissioner (2020), are also recognised as vital for children within the YJS with regards to pro-social modelling and engagement with interventions (Creaney, 2014; Drake et al, 2014).

Despite an inquiry into the WFGWA finding that many public bodies have not aligned their organisational culture to the principles of the Act (Public Accounts Committee, 2021), there has been a flux of activity centred around trauma and trauma-informed practice in Wales, particularly within the CJS (Beer et al, 2020; Glendinning et al, 2020). Much of this activity results from the Welsh Government's commitment to tackling adverse childhood experiences and the intention expressed in *Prosperity for All: The National Strategy* (Welsh Government, 2017). This included the Welsh Government's adverse childhood experiences policy development, which was reviewed in order to support future orientation, focusing on the policy contribution towards the overarching aim of Welsh Government to ensure all children in Wales have the best possible start in life and are given ample opportunity to fulfil their potential. It also explored the language surrounding adverse childhood experiences and the impact of preventative mechanisms to address these experiences. The review found consistent evidence to support the adverse childhood experiences framework from numerous studies which indicated a relationship between adverse childhood experiences and potential outcomes on the life trajectory (for example, Bellis et al, 2015; Hughes et al, 2018). This relationship is recognised within some studies as associative, acknowledging that adverse childhood experiences are not a prescription for a challenging life trajectory and should, therefore, avoid being framed as causal of certain health/social consequences (Kelly-Irving and Delpierre, 2019). However, criticisms were also found regarding language surrounding adverse childhood experiences as deterministic and lacking in clarity, plus the perception that there was a restrictive undertone within the ten recognised adverse childhood experiences (Welsh Government, 2021). One recommendation was to develop a holistic cross-governmental approach, including the consideration of adverse childhood experiences, alongside broader childhood adversity, to enhance life outcomes (Welsh Government, 2021). To address some of the recommendations, the Adverse Childhood Experiences Hub Wales and Traumatic Stress Wales in tandem with an expert reference group, created a National Trauma Practice Framework for Wales titled *Trauma-Informed Wales: A Societal Approach to Understanding, Preventing and Supporting the Impacts of Trauma and Adversity* (Adverse Childhood Experiences Hub Wales and Traumatic Stress Wales, 2022).

The National Trauma Practice Framework for Wales was subject to public consultation. From a trauma-informed perspective, empowerment in social policy should take place via shared power of decision-making abilities to recipient populations (Bowen and Murshid, 2016). Therefore, public consultation may be considered a mechanism to allow societal input but requires careful perusal in order to increase facilitation and decrease barriers around community engagement

(Harden et al, 2015). The National Trauma Practice Framework for Wales aims to ensure consistency among services in Wales who are on a trauma-informed journey, thus, if utilised, may support the Welsh YJS to develop and implement a consistent trauma-informed approach within all service layers to meet the YJ Blueprint 2019 ambition (Ministry of Justice and Welsh Government, 2019).

Conclusion

Many theories exist which seek to understand the developmental trajectory from a trauma-offending lens. An association, non-causal in nature, between childhood trauma, developmental outcomes and criminality remains, suggesting that an understanding of trauma should inform practice. Derived from this, the Welsh YJS has committed to work via a trauma-informed lens against a background of Welsh social policy embodying trauma-informed practice. To be considered as trauma-informed, organisations must understand the responses and consequences which trauma may have on an individual (Bent-Goodley, 2019). The legislated understanding of trauma requires further work to reflect consistency of application across spheres and lived experience which may be alleviated through the National Trauma Practice Framework for Wales. A universal definition, provided by the framework, may support organisations across Wales to work towards shared values/visions while appreciating and responding to individual needs of the Welsh population.

Messages for practice

- An implication for practice may lie in the YJS itself being part of the CJS, thus, there may be challenges in such settings implementing trauma-informed approaches, particularly when elements/practice within the system may be traumatising or re-traumatising in their own right (Covington and Bloom, 2008; Petrillo, 2021).
- Caution should also be applied when working through a trauma-informed lens based on criticisms including the potential to characterise individuals as victims only, rather than seeing them as a whole person (Evans and Coccoma, 2017) and the lacking direction of comprehensive practice (Becker-Blease, 2017). Trauma-informed approaches are not a one-size-fits-all and require rich understanding alongside continuous reflection of recognised potential critiques.

Further resources
1. Glendinning, F., Rodriguez, G.R., Newbury, A. and Wilmot, R. (2021) 'Adverse childhood experience (ACE) and trauma-informed approaches in youth justice services in Wales: An evaluation of the implementation of the ECM project', Public Health Collaborating Unit: Bangor University. https://yjresourcehub.uk/images/Partners/Bangor%20University/Bangor_University_ECM_Evaluation_Report_March_2021.pdf

2. Substance Abuse and Mental Health Services Administration (2014) *SAMHSA's Working Concept of Trauma and Framework for a Trauma-informed approach*, Rockville, MD: National Centre for Trauma-Informed Care.
3. Willmot, P. and Jones, L. (eds) (2022) *Trauma-Informed Forensic Practice: Issues in Forensic Psychology*, London: Routledge.

References

Adverse Childhood Experiences Hub Wales and Traumatic Stress Wales (2022) *Trauma-Informed Wales: A Societal Approach to Understanding, Preventing and Supporting the Impacts of Trauma and Adversity*. Public Health Wales NHS Trust.

Almeida, D.M. and Wong, J.D. (2009) 'Life transitions and daily stress processes', in G.H. Elder and J.Z. Giele (eds) *The Craft of Life Course Research*, New York: Guilford, pp 141–162.

Baglivio, M.T., Wolff, K.T., Piquero, A.R. and Epps, N. (2015) 'The relationship between adverse childhood experiences (ACE) and juvenile offending trajectories in a juvenile offender sample', *Journal of Criminal Justice*, 43(3): 229–241.

Becker-Blease, K.A. (2017) 'As the world becomes trauma-informed, work to do', *Journal of Trauma and Dissociation*, 18(2): 131–138.

Beer, J., Janssen, H., Glendinning, F. and Newbury, A. (2020) *An Evaluation of the Criminal Justice Adverse Childhood Experiences (ACEs) Training and Trauma Awareness Training (TAT): National Roll Out to Members of Her Majesty's Prison and Probation Service (HMPPS) across Wales*. Public Health Wales. https://phwwhocc.co.uk/wp-content/uploads/2021/05/PHW-EAT-ACEs-Criminal-Justice-TAT-report-Eng.pdf

Bellis, M.A., Ashton, K., Hughes, K., Ford, K., Bishop, J. and Paranjothy, A. (2015) *Adverse Childhood Experiences and Their Impact on Health-harming Behaviours in the Welsh Adult Population*. Cardiff: Centre for Public Health, Public Health Wales.

Bent-Goodley, T. (2019) 'The necessity of trauma-informed practice in contemporary social work', *Social Work*, 64(1): 5–8.

Bloom, S.L. and Farragher, B. (2011) *Destroying Sanctuary: The Crisis in Human Service Delivery Systems*, Oxford: Oxford University Press.

Bowen, E.A. and Murshid, N.S. (2016) 'Trauma-informed social policy: a conceptual framework for policy analysis and advocacy', *American Journal of Public Health*, 106(2): 223–229.

Brewster, D. and Jones, R. (2019) 'Distinctly divergent or hanging onto English coat-tails? Drug policy in post-devolution Wales', *Criminology and Criminal Justice*, 19(3): 364–381.

Case, S. and Haines, K. (2015) 'Children first, offender second: the centrality of engagement in positive youth justice', *The Howard Journal of Criminal Justice*, 54(2): 157–175.

Casey, S. (2011) 'Understanding young offenders: developmental criminology', *The Open Criminology Journal*, 4(1-M1): 13–22.

Cordis Bright (2017) *Evaluation of the Enhanced Case Management Approach*, Welsh Government. https://www.cordisbright.co.uk/admin/resources/170328-evaluation-enhanced-case-management-approach-en.pdf

Covington, S. and Bloom, B. (2008) 'Gender-responsive treatment and services in correctional settings', *Women and Therapy*, 29(3): 9–33.

Creaney, S. (2014) 'The position of relationship based practice in youth justice', *Safer Communities*, 13(3): 120–125.

Drake, D.H., Fergusson, R. and Briggs, D.B. (2014) 'Hearing new voices: reviewing youth justice policy through practitioners' relationships with young people', *Youth Justice*, 14(1): 22–39.

Drakeford, M. (2010) 'Devolution and youth justice in Wales', *Criminology and Criminal Justice*, 10(2): 137–154.

Elder, Jr. G.H. and Giele, J.Z. (2009) *The Craft of Life Course Research*, New York: Guilford.

Evans, A. and Coccoma, P. (2017) *Trauma Informed Care: How Neuroscience Influences Practice*, New York: Routledge.

Evans, J., Kennedy, D., Skuse, T. and Matthew, J. (2020) 'Trauma-informed practice and desistance theories: competing or complementary approaches to working with children in conflict with the law?', *Salus Journal*, 8(2): 55–76.

Ford, K., Barton, E.R., Newbury, A., Hughes, K., Bezeczky, Z., Roderick, J. and Bellis, M.A. (2019) *Understanding the Prevalence of Adverse Childhood Experiences (ACEs) in a Male Offender Population in Wales: The Prisoner ACE Survey*. https://phw.nhs.wales/files/aces/the-prisoner-ace-survey/

Future Generations Commissioner for Wales (2020) *Future Generations Report 2020, Chapter 5: Areas of Focus*. Cardiff: Office of the Future Generations Commissioner for Wales. https://www.futuregenerations.wales/wp-content/uploads/2020/06/Chap-5-ACEs.pdf

Glendinning, F., Barton, E.R., Newbury, A., Janssen, H., Johnson, G., Rodriguez, G.R., et al (2020) *An Evaluation of the Adverse Childhood Experience Trauma-Informed Multi-agency Early Action Together (ACE TIME) Training: National Roll Out to Police and Partners*. Public Health Collaborating Unit: Bangor University. http://researchonline.ljmu.ac.uk/id/eprint/12953/1/PHW%20ACEs%20training%20report.pdf

Glendinning, F., Rodriguez, G.R., Newbury, A. and Wilmot, R. (2021) *Adverse Childhood Experience (ACE) and Trauma-informed Approaches in Youth Justice Services in Wales: An Evaluation of the Implementation of the Enhanced Case Management (ECM) Project*. Public Health Collaborating Unit: Bangor University. https://yjresourcehub.uk/images/Partners/Bangor%20University/Bangor_University_ECM_Evaluation_Report_March_2021.pdf

Goodman, R. (2017) 'Contemporary trauma theory and trauma-informed care in substance use disorders: a conceptual model for integrating coping and resilience', *Advances in Social Work*, 18(1): 186–201.

Harden, A., Sheridan, K., McKeown, A., Dan-Ogosi, I. and Bagnall, A.M. (2015) *Evidence Review of Barriers to, and Facilitators of, Community Engagement Approaches and Practices in the UK*. London: Institute for Health and Human Development, University of East London.

Harris, M. and Fallot, R.D. (2001) 'Trauma-informed inpatient services', *New Directions for Mental Health Services*, 89: 33–46.

Herman, J.L. (1992) *Trauma and Recovery: The Aftermath of Violence – from Domestic Abuse to Political Terror*, New York: Basic Books.

Hopper, E., Bassuk, E. and Olivet, J. (2010) 'Shelter from the storm: trauma-informed care in homelessness services settings', *The Open Health Services and Policy Journal*, 3(2): 80–100.

Hughes, K., Ford, K., Davies, A.R., Homolova, L. and Bellis, M.A. (2018) *Sources of Resilience and their Moderating Relationships with Harms from Adverse Childhood Experiences, Report 1: Mental Illness.* Welsh Adverse Childhood Experience (ACE) and Resilience Study, Public Health Wales NHS Trust. http://www.wales.nhs.uk/sitesplus/documents/888/ACE%20&%20Resilience%20Report%20(Eng_final2).pdf

Jung, H., Herrenkohl, T.I., Kilka, J.B., Lee, J.O. and Brown, E.C. (2014) 'Does child maltreatment predict adult crime? Re-examining the question in a prospective study of gender differences, education, and marital status', *Journal of Interpersonal Violence*, 30(13): 2238–2257.

Kelly-Irving, M. and Delpierre, C. (2019) 'A critique of the adverse childhood experiences framework in epidemiology and public health: uses and misuses', *Social Policy and Society*, 18(3): 445–456.

Llewellyn, M., Verity, F., Wallace, S. and Tetlow, S. (2022) 'Expectations and Experiences: Service User and Carer Perspectives on the Social Services and Well-being (Wales) Act'. Cardiff: Welsh Government, GSR report number 16/2022. https://gov.wales/sites/default/files/statistics-and-research/2022–03/expectations-and-experiences-service-user-and-carer-perspectives-on-the-social-services-and-well-being-wales-act.pdf

Lussier, P., Corrado, R. and McCuish, E. (2016) 'A criminal career study of the continuity and discontinuity of sex offending during the adolescence-adulthood transition: a prospective longitudinal study of incarcerated youth', *Justice Quarterly*, 33(7): 1123–1153.

Malvaso, C.G., Delfabbro, P. and Day, A. (2015) 'The maltreatment-offending association: a systematic review of the methodological features of prospective and longitudinal studies', *Trauma, Violence and Abuse*, 19(1): 20–34.

Maruna, S. and LeBel, T. (2010) 'The desistance paradigm in correctional practice: from programs to lives', in F. McNeil, P. Raynor and C. Trotter (eds) *Offender Supervision: New Directions in Theory, Research and Practice*, Cullompton: Willan Publishing, pp 65–87.

Maruna, S., LeBel, T.P., Naples, M. and Mitchell, N. (2009) 'Looking-glass identity transformation: Pygmalion and Golem in the rehabilitation process', in B.M. Veysey, J. Christian and D.J. Martinez (eds) *How Offenders Transform Their Lives*, Cullompton: Willan Publishing, pp 30–55.

McNeil, F., Batchelor, S., Burnett, S. and Knox, J. (2005) *21st Century Social Work. Reducing Reoffending: Key Practice Skills*, Edinburgh: The Scottish Executive.

Menchuner, C. and Maul, A. (2016) 'Key ingredients for successful trauma-informed care implementation', *Advancing Trauma-informed Care*, Centre for Health Care Strategies.

Ministry of Justice and Welsh Government (2019) *Youth Justice Blueprint for Wales*. London and Cardiff: Ministry of Justice and Welsh Government.

Petrillo, M. (2021) 'We've all got a big story: experiences of a trauma–informed intervention in prison', *Howard Journal of Crime and Justice*, 60(2): 232–250.

Public Accounts Committee (2021) *Delivering for Future Generations: The Story So Far*. Cardiff: Welsh Parliament. https://business.senedd.wales/documents/s500006899/Committee%20Report%20-%20Delivering%20for%20Future%20Generations%20The%20story%20so%20far%20March%202021.pdf

Shemmings, D. and Shemmings, Y. (2011) *Understanding Disorganised Attachment: Theory and Practice of Working with Children and Families*, London: Jessica Kingsley Publishers.

Silvester, N. (2022) 'Developing trauma-informed youth justice services', in P. Willmot and L. Jones (eds) *Trauma-Informed Forensic Practice*, London: Routledge, pp 333–348.

Skuse, T. and Matthew, J. (2015) 'The Trauma Recovery Model: sequencing youth justice interventions for young people with complex needs', *Prison Service Journal*, 220: 16–25.

Smith, R. and Gray, P. (2019) 'The changing shape of youth justice: models of practice', *Criminology and Criminal Justice*, 19(5): 554–571.

Substance Abuse and Mental Health Services Administration (2014) *SAMHSA's Working Concept of Trauma and Framework for a Trauma-informed Approach*, Rockville, MD: National Centre for Trauma-Informed Care.

Thomas, S. (2015) 'Children first, offenders second: an aspiration or a reality for youth justice in Wales' [Professional Doctorate in Leadership in Children and Young People's Services], University of Bedfordshire.

van der Kolk, B.A. (2014) *The Body Keeps the Score: Brain, Mind, and Body in the Healing of Trauma*, New York: Penguin Group.

Welsh Assembly Government and Youth Justice Board (2004) *All-Wales Youth Offending Strategy*. Cardiff: Welsh Assembly Government/Youth Justice Board.

Welsh Government (2014) *Social Services and Well-being (Wales) Act 2014*. Cardiff: Welsh Government.

Welsh Government (2015) *Well-being of Future Generations (Wales) Act*. Cardiff: Welsh Government.

Welsh Government (2017) *Prosperity for All: The National Strategy: Taking Wales Forward*. Cardiff: Welsh Government. https://wcva.cymru/wp-content/uploads/2020/01/Prosperity-for-all.pdf

Welsh Government (2021) *Review of Adverse Childhood Experiences (ACE) Policy: Report: How the ACE Policy Has Performed and How it Can Be Developed in the Future*. Cardiff: Welsh Government. https://gov.wales/sites/default/files/pdf-versions/2021/3/3/1615991408/review-adverse-childhood-experiences-ace-policy-report.pdf

Welsh Government and Youth Justice Board (2014) *Children and Young People First: Welsh Government/Youth Justice Board Joint Strategy to Improve Services for Young People from Wales at Risk of Becoming Involved In, or In, the Youth Justice System*. Cardiff: Welsh Assembly Government/Youth Justice Board.

Widom, C.S. (1989) 'The cycle of violence', *Science*, 244(4901): 160–166.

Youth Justice Board (2014) *Policy Implementation Guidance: Addressing Mental Health Problems of Children and Young People in the Youth Justice System*. https://gov.wales/sites/default/files/publications/2019–05/addressing-mental-health-problems-of-children-and-young-people-in-the-youth-justice-system.pdf

Youth Justice Board (2020) *Enhanced Case Management and Child First Principles*. London: Youth Justice Board. https://yjresourcehub.uk/trauma-and-wellbeing/item/807-enhanced-case-management-and-child-first-principles-september-2020.html%20

Youth Justice Board (2021) *Strategic Plan 2021–2024*, Report. London: Youth Justice Board. https://assets.publishing.service.gov.uk/government/uploads/system/uploads/attachment_data/file/966200/YJB_Strategic_Plan_2021_-_2024.pdf

14

Social care with older people: embedding and sustaining practice – the cARTrefu project

Penny Alexander, Diane Seddon, Katherine Algar-Skaife, Gill Toms, Sarah Lord and Kelly Barr

Chapter objectives

- To provide an understanding of why older people in Wales are an important demographic in social care.

- To offer an example of how distinctive social care legislation in Wales has been put into practice to support older people.

- To illustrate a creative project supporting older people in Wales, called cARTrefu, and information about how a research and practice collaboration seeks to achieve positive change for older people and those involved in supporting them.

- To provide information about how different sectors have come together to make these practice changes.

Introduction

This chapter considers the challenges and opportunities of embedding and sustaining creative social care practice with older people, including people who are living with dementia. It is informed by a successful collaboration involving academia, social care practitioners and the arts. To set the scene we consider the demographic characteristics in Wales and the Welsh Government's vision for social care policy and practice for older people. We highlight key messages for future social care policy and practice and signpost to some helpful resources.

Demographic characteristics

Wales has the highest proportion of older people and older unpaid carers in the United Kingdom (Social Care Institute for Excellence, 2018). While dementia is not a natural part of ageing, the incidence of dementia increases with age (United Nations, 2020). An estimated 45,000 people live with dementia in Wales and dementia costs the Welsh economy £1.4 billion, with £196 million of this spent on health care costs annually, £535 million spent on social care costs (publicly and privately funded) annually, £622 million contributed by the work of unpaid carers and £6 million spent on other costs such as advocacy services (Alzheimer's Society, 2015). Increased longevity is to be celebrated, however, the challenges associated with ageing and with supporting an ageing population are well documented (Mitchell and Walker, 2020). The care home sector is a key provider of social care in Wales. Rising demand for care home places (Housing Learning and Improvement Network, 2020), coupled with financial pressures (Jones et al, 2018) present key challenges that require innovative policy and practice responses.

Social care policy for older people in Wales

To meet the needs of this ageing population, the Welsh Government is committed to improving the well-being and quality of life of older people engaging with social care services in Wales. Realising positive change for older people requires integration between social care providers and other partners, a focus on prevention and a shift to thinking more creatively about ways of supporting older people. It also requires collaboration and a strong voice for older people engaging with social care services if personalised support is to be provided as indicated in the Social Services and Well-being (Wales) Act (SSWWA) (Welsh Government, 2014); Well-being of Future Generations (Wales) Act (WFGWA) (Welsh Government, 2015); *A Healthier Wales* (Welsh Government, 2018a); and the *Dementia Action Plan for Wales* (Welsh Government, 2018b). Collaboration and a stronger voice could be achieved through coproductive approaches.

The Welsh way

The SSWWA introduced a distinctive social care policy agenda emphasising personalised and outcomes-focused approaches. It also consolidated the shift in emphasis towards preventative approaches and community-based services that help older people to remain living in their communities when this is their preferred option. The drive for personalised support approaches has been echoed in the Welsh Government's *Dementia Action Plan for Wales 2018–22*. At the same time, the WFGWA, seeking to protect the sustainability of services, has emphasised the benefits of co-developed approaches and cross-sector working. This policy context provides a rich environment for creative, collaborative initiatives in social care for older people. The compact geography of Wales (Wales has a smaller land area than England or Scotland), enhanced by the population concentrations in metropolitan areas, also fosters collaboration as partners are, quite literally, often closer together.

Social care practice for older people in Wales

Strengths-based approaches (Smale et al, 1993; Nelson-Becker et al, 2020) are key to implementing the vision for personalised, outcomes-led social care practice in Wales. Such approaches recognise that every older person has strengths and can manage change positively, growing and learning from their experiences.

Many older people in Wales remain living in their own home and local community. Support can be provided through domiciliary care services and the help of unpaid carers. Older people might also draw on community activities and groups, such as befriending services, men's sheds, and meal clubs (further materials on some of these initiatives are provided in the complementary resources). These provisions help older people remain connected, offering social opportunities and meaningful activities. Peer support and opportunities for shared experiences are especially important for those living with dementia (Improvement Cymru, 2021). However, a significant number of older people require the support of residential or nursing home care. In both scenarios, many older people in Wales fund part (or all) of their care and support.

There is increasing evidence confirming the long-term benefits of the arts for older people, including for those living with dementia, and for the unpaid and paid carers who support them (All-Party Parliamentary Group on Arts, Health, and Wellbeing, 2017; Arts Council of Wales, 2018; Camic et al, 2018; Fancourt and Finn, 2019; Algar–Skaife et al, 2020; Windle et al, 2020; Dowlen and Gray, 2022).

Arts-based, creative approaches are valued-based. They are underpinned by person-centred and relational approaches that strengthen relationships. They are respectful philosophies that recognise people's skills and abilities and encourage people to enhance their capabilities and confidence. Arts-based approaches can be transformative in promoting creative ways of thinking about and working with older people, challenging negative, stereotypical perceptions about older people, enhancing communication with older people and facilitating interconnectedness for older people (Zeilig and West, 2020). Research suggests that the arts should be integral to residential care provision (Broome et al, 2017; Windle et al, 2019) and the role of care home staff is highlighted as key to the successful delivery of the arts in care settings (Zeilig and West, 2020). An arts-based service would use creativity to engage older adults and help form relationships between residents. However, older people living in care homes may be one of the hardest groups to reach with new models of social care support (Toms et al, 2020).

cARTrefu

cARTrefu is a project which helps people achieve their personal well-being outcomes. It is an example of a creative arts-based approach for older people living in care homes that aligns with the progressive legislative agenda in Wales.

Inspired by the people living in, working in, and visiting care homes, cARTrefu was launched in 2015 with funding from the Arts Council of Wales and the

Baring Foundation. cARTrefu means *to reside* in Welsh and it is Age Cymru's flagship programme providing arts in care settings that aims to:

- improve access to creative, participatory art activities for older people in residential care, that can support them to achieve personal well-being outcomes;
- develop artists' professional practice in facilitating creative arts sessions through the opportunity to work with groups of people with whom they may have little vocational experience;
- foster a greater appreciation of the arts among care home staff and develop new skills which staff can share and practise in their daily work with residents.

cARTrefu offered bespoke art residencies for artist practitioners in care homes across Wales. Artist practitioners are professional creatives who have specialist training in their field. Their work can focus on any creative medium including the visual arts, crafting, music and performance. They use their creativity to engage with individuals or groups in public settings (Arts Council England, 2022). cARTrefu was delivered in three phases. In Phase one, 16 artist practitioners delivered eight sessions (two hours per week for eight weeks) with residents. In Phase two, 12 artist practitioners delivered six 12-week residencies, focusing on staff engagement to continue creative activities within the home, and in Phase three, artist practitioners worked in 47 care homes for one month, developing a cARTrefu Activity Plan to empower staff to improve the quality and range of creative provision within the home. Care home staff (N=36) and artists (N=16) also attended one-day workshops.

The COVID-19 pandemic and associated restrictions had a considerable impact on Phase three, as artists were no longer able to go into care homes. The cARTrefu team adapted by delivering online sessions to offer support to care homes and to allow the continuation of programme objectives. They developed a fortnightly e-newsletter with suggestions of creative sessions, suitable for group sessions or one-to-one work for residents having to isolate and signposted to free online creative and cultural resources and events.

cARTrefu is recognised as the largest project of its kind in Europe. Between 2015 and 2022, cARTrefu provided over 4,060 hours of engagement to over 3,800 residents, staff and family members in 225 care homes across Wales. It represents a partnership between the third sector (Age Cymru), the arts (the funders and cARTrefu artists), and social care (care homes). There is also a research partnership with Bangor University to inform the evidence base relating to the contribution of the arts to the well-being and quality of life of older people. This long-standing, co-designed research collaboration is a success of the cARTrefu programme (Algar-Skaife et al, 2020), and it has evolved in response to the needs of the cARTrefu programme.

An independent evaluation of Phase one (Algar-Skaife et al, 2017) confirmed that participating in the cARTrefu programme had a significant impact on older people's well-being and staff attitudes towards residents, especially those living with dementia. Staff also gained the confidence to lead creative activities themselves. A retrospective Social Return on Investment (SROI) analysis demonstrated the social value of the programme in bringing about significant positive changes for care home residents, staff and artist practitioners. A summary animation of the SROI analysis can be found on the cARTrefu website. A touring and virtual exhibition of work created with and inspired by people living in, working in, and visiting care homes also gave a voice to older people and those who support them.

cARTrefu is highly valued by those involved and other organisations in the social care sector are keen to emulate its success (Algar-Skaife et al, 2020). The delivery and research teams have shared implementation and evaluation insights on national and international platforms and the evaluation report and accompanying animation have been widely disseminated. At a strategic level, evidence from the cARTrefu Evaluation Report 2015–17 was used in Age Cymru's responses to the *Parliamentary Review for Health and Social Care in Wales*, *Count Me In*, and the *Connected Communities: Welsh Government Consultation on Tackling Loneliness and Social Isolation*.

Since 2020, Age Cymru has worked collaboratively with researchers at Bangor University to explore the opportunities for embedding and sustaining the cARTrefu approach within the social care sector. This work was supported by a Knowledge Economy Skills Scholarship (KESS II). In the next section we look at the barriers and facilitators to embedding and sustaining arts-based approaches within the social care sector.

Embedding and sustaining the cARTrefu approach in social care practice

First, we conducted a rapid evidence review which retrieved 24 papers/ examples of emerging practice, models and innovations in the social care sector which can be applied to the creative arts. We explored this literature, looking for barriers and facilitators to embedding projects and sustaining arts provision in social care settings. Facilitators included training, which is essential to help care homes understand the need for and potential of arts in social care settings. Communication and jargon could facilitate or inhibit arts engagement for residents and staff, and person-centred, resident-led, and co-designed approaches were beneficial. Buy-in was a key enabler and attitudes within care homes and managerial influence could be further important facilitators. One barrier identified was staffing issues, especially staff confidence which influences the levels of engagement in arts provision.

To explore these barriers and facilitators further and their implications for cARTrefu, three workshops and five qualitative interviews were held with strategic and operational staff from across Wales. We investigated how the cARTrefu programme supports older people living with dementia in care home settings to achieve personal well-being outcomes. Areas of vulnerability and strength within cARTrefu in terms of sustainability were also considered. Informants included artists, care staff, managers and local authority commissioners. These informants identified that the sustainability of cARTrefu is challenged by resource issues, the language used to describe the arts and a lack of awareness of what the arts can involve. Informants reported that sustainability is facilitated by staff engagement in planning and delivering creative activities and collaborative working with arts providers. These learning points are transferable to other arts-based provision for older people in Wales. We discuss these challenges and facilitators next.

Challenges

Releasing resources

A key challenge to art-based approaches is the concomitant staffing and financial implications of freeing up paid carers to provide creative activities or to access support linked with the arts. This was noted both in the rapid evidence review and in the workshops.

Many care homes understand the importance of creative provision, but immediate personal care needs must be prioritised, and this often prevents more creative activities. This was a theme in the workshops. Although the well-being needs of older people were acknowledged, this was perceived as an optional extra: "That well-being thing is kind of an extra, isn't it? Well, it shouldn't be, but it is" (Activities Coordinator).

Buy-in from management would significantly bolster the status of the arts in care home settings, enabling staff and residents to benefit from the well-being and relationship strengthening merits of arts provision within the home. Managers possess the authority and oversee the resources to enable staff to attend training and to explore and implement creative approaches. The need for buy-in was noted in both the rapid evidence review and in the workshops.

Access to funding to support creative approaches is vital. As one workshop participant explained: "Anything is sustainable even for a very long period if you can find someone that is willing to pay" (Strategy Lead). One suggestion in the workshops was to consider if cultural funding opportunities could subsidise creative approaches in care homes, as cultural engagement activities share the same values as creative provision. This supports evidence found during the cARTrefu Phase one evaluation (Algar-Skaife et al, 2017). However, participants identified no viable long-term funding solutions, although short-term funding suggestions included grants, donations, fundraising and Arts Council Wales funding.

Language barriers and awareness

The language surrounding the arts can be a barrier for care home management, paid carers, families and residents. The arts are often interpreted as elitist, and this can result in disengagement from those who lack confidence in their creative capability. Without an understanding of the vocabulary or an awareness of what the arts can involve and its breadth, many within social care struggle to engage with the arts as something that can improve the well-being of older people. This was referenced in the rapid evidence review, but the workshops provided more detailed information and there were connections drawn between activities with a focus on culture and the opportunity for sustainability. Buy-in from residents and staff who perceive cultural activities as being accessible through care homes can enhance sustainability. One workshop respondent suggested cultural bodies should play a bigger part in engaging with all members of society, including those in care homes: "I think there is a responsibility on people providing cultural and artistic experiences to include people in care homes, who can't physically come out. That's one way of sustaining it" (Strategic Officer).

Language barriers are not one sided. Communication between staff members and those bringing the arts into the home was identified as a significant barrier if handled incorrectly. Art providers need to understand the roles of care home staff and how a care home functions. A lack of a shared understanding between artists and care home staff significantly impedes the delivery and continuance of arts provision in a care home setting. Again, although this challenge was noted in the rapid evidence review, the workshops provided more detail about how this challenge is experienced.

Facilitators

Engagement

The success of creative programmes hinges on the engagement of all staff in the planning and creative stages. This includes the joint working of care staff, coordinators and care home managers. One example of this comes from a study included in the rapid evidence review (Kinley et al, 2017) which found that involving managers in planning and delivering creative approaches led to incremental positive effects relating to the ways that managers bought into and supported projects. Building relationships between art providers and care home managers is essential. Equally, respondents in the workshops saw the involvement of care home residents and unpaid carers in planning art and cultural activities through co-design as a key facilitator. They reflected on how handing over 'power' to residents could have a significant and meaningful impact on staff: "The starting point was from the residents; what excited or interested them. It was meaningful and one of those days you remember forever. What was so special about it was that it all came from the residents and their imaginations" (Strategic Officer).

Support

Many care home teams already contain skilled creative staff, but some teams lack these skills or lack the support they need to initiate and/or sustain creative provision. Workshop participants thought that support from cARTrefu artists was helpful in encouraging care home staff, enabling them to flourish and grow in confidence. However, these (and similar opportunities) were seldom available.

Although support was facilitative, 'formal training' was reported by workshop participants to be 'off-putting' for care staff and burdensome. Recommendations in the workshops included non-mandatory training, but there was a recognised tension as offering training accreditation was seen as a key incentive for some stakeholders. For instance, accreditation, especially from national organisations such as Age Cymru and academic institutions afforded credibility. This was especially relevant for managers who would need to release financial and staff resources to enable paid carers to attend.

The staff well-being agenda

Workshop participants identified that creative provision could support paid carer as well as resident and unpaid carer well-being. The coronavirus pandemic has created a heightened awareness of the well-being needs of social care staff (Social Care Wales, 2022). The opportunity to sustain arts-based approaches through the staff well-being agenda was identified by workshop participants as potentially offering a foothold as the care sector experiences increasing cuts.

Conclusion

Creative approaches are underpinned by relational and strengths-based working. They are one way to implement policy intentions in Wales to support the well-being of older people, including older people residing in care homes. This way of working has been seen to improve care standards and staff satisfaction, and to build collaborative working relationships. Creative approaches can positively impact the care culture within care homes. As one workshop participant summarised: "Art is so broad and actually, in some ways, it's a way of doing things as opposed to a thing you are doing; it's not about what you do, it's about how you do it!" (Strategic Lead).

The sustainability of arts-based, creative approaches to support the well-being of older people depends on tackling the identified challenges and promoting the facilitating factors. This will involve training and education, developing effective communication and valuing staff members and residents. It will require the support of care home managers and the buy-in of residents, paid carers and unpaid carers. Collaborative working across multiple sectors is essential to facilitate a creative environment. By embedding creative approaches, Wales will be in a good position to achieve the policy intention that older people (wherever they reside) can experience good well-being.

Messages for practice

- Person-centred and relational care are important in social care for older people. These forms of care will help achieve the Welsh Government policy intentions for older people. Creative approaches can establish and maintain this care culture.

- Interventions that help achieve personal well-being outcomes are critical to realising social care policy ambitions for older adults. The cARTrefu approach is one innovative solution to meeting personal well-being outcomes and we have detailed some other exemplar interventions (for example, men's sheds).
- Long-term funding is needed to support and embed new care approaches in older adult social care.
- Involving older people and managers in co-designing their support is important. Their involvement in co-developing art and cultural activities is particularly important if these activities are to become mainstream in care environments for older people.
- Communication and language barriers need addressing to ensure that no one feels excluded. This is pertinent in art and cultural activities where the language used can form a barrier to some people's engagement.
- Collaboration is critical for ongoing innovation in older adult social care. Long-standing research and practice collaborations are successes of the cARTrefu programme.

Further resources
1. Algar-Skaife, K., Seddon, D., Barr, K. and Lord, S. (2020) 'Implementing, researching and evaluating a Wales-wide arts in residential care programme: reflections from the cARTrefu programme', *FPOP Bulletin, Special Edition Creative Ageing*, 152: 12–19.
2. Fancourt, D. (2017) *Arts in Health: Designing and Researching Interventions*, Oxford: Oxford University Press.
3. Windle, G., Algar-Skaife, K., Caulfield, M., Pickering-Jones, L., Killick, J., Zeilig, H. and Tischler, V. (2019) 'Enhancing communication between dementia care staff and their residents: an arts inspired intervention', *Aging and Mental Health*, 24(8): 1306–1315.

Complementary resources
1. The cARTrefu website: www.agecymru.org.uk/cartrefu
2. Age Cymru telephone befriending service, called 'Friend in Need'. https://www.ageuk.org.uk/cymru/our-work/friend-in-need/
3. Men's Sheds Cymru. https://www.mensshedscymru.co.uk/
4. Age Connects Torfaen lunch and befriending clubs. https://ageconnectstorfaen.org.uk/services/?tab=clubs-and-classes

References
Algar-Skaife, K., Caulfield, M. and Woods, B. (2017) *cARTrefu: Creating Artists in Residents. A National Arts in Care Homes Participatory and Mentoring Programme. Evaluation Report 2015–2017*. UK: DSDC Wales and Age Cymru.

Algar-Skaife, K., Seddon, D., Barr, K. and Lord, S. (2020) 'Implementing, researching and evaluating a Wales-wide arts in residential care programme: Reflections from the cARTrefu programme', FPOP Bulletin, Special Edition Creative Ageing, 152: 12–19.

All-Party Parliamentary Group on Arts, Health and Wellbeing (2017) Creative Health: The Arts for Health and Wellbeing. UK: All-Party Parliamentary Group on Arts, Health and Wellbeing.

Alzheimer's Society (2015) The Hidden Costs of Dementia in Wales. London: Alzheimer's Society.

Arts Council England (2022) Financial Support for Artists, Creative Practitioners, and Freelancers. https://www.artscouncil.org.uk/funding/financial-support-arti sts-creative-practitioners-and-freelancers#section-1

Arts Council of Wales (2018) Arts and Health in Wales: A Mapping Study of Current Activity. Cardiff, UK: Arts Council of Wales.

Broome, E., Dening, T., Schneider, J. and Brooker, D. (2017) 'Care staff and the creative arts: exploring the context of involving care personnel in arts interventions', International Psychogeriatrics, 29(12): 1979–1991.

Camic, P., Crutch, S., Murphy, C., Firth, N., Harding, E., Harrison, C., et al (2018) 'Conceptualising and understanding artistic creativity in the dementias: interdisciplinary approaches to research and practise created out of mind team', Frontiers in Psychology, 9: 1842.

Dowlen, R. and Gray, K. (2022) Research Digest: Older people – Culture, Community, Connection. Version 1, March 2022. Leeds: Centre for Cultural Value. Research-digest-older-people-v1.pdf (culturehive.co.uk).

Fancourt, D. and Finn, S. (2019) What Is the Evidence on the Role of the Arts in Improving Health and Well-being? A Scoping Review. Copenhagen: WHO Regional Office for Europe.

Housing Learning and Improvement Network (2020) Assessment of the Demand for Specialist Housing and Accommodation for Older People in Wales. Report for the Welsh Government. UK: Housing Learning Improvement Network.

Improvement Cymru (2021) All Wales Dementia Care Pathway of Standards: High Level Standard Descriptors. Wales, UK: Improvement Cymru.

Jones, C., Windle, G. and Edwards, R.T. (2018) 'Dementia and imagination: a social return on investment analysis framework for art activities for people living with dementia', The Gerontologist, 60(1): 112–123.

Kinley, J., Stone, L., Butt, A., Kenyon, B. and Lopes, N.S. (2017) 'Developing, implementing and sustaining an end-of-life care programme in residential care homes', International Journal of Palliative Nursing, 23(4): 186–193.

Mitchell, E. and Walker, R. (2020) 'Global ageing: successes, challenges and opportunities', British Journal of Hospital Medicine, 81(2): 1–9.

Nelson-Becker, H., Lloyd, L., Milne, A., Perry, E., Ray, M., Richards, S., et al (2020) 'Strengths-based social work with older people: a UK perspective', in A.N. Mendenhall and N.M. Carney (eds) Rooted in Strengths: Celebrating the Strengths Perspective in Social Work, Lawrence, KS: University of Kansas Libraries, pp 227–46. https://kuscholarworks.ku.edu/handle/1808/30023

Smale, G., Tuson, G., Biehal, N. and Marsh, P. (1993) *Empowerment, Assessment, Care Management and the Skilled Worker*, London: HMSO.

Social Care Institute for Excellence (2018) *Preventative Support for Adult Carers in Wales: Rapid Review*. UK: Social Care Institute for Excellence.

Social Care Wales (2022) 'Your health and well-being'. https://socialcare.wales/service-improvement/health-and-well-being-resources-to-support-you-during-the-coronavirus-covid-19-pandemic

Toms, G., Green, S., Orrell, A., and Verity, F. (2020) 'Building relational research capacity in care homes in the COVID-19 era: applying recognition theory to the research agenda', *Quality in Ageing and Older Adults*, 21(4): 229–39.

United Nations (2020) 'World Population Ageing 2020 Highlights: Living arrangements of older person' https://www.un.org/development/desa/pd/sites/www.un.org.development.desa.pd/files/undesa_pd-2020_world_population_ageing_highlights.pdf

Welsh Government (2014) Social Services and Well-being (Wales) Act 2014.

Welsh Government (2015) Well-being and Future Generations (Wales) Act 2015.

Welsh Government (2018a) *A Healthier Wales: Our Plan for Health and Social Care*, UK: Welsh Government.

Welsh Government (2018b) *Dementia Action Plan for Wales 2018–2022*, UK: Welsh Government.

Windle, G., Algar-Skaife, K., Caulfield, M., Pickering-Jones, L., Killick, J., Zeilig, H. and Tischler, V. (2019) 'Enhancing communication between dementia care staff and their residents: an arts inspired intervention', *Aging & Mental Health*, 24(8): 1306–1315.

Windle, G., Caulfield, M., Woods, B. and Joling, K. (2020) 'How can the arts influence the attitudes of dementia caregivers? A mixed-methods longitudinal investigation', *The Gerontologist*, 60(6): 1103–1114.

Zeilig, H. and West, J. (2020) 'Diverse rhythms: co-creativity and wellbeing in dementia care home settings', *FPOP Bulletin, Special Edition Creative Ageing*, 152: 20–26.

PART III

Current challenges

15

A holistic approach to self-care, resilience and well-being

Neil Thompson

Chapter objectives

- To appreciate the significance of workplace well-being.
- To recognise the need to look beyond the individual level in seeking to understand organisational responses to stress and related problems.
- To consider the challenges such matters present in Welsh social work.

Introduction

The focus of this chapter is on workplace well-being and the challenges presented by the increase in workload pressures brought about by changes in the wider world of work arising largely from neoliberalism, and owing much to the austerity measures imposed by the United Kingdom (UK) Government.

I begin by considering the Welsh context before exploring the significance of the concept of well-being as applied to social work professionals in terms of the currently hot topic of 'employee wellness'. This is followed by a critique of dominant approaches to workplace health and well-being which tend to be atomistic and thereby fail to address the wider picture. A holistic, sociologically informed approach is proposed as an alternative.

The Welsh way

As Gwilym and Williams (2021) highlight, Welsh social policy has been diverging steadily from the rest of the UK since the onset of devolution. This is in part a reflection of the distinctive nature of Welsh culture that has given rise to what is increasingly being referred to as 'the Welsh way' – that is, approaches to social and public policy that focus specifically on Welsh needs and circumstances which are so often different from the rest of the UK.

The Social Services and Well-being (Wales) Act 2014 has been described as a 'landmark' piece of legislation. This is because it was intended not as a simple adjustment or addition to existing law, but as a shift to a new foundation of social welfare practice premised on the key concept of well-being.

At the same time, we have seen a significant growth of interest in the concept of workplace well-being in recognition of the potential for stress to arise as a result of immense pressures on social workers and on social care staff more broadly. These pressures are due to increasing demand as a result of demographic factors (the ageing population) and increased levels of awareness of safeguarding issues in relation to both children and vulnerable adults (Cheese, 2021).

Stress and its challenges

Traditionally, stress is conceptualised in individual terms. However, in this chapter it is argued that both stress and well-being need to be understood more holistically. This involves taking account of micro-level factors, but complementing these with consideration of macro-level factors, such as the way neoliberalism has created a context inimical to public service in general and social work in particular (Thompson, 2019a; Costello, 2020; Thompson and McGowan, 2020). As part of this, austerity has created the 'double whammy' of increased demand (related to increased poverty and associated social problems) and decreased supply (due to significant reductions in public spending).

What has been happening in social work and social care in Wales is a reflection of changes taking place in the world of work more broadly – including a shift towards 'agile working' and a pandemic-induced focus on remote, home-based working. The key message of this chapter is that, while an emphasis on self-care, resilience and well-being is to be welcomed, it needs to be understood holistically. If not, it could be dismissed as a victim-blaming atomistic approach that fails to do justice to the wider cultural and structural factors that have a central role to play. To illustrate this point the continuum of well-being interventions framework is introduced. This conceptualisation presents well-being measures along a continuum from individualistic, therapy-style approaches, through team support to organisational strategy and culture and eventually to the very nature and organisation of work in contemporary society.

It is argued that an effective approach to employee well-being needs to go beyond the individual level, to address team and organisational factors and, ideally, make a contribution to how work operates in society.

The Welsh context also needs to be understood in terms of the concept of 'internal colonialism' – that is, the hierarchical and exploitative nature of the social, economic and political relations between Wales as a 'province' and England as a significant international power base (Price, 2020). Although Wales has its own government in the form of the Senedd, in many ways this is subservient to the UK Government which, at the time of writing, continues a long, well-established tradition of embracing right-wing ideology and associated policies, far removed from the working-class solidarity traditionally associated with Wales.

Devolution and the role of the Senedd, while very much to be welcomed in terms of promoting policies and practices more in keeping with social work values, has to be understood as having significant limitations due to the hierarchical nature of internal colonialism.

The modern workplace

The world of work has changed significantly in recent decades. The development of the gig economy and the demise of the concept of a job for life; privatisation of public services; the cost-cutting aspirations of 'agile' working; and, more recently, the rise of remote and hybrid working in response to the COVID-19 pandemic have all played a part in transforming the world of work. It can be argued that these changes have their roots in the Thatcherite weakening of trade unions which shifted the balance of power very much in favour of the employers, and largely at the expense of employees. This has contributed toward an approach to workplace relations based on getting the *most* out of employees (an exploitation model), rather than seeking to get the *best* out of them (an empowerment model), a point to which I shall return next.

Other forces have been involved too – for example, developments in technology. We are living in a world of high-speed information, where we are constantly bombarded with data. This can affect levels of well-being and lead to stress, anxiety and depression. As Hari (2022) convincingly argues, modern communication technologies have created an 'always on' culture which creates a wealth of interruptions and distractions that have an adverse effect on concentration, productivity and, indirectly at least, our health and well-being. In a job such as social work where we are dealing with complex and sensitive issues, the ability to concentrate is an essential part of critically reflective practice as a basis for safe and effective interventions (Thompson and Thompson, 2023).

The well-being reaction

In recent years, the concept of well-being has been gaining considerable traction in the workplace, mirroring the broader emphasis upon it in social work in Wales. There is now a significant literature on the subject of health and well-being in the workplace (Van Veldhoven and Peccei, 2015; Miller et al, 2018; Costello, 2020; Bevan and Cooper, 2022), the topic is receiving considerable media coverage across academic, professional and lay communities and has become a major focus of interest for many organisations.

Part of this development is owed to the independent *Good Work* report commissioned by the UK Government (Taylor, 2017). This notion of 'good work' can be understood, in part, as being a key element in a broader movement to highlight and rectify the problems that have arisen from the shift of power from employees to employers that I mentioned earlier. This shift enabled a high proportion of employers to exploit their employees to the full. The technical term for this is 'business process re-engineering' (Hammer and Champy, 1993). It is based on the idea of treating staff like other resources and seeking to gain the maximum return on investment through optimal efficiency (for example, by reducing staff numbers but expecting the same level of productivity, if not higher).

It amounts to focusing on employees as human resources, with the emphasis on the *resources* element of the term, rather than the *human*. It is a matter of exploiting employees as a resource (with all the alienating consequences of doing so) by seeking to get the *most* out of them (Jaffe, 2021). But this is not the only way of seeking optimal return on investment. An alternative approach is to focus on getting the *best* out of employees by focusing on them as human beings who will be very resourceful if treated well. In this latter scenario, what is being exploited is the potential for employers and employees to get the best results by working in partnership. This is what is at the heart of the empowerment approach to human resources (Huq, 2015; Bloom, 2021). This latter approach clearly has far more potential for promoting health and well-being and, arguably, is likely to be far more productive for the employing organisation in terms of reduced sickness absence and staff turnover and fewer stress-related problems.

What we have also seen as part of this reaction against the getting the most out of people approach is an increasing emphasis on leadership. The need for leadership to be developed to the full is now recognised, with more and more organisations focusing on enhancing the quality of their leadership and rising to the challenges involved. A significant element of leadership capability is the ability to influence the culture in a positive direction. This will include shaping the culture to have a clearer focus on employee wellness and the promotion of equality, diversity and inclusion – discrimination being a major negative factor in relation to both physical and mental health (Thompson, 2019b).

The combination of an emphasis on leadership and the surge of interest in health and well-being in the workplace can therefore be understood as, in large part, a backlash against the dehumanising developments in workplace strategy that have been establishing themselves more firmly over the years. While this shift toward developing more user-friendly workplaces is very much to be welcomed, it is not without its problems.

The well-being interventions continuum

Webster (2021) argues that our current system sets up the ability to attain good well-being as something only individuals can achieve. She points out that:

> It commercialises and outsources what could be a collectively supported and maintained experience if we designed our society to work towards it.

> Within this scenario, personal resilience and wellbeing become the weapons of choice against poor wellbeing, leaving an absence of systemic support and coordination. Without coordinated and active design towards improved wellbeing, and with this absence filled with individual responsibility, we see instead that inequalities within and between places are allowed to emerge and proliferate. (p 25)

This is something I have been aware of for quite some time, recognising through my training and consultancy role that it is becoming increasingly commonplace for organisations to limit their focus largely to the individual level. Well-being interventions tend therefore to focus mainly, if not exclusively, on the individual (a focus on healthy eating, exercise and so on). There are two main dangers with this approach:

1. Wider issues are largely being ignored, and so the effectiveness of the interventions is likely to be very limited.
2. If employees who are under high levels of relentless pressure are given the impression that the responsibility for improving health and well-being by reducing stress levels is in their own hands, with little or no reference to the organisation's role in making necessary changes (in line with health and safety legislation, for example), then the likely result is a degree of cynicism that contributes to a sense of alienation.

At best, then, we are looking at limited effectiveness and, at worst, a counterproductive outcome in terms of employee disaffection that is likely to add to the pressures and lead to a vicious circle (Thompson, 2019a).

What I have found particularly concerning is the reductionist use of the concept of resilience as a weapon to beat overstretched employees with. For example, a situation I have come across a number of times, sadly, is one whereby stressed employees are told that they need to build their resilience, as if resilience is some sort of personality trait on the part of the individual, rather than a complex multidimensional phenomenon that relies on a number of factors – the level of support, for example (Thompson and Cox, 2020). In the worst cases, such a perceived 'resilience deficit' is regarded as a basis for invoking capability procedures (rather than looking holistically at the circumstances that are contributing to the experience of stress). Costello (2020) captures this point well in arguing that:

> people who experience stress at work are seen as weak, having some character flaw or lacking backbone. Thinking of stress in this way is inappropriate and potentially dangerous. It forces the issue underground for some, and promotes a culture of shame in others that gets in the way of people either asking for help, or taking time off to get better. (p 5)

Figure 15.1 The well-being interventions continuum

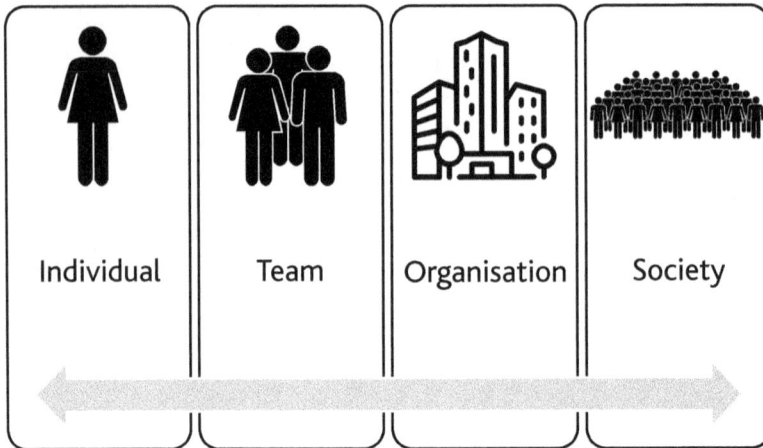

Individual   Team   Organisation   Society

There is a certain irony that I have seen this happening in social work organisations in which presenting an individual citizen who is struggling with their life pressures in purely individualistic terms as some sort of resilience deficit on their part (rather than looking holistically at the wider set of circumstances) would be considered judgemental and therefore professionally inappropriate – and yet, the same resilience deficiency logic seems to be applied to employees in many cases.

What is needed, therefore, is a much broader perspective on workplace well-being and employee wellness, which is where the well-being interventions continuum comes into the picture (Figure 15.1).

There are certainly steps that individuals can take at the micro level in terms of self-care – for example, by eating a healthy diet, exercising regularly and getting enough sleep. However, while these factors can help to avoid stress, there are two important points to note:

1. They are not enough on their own. As we shall see, we need to consider – and address – a range of other factors.
2. Being stressed in itself presents an obstacle to self-care. For example, it is common for people who are experiencing stress to seek comfort in fatty and sugar-soaked foods, to feel too worn out to exercise and too anxious to sleep well. This is the basis of a vicious circle – the problem stands as an obstacle to the solution and thereby perpetuates itself. This can lead to a further vicious circle whereby the resilience deficit model of stress leads to a sense of shame and stigma, a reluctance to ask for support and thus a sense of feeling trapped that can lead to more anxiety and even depression (Thompson, 2019a).

We can therefore conclude that there is a role for the individual at the micro level, but it is highly problematic and dangerous to focus exclusively on the individual level.

The first step in terms of the continuum is to understand the individual in the broader context of the team. The vast majority of social workers work in teams. The team context can be make or break in terms of health and well-being. That is, a supportive, nurturing and empowering team can be an excellent resource that will boost confidence, energy and resilience. The sense of camaraderie, solidarity and safety can be an immense asset when it comes to coping with pressures and keeping stress at bay.

By contrast, where such positives are absent from a team or, worse still, the team has a toxic atmosphere and/or is riven by unresolved conflicts, ill-feeling and spite, the negative effects can be devastating, serving as not only an obstacle to health and well-being, but also a source of additional pressures that can lead to team members crossing the line from a high but manageable level of pressure to health-affecting stress.

Well-being interventions that do not consider the role of the team context are therefore likely to present a distorted picture of the situation and fail to consider possible positive ways forward.

We can therefore broaden our understanding of self-care and resilience beyond the individual level and appreciate that the team context will either facilitate self-care and boost resilience or stand as an obstacle to self-care and undermine resilience (for example, by undermining confidence and/or increasing anxiety).

The next step is to seek to understand the role of the team as part of the even wider context of the organisation itself. Teams will generally have a subculture of their own, but, by and large, they will be strongly influenced by the culture of the organisation. Cultures are simply sets of habits, unwritten rules and taken-for-granted assumptions, but they are extremely powerful because they influence us without our knowing it most of the time – we become 'embedded in the culture' and become socialised into it very quickly.

Just as the team context can make or break, so too can the organisational culture. Cultures give powerful messages that we are oblivious to most of the time, but they nonetheless affect us quite strongly. Such messages will include:

- 'We are here to support you' or 'We expect you to press on with minimal support'.
- 'We value you and appreciate the contribution you make' or 'We take you for granted'.
- 'We strive to make you feel safe and will seek to protect you if anything goes wrong' or 'We will look for someone to blame if something goes wrong'.

In terms of health and well-being, these add up to a message of either: 'We are genuinely committed to promoting your health and well-being as resourceful humans in a spirit of partnership, empowerment and mutual benefit' or 'We make tokenistic noises about health and well-being to avoid criticism, while seeking to exploit you to the full'.

Such 'culture messages' need to be taken quite seriously, as they will have a profound and far-reaching impact on morale. High morale will give staff under pressure a significant boost and offer the basis of a virtuous circle – the higher morale is, the more productive employees will be; the more productive and engaged they are, the higher their morale will be. By contrast, low morale will sap energy and leave people feeling drained and struggling to cope with their pressures, thereby triggering yet another vicious circle.

This brings us back to the topic of leadership and the role of leaders in shaping a positive culture – that is, a culture with high morale where employees feel supported, valued and safe. In terms of self-care and resilience, therefore, we can now see that much depends on leadership. And, of course, while some people are paid as managers to take an active role in shaping a positive culture, everyone has some degree of responsibility in terms of the part they play in either sustaining or transforming a culture – cultures only exist because each day members of that culture contribute to reinforcing it. Cultures do not have a life of their own; they exist through the actions and attitudes of their members (all members, not just those paid to occupy formal leadership roles).

The third and final step in terms of the well-being interventions continuum is to understand the organisation in the context of the wider society and the social structures, processes, institutions, discourses, expectations and relations that contribute so much to shaping what we generally refer to as the 'world of work'.

As we noted earlier, the world of work has been changing in significant ways for quite some time and continues to do so. One driving factor in this regard has been the predominance of neoliberal thinking. The neoliberal emphasis on the need to give free rein to 'market forces' and the minimisation of the role of the state and public services has contributed to considerably increased inequality combined with additional pressures on public servants, not least social workers.

What we have seen at this societal level, therefore, has been what I referred to earlier as a 'double whammy' for social workers in terms of pressure and stress and their health and well-being. Austerity-driven cuts in public services have led to increased demand (through increased poverty and social problems (Thompson, 2017)) accompanied by decreased supply. The unrelenting pressures have acted as both a source of increased health and well-being challenges and an even greater need to take employee wellness seriously and make substantial investments in well-being interventions across the board.

In Wales, we have had the 'cushion' of a Senedd that has sought to move away from the deeply neoliberal approach to social welfare adopted in England, although Evans et al (2021) are critical of what they see as the persistence of neoliberalism within 'the Welsh way'. The constitutional subservience of the Senedd to the UK Government also makes the full rejection of neoliberalism impossible.

Conclusion

Bevan and Cooper (2022: 5) make the point that 'promoting well-being at work … is an idea whose time has come'. This is a promising position to be in, given the deterioration over many years of working conditions and the increase in terms of workload expectations. However, there is a danger that approaches that fail to go beyond the level of the individual will not only have very limited effectiveness, but will also run the very significant risk of making a bad situation worse by alienating employees who feel they are being given responsibility for problems that have their roots in the much wider macro-level context, even to the extent of being inappropriately blamed for structural, cultural and systemic problems.

The answer is not to shift the blame to the organisation, as that is based on too superficial an understanding of the complex multidimensional dynamics that are shaping the modern workplace in general and social work in particular. Once again, Costello's insights are valuable: 'Organisations are not wholly responsible for the stress we experience at work. It is too simplistic to attach blame to either the individual or a faceless monolith. Instead, stress has to be understood in terms of a multi-layered physiological, social and political phenomenon' (2020: 8).

This reflects what I mean by a holistic approach. If we want to develop an adequate understanding of employee wellness, then we need to look at the bigger picture to incorporate all four elements of the well-being interventions continuum: the individual, the team, the organisation and society. Self-help and resilience have an important part to play, but they need to be understood as part of the wider context. Without this holistic perspective, there is a danger that an atomistic focus on self-help and resilience will serve to pathologise the individual.

Social work has an important role to play in developing and sustaining a more humane and inclusive Wales in keeping with our national traditions of community support and progressive politics. We need to make sure that a failure to engage with the complexities of health and well-being in the workplace does not undermine social work's effectiveness or blunt its capacity to contribute to social justice and well-being.

Messages for practice

- Stress, self-care and resilience need to be understood holistically in order to avoid 'victim blaming'.
- Contributing to positive teamwork can be of significant benefit in terms of promoting health and well-being.
- Developing awareness of organisational culture and seeking to influence it in a positive direction can help to create an atmosphere conducive to employee wellness as a basis for safe and effective practice.

Further resources
1. Costello, J. (2020) *Workplace Wellbeing: A Relational Approach*, London: Routledge.
2. Thompson, N. (2019) *The Managing Stress Practice Manual*, Wrexham: Avenue Media Solutions.
3. Thompson, N. and McGowan, J. (2020) *How to Survive in Social Work*, Wrexham: Avenue Media Solutions.

References

Bevan, S. and Cooper, C.L. (2022) *The Healthy Workforce: Enhancing Wellbeing and Productivity in the Workers of the Future*, Bingley: Emerald Publishing.

Bloom, D.T. (2021) *Employee Empowerment: The Prime Component of Sustainable Change Management*, New York: Routledge.

Cheese, P. (2021) *The New World of Work: Shaping a Future that Helps People, Organizations and Our Societies to Survive*, London: Kogan Page.

Costello, J. (2020) *Workplace Wellbeing: A Relational Approach*, London: Routledge.

Evans, D., Smith, K. and Williams, H. (eds) (2021) *The Welsh Way: Essays on Neoliberalism and Devolution*, Cardigan: Parthian.

Gwilym, H. and Williams, C. (eds) (2021) *Social Policy for Welfare Practice in Wales* (3rd edn), Birmingham: BASW.

Hammer, M. and Champy, J. (1993) *Reengineering the Corporation: A Manifesto for Business Revolution*, New York: Harper Business.

Hari, J. (2022) *Stolen Focus: Why You Can't Pay Attention*, London: Bloomsbury.

Huq, R.A. (2015) *The Psychology of Employee Empowerment: Concepts, Critical Themes and Frameworks for Intervention*, Farnham: Gower.

Jaffe, S. (2021) *Work Won't Love You Back: How Devotion to Jobs Keeps Us Exploited, Exhausted and Alone*, London: Hurst & Co.

Miller, R., Williams, P. and O'Neill, M. (2018) *The Healthy Workplace Nudge*, Hoboken, NJ: Wiley.

Price, A. (2020) 'Wales, colonised and coloniser: a reflection'. Opinion piece, Nation Cymru. https://nation.cymru/opinion/wales-colonised-and-coloniser-a-reflection/

Taylor, M. (2017) *Good Work: The Taylor Review of Modern Working Practices*, London: Department for Business, Energy and Industrial Strategy.

Thompson, N. (2017) *Social Problems and Social Justice*, London: Bloomsbury.

Thompson, N. (2019a) *The Managing Stress Practice Manual*, Wrexham: Avenue Media Solutions.

Thompson, N. (2019b) *Mental Health and Well-being: Alternatives to the Medical Model*, New York: Routledge.

Thompson, N. and Cox, G.R. (eds) (2020) *Promoting Resilience: Responding to Adversity, Vulnerability and Loss*, New York: Routledge.

Thompson, N. and McGowan, J. (2020) *How to Survive in Social Work*, Wrexham: Avenue Media Solutions.

Thompson, S. and Thompson, N. (2023) *The Critically Reflective Practitioner* (3rd edn), London: Bloomsbury.

Van Veldhoven, M. and Peccei, R. (eds) (2015) *Well-being and Performance at Work: The Role of Context*, London: Psychology Press.

Webster, H. (2021) 'A local focus', *RSA Journal*, 3: 25–29.

16

Social work with transgender children and their families

Naomi Parry and Ceryl Teleri Davies

Chapter objectives

- To identify and explore the nature of social work with transgender children and families within a Welsh context.

- To explore the link between the response to transgender children and their families and Welsh social work practice.

- To advance knowledge to inform the development of social work practice.

Introduction

The understanding of the needs of the transgender community in Wales and beyond remains unclear (Welsh Government, 2021). The commonly used term trans, derives from the word transgender, which is the umbrella term describing individuals whose gender 'is not the same as or does not sit comfortably with the sex they were assigned at birth' (Stonewall, 2019). Defining the key terms of sex and gender can be challenging and social work use of them should consider a range of cultural and social dynamics.

The UK Government definition of *sex* focuses on 'referring to the biological aspects of an individual as determined by their anatomy' (Office for National Statistics, 2019). The sex of an individual is legally assigned onto certification at birth and is dependent on biological differences and expectations which are then categorised into one of two groups, male or female (Lips, 2020). The two groups are perceived as binary opposites and qualities assigned based on the category in which they are classified, resulting in sex stereotypes which are powerful in influencing and interpreting behaviour (Lips, 2020). The concept of *gender* is defined as 'a social construction relating to behaviours and attributes based on labels of masculinity and femininity' (Office for National Statistics, 2019). Although the gender may have emerged from the binary sex categories, it is experienced as a fluid concept that can change in line with societal expectations and social norms. Therefore, gender as opposed to sex is a more marked social construct.

As a result, defining the term trans is complex due to the increasing number of expressions that have been socially developed (Cruz, 2014). Conceptualising our definition(s) of transgender should be adaptable to changes in our social construction of 'everyday' life, including the fluidity of gendered identities. Consequently trans discourse from a wider 'societal liberalisation' develops as trans issues are evolving, and it can be expected that defintions, language and terminology will continue to evolve (Pearce et al, 2019). For the purpose of this chapter, the trans(gender) definition offered by Hines and Sanger (2010: 10) will be adopted: 'a range of gender experiences, subjectivities and presentations that fall across, between or beyond stable categories of "man" and "woman".' This defintion encompasses the concept of gender as a spectrum focused on individual subjectivity and expression. Adopting a 'spectrum of terminologies' that sit under the umbrella term 'trans' is inclusive of all individuals with gendered identity differences (Office for National Statistics, 2022a). As Social Care Wales (2017) refer to those in receipt of care and support as 'individuals', the term 'trans individuals' and 'trans children' will be the terminology used.

Although the Office for National Statistics adopts a 'spectrum of terminologies', the complexities of trans classification and data gathering suggest that limited specific prevalence data are gathered in the UK (Office for National Statistics, 2022b). The Government Equalities Office (2018) estimated that there are between 200,000 and 500,000 trans individuals in the UK. The variation in this figure is significant, reflecting the issues and complexity in defining and thus measuring the trans population across the UK. This absence of data also prevents measurement of levels of discrimination and inequality experienced by the UK trans community and, by consequence, the level of need and discrimination experienced. This results in the maintenance of this complex issue as a 'hidden' and stigmatised social problem.

The origins of this chapter resided within a MA dissertation project that identified this gap in data, and additional limited amounts of literature and social work practice in relation to the needs of trans individuals in Wales. This study reinforced the high level of stigma and shame experienced by the trans community (Parry, 2020). It further analysed the available identified literature using Goffman's conceptual framework as the analytical lens. This chapter continues to adopt this lens. Goffman's (1959) perception of stigma and 'presentation of self', is relevant to the topic of trans and gendered identity to provide theorisation and focus to the discussion (Deegan, 2014). Goffman describes individuals as performers, with society as the audience. The communication with the audience is the performance, with the expression of 'self' often fluid to the desires of the audience. This presentation of 'self' is the 'front stage' performance with the 'backstage' or often 'hidden' identity representing the performers' true identity. It must be emphasised here that there is no intention to imply gender expression is a performance in literal terms. The aim is to draw on Goffman's concept: that expression of self can be concealed as well as displayed and that the reaction of society to an individual's expression can influence the individual's freedom to express their true self or identity. With regard to trans matters, the stigma a trans individual experiences from society, can impact how comfortable they are to express their gendered identity and, thus, can lead to the negative consequences of oppression (White-Hughto et al, 2015).

Social work practice with trans children and their families

There has been an increase in public awareness and visibility of the trans community and gender identity issues in recent years (Mallon, 2018; Office for National Statistics, 2022a). High-profile celebrities in the media, such as Olympic athlete and reality TV celebrity Caitlyn Jenner, Olympic athlete Chris Mosier and also the appearance of trans actors and characters in soaps have contributed to this increased visibility in mainstream media (Austin, 2017; Beumont, 2021; Office for National Statistics, 2022a). This growth in public awareness has increased the call for trans-informed social work practice (Hudson-Sharp, 2018a). The demand for more attuned social work practice is expected to gather further momentum (Austin, 2017) alongside the inequality and discrimination faced by trans individuals and higher rates in mental health and well-being needs (Hudson-Sharp, 2018b).

In 2015, the rates of children and young people being referred to the Gender Identity Development Service (GIDS) with mental health and well-being needs was 1,408 across the UK and 42 in Wales. By 2020 the figure across the UK had risen to 2,728 and 138 in Wales (NHS, 2022a), possibly reflecting the increasing visibility of the trans community. Gendered identity issues for children is an emotive topic (Gregor et al, 2015), with increased public awareness bringing both benefits and limitations to the trans community. A perceived benefit is the support offered to the trans community to become increasingly accepted (Dee, 2010). However, with increased awareness come prejudice, discrimination, negative attitudes and stigma, particularly toward families that support a child's transition (Capous-Desyllas and Barron, 2017).

To inform effective practice and improve outcomes, social workers supporting trans children and their families need robust and sensitive awareness of this complex topic (Capous-Desyllas and Barron, 2017; Mallon, 2018). Awareness and knowledge of gender identity issues enable social workers to identify where support is needed with development in a range of areas, including family and community life, self-image, self-esteem and gender identity (Jowitt and O'Laughlin, 2005). To achieve positive self-image and self-esteem, a sense of secure identity, belonging and acceptance by family, peers and wider society, is important for the well-being and development of children (Jowitt and O'Laughlin, 2005). For children who are care experienced or in need of care and support, their sense of self and identity may require particular attention due to disruptions they may have experienced (Fahlberg, 2004). In response to some of these issues, the Welsh Government (2021) has developed an Action Plan, which, while it highlights good practice in several key areas (for example, education and health outcomes), does not contain any direct consideration of what is required to improve social outcomes or social work support to advance LGBTQ+ equality.

The Welsh way

The Welsh Government (2021) has emphasised the importance for social work practice to be aware of the Welsh LGBTQ+ Action Plan. This plan provides action for Welsh Government and agencies to follow in tackling inequality and improving the experiences of LGBTQ+ individuals in Wales. The Action Plan emphasises the urgent need to understand and mitigate disproportionalities experienced. It suggests this can be done by training professionals to adequately support LGBTQ+ young people in tackling discrimination, alongside Social Care Wales in reviewing the Codes of Practice and statutory guidance provided by the Social Services and Well-being (Wales) Act 2014. The Welsh way also includes action to target funding into research in this area of need (Welsh Government, 2021).

Family attitudes and support

Families clearly play a significant role in the lives of children. As such, familial support and attitudes toward gendered identity development of children is a key issue in healthy development. There is a correlation between family support and the mental well-being of trans children (Schlehofer et al, 2022). This includes the support received by the family and the support the family is able to provide the child (Capous-Desyllas and Baron, 2017; Davy and Cordoba, 2019). Active family support toward trans children is more common than suggested by some stereotypes (Keisling et al, 2011). It should, however, be noted that families can also experience loss and grief when a child transitions or experiences changes in their gender identity (Coolhart et al, 2018). They may also encounter the discrimination experienced by a trans child (Catalpa and McGuire, 2018). Some parents and carers of trans children often feel a need to advocate, defend and promote their child's decisions and needs, including educating professionals in various settings such as social services, education and health. Due to the worry and anxiety surrounding the stigma and discrimination their child may face, parents often feel the need to build their child's resilience and prepare them for the anticipated bullying and rejection, as well as support them to deal with the emotional consequences of this (Capous-Desyllas and Baron, 2017; Davy and Cordoba, 2019).

Other parents often share feelings of confusion when considering their child's emerging gender identity. Parents report feeling confused as to whether or not what their child is experiencing is a gender identity issue and how to balance their child's need to express and explore their gender identity, along with their own fears and anxieties around their child being exposed to and vulnerable to the potential negative reactions of society (Vanderburgh, 2008; Gregor et al, 2015). Parents have reported feeling confused regarding their own feelings of grief and loss when supporting children who are exploring gender identity and gender fluidity (Gregor et al, 2015).

The issue of gender expression and the negative consequences of supressing this when discussing 'coming out' as trans are highlighted in the literature. This, to a degree, echoes parental concerns around understanding their child's gender expression. Schlehofer et al (2022: 40) found that the method of *disclosure or coming out* for trans children and their parents fell into two main categories. First, the category of 'explicit direct disclosure' where parents communicate the information in written form through message, email or letter, thus sharing the information in a controlled and organised way. The second method is described as 'casual unfolding disclosure', meaning the family became aware naturally as the gender identity developed. Other factors that were also considered in disclosing a trans child's gender are level of conservativeness, religion, age, geographical and emotional distance (Schlehofer et al, 2022). Olson et al (2015) provide valuable insight into the impact of issues around 'coming out', which identified that, on average, participants were aware of gender incongruence by age eight, however, they did not come out to their families until age 17, suggesting that there are significant barriers to children feeling able to disclose their gender identity.

It is also important to expand the discussion, from parents to the significance of support of any extended family. For a trans child, disclosing their gender differences to extended family can be extremely difficult. Schlehofer et al (2022) describe extended family members and their immediate and ongoing responses to a child's chosen gender identity as 'stressors' or 'supporters'. Parents engage in a variety of ways to either utilise the welcoming of the 'supporters' or mitigate the difficulties of the 'stressors'. For example, one young person within Schlehofer et al's (2022) research explained how an uncle, who is part of the gay community, felt he could offer support due to his own experiences. He admitted he did not understand it, but wanted to learn with them on their journey and support the family, and their parents were keen to utilise this. Some parents found that they distanced themselves from family members who had negative responses and attitudes toward the child's gender incongruence, to protect the child from being exposed to it.

Some families appear to adapt more easily than others to a child's gender differences and fluidity. Vanderburgh (2008) provides a list of practical approaches that assist parents to support their trans child, for example: information about trans identities of various kinds, information on appropriate support structures, information about support groups and organisations and information about the physical realities of transition. This support list provides a really useful starting point for social work practitioners, in working with parents and families of transgender children.

Mental and emotional well-being

Gender dysphoria is described by the NHS (2022b) as a 'sense of unease an individual experiences due to a mismatch between their biological sex and gender identity' that can lead to 'depression, anxiety and have a harmful impact on daily life'. GIDS is a specialist service for children and young people with gender identity-related issues. They have reported increasing numbers of referrals being made to their clinics in recent years, with consequential significant waiting times from referral to initial appointment (GIDS, 2022).

Access to such specialist support and information around gender dysphoria, particularly for children in Wales, can be a challenge. In order to be diagnosed with gender dysphoria, a child must be referred to the GIDS. There is currently no GIDS provision for children and young people within Wales. To access gender identity support, Welsh children are required to apply for funding to access a Tavistock Clinic in London or Leeds (NHS, 2019b). This means that access to support protected by Welsh language legislation and guidance such as 'The Active Offer' which ensures they are able to discuss such sensitive and emotive issues in the language of their choice (Welsh Government, 2016) is not available. A lack of a Welsh service also affects broader issues such as a sense of 'belonging' to the community as a whole, potential cost implications of travelling to clinics and the lack of preventative services.

Olson et al (2015) identified high levels of mental health and gender dysphoria concerns among the characteristics of transgender children being supported by a gender clinic. Thirty-five per cent of individuals reported symptoms of depression, half reported having experienced suicidal ideation and a third of participants had made at least one suicide attempt. Olson et al (2015) concluded that participants are more prone to exhibiting risk and increased vulnerability of harm. These issues are vital considerations for social work practitioners working with trans children and their families.

This is echoed in a study into the impact of minority stressors such as discrimination, prejudice and anti-trans attitudes by Tebbe and Maradi (2016), who found that rates of poor emotional well-being were high, including 68.5 per cent meeting the threshold for clinical depression, 71.9 per cent who had thought of suicide in their lifetime and 28.1 per cent who had attempted suicide. Tebbe and Maradi (2016) highlighted that discrimination and oppression on a sociocultural level acts as a stressor which contributes to depression and suicide risk among the trans community, concluding that an increase in acceptance of trans individuals within society and developing wider social networks become ways of reducing these risk factors. Olson et al (2015) also noted this connection between the correlations of high mental health concerns and discrimination.

The response to these experiences, including the suppressing of a profound element of the core self, is often the development of a range of coping mechanisms, including substance use and self-harm (Olson et al, 2015). Understanding these mechanisms and their potential risks is an important consideration for social workers when working with trans children (Budge et al, 2018). Budge et al (2018) introduced a model outlining some of the coping mechanisms adapted by trans children. These included emotional relief, social support, personal solace, negotiating gender, avoidance and activity. Developing an understanding of the coping strategies, both positive and negative, can also help to better understand protective factors and resilience. It is vital for social work practitioners to be aware of the various coping strategies adopted by transgender children, as it is possible for behaviours such as aggressive outbursts, self-isolation, avoiding communication and excessive crying to be overlooked or misinterpreted by caregivers and professionals.

Whyatt-Sames (2017) explored the gender identity and mental well-being with care experienced children. Some of the issues identified which were unique to care experienced children were meeting the biological family following changes in appearance, the importance of life journey work, along with the foster carers' anxiety around causing distress by showing the child photographs pre-transition. Whyatt-Sames' (2017) valuable insights concluded by offering a gender affirmative approach model. This usefully highlights:

• Gender presentations are diverse across cultures, requiring cultural sensitivity.
• Gender identity involves interweaving of biology, development, socialisation and culture, all of which have a bearing on gender health.
• Gender is fluid.
• Pathology does not stem from within the child, but from cultural reactions such as transphobia, homophobia and sexism.

This affirmative approach aligns to the key principles of the Social Services and Well-being (Wales) Act 2014, with the aim of protecting the well-being of children and their families, listening to the voices of children, and coproducing care and support plans with families in a multi-agency manner.

Messages for practice

• Education and awareness improvements are required on various levels within social work practice, from an understanding of the language and terminology to the more specific issues related to social work practice.
• There is a need to consider explicit, specific and focused content on trans awareness as part of social work education.
• Social workers should take practical measures to ensure trans children and their families are being supported by an inclusive, anti-discriminatory and anti-oppressive service. This should include:
  ◦ an affirmative practice approach in supporting trans children and their families;
  ◦ a focus on the link between stigma, discrimination and experiences of oppression;

- a focus on making the connection between mental health and the challenges faced by trans children and their families;
- an approach focused on giving time and space to listen without judgement to the voices of children and their families;
- a focus on a whole family and strengths-based approach;
- a focus on multidisciplinary working;
- raising awareness, for example, posters and leaflets with information for trans children and their parents on display in public areas, including the use of gender-sensitive paperwork.

Conclusion

There is a sparsity of evidence, research and data with regard to trans issues, trans children and their families, including within Wales. This deprives the profession of a depth of information to provide an accurate picture of the nature of need across Wales. Despite this, it is clear that stigma and shame continue to restrict transgender children in Wales from expressing their gender identity. Concealing this aspect of their identity is having a negative impact on their well-being. The adoption of an approach by Welsh social workers, which is accepting, supportive, encouraging and strengths-based, can help improve this situation.

Policy and research have begun to move in a more positive direction, with an increased focus on raising awareness on the nature and impact of this issue. This includes some of the messages for social work practice highlighted in this chapter. To enable social work practitioners to better deliver practice with such an increased awareness and understanding, improved specific input into social work education and training is required. Robust awareness of transgender considerations should be integrated through all social work anti-discriminatory practice. The adoption of such affirmative social work practice is aligned with core social work values, particularly those focused on integrity, dignity and promoting social justice.

Further resources
1. Lips, H. (2020) *Sex and Gender: An Introduction* (7th edn), Illinois: Waveland Press.
2. Hudson-Sharp, N. (2018) *Transgender Awareness in Child and Family Social Work Education: Research Report.* Department for Education, Social Sciences. https://www.niesr.ac.uk/wp-content/uploads/2021/10/Transgender_awareness_in_child_and_family_social_work_education.pdf
3. Welsh Government (2021) *LGBTQ+ Action Plan for Wales* [online]. https://www.gov.wales/sites/default/files/consultations/2021-07/lgbtq%2B-action-plan.pdf

References
Austin, A. (2017) 'Transgender and gender diverse children: considerations for affirmative social work practice', *Child Adolescent Social Work Journal*, 35: 73–84.

Beumont, T. (2021) 'Sam Smith excluded from gendered categories at 2021 Brit awards'. *The Guardian* [online]. https://www.theguardian.com/music/2021/mar/12/sam-smith-gender-2021-brit-awards

Budge, S.L., Conniff, J., Belcourt, W.S., Parks, R.L., Pantalone, D. and Katz-Wise, S.L. (2018) 'A grounded theory study of the development of trans youths' awareness of coping with gender identity', *Journal of Child and Family Studies*, 27: 3048–3061.

Capous-Desyllas, M. and Barron, C. (2017) 'Transgressing the gendered norms in childhood: understanding transgender children and their families', *Journal of LGBT Family Studies*, 13(5): 407–438.

Catalpa, J. and McGuire, J. (2018) 'Family boundary ambiguity among transgender youth', *Family Relations*, 67(6): 88–103.

Coolhart, D., Ritenour, K. and Grodzinski, A. (2018) 'Experiences of ambiguous loss for parents of transgender male youth: a phenomenological exploration', *Contemporary Family Therapy*, 40(28): 28–41.

Cruz, T. (2014) 'Assessing access to care for transgender and gender nonconforming people: a consideration of diversity in combating discrimination', *Social Science and Medicine*, 110: 65–73.

Davy, Z. and Cordoba, S. (2019) 'School cultures and trans and gender-diverse children: parents' perspectives', *Journal of GLBT Family Studies*, 16(4): 349–367.

Dee, H. (2010) *The Red in the Rainbow: Sexuality and Sexism and LGBT Liberation*, London: Bookmarks Publications.

Deegan, M.J. (2014) 'Goffman on gender, sexism, and feminism: a summary of notes on a conversation with Erving Goffman and my reflections then and now', *Symbolic Interaction*, 37(1): 71–86.

Fahlberg, V. (2004) *A Journey through Placement*, London: BAAF.

Gender Identity Development Service (GIDS) (2022) *How Long is the Wait for a First Appointment at GIDS?* https://gic.nhs.uk/appointments/waiting-times/

Goffman, E. (1959) *The Presentation of Self in Everyday Life*, New York: Anchor Books.

Government Equalities Office (2018) *Trans People in the UK* [online]. https://assets.publishing.service.gov.uk/government/uploads/system/uploads/attachment_data/file/721642/GEO-LGBT-factsheet.pdf

Gregor, C., Hingley-Jones, H. and Davidson, S. (2015) 'Understanding the experience of parents of pre-pubescent children with gender identity issues', *Child and Adolescent Social Work Journal*, 32(3): 237–246.

Hines, S. and Sanger, T. (2010) *Transgender Identities (Open Access): Towards a Social Analysis of Gender Diversity*, Florence: Routledge.

Hudson-Sharp, N. (2018a) 'Promoting transgender equality: social workers are up for the challenge but can't do it alone'. Blog. https://www.niesr.ac.uk/blog/promoting-transgender-equality-social-workers-are-up-for-the-challenge-but-cant-do-it-alone

Hudson-Sharp, N. (2018b) *Transgender Awareness in Child and Family Social Work Education: Research Report*. Department for Education, Social Sciences. https://www.niesr.ac.uk/wp-content/uploads/2021/10/Transgender_awareness_in_child_and_family_social_work_education.pdf

Jowitt, M. and O'Loughlin, S. (2005) *Social Work with Children and Families*, Exeter: Learning Matters.

Keisling, M. (2011) *Injustice at Every Turn: A Report of the National Transgender Discrimination Survey*, Washington, DC: National Centre.

Lips, H. (2020) *Sex and Gender: An Introduction* (7th edn), Illinois: Waveland Press.

Mallon, G. (2018) *Social Work Practice with Lesbian, Gay, Bisexual and Transgender People* (3rd edn), London: Routledge.

NHS (2019a) *Gender Identity Clinic*. https://gic.nhs.uk/

NHS (2019b). *Tavistock and Portman: Gender Identity Development Service Statistics*. https://tavistockandportman.nhs.uk/documents/408/gids-service-statistics.pdf

NHS (2022a) *Tavistock and Portman: Gender Identity Development Service Referrals in 2019–20 Same as 2018–19*. https://tavistockandportman.nhs.uk/about-us/news/stories/gender-identity-development-service-referrals-2019-20-same-2018-19/

NHS (2022b). *Gender Dysphoria: An Overview*. https://www.nhs.uk/conditions/gender-dysphoria/

Office for National Statistics (2009) *Trans Data Position Paper*. https://www.ons.gov.uk/file?uri=/methodology/classificationsandstandards/measuringequality/genderidentity/transdatapositionpaperfinaltcm77180898.pdf

Office for National Statistics (2019) *What Is the Difference between Sex and Gender?* [online]. https://www.ons.gov.uk

Office for National Statistics (2022a) *Gender Identity Update: An update to our 2009 Trans Data Position Paper, detailing changes and progress around the topic of gender identity*. https://www.ons.gov.uk/methodology/classificationsandstandards/measuringequality/genderidentity/genderidentityupdate

Office for National Statistics (2022b) *Transgender Statistics*. Transgender population figures – Office for National Statistics. www.ons.gov.uk

Olson, J., Schrager, S.M., Belzer, M., Simons, L.K. and Clark, L.F. (2015) 'Baseline physiologic and psychosocial characteristics of transgender youth seeking care for gender dysphoria', *Journal of Adolescent Health*, 57: 374–380.

Parry, N. (2020) 'How can social workers respond to the needs of transgender children and their families?' [Unpublished MA Dissertation], Bangor University.

Pearce, R., Steinberg, D.L. and Moon, I. (2019) 'Introduction: the emergence of "trans"', *Sexualities*, 22(1–2): 3–12.

Schlehofer, M., Cortez Regan, M. and Harbaugh, J. (2022) '"If extended family can't deal …": disclosing trans and gender non-conforming children's identity', *Child & Adolescent Social Work Journal*, 39(1): 29–43.

Social Care Wales (2017) *Code of Professional Practice for Social Care* [online]. https://socialcare.wales/cms-assets/documents/Code-of-Professional-Practice-for-Social-Care-web-version.pdf

Social Care Wales (2020) *Codes of Practice and Guidance*. https://socialcare.wales/dealing-with-concerns/codes-of-practice-and-guidance

Stonewall (2019) *Glossary of Terms*. https://www.stonewall.org.uk/help-advice/glossary-terms

Tebbe, E.A. and Moradi, B. (2016) 'Suicide risk in trans populations: an application of minority stress theory', *Journal of Counselling Psychology*, 63(5): 520–533.

Vandeburgh, R. (2008) 'Appropriate therapeutic care for families with pre-pubescent transgender/gender-dissonant children', *Journal of Child and Adolescent Social Work*, 26: 135–154.

Welsh Government (2016) *More Than Just Words: Delivering the 'Active Offer' Information Pack – Health*. https://www.gov.wales/more-just-words-welsh-language-plan-health-and-social-care.

Welsh Government (2021) *LGBTQ+ Action Plan for Wales*. https://www.gov.wales/sites/default/files/consultations/2021-07/lgbtq%2B-action-plan.pdf

White-Hughto, J., Reisner, S. and Pachankis, J.E. (2015) 'Transgender stigma and health: a critical review of stigma determinants, mechanisms, and interventions', *Social Science and Medicine*, 147: 222–231.

Whyatt-Sames, J. (2017) 'Being brave: negotiating the path of social transition with a transgender child in foster care', *Journal of LGBT Family Studies*, 13(4): 309–332.

17

Young intimate relationships: messages from research for practice

Ceryl Teleri Davies

Chapter objectives

- To identify and explore the impact of social norms on the nature of young people's intimate relationships.

- To understand the Welsh experience in relation to abuse and young people's intimate relationships.

- To highlight the role of social work in supporting young people to address abuse in young intimate relationships.

Introduction

Though our understanding of abuse in young intimate relationships has grown over the years, there has been limited opportunity for the voices of young women (older children 15–18 or young adults 18–24) to explain how they negotiate issues of identity and power within their intimate relationships. The ongoing debates on related matters, such as the age of sexual consent, the non-consensual circulation of sexualised images, the exploitation of young women and the #MeToo movement present the ideal context to explore the issue.

Young women are particularly impacted by specific forms of gender-based violence (GBV), which have a negative impact on their well-being across the life cycle. In 2021, the All-Party Parliamentary Group for United Nations Women, established to drive gender equality and policy changes to address women's safety, produced a report on sexual harassment. Their findings revealed that 86 per cent of women aged 18–24 in the United Kingdom (UK) had been sexually harassed in public spaces, with only 3 per cent of women stating that they did not recall ever having experienced sexually harassing behaviour. Additionally, one in five UK young women report that they had experienced abuse and harassment online (Ipsos MORI, 2017). Young women from minority ethnic backgrounds are more likely to suffer sexual harassment at school (Girlguiding, 2021) and university (Ending Violence Against Women and Girls, 2021). The UK charity Co-ordinated Action Against Domestic Abuse (2013) has identified that there is elevated normalisation of abuse

203

and controlling behaviour among young people. European research on this form of abuse has grown during recent years, with the degree of harm clearly evidenced, as is this gendered nature of this harm (Barter et al, 2009; Sundaram, 2014).

While there is an emerging body of research covering diverse aspects of the dynamics of such relationships, particular categories of young people, such as pregnant young women, young mothers, young women in secure settings and disabled young women, are yet to receive detailed research attention. This chapter examines one such study, that addressed by exploring how young Welsh women aged 15–18 discuss their attitudes toward, and experiences of, intimate relationships (Davies, 2019). The research was conducted during a period when the focus and importance of GBV was increasing in Wales, as a result of the implementation of the Violence against Women, Domestic Abuse and Sexual Violence (Wales) Act 2015, and where there was hope of further change on the horizon with the then pending Domestic Abuse Act (2021).

Terminology

Defining key terms, such as GBV and domestic abuse, can be a challenge. For young people, intimate relationships, 'going out', relationship exclusivity, 'courtship' or 'dating' morph into different forms, depending on several factors such as local norms, age group and peers. The majority of young people begin initiating intimate relationships during early adolescence, between the ages of 10 and 13 (Stonard et al, 2017; Davies, 2019). Young intimate relationships differ from adult intimate relationships, specifically with regard to the roles played by expectations, degree of intimacy, duration and everyday routines (Hickman et al, 2004; Davies, 2019). While a range of intersectional factors influence the presence of abuse within intimate relationships, the primary focus of this chapter is the influence of gendered social norms.

A broad range of terminology is used to conceptualise forms of GBV. These include domestic violence and/or domestic abuse, intimate partner violence and/or abuse and violence against women and girls. Domestic abuse is when a person over the age of 16 years old inflicts abuse (physical, sexual, controlling, coercive, emotional, psychological or economic abuse) on another person over the age of 16 years old, when the individuals are personally connected (intimate relationship or relatives) (Domestic Abuse Act, 2021). The UN Declaration on the Elimination of Violence against Women (1994) defines violence against women as a broad range of abuse, including coercion. GBV is a social problem embedded across societies. GBV takes a range of behaviours across a spectrum of harm based on perceived sex, gender, sexual orientation and/or gender identity (Council of Europe, 2022). It is rooted in the inequity of power based on gender, and is supported by institutional structural power, laws and policies dictated and shaped by gendered social norms. GBV continues due to the acceptance of social norms, and the unequal societal power structures favouring masculinity. Of course, not all men are abusive, but the power men acquire throughout societal settings is evident as part of their status. As a result, this power and control accorded to men ensures that GBV is both supported and perpetuated.

Messages for practice

- It must be remembered that the concept of 'dating', 'going out', 'seeing someone', being in an intimate relationship and a sense of courtship differs across cultures, lifestyles and places.
- Social workers need to consider the dynamics of both online and offline intimate relationships, in particular when evaluating the similarities and differences between both forms of abuse.
- How we define intimate relationships, being a 'young person' and indeed abuse can also differ across spaces and cultures. The definitions adopted should consider cultural dynamics and the context and nature of abuse.

Social norms and the nature of young intimate relationships

Social norms are the informal and often unwritten rules that define and determine what society perceives as acceptable or appropriate standards of behaviour (Cislaghi and Heise, 2018). Existing research on young intimate relationships has neglected to draw upon the ways in which attitudes and gender norms shape the embodiment of gendered roles for young people. In order to understand the nature of young people's intimate relationships, it is necessary to understand the social and gendered context of their 'everyday' lives. How young women conceptualise gender and its subsequent impact on their attitudes toward GBV is key to understanding their consideration of what 'counts' as abuse. Analysing young women's experiences can assist us in understanding gendered 'scripts', the social stereotypes perpetuating these 'scripts' and the reinforcement of these 'scripts' by young people. The traditional role of young women within intimate relationships has been associated with passivity and respectability (Connell, 1987). The normative socialisation of young women enforces the idea of males as 'strong' and 'in control', and females as 'weak' and 'compliant', reinforcing gendered responsibility within relationships. Evaluating the social construction of gender gives us an understanding of social stereotypes and what is considered as the 'doing of gender' (West and Zimmerman, 1987).

The research

Research by Davies (2019) explored how young Welsh women, aged 15–18, discussed their attitudes toward, and experiences of, intimate relationships. It considered potential gaps between young women's expectations and their lived experiences. It involved young women drawn from seven schools and the Youth Justice Services in North Wales. Data were collected using questionnaires (n=220) and semi-structured interviews (n=25). All the names within this chapter are pseudonyms, as chosen by the young women.

Sexual intimacy

Despite a consensus across the views of participants that an intimate relationship equated to 'going out', there was no consensus on the point at which it developed from 'going out' into an intimate relationship. This was reflected in, first, the challenge of defining 'going out'; and second, the urgency to discuss their intimate relationships with reference to sexual intimacy, rather than in light of the progression of their relationship and the stages of 'going out'. That is, the importance of their intimate relationships was measured with reference to sexual intimacy, which was seen as a key component to the definition of the seriousness of a relationship. There was a general ambiguity as to what actually constituted sexual intimacy, with particular behaviours outside this definition (kissing, touching), while other actions were conceptualised as 'sex' (intercourse). The young women shared that the degree of intimacy, emotions and the regularity of sex factored in whether the sexual intimacy could be defined as part of an intimate relationship.

Intimate relationships were automatically assumed by the participants to be within the framework of heterosexuality. The formation of a 'couple' and a 'relationship' was based on its length, publicity and the social identity of both individuals as a 'couple'. Ultimately, the narratives revealed the young men as formulating the pace, boundaries and expectations of the relationship. As such, coercion also played a key role, with young women describing circumstances of overt and explicitly sexual coercion. Sexual pressure was expressed as intensifying with age, in particular for young men, with this pressure often excused and nominated as the factor influencing the male sexual priority within intimate relationships. Young men were described as having to 'live up' to the expectation that they would want to have sex, to want to have it all the time; with the possibility of leaving school as a virgin ridiculed by their peers. The desperation and pressure to have sex was normalised as the expected masculine role, while this perceived male sexual drive was not seen as having the potential to translate into manipulation, pressure or sexual coercion. The pressure on young men to perform was also visible, as there was a sense of the gendered and heteronormative expectation, as one young woman noted: "You're gay if you don't have an interest in sex" (Chloe).

The challenge of the 'ideal' relationship

There was a sense from the young women that attraction was measured by the ability to be in, and have, an intimate relationship; a measure of their heterosexual performance. The young women revealed the pressure to conform to the perceived ideal image of attractiveness, reinforced by their peers and the online community. There were examples of the young women adapting their appearance and personalities to attract a boyfriend and to maintain their intimate relationship. The young women described how they adopted Goffman's techniques of 'impression management' to stage and maintain their performance as this 'ideal girlfriend'. Goffman (1959) conceptualised 'impression management' as a desire to manipulate our presentation of self to others as part of our social interactions. For example, Chloe described how she wanted the "ideal relationship", which she described as "going out for meals together".

Some participants reflected a belief that they should feel 'lucky' to be in an intimate relationship, with a sense of loss and embarrassment if this aim had not been achieved. There was a general sense of 'success' when a young woman was 'selected' to undertake the 'girlfriend role' and that she should therefore settle for a boy willing to be part of a relationship. This reinforced the belief that young women valued relationships more than young men, as it is the role of young men to do the asking and for the young women to accept their offer. It can be argued that such a sense of gratefulness, as well as the impression of a relationship, in defining success can result in young women remaining in unhealthy relationships. In comparison, young men were described as having a sense of entitlement, which placed them in a position of power, as the young women generally felt fortunate when they committed to an intimate relationship. This perceived 'luck' was expanded further when there was a sense that their social position within their peer group was improved, resulting in party invitations and inclusion in the conversations about sex and relationships. The absence of an intimate relationship was conceptualised as a void, which resulted in a natural exclusion from the conversation and had a knock-on effect on their popularity and visibility. This was also seen as a measure of individual maturity and preparation for adulthood. Conversely, this increased participation often came at a price, as several narratives illustrated that increased attendance at parties or social events often led to arguments, jealousy and close surveillance by their boyfriends. The pressure to gain relationship experience and avoid exclusion from peer conversations was unavoidable, due to its overwhelming presence in all forms of online and offline spaces.

Social norms

When articulating their opinion, the foremost focus was on mutual trust and "no lying, I hate being lied to" (Bonnie), with all the respondents commenting on its importance as the foundation of a healthy relationship. There was also a sense of the need to "feel close and be there for each other" (Chloe) and the need to be able to rely on each other. This was aligned to the notion of the importance of honesty, being able to "be yourself" (Becky), feel comfortable with each other and have a general feeling of a "strong bond" (Aleysha), loving and being loved. Within the young women's accounts there was a focus on honesty and communicating effectively ("tell everything" (Lowri) to your partner), and a general need for respect. There was also a sense of the importance of attraction and gaining enjoyment and pleasure from intimate relationships, not only in a physical or sexual manner, but also in the sense of mutual belonging, partnership and the security of "being there for each other" (Chloe). Importance was also placed on being attractive to the opposite sex; in particular, having the perceived body image of what they thought men found attractive in women, for example, "big boobs, shapely bum and a slender waist" (Glesni). The wants and desires as part of sexual attraction and relationship desires were framed in a gendered manner. Young men were described as hyper-sexual, with their focus on the female body and looks. This was further perpetuated by the notion that young women were judged on their body image; in particular, whether they were fat, which drove their desire to "look better for their boyfriends" (Mali). However, young men were expected to conform to the body image of being strong and masculine ("It's a bit weird if a boy is shorter than me" (Glesni)), and that young men should not demonstrate their body insecurities.

The 'check and balance' on relationship status and progression was gendered. Primarily, the young women checked the status; specifically, if the relationship was established and monogamous, as this was a "typical girl thing" (Alyesha). Additionally, this was packaged in a manner which further drew on traditional gendered discourses by explicitly noting that boys and girls played a different role in intimate relationships, with young men wanting and needing the freedom to go out more. There was a 'mixed' response initially to the planning of activities within relationships, with a few explicit answers that their boyfriends led on the planning front as "he likes planning, so he decides" (Becky). On the surface it appeared that boys were more 'laid back', and therefore activities were negotiable; when unpicking further it became apparent that this negotiable space was limited by 'his mood'.

Mostly, the young women indicated that the progression of their relationship was largely controlled by their boyfriends. This behaviour was located within a framework of justification and naturalisation of the male role, rather than as controlling behaviour. Young women did not express any desire to take more of an active role in determining the progress of their intimate relationships. This was because seeming to be keen could have negative implications, such as rejection – "They won't want you" (Alyesha) – or "being used for sex" (Michelle). Young men's desire for an exclusive relationship, or any degree of commitment, was seen as ambivalent, to say the least. When a degree of commitment was offered, this often crossed the boundary to become controlling and oppressive.

Primarily the young women drew upon traditional dominant discourses of (hetero)sexuality by positioning themselves as focused on wanting commitment and love from intimate relationships, in particular the concept of becoming a couple and conforming to relationship expectations focused on romantic ideals, and the need to "feel special" (Collette) and "be together" (Julie). It also became apparent that their agency was limited through the dominance of these normative discourses, and the notion of their role as passive and secondary to their boyfriends'.

Healthy relationships

Education

Across the narratives there was a general lack of reflection on the discrepancy between their perception of a healthy relationship and their actual relationship experiences. The focus of preventative education for young people should be on recognising the impact of everyday forms of GBV as a continuum of naturalised harassment and abuse of women by men, rather than as a 'sledgehammer', or abuse perpetrated by a minority of dominant men (Stanko, 1985). Young people should be educated on understanding the impact of everyday harassment and abuse experienced by known perpetrators from their own intimate relationships, and therefore a focus should be on understanding young people's lived experiences of abuse within their own intimate relationships. Young women should be educated on the norms associated with our gendered roles; specifically, young men's power and entitlement to young women's bodies, their feelings and thoughts. The foundation of prevention education with young people should focus on normative gendered power dynamics and its impact on their experiences of the everyday routines of their intimate relationships, including the established scripts of the progression of their relationships, how they experience intimacy, coercion and abuse, and how these experiences differ as a result of their individual needs, well-being and personal profile; therefore, identifying the connections in the ways that young women experience abuse within their intimate relationships, while also identifying the impact of their individualised needs on their own subjective experiences.

The need to implement evidence-based domestic abuse/healthy relationship interventions aimed particularly at young people in the UK is now acknowledged. Evidence reflects that schools do not prioritise personal and social education in Wales and, as a result, the content and delivery of healthy relationships education has varied significantly across Wales (Estyn, 2017). Through the Sex and Relationships Education Expert Panel, the debate gathered new momentum in Wales following the publication of the report on the future of sex and relationship education in Wales in early 2018 (Renold and McGeeney, 2017). This report concluded that the current provision of sex and relationship education in Wales is inadequate, is too focused on the biological aspects of relationships and is not inclusive of a range of needs, young people's views or their everyday experiences (Renold and McGeeney, 2017: 30). As a result, the Welsh perspective has diverged from the English approach, with education, social and health matters devolved as a power to the Welsh Government.

The Welsh way

The key principles of the revised Welsh approach are focused on adopting an interdisciplinary, whole-school approach and inclusive rights-based approach.

The focus is also on schools understanding the needs profile of their student body, in order to address their support needs in a bespoke manner based on their particular needs and protected characteristics. Most schools continue to be confused as to which personal, social, health and economic (PSHE) guide to follow (Estyn, 2017), and the Welsh Government guidance on the Curriculum for Wales – Relationships and Sexuality Education Code (2021) continues to be in draft format. The current PSHE framework in Wales has a well-being theme, primarily due to the policy and legislative focus on well-being across community health and social care services in Wales. For example, see the Social Services and Well-being (Wales) Act 2014. This theme includes a focus on understanding safe relationships, living safe and healthy lives and inequalities and respect. Evidence suggests that this preventative approach in Wales has primarily focused on sporadic 'one-off' sessions on particular aspects of domestic abuse (Robinson, 2012; Estyn, 2017; Renold and McGeeney, 2017), while a 'whole-school approach' is regarded as a more effective method of shifting attitudinal beliefs (Hester and Westermarland, 2005; Maxwell et al, 2010; Renold and McGeeney, 2017).

From school to a whole-community approach

A 'whole-school approach' provides a comprehensive framework for healthy relationship education, goes beyond classroom learning and aims to shift the overall attitudes toward equality, gender and relationships across the whole community in order to achieve sustained change on an individual and structural level (Renold and McGeeney, 2017). Such an approach would entail the use of teaching tools/prevention packages, including a focus on gender stereotyping and the tackling of embedded beliefs of gender inequality and sexism. Recent evidence indicates that those schools that are most effective in delivering healthy relationships education do so within a culture of gender equality and respect for the rights of others (Estyn, 2017; Renold and McGeeney, 2017).

However, there is a need for a 'whole-community approach' rather than a 'whole-school approach', with a core aim of tackling the harmful attitudes that scaffold this form of abuse and the perpetration of abuse, as both a social problem and a well-being issue. The role of social workers as part of a 'whole-community approach' is crucial in supporting the needs of young people in an inclusive and safe manner. This idea of a 'whole-community approach' is based on the principles of an ecological model and focuses on addressing the root cause of abuse in young people's intimate relationships, and the impact of harmful gendered social norms across local communities, by adopting a culture of cooperation, multi-agency working and effective communication in order to evaluate and address this social problem in a bespoke manner across diverse communities (for further details on this model see Davies, 2023). The core of prevention and early intervention work with young people on a multi-agency basis should focus on the transformation of unequal power relationships, and the attitudes and behaviours that underpin these.

If we are to understand the nature and patterns of abuse in teenage relationships, then we must acknowledge how young people construct meanings about their sexual selves, their relationship aspirations, their understanding and their attitudes toward 'good' and 'bad' relationships. The attitudes of the young Welsh women were focused on an ideology of equality, whereas their intimate relationship experiences generally revealed their limited and unequal power base. This indicates the challenges posed by a post-feminist discourse, where narratives and expectations about equalisation and aspirations are far removed from their real positions in intimate relationships. There was a general resistance toward, as well as a justification of, somewhat subtle forms of coercion, harassment and control. The extent of acceptability was shaped by their image of traditional gendered norms and expectations.

The young women's narratives illustrated the task of challenging young men's power due to the cultural attitudes that perpetuate established static gendered identities, which favour men over women. Preparing young men to relinquish their power needs to be incorporated as part of prevention education. Furthermore, when re-evaluating the balance of power between young women and young men, young women's confidence and agency require further consideration. This re-evaluation will assist young women to construct their position in a manner that reduces the likelihood that any form of negotiation and power comes at a cost. This cost was seen within their narratives as the emotional work of the management of this power imbalance, due to the lack of negotiating space within their intimate relationships.

Messages for practice

- Social workers need to consider and understand the influence of gendered social norms on young people's identity and power within the intimate relationships.
- Social workers need to focus on giving young people a 'safe' and confidential space to share their experiences and questions around their intimate relationships.
- The community as a whole should work to promote healthy relationships support as a multi-agency 'whole-community approach' (see Davies, 2023: for further information on this approach).

Further resources

1. Davies, C.T. (2019) 'This is abuse? Young women's perspectives of what's "OK" and "not OK" in their intimate relationships', *Journal of Family Violence*, 34: 479–491. https://doi.org/10.1007/s10896–019–00038–2
2. Davies, C.T. (2023) *Understanding Abuse in Young People's Intimate Relationships: Female Perspectives on Power, Control and Gendered Social Norms*, Bristol: Policy Press.

3. Sundaram, V. (2018) 'A continuum of acceptability: understanding young people's views on gender-based violence', in A. Sundari, R. Lewis and R. Jones (eds) *Gender Based Violence in University Communities*, Bristol: Policy Press, pp 23–40.

References

All-Party Parliamentary Group for United Nations Women (2021) *Prevalence and Reporting of Sexual Harassment in UK Public Spaces*. https://www.unwomenuk.org/site/wp-content/uploads/2021/03/APPG-UN-Women-Sexual-Harassment-Report_Updated.pdf

Barter, C., McCarry, M., Berridge, D. and Evans, K. (2009) *Partner Exploitation and Violence in Teenage Intimate Relationships*. http://www.womenssupportproject.co.uk/userfiles/file/partner_exploitation_and_violence_report_wdf70129.pdf

Cislaghi, B. and Heise, L. (2018) 'Theory and practice of social norms interventions: eight common pitfalls', *Global Health*, 14(1): 83.

Connell, R.W. (1987) *Gender & Power*, Oxford: Blackwell Publishers.

Co-ordinated Action Against Domestic Abuse (2013) *CAADA Insights Factsheet: Teenage Victims of Domestic Violence*. https://safelives.org.uk/sites/default/files/resources/SafeLives%20Insights%20factsheet%20-%20teenage%20victims%20of%20domestic%20abuse.pdf

Council of Europe (2022) *Istanbul Convention: Treaty to End Violence against Women*. https://www.coe.int/en/web/istanbul-convention/key-facts

Davies, C.T. (2019) 'This is abuse? Young women's perspectives of what's "OK" and "not OK" in their intimate relationships', *Journal of Family Violence*, 34: 479–491.

Davies, C.T. (2023) *Understanding Abuse in Young People's Intimate Relationships: Female Perspectives on Power, Control and Gendered Social Norms*, Bristol: Policy Press.

Ending Violence Against Women and Girls (2021) 'Violence Against Women and Girls (VAWG) strategy 2021 to 2024: call for evidence'. https://www.gov.uk/government/consultations/violence-against-women-and-girls-vawg-call-for-evidence/violence-against-women-and-girls-vawg-strategy-2021–2024-call-for-evidence

Girlguiding (2021) *Sexual Harassment: Support for Girls and Leaders*. https://www.girlguiding.org.uk/girls-making-change/ways-to-take-action/past-actions-and-campaigns/campaign-to-end-sexual-harassment/sexual-harassment--and-where-to-get-support/

Goffman, E. (1959) *The Presentation of Self in Everyday Life*, New York: Anchor Books.

Hester, M. and Westmarland, N. (2005) *Tackling Domestic Violence: Effective Interventions and Approaches*. Home Office Research Study No. 290. London: Home Office.

Hickman, L.J., Jaycox, L.H. and Aronoff, J. (2004) 'Dating violence among adolescents: prevalence, gender distribution, and prevention program effectiveness', *Trauma, Violence & Abuse*, 5(2): 123–142.

Ipsos MORI (2017) 'Ipsos survey for Amnesty International on online abuse and harassment' [online]. https://www.ipsos.com/en-uk/online-abuse-and-harassment

Maxwell, C., Chase, E., Warwick, I., Aggleton, P. and Wharf, H. (2010) *Preventing Violence, Promoting Equality: A Whole-school Approach*, WOMANKIND Worldwide: London.

Renold, E. and McGeeney, E. (2017) *Informing the Future of the Sex and Relationships Education Curriculum in Wales. Project Report.* Cardiff: Cardiff University.

Robinson, K.H. (2012) 'Sexual harassment in schools: issues of identity and power – negotiating the complexities, contexts and contradictions of this everyday practice', in S. Saltmarsh, K. Robinson and C. Davies (eds) *Rethinking School Violence*, Auckland: Palgrave Macmillan, pp 71–93.

Stanko, E.A. (1985) *Intimate Intrusions*, London: Unwin Hyman.

Stonard, K., Bowen, E., Walker, K. and Price, S.A. (2017) 'They'll always find a way to get to you: technology use in adolescent romantic relationships and its role in dating violence and abuse', *Journal of Interpersonal Violence*, 32(14): 2083–2117. doi: 10.1177/0886260515590787

Sundaram, V. (2014) ' "You can try, but you won't stop it. It'll always be there": youth perspectives on violence and prevention in schools', *Journal of Interpersonal Violence*, 31(4): 652–676.

West, C. and Zimmerman, D. (1987) 'Doing gender', *Gender and Society*, 1(2): 125–151.

18

Anti-racist social work practice in Wales

Jade Forbes and Abyd Quinn Aziz

Chapter objectives

- To consider the impact of race and racism on BME people involved in social work in Wales.

- To examine racism and anti-racism in social work education.

- To suggest useful practices in developing anti-racist social work in Wales.

Introduction

When discussing BME people in Wales, it is important to recognise this 'community' is made up of a vast, culturally diverse, rich, uniquely distinguishable set of individuals and so we do not claim to speak for all of them. The ideas for this chapter come from our personal experiences, conversations with other social workers and social work students as well as from relevant literature. Anti-discriminatory and anti-racist practice is central to the social work profession and the global definition of social work includes 'social justice, human rights, collective responsibility and respect for diversities' as central values (International Federation of Social Workers, 2014). In Wales, the professional regulator, Social Care Wales (SCW) (2017: 14), requires social workers to 'ensure people are not discriminated against'.

Conversations about anti-racism are both continuous and fast moving. This chapter begins with a snapshot of some personal experiences on race based on conversations a collective of BME people professionally involved in social work in Wales had, when setting up the new BASW Cymru anti-racism group, of which the chapter authors are members. We do not claim to be addressing the most up-to-date event, as we see and read examples every day, and we must point out our focus is on Black and brown people. While we explore this in the Welsh context, we refer to similar accounts and experiences from the rest of the United Kingdom (UK) (Reid and Maclean, 2021) and other nations such as the United States of America, where there is a wealth of literature on this topic (Pierro, 2022).

Statistics show 4.9 per cent of the population of Wales identified as BME, rising to 15.8 per cent in Cardiff and 12.5 per cent in Newport (StatsWales, 2021). Cardiff has one of the oldest Black communities in Britain with the Somali population having settled here in the 19th century (Williams et al, 2015). When entering social work practice, many of us had ideals of becoming facilitators of positive change, often motivated by ingrained human rights-based approaches to practice and in seeing individuals and families as distinct and unique beings. Living in places with significant BME populations enables people to gain some knowledge of cultures and some of the small nuances within cultures, and perhaps even the confidence to ask about the context of culture and identify what this might mean to individuals.

As BME social workers we feel ourselves to be in various positions of protector and victim while feeling subject to covert, direct and indirect oppressive racism in our daily practice. We also feel that policies, practices and service delivery are often more sensitive and inclusive in workplaces with higher proportions of BME workers and citizens. This made us wonder how many other BME people involved in social work have similar experiences and uphill battles with racism while themselves adhering to professional standards, underpinned by social justice, challenging oppression and discrimination for equity, not just equality of opportunity. BME women spoke of being labelled 'angry Black' when being assertive, especially when having darker skin, as well as experiencing stereotypical tropes, such as a focus on physicality rather than intellect, of being loud, good dancers, and so on. This reinforces the need to change fundamental aspects of our authentic selves at work to fit more socially prescribed and acceptable narratives. We also looked at how this can be damaging both physically and emotionally as expressions of anger, frustration and hurt were covered up as not being allowed, through historical processes such as slavery and colonisation. Generational experiences of this, though diluted, leave ongoing trauma, impact mental health and create other manifestations of inequality through this self-editing (Obassi, 2022) and we feel this requires a robust understanding of the adverse experiences, challenges and barriers encountered by BME people, which we address later.

The effects of racism surfaced recently following the 2020 brutal, public murder of George Floyd in the USA. Committed by a police officer, the ugly reality and horror of racism and the abuse of power was thrust into public view, creating dialogue that highlighted racism and its effect more broadly. We discussed recent local incidents which caused concern in Welsh BME communities. These included the deaths of two young Black men following contact with the police, Mouayed Bashir (29) and Mohamud Hassan (24), the death of Christopher Kappesa (13) where the Crown Prosecution Service decided not to charge a 14-year-old boy who allegedly caused his death, and the imprisonment of Siyanda Mngaza who claimed she was defending herself from a racist attack. These events highlighted that this was not solely a problem elsewhere in the world – and reminded us of our experiences here.

Understanding race and racism

We acknowledge there is no generally agreed term in use to define people of ethnicities apart from white. For this chapter, we use the term Black and minority ethnic (BME) (Gunaratnum, 2003), to denote people of colour, racialised minorities, global majorities and other developing terms, while recognising these remain contested (Arday, 2021). There are pros and cons of using categories as '[c]ounting and categorisation is a double-edged sword; as well as offering a basis for "ethnic pride" and national identification, we know that such markers of difference, through processes of "othering" have acted as a proxy for determining moral worth, superiority/inferiority, and belonging/non-belonging' (Costa et al, 2021: 11). At a consultation on the use of terms on race and ethnicity as part of the Anti-racist Wales Action Plan (Welsh Government, 2022), community groups recommended that the term Black, Asian and Minority Ethnic (BAME) should no longer be used, and the Welsh Government has also consulted on appropriate terminology in the Welsh language. The report by the Commission on Race and Ethnic Disparities (Sewell, 2021: 33) also suggested ending the use of BAME as it obscured 'significant differences in outcomes between ethnic groups'.

The notion of race is contested as a social construct. Singh (2020: 16) suggests 'its emergence as a scientific tool for sifting out, categorising, organising and brutalising human populations really began to gain prominence in the late seventeenth century'. He outlines the developing meaning given to race through the different phases of thinking through the centuries, such as scriptural, scientific, cultural and sociological, as well as the different perspectives that can be taken on race. Alexander (2018: 1038) suggests two more recent phases, the 1960s to the 1980s and then 1980s to the early 2000s, the former being a 'political stance, and represents a coalition of groups and concerns, the second privileges identity, and sees the fracturing of this coalition around questions of ethnicity and later religion'. Alexander (2018) says, within race studies in the UK, there was further differentiation where Asian communities were shown by looking at their migration, focusing on rituals and practices but African-Caribbean communities' structural disadvantage and discrimination were highlighted, reinforcing the hierarchy of colour.

Singh (2020: 31) outlines some of the 'theoretical, ideological and political tensions surrounding the theorisation of "race"' and suggests the contested nature of the term 'race' leaves it without meaning for some, but for others maintains a focus on racism. We can see that race impacts society and so within social work there is a notion of addressing inequality by centring anti-discriminatory practice in social work. As well as suggesting race is a social construct, we should look at who it benefits.

The impact of racism

The impact on BME populations is noted, such as the Joint Non-Governmental Organisation Shadow Report on Racial Inequality in Wales (Race Equality First, 2021: 5), which argues:

> an integral part of understanding ethnic disparities in Wales, and across the UK, comes from understanding structural inequality and

systemic/institutional racism, and how it affects ethnic minority populations. Structural inequalities emerge when laws and institutional practices, customs and guiding ideas combine to harm ethnic minority populations in ways the White population does not encounter.

Key in this is not just the impact on individuals or because of individual actions, but how 'structural inequalities are maintained across institutions such as education, employment, housing, and healthcare and inhibit the enjoyment of economic and social, civil and political rights for ethnic minorities' (Race Equality First, 2021: 6). The report identifies impacts on media, hate crimes, criminal justice, political and civil rights and economic and social rights as well as in access to justice. Many reports outline further concerns specifically in employment (Ashe et al, 2019), schools (Show Racism the Red Card, 2020), higher education (Equality and Human Rights Commission, 2019), health (British Medical Association, 2022), policing (Race Alliance Wales, 2022) and participation in the economy (Turkmen, 2019). In higher education, despite increased numbers of BME students, disparities and inequalities remain in where BME students gain places and their completion rates (Office for Students, 2018). Differences in those attaining a 'good' (first- or upper second-class) degree show white graduates make up the highest proportion (82 per cent) and Black graduates the lowest (60 per cent), also impacting future employment opportunities.

Specifically in social work

There are different outcomes for people using services due to their race, for example Webb et al (2020: 11), identify 'significant differences in child protection practice between ethnic groups … while ethnicity itself has a large influence'. They do caution that these relationships are not straightforward and remain 'complex and differ both based on the intensity of the child protection intervention and level of deprivation' (Webb et al, 2020: 11) and that there are gaps in our knowledge of inequalities among and within the ethnic minorities. Waddell et al (2022) reported the views of parents and children involved with family support, supporting children to realise their potential by increasing protective factors in their lives. They found 'stark and persistent inequalities in outcomes for children from minority ethnic groups' (Waddell et al, 2022: 6) and parents and young people reporting experiences of racism when accessing services and in the support offered. As well as experiencing racism, Graham (2000: 434) feels the models we use in social work are based on Eurocentric notions and support 'a subtle form of cultural oppression which negates the legitimacy and validity of alternate world views'. Discussing the current state of race and ethnicity in social work research, Williams (2020) highlights that thorough study and analysis is even more necessary with continuing global inequalities, the 'migrant crises' and increasing populist political discourse, fed by neoliberal government.

A small survey by the BASW Anti-Racist Social Work Practice Group presents a snapshot. They concluded that racism exists in social work in Wales, in employment and education and is 'experienced by practitioners, managers and those who use services' (BASW, 2022: 5). The survey also found evidence of the impact on BME workers and found that racism was not addressed when reported, and that the process was not transparent. Respondents felt notions of whiteness, such as white privilege, were not discussed and anti-racist values were not promoted, concluding much more needed to be done to address this. A study by Bunce et al (2019) found a recurring theme throughout the literature of a feeling of 'otherness' experienced by BME students and explored this in more detail with health and social care students. They conclude the need for 'universities ... to undergo a significant transformation' (Bunce et al, 2019: 12) to be able to offer BME students the life-changing experience university aims to provide all students.

What is anti-racism in social work?

Being anti-racist requires ideas and action. Kendi (2019) argues there is no middle non-racist position. Butler et al (2003) underline that racism does not only exist or require attention when BME workers or users of services are present. Attention is required on white internalised attitudes and socially constructed superiority and of racist dynamics which can be prevalent in white-dominated social and professional discourse. Kendi (2019) also makes the point that racism is internalised by all, not just white people, and confesses that he had to address his own racism at the start of his journey. It is important to be clear about defining what we mean by anti-racism, differentiating this from the generic cultural competence or inclusive practices that have emerged.

The power of socialisation through the media is further commented on by hooks (1992) on the irony of Black individuals who 'succeed' often by giving up their Black culture and taking on white supremacist ways of thinking. hooks (1992: 18) feels that merely celebrating Black culture without actively struggling for anti-racism to transform society does not, in itself, intervene 'on white supremacist socialization'. To help better understand racism, Eddo-Lodge (2017) offers tools for critical thinking to challenge racism and suggests the need to recognise structural racism, to listen better to marginalised perspectives, to work collectively and take individual responsibility to address inequalities.

Many commentators, Black activists and professionals emphasise the need for social work education to address racism. The Central Council for the Education and Training of Social Workers (CCETSW) recognised this need throughout the social work curriculum, leading to the Regulation and Rules for the Diploma in Social Work (CCETSW, 1991; also known as Paper 30). This gave social work students consciousness of structural and institutional racism and developed competence in anti-racist practice. Lavalette and Penketh (2014) described 1980s' and 90s' developments together with challenges and resistance by politicians and professionals, 'which denied the structural and institutional nature of racism and accused CCETSW of being taken over by groups of obsessed zealots whose major concern was to express rigid "politically correct" values' (Lavalette and Penketh, 2014: 10).

Lavalette and Penketh (2014: 1) described the views of politicians and the media that social work 'is dominated by political correctness' and that there is too much 'focus on issues such as "race", ethnicity and discrimination within social work'. Notwithstanding this, their survey of social work journals and books showed a relative absence of these conversations within social work education and research. They highlight that the move to looking at 'diversity, difference, equality and rights' diluted anti-racism towards a range of oppressions and non-discriminatory practice in the 2000s (Graham, 2000). In a context where racism continues to impact BME communities across the UK and the world, we suggest understanding structural discrimination is key for social workers.

The murder of George Floyd and the re-emergence of Black Lives Matters led to social workers and social work educators looking again at anti-racism and decolonisation (for an introduction on decolonising social work, see Tascón and Ife, 2020), demanding now is the time for action (Reid, 2020; Bentick and Shodeinde, 2021). Some displays of support for Black Lives Matter have been criticised as performative, with 'some cringe statements, some nauseatingly feeble blogs and some noteworthy silences. Unfortunately, there remains a scarcity of cast-iron and *explicit* actions and/or commitments to anti-racism' (Reid, 2020).

Regarding diversity on social work courses, the proportion of Black applicants accepted across the UK is high compared to other programmes, which might reflect the numbers of BME people working in social care (Fairtlough et al, 2014). In 2019, social work had the highest proportion of Black applicants (21 per cent) of any subject, followed by nursing (20 per cent) (University and Colleges Admissions Service (UCAS), 2020). Despite growing awareness of racism, studies have highlighted the discrimination experienced by BME students in social work education (Penketh, 2000). Fairtlough et al (2014) explore data from 1994 where the Runnymead Trust found BME students were more likely to fail than white students, and by Hussein et al (2008 and 2009), that progression for BME students (enrolled 1995–98) was poorer and that BME students (enrolled in 2002/04 and 2004/05), were less likely to pass on time and were more likely to fail or be referred. In Scotland, Hillen and Levy (2015: 795) found 'the central tenets of a strengths-based perspective: of valuing strengths, capacity, resilience and knowledge; are too frequently absent from BME social work students' learning journey'. They also call for race and whiteness to be talked about, to educate staff and students to other ways of seeing the world.

A Welsh Government study supporting the Race Equality Action Plan analysed evidence on racial inequality in health and social care for both workers and people using services (Hatch et al, 2020), making recommendations on reducing bias in recruitment and progression and creating inclusive and psychologically safe workplaces. They recognised that several steps were required for behavioural change and recommended mandatory training beyond 'cultural competence' and unconscious bias, to look at anti-racism and to enable staff to raise concerns. This required strategies to support equality for people using services, with sensitive services and an explicit anti-racist delivery, supported by training and organisational frameworks. It suggested working with third sector organisations to engage community, meaningful data gathering and visible leadership to systematically unpick the 'underlying racist institutional policies, processes, procedures, norms, and attitudes which maintain the status quo' (Hatch et al, 2020: 4).

The lack of BME people in leadership and senior management roles in Wales is also of concern and echoes calls in England (Carter, 2020) for 'visible leadership' to tackle race discrimination in the profession, including tackling issues such as the lack of career progression for BME individuals. A workforce race equality pilot (Samuel, 2020a) recognised that England has a good proportion (14 per cent) of BME practitioners compared with its population, with 25 per cent of practitioners in adults' services, 22 per cent in children's services and 18 per cent in National Health Service mental health roles. However, Samuel (2020a) also expressed several concerns. These include: the suggestion that these are still not representative of the communities served; the lower proportion of BME practitioners in senior management than at the front line; the high proportion of Black social workers in agency work; and inequalities among student numbers on different qualifying routes. The study also showed disproportionately high referrals of BME practitioners to fitness to practice investigations and asked Social Work England to record the ethnicity of referred people and of the panel, to 'inform how best to support social workers already traumatised through such processes and feed into social work employer's anti-racist and equality, inclusion and diversity policy/plans/evaluation' (Samuel, 2020b).

Anti-racism training in social work courses

Graham (2000) summarises previous authors (Ahmad, 1990; Dominelli, 1997; Thompson, 1997) to offer some principles for anti-racist social work, beginning with the necessity to recognise the ideological social construction of race which maintains the belief of a superiority of one race. This can be seen in inequality throughout social life, and this understanding is central in organising for social change and to critically look at how institutional racism 'produces an over-representation of black people subject to the social control functions of social work institutions' (Graham, 2000: 425). It is also important to understand the intersections of all other forms of social oppression, for workers to become aware of their personal biases, attitudes and stereotypes and to be prepared to challenge institutions and others.

Many studies have highlighted that social workers might struggle to work with BME people who use services. Butt (2006) summarised how white social workers may hold stereotypical notions of other races and work to unconscious biases, such as a belief that Asian families always look after their own. Butt (2006) also found white workers feeling they did not have the skills to work with BME families and managers not able to direct BME workers. There was also the myth of white workers fearing being labelled racist for intervening with BME communities, such as in Rotherham, where some suggested child abuse was ignored due to 'the fear of officials that by intervening appropriately in cases where the suspects were Pakistani Muslims, they themselves would be castigated as racist' (Muir, 2014).

Bentick and Shodeinde (2021) demonstrate the impact of racism by referring to studies comparing outcomes for BME students across courses in the university which found an 'attainment gap' of 13 per cent (Universities United Kingdom, 2019), and Fairtlough et al (2014) and Hillen and Levy (2015) show this specifically on social work programmes. Thomas, Howe and Keen (2011) describe the lack of robust investigation of BME students' complaints when experiencing unfair or discriminatory treatment on placement. These are supported by the latest figures that show 3.2 per cent of BME social workers did not complete their Assessed and Supported Year in Employment compared to 0.9 per cent of white social workers. Furthermore, BME social workers comprised over half of the failures despite only representing a quarter of the total participants (Skills for Care, 2021).

Singh (2019) suggested that teaching creates an awareness where racism is made visible and is spoken about and challenged. Hollinrake et al (2019) found that student perspectives asked for more sensitive approaches to considering cultural differences and for white lecturers to take more responsibility in exploring white privilege and its impact. The students also asked for safe spaces to manage emotional responses to oppression so they could exchange their experiences and enable learning about different norms and values. In Wales, there is no explicit mention of anti-racist practice in the Social Work Regulator's guidance concerning the National Occupational Standards for social work (Social Care Wales, 2011). Williams and Parrott (2012: 1291) showed 'any specific focus on anti-racist approaches, including cultural diversity training, to be marginal' and identified the need to more strategically embed this into social work training. In our conversations we found no tangible examples of how this was done, although we did hear about different examples of training on the different programmes in Wales.

Anti-racist practice in Wales

In the foreword to An Anti-Racist Wales Action Plan, the First Minister recognises:

> It is time for change. Our vision is of a Wales that is proudly anti-racist, where everyone is treated as an equal citizen. We want to make meaningful changes to the lives of Black, Asian and Minority Ethnic people in a transparent way that uses their lived experiences and respects their rights as citizens of Wales. (Welsh Government, 2021: 3)

The Welsh Government is aiming to become an anti-racist nation and has outlined the plan and steps toward this in the Race Equality Action Plan. This looks to move from rhetoric to taking meaningful action and highlights the need for organisations and structures to be accountable to meeting identified timelines on goals, actions and outcomes. Professor Ogbonna, co-chair of the Race Equality Action Plan working group discusses anti-racism and the importance of individuals and organisations learning how racism persists and can 'become ingrained in societal and organisational cultures in ways that become taken-for-granted, and guide behaviours in everyday life' (Welsh Government, 2021: 5). The Race Equality Action Plan usefully summarises goals for social care – specifically for people using services, the workforce and leadership – as well as recognising the need for accountability and gathering data. For the people using services, an aim is to provide accessible, dignified and culturally appropriate care and support which is supported by ensuring the workforce develops cultural competence as well as making sure it is delivered with zero tolerance of racism or discrimination. Along with training the workforce, it aims to address the barriers to BME people trying to make a career in social care and ensure they feel safe in their workplaces around anti-racism. To support this needs leadership to champion and deliver these changes and actions on accountability; actions and behaviours that must be embedded across the care sector with data gathering to inform progress, including the voices of BME people.

Positive steps

There are some positive developments to report in addressing racism, although many initiatives have been identified previously. Across higher education, the Closing the Gap report (Universities United Kingdom, 2019) made useful suggestions for universities. These included leadership, holding conversations about race, changing their cultures, increasing the racial diversity of the workforce and creating more inclusive environments, and specifically, gathering and analysing data to support an understanding of what works. Bhatti-Sinclair (2015) also discusses culturally appropriate interventions in social work and Tedam (2010) developed the MANDELA model of supervision with a distinctly African flavour to better engage and work with BME students.

The Welsh way

In Wales, legislation and principles, as mentioned in previous chapters, highlight the 'Welsh context', strengths-based approaches, coproduction, partnership and voice and control and these facilitate taking an anti-racist approach. Organisations such as Coleg Cymraeg (Coleg Cymraeg, 2022) demonstrate an anti-racist stance by appointing an Equality, Diversity and Anti-racism Coordinator and signing up to the Zero Racism Wales policy

(Race Council Cymru, 2022), as have Cardiff University, who also formally became supporters of Race Alliance Wales. The Welsh Government has also launched a resource to inform anti-racist children's safeguarding practice (Davis and Hallett, 2022).

Anti-racist social work practice is being discussed more in Wales with the advent of supportive groups and discussions, and these are supported by broader changes, such as the mandatory teaching of Black history in schools (Welsh Government, 2022). There are also provisos about it not being left to BME people to fix, and a need for consideration of recruitment, systems and data gathering, together with anti-racist education, allyship, reverse mentoring and leadership programmes to counter the white ceiling (Reid, 2020). BASW Cymru has followed BASW UK with positive steps in setting up an anti-racism working group and its initial report makes some useful recommendations (BASW Cymru, 2022) which we look forward to developing.

The appointment of Hanah Issa, an Iraqi, Welsh, Muslim woman as National Poet and the unveiling in Cardiff of a statue to Betty Campbell, the first Black headteacher in Wales also point to a changing culture, which augurs well for future development.

Messages for practice

- Some basic steps, which have been previously identified, need to now be carried out, including accepting that social work values are undermined by racism and hence the need for effective anti-racism education and training involving workers, students and people with lived experience.
- To work toward more diverse leadership and robust processes to deal with racism and discrimination to working towards zero tolerance of it.
- The BASW anti-racist working group will continue to develop these and work with the Welsh Government to embed this into social work education and practice.

Further resources

1. Singh, G. and Masocha, S. (eds) (2020) *Anti-racist Social Work: International Perspectives*, London: Red Globe Press.
2. Thompson, N. (2021) *Anti-racism for Beginners*, Wrexham: Pavilion Publishers.
3. Reid, W. and Maclean, S. (eds) (2021) *Outlanders: Hidden Narratives from Social Workers of Colour*, Litchfield: Kirwan Maclean Publishers.

References

Ahmad, B. (1990) *Black Perspectives in Social Work*, Birmingham: Venture Press.
Alexander, C. (2018) 'Breaking black: the death of ethnic and racial studies in Britain', *Ethnic and Racial Studies*, 41(6): 1034–1054.

Arday, J. (2021) *Improving Race Equality in Education*, Cardiff: Wales Centre for Public Policy.

Ashe, S.D., Borkowska, M. and Nazroo, J. (2019) *Racism Ruins Lives*, Manchester: Trades Union Congress.

Bentick, P. and Shodeinde, P. (2021) 'Why anti-racism is needed in social work education', *Professional Social Work Magazine*, Birmingham: BASW.

Bhatti-Sinclair, K. (2015) 'Culturally appropriate interventions in social work', in *International Encyclopaedia of the Social & Behavioural Sciences* (2nd edn), Volume 5. Elsevier, pp 516-522.

British Association of Social Workers Cymru (2022) *Racism in Social Work: From Words to Action, Summary Report*. Birmingham: BASW.

British Medical Association (2022) *Delivering Racial Equality in Medicine*. London: British Medical Association.

Bunce, L., King, N., Saran, S. and Talib, N. (2019) 'Experiences of black and minority ethnic (BME) students in higher education: applying self-determination theory to understand the BME attainment gap', *Studies in Higher Education*, doi: 10.1080/03075079.2019.1643305

Butler, A., Elliot, T. and Stopard, N. (2003) 'Living up to the standards we set: a critical account of the development of anti-racist standards', *Social Work Education*, 22(3): 271–282.

Butt, J. (2006) *Are We There Yet? Identifying the Characteristics of Social Care Organisations that Successfully Promote Diversity*, Bristol: Policy Press.

Carter, C. (2020) 'Chief social workers: "visible leadership" needed to tackle race discrimination in profession', Community Care. https://www.communitycare.co.uk/2020/10/26/chief-social-workers-visible-leadership-needed-tackle-race-discrimination-profession/

Central Council for Education and Training in Social Work (1991) *One Small Step towards Racial Justice: The Teaching of Anti-racism in Diploma in Social Work Programme*. London: CCETSW.

Coleg Cymraeg (2022) ' "Identities: Welshness" A new series discussing Wales in all its diversity'. https://www.colegcymraeg.ac.uk/en/aboutus/news/pennawd-12720-en.aspx

Costa, C., Dixon-Smith, S. and Singh, G. (2021) *Beyond BAME: Rethinking the Politics, Construction, Application, and Efficacy of Ethnic Categorisation*, Higher Education research Action Group (HERAG). https://drive.google.com/file/d/1jb0k6kk1jv0jIC8ldePJatAcKNL1vrsU/view?usp=sharing

Davis, J. and Hallett, S. (2022) *Check Your Thinking: Anti-racist Practice in Children's Safeguarding*, Welsh Government. https://www.checkyourthinking.org/anti-racism/

Dominelli, L. (1997) *Anti-racist Social Work* (2nd edn), Basingstoke: Macmillan.

Eddo-Lodge, R. (2017) *Why I Am No Longer Talking to White People about Race*, London: Bloomsbury Publishing.

Equality and Human Rights Commission (2019) *Tackling Racial Harassment: Universities Challenged*, IFF Research.

Fairtlough, A., Bernard, C., Fletcher, J. and Ahmet, A. (2014) 'Black social work students' experiences of practice learning: understanding differential progression rates', *Journal of Social Work*, 14(6): 605–624.

Graham, M. (2000) 'Honouring social work principles: exploring the connections between anti-racist social work and African-centred worldviews', *Social Work Education*, 19(5): 423–436.

Gunaratnum, Y. (2003) *Researching 'Race' and Ethnicity*, London: Sage.

Hatch, S., Woodhead, C., Moriarty, J., Rhead, R. and Connor, L. (2020) *Improving Race Equality in Health and Social Care*. Cardiff: Wales Centre for Public Policy.

Hillen, P. and Levy, S. (2015) 'Framing the experiences of BME social work students within a narrative of educating for a culturally diverse workforce', *Social Work Education*, 34(7): 785–798.

Hollinrake, S., Hunt, G., Dix, H. and Wagner, A. (2019) 'Do we practice (or teach) what we preach? Developing a more inclusive learning environment to better prepare social work students for practice through improving the exploration of their different ethnicities within teaching, learning and assessment opportunities', *Social Work Education*, 38(5): 582–603.

hooks, b. (1992) *Black Looks: Race and Representation*, Boston, MA: South End Press.

Hussein, S., Moriarty, J., Manthorpe, J. and Huxley, P. (2008) 'Diversity and progression among students starting social work qualifying programme in England between 1995 and 1998: a quantitative study', *British Journal of Social Work*, 38(8): 1588–1609.

Hussein, S., Moriarty, J. and Manthorpe, J. (2009) 'Variations in progression of social work students in England: using student data to help promote achievement: undergraduate full-time students' progression on the social work degree'. Project report. King's College London.

International Federation of Social Workers (2014) *Global Definition of Social Work*. https://www.ifsw.org/what-is-social-work/global-definition-of-social-work/

Kendi, I.X. (2019) *How to Be an Antiracist*, London: Vintage Publishing.

Lavalette, M. and Penketh, L. (2014) *Race, Racism and Social Work: Contemporary Issues and Debates*, Bristol: Policy Press.

Muir, H. (2014) 'Blaming the Rotherham abuse on a fear of being branded a racist is ludicrous'. *The Guardian* [online]. https://www.theguardian.com/commentisfree/2014/aug/29/rotherham-abuse-political-correctness-ludicrous

Obassi, C. (2022) 'Black social workers: identity, racism, invisibility/hypervisibility at work', *Journal of Social Work*, 22(2): 479–497.

Office for Students (2018) *Differences in Student Outcomes*. https://www.officeforstudents.org.uk/data-and-analysis/differences-in-student-outcomes/ethnicity/

Peirro, L. (2022) 'Over a quarter of social workers faced racism from colleagues or managers in 12-month period, finds survey'. Community Care. https://www.communitycare.co.uk/2022/03/18/one-third-of-social-workers-faced-racism-from-colleagues-or-managers-in-past-year-finds-survey/

Penketh, L. (2000) *Tackling Institutional Racism: Anti-Racist Policies and Social Work Education and Training*, Bristol: Policy Press.

Race Alliance Wales (2022) *What's Going On? Experiences of Young Racialised People on Policing in Wales.* https://racealliance.wales/wp-content/uploads/2022/09/RAW_Police-Report-180522-2.pdf

Race Council Cymru (2022) *Zero Racism Wales: Now is the Time to Take a Stand.* Cardiff: RCC. https://zeroracismwales.co.uk/

Race Equality First (2021) *Joint NGO Shadow Report on Racial Inequality in Wales.* https://raceequalityfirst.org/CERD-Shadow-Report-for-Wales.pdf

Reid, W. (2020) 'Anti-racism in social work: no more questions, just actions please', *Community Care.* https://www.communitycare.co.uk/2020/12/16/anti-racism-social-work-questions-just-actions-please/

Reid, W. and Maclean, S. (2021) *Outlanders: Hidden Narratives from Social Workers of Colour*, Lichfield: Kirwan Maclean Associates.

Samuel, M. (2020a) 'Chief social workers to pilot workforce race and equality standard', *Community Care.* https://www.communitycare.co.uk/2020/10/05/chief-social-workers-pilot-workforce-race-equality-standard/

Samuel, M. (2020b) 'Black and ethnic minority social workers disproportionately subject to fitness to practise investigations', *Community Care.* https://www.communitycare.co.uk/2020/07/31/black-ethnic-minority-social-workers-disproportionately-subject-fitness-practise-investigations/

Sewell, T. (2021) *Commission on Race and Ethnic Disparities: The Report, March 2021.* London: Commission on Race and Ethic Disparities. https://assets.publishing.service.gov.uk/government/uploads/system/uploads/attachment_data/file/974507/20210331_-_CRED_Report_-_FINAL_-_Web_Accessible.pdf

Show Racism the Red Card (2020) *Racism in Wales? Exploring Prejudice in the Welsh Education System.* https://www.theredcard.org/wp-content/uploads/2023/01/RacisminWales-ExploringracismtheEducationsystemMay2020F.pdf

Singh, G. (2020) ' "Race" racism and resistance: theory and politics', in G. Singh and S. Masocha (eds) (2020) *Anti-Racist Social Work: International Perspectives*, London: Red Globe Press, pp 13–34.

Singh, G. and Masocha, S. (eds) (2020) *Anti-Racist Social Work: International Perspectives*, London: Red Globe Press.

Singh, S. (2019) 'What do we know the experiences and outcomes of anti-racist social work education? An empirical case study evidencing contested engagement and transformative learning', *Social Work Education*, 38(5): 631–653.

Skills for Care (2021) *Assessed and Supported Year in Employment (ASYE) Child and Family Annual Report to the Department for Education.* London: DfE.

Social Care Wales (2011) *National Occupational Standards.* Cardiff: Social Care Wales. https://socialcare.wales/nos-areas/social-work

Social Care Wales (2017) *Code of Professional Practice for Social Care.* Cardiff: Social Care Wales.

StatsWales (2021) *Ethnicity by Area and Ethnic Group.* Cardiff: Welsh Government.

Tascón, S.M. and Ife, J. (2020) *Disrupting Whiteness in Social Work*, London: Routledge.

Tedam, P. (2010) 'The MANDELA model of practice learning: an old present in new wrapping', *Journal of Practice Teaching & Learning*, 11(2): 60–76.

Thomas, G.T., Howe, K. and Keen, S. (2011) 'Supporting black and minority ethnic students in practice learning', *Journal of Practice Teaching & Learning*, 10(3): 37–54.

Thompson, N. (1997) *Anti-discriminatory Practice* (2nd edn), Basingstoke: Macmillan.

Thompson, N. (2021) *Anti Racism for Beginners*, Wrexham: Avenue Media Solutions.

Turkmen, H. (2019) *Triple Glazed Ceiling, Barriers to Black, Asian and Minority Ethnic (BAME) Women Participating in the Economy*. Cardiff: Chwarae Teg.

Universities United Kingdom (2019) *Black Asian and Minority Ethnic Student Attainment at UK Universities: #CLOSINGTHEGAP*. London: Universities United Kingdom and National Union of Students.

University and Colleges Admissions Service (UCAS) (2020) *Insight: Social Care Course Admissions*. https://www.ucas.com/corporate/news-and-key-docume nts/news/new-ucas-insight-shows-health-and-social-care-professions-among-most-diverse-and-welcoming-courses

Waddell, S., Sorgenfrei, M., Freeman, G., Gordon, M., Steele, M. and Wilson, H. (2022) *Improving the Way Family Support Services Work for Minority Ethnic Families*, London: Early Intervention Foundation

Webb, C., Bywaters, P., Scourfield, J., Davidson, G. and Bunting, L. (2020) 'Cuts both ways: ethnicity, poverty, and the social gradient in child welfare interventions', *Children and Youth Service Review*, 117.

Welsh Government (2021) *An Anti-racist Wales, Race Equality Action Plan, Summary*. Cardiff: Welsh Government. https://www.gov.wales/anti-racist-wales-act ion-plan

Welsh Government (2022) *Education Is Changing*. https://www.gov.wales/educat ion-is-changing

Williams, C. (2020) 'Politics, preoccupations, pragmatics: a race/ethnicity redux for social work research', *European Journal of Social Work*, 23(6): 1057–1068.

Williams, C. and Parrott, L. (2012) 'Anti-racism and predominantly "white areas": local and national referents in the search for race equality in social work education', *British Journal of Social Work*, 44(2): 290–309.

Williams, C., Evans, N. and O'Leary, P. (eds) (2015) *A Tolerant Nation? Revisiting Ethnic Diversity in a Devolved Wales* (2nd edn), Cardiff: University of Wales Press.

19

Supporting sanctuary seekers in Wales

*Tracey Maegusuku-Hewett, Haddy Sallah, Joanne Pye,
Beth Pearl and Natacha Leao de Silva*

Chapter objectives

- To gain an understanding of the contemporary contexts in which people seek sanctuary in the United Kingdom (UK) and Wales.

- To get to grips with the Welsh way of supporting people who seek sanctuary, while raising awareness of non-devolved immigration legislation, how this intersects with existing devolved policy and practice, as well as some of the challenges it presents.

- To contemplate sanctuary seekers' needs, how social workers can and do respond, and to identify key messages for social work.

Introduction

Who are sanctuary seekers and refugees, and why does this chapter focus on them?

Within the chapter, we focus only on those who seek sanctuary and refugees. We use the term 'sanctuary seeker' to refer to an individual who has arrived in the UK, and who, in Home Office terms, has 'made a claim for asylum'. This is granted if the individual meets the definition of a refugee, as defined within Article 1.2 of the United Nations (1951) Refugee Convention as anyone who is outside of their country of origin and is 'unable to return owing to a well-founded fear of being persecuted for reasons of race, religion, nationality, membership of a particular social group or political opinion'.

Sanctuary seekers may be single adults, families or unaccompanied children and young people. Typically, sanctuary seekers arrive with a range of forced migratory experiences, and immediate and longer-term health, well-being and practical support needs. They may also be depleted of familial and material resources (Social Care Institute for Excellence (SCIE), 2015). Until granted refugee status, sanctuary seekers are 'processed' within a contentious but politically legitimised immigration system that controls and monitors them, and excludes them from fundamental rights, for example, prohibition from employment (James, 2021). As sanctuary seekers, they are, in many respects, powerless and least able to advocate for social justice and their empowerment. Social workers need to be adequately prepared for their encounters with sanctuary seekers and refugees, particularly in the current era of increasing migrant flows and a more enriched and culturally diversified Wales. This chapter hopes to provide insight into the experiences and presenting needs of sanctuary seekers and refugees along with theoretical, ethical and practical considerations that can help provide a culturally competent response.

Why do people migrate to the UK?

At a rudimentary level, people can be understood as migrating for push and pull factors. Push factors may be a consequence of war, persecution and climate catastrophe. Alternatively, pull factors could be the prospect of employment, education, abject poverty alleviation and wealth generation. While this is a crude binary, as reasons for migration are multifaceted and nuanced, it nonetheless fits with the ways in which the UK Government manages migration by way of the legal categorisation of people. So those who are seemingly 'pushed' here may be seeking sanctuary by way of an asylum claim. Others may be 'pulled' to the UK as desirable human commodities to fill an occupational skills shortage, or study opportunity. Such categorisation affords certain civil and human rights, incurs specific responsibilities, and legitimises the inclusion or exclusion of certain categories of 'others' from the territory and British/Welsh society. The Migration Observatory (2020) notes that statistics since 1991 show that in most of these years, people came to the UK for work, followed by those who came for study and those who joined their family. Apart from unprecedented numbers in 2002, when there were 95,900 claims for asylum, sanctuary seekers made up, and continue to account for, the fewest number of migrants. As for irregular migrants (sometimes referred to as illegal immigrants), there are no reliable statistics on how many live in the UK, though estimates range from 800,000 to 1,200,000 in 2017 (Walsh, 2020).

Sanctuary seekers and refugees arriving in the UK and Wales

Refugee quota programmes

Historically, since the 20th century, the UK has hosted refugee 'groups' via organised quota programmes. Kushner and Knox (1999), Robinson (2003) and Teichmann (2002) have variously chronicled the reception, support and lived experiences of Jewish children, Basque 'ninos', Hungarians, Czechoslovakians, Ugandan Asians, Chileans and the Vietnamese, in some detail up until the 1980s. Of note, by the 1990s it could be seen that the UK had reduced its commitment to receiving and resettling quotas of recognised refugees. For example, in the case of the Balkan crisis in 1992, the UK gave only temporary shelter to a meagre 4,000 of an estimated two million displaced Bosnians (Teichmann, 2002). Worse still, by the turn of the 21st century, quotas dwindled to several hundred a year at best, through schemes such as the United Nations High Commissioner for

Refugees (UNHCR) Refugee Mandate Scheme and the Gateway Protection Programme. On average, the two schemes saw 661 refugees resettled per year (Sturge, 2022). It was not until the so-called 'migrant crisis' of 2015 that the UK once again recognised the need for a greater commitment to refugee quotas (while also navigating a referendum on Brexit). The insurmountable global crisis led to the UK Government agreeing to the resettlement of displaced nationals from Syria and Afghanistan, and a small number of unaccompanied children from the migrant camps of Calais and elsewhere in Europe (Sturge, 2022).

By 2020, the UK Government had announced there would be a consolidation of quotas into three distinct schemes going forward. These were the 'UK Resettlement Scheme', the 'Mandate Scheme', and the 'Community Sponsorship Scheme' (Home Office, 2021: 3). Subsequently, with the unfolding crisis in Afghanistan, came the Afghanistan Assistance and Resettlement Policy, and, by early 2022, the Afghanistan Citizens Resettlement Scheme. Likewise, with Russia's invasion of Ukraine, the family and community sponsor scheme 'Homes for Ukraine' came into fruition.

Spontaneous sanctuary seekers

All of these quota schemes are afforded to recognised refugees under the United Nations (1951) Refugee Convention. However, thousands of sanctuary seekers have arrived in the UK of their own volition (in the absence of being privy to such schemes). In 2021 the UK received 48,540 claims for asylum and 3,762 claims made by unaccompanied children and young people (94 per cent of whom were males). The number of sanctuary seekers during this year was an increase on the figure for 2020 (Refugee Council, 2022). Sturge (2022) highlights this is due to the challenges of seeking sanctuary during a global pandemic.

Mapping sanctuary seekers and recognised refugees in Wales

For a valuable insight into earlier migration to Wales, you are directed to Williams et al (2015) who provide a detailed overview of historical cultural diversity, antipathy and lived experiences. Notwithstanding the size of the Welsh population, the nation has, and continues to receive its share of quota refugees and sanctuary seekers. In the 1990s, Robinson (1998) was tasked with estimating the size and make-up of the refugee population of Wales. This is something that he cautioned was not an exact science due to the lack of data. Following a survey of all organisations that may encounter sanctuary seekers and refugees, he estimated there to be around 3,500 to 3,600 people living mainly within Cardiff, Swansea and Newport. There were thought to be 15 nationality groups; the prominent ones being Somalian (70 per cent), Vietnamese (9.3 per cent) and Iranian (6 per cent).

By the 2000s, and due to a newly introduced dispersal scheme under the Immigration and Asylum Act (1999), sanctuary seekers were dispersed to Cardiff, Newport, Swansea and Wrexham. Payson (2015) notes how at this point there were no less than 74 different nationality groups dispersed to Wales. More recently, statistics are better collated. We know that for every 10,000 people in Wales, there are only eight sanctuary seekers. In December 2021, there were 2,605 sanctuary seekers living in Wales, the majority of whom were destitute and therefore given minimal subsistence and housing under Section 95 of the Immigration and Asylum Act 1999. Meanwhile, estimates of unaccompanied children and young people are based on local authority (LA) data for children looked after, and StatsWales (2021) indicates there were only 65 unaccompanied children in care in Wales as of March 2021. Anecdotally, however, this figure is thought to be an underestimate. As for refugees arriving through contemporary quota schemes to Wales, between 2014 and 2021, there were 1,479 refugees resettled. Essential to considerations of Welsh context is the fact that refugees have been resettled across all LAs of Wales, not just the larger cities (House of Commons, 2022).

Wales as a Nation of Sanctuary

Ideological stance on sanctuary seekers and refugees

Immigration is a non-devolved matter, though Wales has its own jurisdiction over social care, housing, health, play and recreation, education, which sanctuary seekers can benefit from. Wales also takes pride in its status as a Nation of Sanctuary, the only UK nation to do so, and this commitment to sanctuary seekers and refugees is articulated in the accompanying Refugee and Asylum Seeker Action Plan (Welsh Government, 2019) and the Race Equality Action Plan (Welsh Government, 2021a).

Policy rhetoric is one of human rights and recognition of the benefits of a culturally diverse nation to the enrichment of Welsh society. The Welsh Government (2022: 225) affirms it is 'committed to reducing the inequalities experienced by asylum seekers and refugees, increasing access to opportunities and improving relations between these communities and wider society'. The Welsh Government has also spoken out against immigration policy that is deemed as lacking in dignity or humanity. For example, in 2021 during the COVID-19 pandemic, the Welsh Government condemned the Home Office's policy of housing male sanctuary seekers in an army barracks in Pembrokeshire. In a Ministerial Statement, Jane Hutt, Deputy First Minister, pointed out that the use of the camp 'is incompatible with the Welsh Government's approach to inclusive and cohesive communities' (Welsh Government, 2021b). That said, ultimately, the Welsh Government recognises the usefulness of dialogue with the UK Government on non-devolved immigration policies and their translation to the Welsh context, though they concede that any proposed Wales-based actions cannot infringe upon the primacy of immigration legislation (Welsh Government, 2019).

The everyday support of sanctuary seekers and refugees in Wales

As noted earlier, the reception and support of sanctuary seekers and refugees is contingent upon their immigration category. So, in Wales, those arriving through the dispersal scheme are supported under 'Section 95', and unaccompanied children are afforded LA care under Part 6 of the Social Services and Well-being (Wales) Act 2014 (SSWWA). As for those who arrive through a quota scheme, they are already afforded refugee status or temporary leave. There is UK and Welsh Government financial 'backing' and reliance on the voluntary sector, charities, faith-based groups and community members to assist in the immediate integration into Welsh society of quota refugees, and to provide ongoing community support to all sanctuary seekers regardless of status, as has been the case historically.

Their contribution is significant. For example, not only providing signposting, advocacy, English for Speakers of Other Languages, access to training and volunteering, social support and inclusion but also dealing with crises, many of which are a consequence of the asylum process, for example, homelessness, destitution, hunger, period poverty, violence and mental ill-health. Maybline and James (2019) as cited in James (2021), highlight that community groups have contributed around £33 million per year in alleviating poverty among refugees across the UK. Wales, for its part, has a well-established network of community support groups, some are localised to a particular LA, for example, Oasis Cardiff, and others may be national such as the Welsh Refugee Council. They offer a broad range of services. Here is one such example.

A case example of community support in action in Wales

The Ethnic Minorities and Youth Support Team Wales (EYST) is a charity that supports sanctuary seekers and refugees. EYST has been supporting Syrians under the UK Vulnerable Persons Resettlement Scheme. This involves supporting refugees to access housing, healthcare and education, contacting solicitors, the Home Office and Migrant Help on their behalf. EYST's support continues until refugees gain their citizenship. EYST also offers well-being, social and emotional support and mentoring.

Community provision such as this chimes with the social enterprise, coproductive and community-based principles underpinning the SSWWA. Yet Zetter, Griffiths and Sigona (2005) caution that social exclusion and crises brought about by restrictive immigration policies have been the catalyst for their emergence. This contrasts with the more optimistic notions around social capital and inclusive communities espoused by governments.

The Welsh way

While adhering to the UK national legislative framework regarding immigration, Wales has adopted a distinct approach to supporting sanctuary seekers and refugees as a Nation of Sanctuary: an approach that is reflective of the core principles of devolved legislation.

There is a reliance on the voluntary sector, community organisations and citizens to provide support to sanctuary seekers and refugees. In reality, this may become more difficult to sustain given the extent of support offered and current economic climate within Wales.

The Welsh way of supporting sanctuary seekers and refugees will continue to evolve and change over time, being influenced by societal attitudes and the political/economic landscape.

The social work role with sanctuary seekers

Social workers within community development and/or voluntary sector roles may have developed their expertise and knowledge of sanctuary seekers' support needs, service availability and of immigration policy. However, statutory social workers may have far less engagement with sanctuary seekers or refugees, possibly only engaging with them in contexts of their specific roles, such as in the assessment of care and support needs for an older adult refugee, a child refugee with disabilities, through domestic violence services, in the accommodation and support of unaccompanied young people, and so on. Maegusuku-Hewett, Kalicinski and Maxwell (2008) carried out research with 131 professionals from multidisciplinary backgrounds in Wales that sought to explore the safeguarding and care practices with children and young people who were trafficked, unaccompanied or arriving in Wales with their families. While there were excellent practices being developed, which were helped by all-Wales forums for practitioners, a lack of encounter was found to be detrimental. That is, practitioners in areas with far fewer sanctuary seekers lacked confidence in their knowledge of immigration and human rights legislations, and of need and service provision. Other findings demonstrated limited knowledge about cultural forms of abuse such as female genital mutilation and honour-based violence. Some professionals expressed concerns about referring child safeguarding concerns for fear of being seen as ethnocentric or racist. Since the research, there have been some practice developments and guidance. This included the provision of a time-limited, all-Wales practitioner information officer funded by the Welsh Government, and the dissemination of specific guidance to promote good practice in the care, support and safeguarding of children and young people. For example, age assessments (Welsh Government, 2021c), the everyday support of unaccompanied children (see Children's Legal Centre, 2019) and safeguarding from trafficking and cultural, traditional or religious forms of abuse. The latter is now integrated into the All Wales Safeguarding Procedures (Wales Safeguarding Procedures Project Board, 2019).

Social work theories as helpful tools to aid culturally competent practice

Theory is integral to social work practice; it helps us to understand behaviours and actions and to work in an evidence-based way with citizens. The following shows brief examples of a few prominent theories that can help students and practitioners to develop their understanding of the needs and circumstances of sanctuary seekers.

Grief and loss

It can be argued that all those requiring support from social workers do so because they are experiencing some form of loss. For example, Doka (1989) considers Disenfranchised Grief. This is grief that is not acknowledged or recognised by society. Boss (2006) considers Ambiguous Loss which is loss where there is no closure (such as separation due to migration).

Attachment Theory (Bowlby)

Bowlby (1969/82) highlights the impact of infants' experiences of attachment to their primary carers and secure base during their formative years and how this impacts upon individuals' ability to form and sustain relationships throughout their life course.

Ecological Systems Theory

Bronfenbrenner (1994) considers the interconnectedness between different individuals and five environmental, bi-directional and interrelated systems. This theory promotes an integrated and holistic understanding of an individual's situation and acknowledges that where there is discord in one system it can affect other systems.

The relevance of these theories is evident for sanctuary seekers, as the different aspects of their lives when settling in a new environment will all come under strain. Theories around loss can help us appreciate the impact of multiple losses such as one's home, country, family and friends, and the feelings associated with unrecognised or unresolved loss. Goede and Boshuizen-van Burken (2019: 725) caution that loss can be so chronic that 'no matter what the host country provides, the overwhelming loss experienced by refugees will still be present'. Attachment theory is particularly helpful when understanding the emotional impact of separation on unaccompanied children and young people. Ecological systems theory helps us to recognise when systems are under strain and the inter-relatedness of different social systems. It also helps to identify strengths that can be drawn upon and the resilience that sanctuary seekers possess (Maegusuku-Hewett et al, 2007).

Developing culturally competent social work practice with sanctuary seekers

The concept of cultural competence is slippery, as it is variably understood and operationalised. Some avoid the term altogether, deeming it to suggest cultural competence as something that may be achieved but without the need for sustained commitment (Lau and Rodgers, 2021; Das and Carter Anand, 2016). Nonetheless, being pragmatic, we draw upon a definition derived from a Wales-based project that sought to create a cultural competence toolkit: 'Cultural competence is the capacity to provide effective services taking into account the cultural beliefs, behaviours and needs of people: it is therefore made up of cultural awareness, knowledge and sensitivity as well as the promotion of anti-oppressive and anti-discriminatory policies' (Diverse Cymru, 2016).

Using this definition as our frame of reference, (while acknowledging its contested nature), cultural competence has three core components. First, 'cultural awareness'. This could entail one's own ongoing reflections on one's values base. For example, it is essential that social work students and practitioners reflect on and are self-aware of their own stance on migration control. Our personal and political views can influence the response we provide to sanctuary seekers asking for our help. We may respond with kindness and compassion (Banks, 2010), act as street-level bureaucrats in the navigation of sanctuary seekers' human rights and the primacy of immigration control (Dunkerley et al, 2005; Kohli, 2005) or, as Humphries (2004: 95) pessimistically declares, 'Social work has been drawn into implementing racist policy initiatives, whilst still maintaining its unreflective, self-deceiving, anti-oppressive belief systems'.

The second element of cultural competence relates to 'cultural knowledge'. Such knowledge may be derived from our own identities, from engagement and learning from the lived experiences of sanctuary seekers or from formal knowledge acquired through education and research. The latter has provided useful research evidence around cultural needs of sanctuary seekers that can inform social work practice with unaccompanied children and young people in care. For example, Kohli, Connolly and Warman (2010) on the importance of food; Ní Raghallaigh (2011) on religion; Ní Raghallaigh and Sirriyeh (2014) on cultural and linguistic needs and differential concepts of children and childhood.

The third and final element is 'cultural sensitivity'. At its simplest, this means being aware of difference and diversity of culture without ascribing negative values. Some would advocate it is more than a mere recognition of cultural difference. Das and Carter Anand (2016) stress that when considering difference, social workers ought to avoid the trap of seeing difference by way of 'othering' wherein the only frame of reference in which to compare is the majority cultural norm, thus perpetuating a Eurocentric positionality. Meanwhile Thompson (2012) advocates that differences in cultures should be celebrated and seen as assets which can also deter the reproduction of oppressive social relations in practice. Lau and Rodgers (2021) refer to respectful engagement with refugees wherein listening, awareness of power, honesty around expectations, as well as limits to confidentiality, were all considered imperative to refugees in building trusting working relationships. These are core social work competencies enshrined in our professional and ethical codes (Social Care Wales (SCW), 2017; British Association of Social Workers (BASW), 2021).

Key messages for ethical culturally competent social work practice

Responses and interventions in relation to sanctuary seekers will invariably be influenced by the neoliberal structures of the organisations within which social workers operate and the prevailing legislation and policies which are in place to manage migration (Devenney, 2019). Social workers may find immigration legislation and policy to be at odds with the professional values base of social work. A particularly ethically fraught aspect of practice relates to the 'hostile environment' and supporting sanctuary seekers who may have failed in their application for asylum and present to housing, social and health care services but with 'no recourse to public funds' (Farmer, 2017).

So contentious is the matter of the social work response, that the profession has had its fair share of critics (Humphries (2004), Crawley (2006), Farmer (2017), to name but a few). Androff and Mathis (2022) advocate that social workers should take a human rights-based approach to their everyday practices with sanctuary seekers, as well as promoting their civil and political rights within wider society. However, this can be challenging without knowledge of asylum, equality and human rights legislation. At the least, having human and children's rights within our sights when making decisions, would be in keeping with existing aspirations of the Welsh Government and social work professional codes and values (SCW, 2017; BASW, 2021). Meanwhile, Article 3 (inhumane and degrading treatment), and Article 8 (right to private and family life) of the European Convention on Human Rights 1950, along with Article 3 (child's best interests) and Article 22 (equity of treatment of refugee children) of the United Nations Convention on the Rights of the Child 1989, are key rights conventions of relevance.

Over the past two decades there have been numerous case law challenges to immigration policy that have illustrated infringement of rights, and which have led to positive and significant changes to how the law is interpreted and how social workers must practise. For example, *Westminster City Council v. National Asylum Support Service*: HL 17 Oct [2002] provided clarity on the obligation of LA social services departments to provide assessment and support for sanctuary seekers with care and support needs.

Messages for practice

- There needs to be a distinct focus on sanctuary seekers within social work education and social care services, supported by up-to-date, regular, freely

accessible social work briefings around research, practice and legislative and case law developments.
- Within Wales, bodies such as SCW, BASW Cymru and the Welsh Government could reinforce the connection between Wales as a Nation of Sanctuary and social work's position and expectations of the profession to engage in human rights-based and culturally sensitive practice.
- We need to recognise the importance of listening to, and learning from, those with lived experience as an integral part of education and practice.

The chapter provides some contextual detail about the historical and current migration of sanctuary seekers and refugees to the UK and Wales. A key consideration is that immigration is a non-devolved matter and, as such, the chapter unravelled how Wales as a 'Nation of Sanctuary', interprets and navigates this terrain with commitment to a rights-based ideology.

Further resources
1. Children's Legal Centre (2022) guidance. *A Best Practice Guide for Social Workers in Wales Supporting Children Who Are Claiming Asylum.* Cardiff: Welsh Government. https://www.gov.wales/sites/default/files/publications/2022-11/children-seeking-asylum-guidance-for-social-workers_1.pdf
2. Diverse Cymru (2016) *Cultural Competency Toolkit. A Practical Guide for Mental Health Professionals, Other Professionals and Front-line Staff Working within the Mental Health, Health and Social Care Sector in Wales.* https://diversecymru.org.uk/wp-content/uploads/2021/11/Cultural-Competency-Toolkit.pdf
3. SCIE (2015) *Good Practice in Social Care for Refugees and Asylum Seekers.* SCIE guide 37. https://www.scie.org.uk/publications/guides/guide37-good-practice-in-social-care-with-refugees-and-asylum-seekers/files/guide37.pdf

References
Androff, D. and Mathis, C. (2022) 'Human rights-based social work practice with immigrants and asylum seekers in a legal service organization', *Journal of Human Rights and Social Work,* 7(2): 178–188.

Banks, S.J. (2010) 'Integrity in professional life: issues of conduct, commitment and capacity', *British Journal of Social Work,* 40(7): 2168–2184.

Boss, P. (2006) *Loss, Trauma, and Resilience: Therapeutic Work with Ambiguous Loss,* New York: W.W. Norton & Company.

Bowlby, J. (1969/1982) *Attachment and Loss, Vol. 1: Attachment* (2nd edn), New York: Basic Books.

British Association of Social Workers (2021) *The BASW Code of Ethics for Social Work.* BASW. https://www.basw.co.uk/system/files/resources/basw_code_of_ethics_-_2021.pdf

Bronfenbrenner, U. (1994) 'Ecological models of human development', *International Encyclopaedia of Education,* 3(2): 1643–1647.

Children's Legal Centre (2019) *Child First: Looking After Unaccompanied Asylum-Seeking Children in Wales.* Welsh Government. https://gov.wales/sites/default/files/publications/2019–08/child-first-looking-after-unaccompanied-asylum-seeking-children-in-wales.pdf

Crawley, H. (2006) *Child First, Migrant Second: Ensuring That Every Child Matters,* London: ILPA.

Das, C. and Carter Anand, J. (2016) '"Pushing theory": applying cultural competence in practice – a case study of community conflict in Northern Ireland', in C. Williams and M. Graham (eds) *Social Work in a Diverse Society: Transformative Practice with Black and Minority Ethnic Individuals and Communities,* Bristol: Policy Press, pp 22–37.

Devenney, K. (2019) 'Social work with unaccompanied asylum-seeking young people: reframing social care professionals as "co-navigators"', *British Journal of Social Work*, 0: 1–18. https://doi.org/10.1093/bjsw/bcz071

Diverse Cymru (2016) *Cultural Competency Toolkit. A Practical Guide for Mental Health Professionals, Other Professionals and Front-line Staff Working Within the Mental Health, Health and Social Care Sector in Wales.* https://diversecymru.org.uk/wp-content/uploads/2021/11/Cultural-Competency-Toolkit.pdf

Doka, K. (ed) (1989) *Disenfranchised Grief: Recognizing Hidden Sorrow*, Lexington, KT: Jossey Bass.

Dunkerley, D., Scourfield, J., Maegusuku-Hewett, T. and Smalley, N. (2005) 'The experiences of front-line staff working with children who are seeking asylum', *Social Policy and Administration*, special issue on migration, 39(6): 640–652.

Farmer, N.J. (2017) '"No Recourse to Public Funds", insecure immigration status and destitution: the role of social work?', *Critical and Radical Social Work*, 5(3): 357–367.

Goede, R. and Boshuizen-van Burken, C. (2019) 'A critical systems thinking approach to empower refugees based on Maslow's theory of human motivation', *Systems Research and Behavioural Science*, 36(5): 715–726.

Home Office (2021) *UK Refugee Resettlement: Policy Guidance.* Home Office. https://assets.publishing.service.gov.uk/government/uploads/system/uploads/attachment_data/file/1011824/Resettlement_Policy_Guidance_2021.pdf

House of Commons (2022) *Resettled Refugees by Local Authority: Cumulative Total. January 2014–June 2021.* House of Commons. https://researchbriefings.files.parliament.uk/documents/SN01403/CBP01403-Annex---Resettlement-by-local-authority.xlsx

Humphries, B. (2004) 'An unacceptable role for social work: implementing immigration policy', *British Journal of Social Work*, 34(1): 93–107.

James, M.L. (2021) 'Can community-based social protection interventions improve the wellbeing of asylum seekers and refugees in the United Kingdom? A systematic qualitative meta aggregation review', *Social Sciences*, 10: 194.

Kohli, R. (2005) The comfort of strangers: social work practice with unaccompanied asylum-seeking children and young people in the UK, *Child and Family Social Work*, 11(1): 1–10.

Kohli, R., Connolly, H. and Warman, A. (2010) 'Food and its meaning for asylum seeking children and young people in foster care', *Children's Geographies*, 8(3): 233–245.

Kushner, T. and Knox, C. (1999) *Refugees in an Age of Genocide*, London: Frank Cass.

Lau, L.S. and Rodgers, G. (2021) 'Cultural competence in refugee service settings: a scoping review', *Health Equity*, 5(1): 124–134.

Maegusuku-Hewett, T., Dunkerley, D., Scourfield, J. and Smalley, N. (2007) 'Refugee children in Wales: coping and adaptation in the face of adversity', *Children and Society*, 21(4): 309–321.

Maegusuku-Hewett, T., Kalicinski, L. and Maxwell, N. (2008) *The Care and Protection of Asylum-seeker and Trafficked Children in Wales: Agenda for Action*, Cardiff: Save the Children Wales.

Migration Observatory (2020) *Who Migrates to the UK and Why?* https://migration observatory.ox.ac.uk/resources/briefings/who-migrates-to-the-uk-and-why/

Ní Raghallaigh, M. (2011) 'Religion in the lives of unaccompanied minors: an available and compelling coping resource', *British Journal of Social Work*, 4193: 539–556.

Ní Raghallaigh, M. and Sirriyeh, A. (2015) 'The negotiation of culture in foster care placements for separated refugee and asylum-seeking young people in Ireland and England', *Childhood*, 22(2): 263–277.

Payson, A. (2015) '"This is the place we are calling home": changes in sanctuary seeking in Wales', in C. Williams, N. Evans and P. O'Leary (eds) *A Tolerant Nation? Revisiting Ethnic Diversity in a Devolved Wales* (2nd edn), Cardiff: University of Wales Press, pp 277–304.

Refugee Council (2022) *Quarterly Asylum Statistics.* https://media.refugeecouncil. org.uk/wp-content/uploads/2022/06/17092544/Asylum-Statistics-June-2022.pdf

Robinson, V. (1998) 'Neither here nor there: refugees in Wales', *Contemporary Wales*, 11: 200–214.

Robinson, V. (2003) 'Croeso i Gymru – Welcome to Wales? Refugees and asylum seekers in Wales', in C. Williams , N. Evans and P. O'Leary (eds) *A Tolerant Nation? Exploring Ethnic Diversity in Wales*, Cardiff: University of Wales Press, pp 179–200.

Social Care Institute for Excellence (SCIE) (2015) *Good Practice in Social Care for Refugees and Asylum Seekers.* SCIE Guide 37. https://www.scie.org.uk/publi cations/guides/guide37-good-practice-in-social-care-with-refugees-and-asy lum-seekers/files/guide37.pdf

Social Care Wales (SCW) (2017) *Codes of Professional Practice.* SCW. https://soc ialcare.wales/cms-assets/documents/Code-of-Professional-Practice-for-Soc ial-Care-web-version.pdf

StatsWales (2021) Unaccompanied Asylum-seeking Children Being Looked After at the 31st March by Local Authority. https://statswales.gov.wales/Catalogue/ Health-and-Social-Care/Social-Services/Childrens-Services/Children-Loo ked-After/unaccompaniedasylumseekingchildrenbeinglookedafteratthe31ma rch-by-localauthority

Sturge, G. (2022) *Asylum Statistics*. SN 01403. House of Commons Library. https://researchbriefings.files.parliament.uk/documents/SN01403/SN01 403.pdf

Teichmann, I. (2002) *Credit to the Nation: Refugee Contributions to the UK*, London: Refugee Council.

Thompson, N. (2012) *Anti-discriminatory Practice: Equality, Diversity and Social Justice* (5th edn), London: Palgrave Macmillan.

United Nations (1951) *Convention Relating to the Status of Refugees*. Geneva: UN.

Wales Safeguarding Procedures Project Board (2019) *Wales Safeguarding Procedures*. All Wales Practice Guides. https://www.safeguarding.wales/chi/index.c6.html

Walsh, P. (2020) *Irregular Migration to the UK*. Migration Observatory. https:// migrationobservatory.ox.ac.uk/wp-content/uploads/2020/09/Briefing-Irregu lar-Migration-in-the-UK.pdf

Welsh Government (2019) *Nation of Sanctuary: Refugee and Asylum Seeker Plan*. https://gov.wales/sites/default/files/publications/2019–03/nation-of-sanctu ary-refugee-and-asylum-seeker-plan_0.pdf

Welsh Government (2021a) *An Anti-racist Wales: Race Equality Action Plan for Wales*. https://gov.wales/sites/default/files/consultations/2022–06/race-equal ity-action-plan-an-anti-racist-wales.pdf

Welsh Government (2021b) *Written Statement: Use of Penally Army Training Camp for Asylum Seekers*. https://gov.wales/written-statement-use-penally-army-train ing-camp-asylum-seekers

Welsh Government (2021c) *Unaccompanied Asylum Seeking Children: Age Assessment Toolkit*. Welsh Government. https://gov.wales/sites/default/files/publications/ 2021–06/unaccompanied-asylum-seeking-children-age-assessment-toolkit.pdf

Welsh Government (2022) *Policy and Strategy: Anti-racist Wales Action Plan. What We Are Going to Do to Make Wales Anti-racist*. https://www.gov.wales/sites/default/ files/pdf-versions/2022/7/3/1658919769/anti-racist-wales-action-plan- contents.pdf

Williams, C., Evans, N. and O'Leary, P. (eds) (2015) *A Tolerant Nation? Revisiting Ethnic Diversity in a Devolved Wales* (2nd edn), Cardiff: University of Wales Press.

Zetter, R., Griffiths, D. and Sigona, N. (2005) 'Social capital or social exclusion? The impact of asylum-seeker dispersal on UK refugee community organizations', *Community Development Journal*, 40(2): 169–181.

20

Community development in social work practice

Fiona Verity

Chapter objectives

- To canvas contemporary conditions that are heralding the 'turn of the tide' for community development in Wales, with implications for social work.

- To situate a discussion of community development in social work within the framework of ideas about 'social amnesia', as articulated by the historian Russell Jacoby.

- To explore what might create an energy to power an incoming tide of community development and social work in Wales, so it can contribute to a progressive social change project.

Introduction

> In the unceasing ebb and flow of justice and oppression we must all dig channels as best we may, that at the propitious moment somewhat of the swelling tide may be conducted to the barren places of life. (Jane Addams 1912: 23–43)

Community development is a named social work method, a collective approach to respond to issues that are relevant to diversely defined 'communities' and potential 'space' for social change (Ife, 1999, Shaw and Martin, 2000; International Federation of Social Work (IFSW), 2014). However, in recent times, community development's place and recognition within social work practice and education has been whittled away (Forde and Lynch, 2015; Forde et al, 2021). There are many interrelated reasons for this dynamic over time; prevailing views about social work, the draw to individual and family focused practice to the exclusion of collective practice, the dominance of statutory work and thinking, and a risk averse sensibility are some of them (Mendes, 2008; Geoghegan and Powell, 2009; Tan, 2009; Forde et al, 2021). Neoliberal informed developments in social care, such as market practices, implemented from the 1990s, have left their imprint in social work and social policy (Williams, 1999).

The starting place for the ensuing discussion is a position in concert with the ISFW's definition of social work; community development is a social work response to injustices and interconnected historically located systemic issues, seen for example in inequalities and poverty (IFSW, 2014). Of course, social work is a broad church and community development is not one thing, nor defined and interpreted in the same way (du Sautoy, 1966; Waddington, 1979; Ife, 1999; Mendes, 2008). Community development may be locality place-based developments, community organisation, consciousness raising and collective social action and organising. Each has underlying theoretical perspectives and models of practice. It can also be pursued for varied intentions: progressive aims, reformist intentions and agendas that are about maintaining a status quo (Thorpe, 1985).

Also, the history of community development more broadly and it within social work is full of mismatches between intentions and outcomes (for example, between espoused aims for citizen engagement, empowerment and social justice, and the outcomes in practice) (Shaw and Martin, 2000). Mowbray and Bryson's (1981) insights on processes of mystification in community initiatives, using the language of 'spray on solutions', are instructive; developments which at face value seem empowering can cover up dominant interests. Diverse ideological positioning has implications for social work's relation and responsiveness to 'communities', the relationship of social work with the state (that is, room to be more than an agent of social control), as well as in respect to solidarity with social movements. Community development's manifestation within social work has reflected prevailing social, political and policy trends, as well as these varied intentions.

We see these various motivations in examples across time and space; 19th-century organising by Octavia Hill in England, and in the USA, in a similar era, Jane Addams' social reform coupled with locality work; socialist, feminist and radical developments, poststructural perspectives and neoliberal-shaped community initiatives. As Clarke et al (2002) describe, in Wales, and back before formalised government community development programmes, there has been a 'Welsh way' in community development. They write of community development responses to political and economic conditions through cooperatives, mutualism, organising, and community initiatives reflecting kinship ties, labour relations, religious faith, culture, and geography (Clarke et al, 2002: 3–6). In recent times the tide has been out on community development in social work in many parts of the developed world (Forde et al, 2021). For example, there is a dearth of direct community development teaching in some university-based social work education across Wales, a not unfamiliar pattern in other places across the world (Mendes, 2008; Forde et al, 2021).

'Harnessing the power of our tides' is the strapline for the Swansea Bay Tidal Power Lagoon Project (Swansea being the second largest city in South Wales), a project to generate electricity through tidal water (Tidal Lagoon Power). The metaphor of tides, of 'swells', withdrawals, and the power of renewal, is commonly used in discussions of trends in social work. In 2015, I gave a conference talk with colleagues using the metaphor of tides and 'incoming waves' in exploring community development; like the tide, a natural movement with ups, downs and serendipitous encounters that potentially can energise change. This can be change for people, within diverse communities, and change at broader macro levels (Verity et al, 2015). The premise of this chapter is that there are recent developments in Wales, to follow the metaphor, an incoming tide of renewal, which can energise community development, and wherein social work can play a part. Social enterprises, locality-based community development, community-instigated social care models and community collaborations are some examples of these developments in practice.

The definition of community development used in this chapter is one articulated by social work and community development writer Jim Ife. He writes that community development is:

> the process of establishing, or re-establishing, structures of human community within which new ways of relating, organising social life and meeting human need become possible. In this context, community work is seen as the activity, or practice, of a person who seeks to facilitate that process of community development. (Ife, 1999: 2)

Ife's community development model is firmly rooted in principles and values of social justice and human rights.

Welsh shifting tidal patterns: policy and practice

A shifting tidal pattern in social policy, with implications for the scope and reach of social work, is evident in the specified duties and values of contemporary Welsh Government legislation, for example in the Social Services and Well-being (Wales) Act 2014 (SSWWA) and the Well-being of Future Generations (Wales) Act 2015. This shift is set against the background of marketised social welfare which has dominated practice for decades (Williams, 1999). The premise of this chapter is that these legislative changes are opening possibilities for an invigorated community development practice in social work in Wales. Set in a human rights framework, Section 15 of the SSWWA lists nine prevention purposes which include '(a) contributing towards preventing or delaying the development of people's needs for care and support; and (b) reducing the needs for care and support of people who have such needs' (2014).

The prevention principle under the SSWWA is interconnected with principles of coproduction, collaboration and voice and control, all required under the Act and essential in community development (see Chapter 7). The Code of Practice related to the prevention duties under the Act is peppered with notions of 'assets and strengths', 'empowerment', 'participation' and 'partnerships' (SSWWA Code of Practice 2, Welsh Government, 2015a). Section 16 of the same Act (2014) sets out duties in respect to supporting the work of civil society and third sector organisations, including the support for the development of user-led services, cooperatives and social enterprises. These third sector developments have a particular historical resonance in Wales; the worldwide cooperative movement has its origin in the ideals and actions of Welsh-born Robert Owen, who believed in a utopian vision of cooperation in communities working for the betterment of society (Kumar, 1990). In 2008, and before the implementation of the SSWWA, a study located 3,056 social enterprise organisations across Wales (Foster et al, 2009: 5).

The Well-being of Future Generations (Wales) Act 2015 is more explicit in the focus on structural factors and developmental process. The backbone in this piece of legislation is the notion of 'sustainable development', defined in this Act as 'the process of improving the economic, social, environmental, and cultural well-being of Wales by taking action in accordance with the sustainable development principle, aimed at achieving the well-being goals' (Welsh Government, 2015b: 3).

The Act requires public sector bodies to work towards seven well-being goals: 'A prosperous Wales', 'A resilient Wales', 'A healthier Wales', 'A more equal Wales', 'A Wales of cohesive communities', 'A Wales of vibrant culture and thriving Welsh language' and 'A globally responsible Wales' (Welsh Government, 2015b: 3–4) (see Chapter 1).

Some of the optimism and sense of the enabling power of Welsh Government legislation, to create space for a different practice, is captured in a process evaluation report of the implementation of the SSWWA (Llewellyn et al, 2020). The Act as a 'catalyst' for new directions is evident in reflections of senior managers about the Act, as seen in one example from this evaluation report: 'I'm sure the Future Generations Act helps that in terms of getting other organisations, other departments within the local authority to think about things more from a preventative model and early intervention' (Senior Manager, LA, Locality 1) (Llewellyn et al, 2020: 44).

In the contemporary policy and social context, examples of government-sponsored initiatives are prevention and early intervention programmes (for example, initiatives such as 'Dementia Friendly Communities') and locality-based community development initiatives (for example, Local Area Coordination models and 'Community Connectors'). As an example, Swansea Council (2022) has a network of Local Area Coordinators, who are based in place communities, and support local people in meeting their needs through 'local resources and networks'. Moreover, there are examples of initiatives which support the development of local community infrastructure and assets.

The support for the development of civil society initiatives includes the Welsh Government requirement to establish Social Value Forums to 'encourage a flourishing social value sector which is able and willing to fulfil service delivery opportunities' (Welsh Government, 2015a: 56). These forums have been the catalyst for community-based initiatives, again some of which are community development. At face value, these initiatives and the policy backdrop seem to signal a swelling tide with implications for a renewal of community development practice within social work.

This incoming tide is rolling onto the shoreline of community developments across Wales, many with deep, culturally distinctive histories (Clarke et al, 2002). It also builds on more recent government initiatives such as the 'Communities First Programme', an initiative in low-income areas across Wales which ran until 2017. Based in community development and participatory approaches, the programme aimed 'at reducing poverty and helping to improve the lives of people who live in the poorest areas' (Communities Directorate–National Assembly for Wales, 2001: 3). Numerous reports identified the community-level successes of 'Communities First', for example, a report by the Welsh National Assembly noted: 'one of the key successes of Communities First is the relationships staff have built up with communities ... relationships that cut across more than one generation and were vital to the programme's ability to help and support people, sometimes in the most challenging circumstances' (National Assembly for Wales, 2017: 15). It further notes the 'life changing impact' of some of this work (2017: 12), and the investments that went into valued local community programmes and projects.

The Welsh way

There is an incoming tide for a renewal of community development within social work. The Welsh Government has placed an emphasis on preventative and community-based programmes. This tide of potential renewal builds on the rich and extensive history of community-led community development in Wales and that supported by governments.

Critical thinking on the 'incoming tide'

Although his work primarily revolved around discussion of the treatment of Freudian psychoanalysis and psychology over time, Russell Jacoby in the 1970s articulated a compelling argument about 'social amnesia', with a call to remember and reconnect with the past to inform analysis and action in the current times. In other words, a critical historical perspective. Broadly speaking, this idea of awakening from 'social amnesia' frames the ensuing discussion of salient lessons from social work to harness the power of the incoming tide of community development. First published in 1975, Jacoby's book *Social Amnesia* (2017) was motivated by an exploration of why certain ideas from the past were dismissed because they were from a different time and therefore seen to be less relevant. In extolling the need for a sharp critical theory, he examines the fluctuating focus in intellectual ideas over the 20th century between attention to subjectivity and/ or objective analysis of the social world, including the exchange between Marx and Freud. Of this dismissal process he writes: 'Today criticism that shelves the old in the name of the new forms part of the *Zeitgeist*; it works to justify and defend by forgetting. In making only a fleeting gesture toward the past, or none at all, social and psychological thought turn apologetic' (2017: 3).

Jacoby's social amnesia is a collective social forgetting, and what he calls a 'pseudo-historical consciousness'. He reminds us to remember the ideas and historically laid down patterns in the social, economic and cultural world, in order to 'think against the grain' in the contemporary times (Jacoby, 1997). These ideas are informed by a Marxist understanding of ideology as 'reification', 'an illusion that is objectively manufactured by society' (2017: 4). Jacoby also cautions against the temptation to reach for ideas that are 'pick[ed] up at the latest drive-in window of thought' (2017: 3).

Based on this premise, what can be remembered from history, from Wales and wider afield, to inform a social work where community development moves more into the centre of practice? It is beyond the scope of this chapter to do justice to this substantial question, so it focuses in the following two areas: (a) reclaiming sociological thinking, and (b) creating space for community development values and practice in neoliberal bureaucratic cultures.

Reclaiming sociological thinking

As has historically been so, the current renewal tides for community development are impelled by injustices that are sociopolitical and economic in origin, and which are unevenly felt by diverse population groups. These social, political and economic issues and the impacts in Wales are the subject of earlier chapters. There are public policy drivers for these developments, plus a sheer desperation for new alternatives. For example, and not dissimilar to other countries, social services in Wales are under immense strain, with repeated calls for new paths. As Clifton, from Senedd Research in the Welsh Parliament notes: 'It's widely *accepted* that fundamental reform of social care is long overdue. There have been numerous Welsh and UK Government papers and reports on reform, but the can has been repeatedly kicked down the road' (Clifton, 2021).

History has shown the tensions and challenges for place-based community development programmes in addressing a constellation of wider structural issues. This is evident in the evaluation of the Welsh Government's 'Communities First' programme. Communities First was 'designed to make sure that local people play a major part in developing the solutions to the problems they face' (Communities Directorate–National Assembly for Wales, 2001: 15). Through community development at a local level, and rooted in community planning, the programme engaged communities in actions about 'jobs and business', 'education and training', 'environment', 'health and well-being', 'active communities' and 'community safety'.

The Bevan Foundation, in a submission to the National Assembly for Wales' 'Equality, Local Government and Communities Committee' Inquiry into Communities First, notes the limitations in an approach to reducing poverty that foregrounded individual or community-level change, such as 'changing the characteristics and behaviours of individuals' (Bevan Foundation, 2017: para 7). This viewpoint is echoed in the National Assembly Inquiry report itself: 'Communities First was set a near impossible task. One single programme, especially one with a community development focus, never had the ability to make significant in-roads into poverty reduction on a local or national scale' (National Assembly for Wales, 2017: 8).

Navigating these tensions is aided with critical thinking about the dynamic interconnections between private spheres and the public realm. In social work this has been variously expressed; what the children's social worker and academic Clare Winnicott, who in the 1930s worked in the Welsh Valleys, stated as a task to 'be altering the structure to meet the individual and helping the individual within the structure ... you can't ever take your hand off either of these things' (1980: 19). Mary Richmond (1917), author of *Social Diagnosis*, and more commonly associated with case work, similarly stated that social work is concerned with people *in* their social and economic environment. Richmond's contemporary, sociologist and social worker Jane Addams explains how the work she was part of was 'fired by a hatred of social injustice' (as cited in Thompson et al, 2019: 10). Her practice was distinctively progressive and developmental, supporting local community building and matters to do with housing improvements, sanitation, education, labour conditions, women's rights and peace.

But there are other challenges with impacts for community development; social work's role within the state and the oscillation between a focus on 'micro' and 'macro' practice (Bartlett, 1970; Thompson et al, 2019; Payne, 2021). Holding this understanding – that social work history, and the place of community development in social work, is a story of tensions (Payne, 2021) – is liberating, as it signals a need to think and look for the ideological dimensions that Jacoby refers to. This opens the window on a critical analysis about power, or as Jacoby writes, thinking needs to be 'against the grain' (Jacoby, 1997: 60).

Continuous engagement with ideas and multiple forms of evidence can deepen the ways in which these tensions are understood, especially so if social work is out of practice in engaging in community development. Dunk-West and Verity (2018), in describing a sociological social work practice, combine the essence of C. Wright Mills' sociological imagination (to think historical, critically and linking micro and macros) with strategies to foster a creative imaginative habit in social work. They write: 'Surrounding ourselves with sources of motivation and encouragement, and "cultivating humanity" will help us keep our social work imaginative fuse glowing' (Dunk-West and Verity, 2018: 51). From a Welsh perspective, there is a rich vein of community development for inspiration. Welsh mutualism and organising, for example Robert Owen's ideas in action about cooperatives and community development, empowerment, human dignity and respect, have inspired global developments and practice, and are a place to start.

Counteracting neoliberal bureaucratic cultures

A further example of tensions in community development within social work is in the everyday dynamics within the organisational contexts of practice, especially statutory social work. For example, performance compliant and risk averse cultures have long been implicated in closing potential spaces for community development practice (Verity, 2011). Waddington, in 1979, speculated about the impact of the neoliberal ideas then hovering on the horizon. He presciently said: 'The new community workers will spend an increasing part of their work in deskbound activities and will do less fieldwork with clients. They will be more involved in management, in making policy, and in controlling budgets and resource allocation' (1979: 208).

Over the last 40 years and propelled by requirements under the rubric of 'managerialism', organisations within Wales (both statutory and non-statutory), like in other countries, have been culturally consumed by neoliberal practices. The evaluation of the Communities First Programme in Wales noted the 'administrative and reporting burdens' on programme recipients (National Assembly for Wales, 2017: 17). At one stage, the programme had over 100 performance indicators.

Jacoby's caution to think more critically about new developments has a particular timbre in an institutional context of social work practice shaped to its core by neoliberal ideas, where there can be a tendency to adopt trends and fashions in practice, that is, programmes imported or replicated from other places. In contrast, community development, I argue, requires repositioning of practice attention firmly in the cultures, needs, perspectives, hopes and imaginations of the people with whom social workers are working. Turning around this organisational context of practice is part of the community development project, to support spaces for social workers to facilitate community-based processes and actions. There is a groundswell of action in Wales to reorient compliance-based organisational cultures to ones that allow for creative and heart-centred practices (Andrews et al, 2020). This includes releasing capacity for processes of working alongside and with people, outside of an 'expert frame' by the social worker and the agency.

Messages for practice

- There is value in social workers connecting to sources of inspiration about the power and hope of community development.
- Social workers should remember historical lessons about the dynamics of institutional power, and its influence on social work's engagement with socially just informed community development.
- Social workers in Wales can actively support organisational change to support cultures that enable empowering community development.
- Social work practice should be in solidarity with others (citizens, community organisations, social movements).

Conclusion

In Wales, there are intersecting drivers of a contemporary tidal surge in community development, with implications for renewal in social work. This is where community development is a core social work task, beyond an optional endeavour by a worker or organisation with passion for this way of working, and more than social analysis of issues or seeing a social context. Community development also has many cautionary examples of good intentions butting up against other agendas; it is part of the change terrain. Again, remembering this has potency in a climate of renewed community development in social work, where, in the contemporary Welsh context, the language of human rights, prevention and early intervention are beacons for a community development approach.

It is within an environment of progressive government legislation informed by clear values, and a strained, underfunded social service system that community development in social work has an urgent contribution to make; a response to the critical issues that face the people, families and communities those social workers support. This can be assisted with a practice that connects to sources of inspiration about the power and hope of community development but also remembers historical lessons about tensions in the dynamics of institutional power, and the implications for a socially just informed community development. Working for organisational change and in solidarity with others (citizens, community organisations, social movements), is intrinsic to community development in social work.

Acknowledgements

My sincere thanks and acknowledgement to my social work colleagues Nick Andrews, Elizabeth Becker and Catherine Launder, and the book editors, for helpful comments on an earlier draft of this chapter.

Further resources

1. Clarke, S., Byatt, A., Hoban, M. and Powell, D. (2002) *Community Development in South Wales*, Cardiff: University of Wales Press.
2. The Co-operative Movement. https://www.wcml.org.uk/our-collections/working-lives/the-cooperative-movement/
3. The Community Development Podcast. https://russelltodd.cymru/en/project/the-community-development-podcast/

References

Addams, J. (1912) *Twenty Years at Hull-House with Autobiographical Notes*, New York: The Macmillan Company.

Andrews, N., Gabbay, J., Le-May, A., Miller, E., Petch, A. and O'Neill, M. (2020) 'Story, dialogue and caring about what matters to people: progress towards evidence-enriched policy and practice', *Evidence & Policy: A Journal of Research, Debate and Practice*, 16(10): 597–618.

Bartlett, H. (1970) *Common Base of Social Work Practice*, New York: NASW.

Bevan Foundation (2017) *Response to the Inquiry into Poverty in Wales: Communities First – Lessons Learnt.* Ymateb gan: Sefydliad Bevan, Senedd Wales.

Clarke, S., Byatt, A., Hoban, M. and Powell, D. (2002) *Community Development in South Wales*, Cardiff: University of Wales Press.

Clifton, A. (2021) *Social Care: A System at Breaking Point?* Senedd Research, 17 May [online]. https://research.senedd.wales/research-articles/social-care-a-system-at-breaking-point/

Communities Directorate–National Assembly for Wales (2001) *Communities First Guidance.* Cardiff.

Du Sautoy, P. (1966) 'Community development in Britain?', in G. Craig, K. Popple and M. Shaw (eds) (2008) *Community Development in Theory and Practice*, Nottingham: Spokesman Books, pp 28–32.

Dunk-West, P. and Verity, F. (2018) *Practising Sociological Social Work*, London: Macmillan.

Forde, C. and Lynch, D. (2015) *Social Work and Community Development: A Critical Practice Perspective*, London: Macmillan.

Forde, C., Lynch, D. and Lathouras, A. (2021) 'Introduction: community development in social work education: themes for a changing world', *Community Development Journal*, 56(4): 561–565.

Geoghegan, M. and Powell, F. (2009) 'Community development and the contested politics of the late modern agora: of, alongside or against neoliberalism?', *Community Development Journal*, 44(4): 430–447.

Ife, J. (1999) *Community Development-creating Community Alternatives: Vision, Analysis and Practice*, New South Wales (NSW): Longman.

International Federation of Social Work (2014) *Global Definition of Social Work.* July [online]. https://www.ifsw.org/what-is-social-work/global-definition-of-social-work/

Jacoby, R. (1997) 'Revisiting *Social Amnesia*', *Culture and Society*, 35: 58–60.

Jacoby, R. (2017) *Social Amnesia: A Critique of Conformist Psychology*, Oxon: Routledge.

Kumar, K. (1990) 'Utopian thought and communal practice: Robert Owen and the Owenite communities', *Theory and Society*, 19(1): 1–35.

Llewellyn, M., Verity, F. and Wallace, S. (eds) (2020) 'Evaluation of the Social Services and Well-being (Wales) Act 2014: Literature Review'. GSR report number 60/2020. Cardiff: Welsh Government.

Mendes, P. (2008) 'Teaching community development to social work students: a critical reflection', *Community Development Journal*, 44(2): 248–262.

Mowbray, M. and Bryson, L. (1981) '"Community": the spray on solution', *Australian Journal of Social Issues*, 16: 255–267.

National Assembly for Wales (2017) *Communities First Lessons Learnt.* Equality, Local Government and Communities Committee, Cardiff.

Payne, M. (2021) *Modern Social Work Theory*, London: Red Globe Press.

Richmond, M. (1917) *Social Diagnosis*, New York: Russell Sage Foundation.

Shaw, M. and Martin, I. (2000) 'Community work, citizenship and democracy: remaking the connections', in G. Craig, K. Popple and M. Shaw (eds) *Community Development in Theory and Practice*, London: Spokesman Books.

Swansea Council (2022) *Local Area Co-ordination*. Swansea.

Swansea University (2016) *Local Community Initiatives in Western Bay*. Formative Evaluation Summary Report, Swansea University. https://lacnetwork.org/wp-content/uploads/2017/04/FINAL-Local-Area-Coordination-Evaluation-Report-2017.pdf

Thompson, J.B., Spano, R. and Koenig, T.L. (2019) 'Back to Addams and Richmond: was social work really a divided house in the beginning?', *The Journal of Sociology & Social Welfare*, 46(2): Article 1. https://scholarworks.wmich.edu/jssw/vol46/iss2/1

Thorpe, R. (1985) 'Community work and ideology: an Australian perspective', in R. Thorpe, J. Petruchina and L. Hughes (eds) *Community Work or Social Change? An Australian Perspective*, Oxford: Routledge.

Verity, F. (2011) 'Community development: in the market's slipstream', in J.P. Rothe, L. Carroll and D. Ozegovic (eds) *Deliberations on Community Development*, New York: Nova Science Publishers, pp 235–247.

Verity, F., Willis, P. and Becker, E. (2015) 'Community development: turning the tide', *New Community*, 14(1): 67–70.

Waddington, P. (1979) 'Looking ahead: community work in the 1980s', in G. Craig, K. Popple and M. Shaw (eds) *Community Development in Theory and Practice*, London: Spokesman Books, pp 66–81.

Welsh Government (2014) *Social Services and Well-being (Wales) Act 2014*. Cardiff: Welsh Government.

Welsh Government (2015a) *Social Services and Well-being Act 2014: Part 2 Code of Practice (General Functions)*. Cardiff: Welsh Government.

Welsh Government (2015b) *Well-being of Future Generations (Wales) Act 2015*. Cardiff: Welsh Government.

Williams, F. (1999) 'Good-enough principles for welfare', *Journal of Social Policy*, 28(4): 667–687.

Winnicott, C. (1980) 'The Cohen Interviews: Clare Winnicott (nee BRITTON) – Interview no 24'. https://warwick.ac.uk/services/library/mrc/archives_online/speakingarchives/socialwork/929.publ_no_24_winnicott.pdf

21

Responses to the COVID-19 pandemic

Christian Kerr, Gillian Macintyre, Robin Sen and Abyd Quinn Aziz

Chapter objectives

- To identify and discuss challenges presented by COVID-19 to groups and communities in Wales.

- To describe how Welsh Government and Welsh communities responded to the crisis, identifying key features of 'the Welsh way'.

- To outline key messages for social work practice.

Introduction

There is a paucity of relevant literature on the impacts of and responses to the COVID-19 pandemic in Wales. This may be because proximity to England tends to lead to the de-emphasis of the unique history and profile of Wales. In discussing a pandemic which is, by nature, global in scale, yet intensely personal and close to home in its impact, it is important to parse out issues as they relate to people and communities in Wales.

While the pandemic is largely referred to in the past tense, including in this chapter, due to the widely-held view that 'the worst is over', it is important to remember that we are in its latest phase, having seen several surging variants across the UK. Many people with suppressed or compromised immune systems are still 'shielding' due to the heightened risks associated with contracting COVID-19 (Daniels, 2022) and we are all, in various ways, still dealing with the ongoing impacts of the pandemic (The British Academy, 2021).

Impact of COVID-19

COVID-19 and Wales

At time of writing, Wales is currently 'Covid stable' (Duffy, 2022) with no current restrictions in place (Welsh Government, 2022a). Statistics show the age-standardised mortality rate for deaths *involving* COVID-19 is slightly lower in Wales (130.7 deaths per 100,000) than in England (130.8), with Scotland (119.8) and Northern Ireland (120.7) both lower in the 28 months to the end of June 2022 (Duffy, 2022). The age-standardised mortality rate *due to*

COVID-19 – COVID-19 being the primary, underlying cause of death – is also lower than in England (Duffy, 2022). Peaks and troughs in infection and death rates broadly match those in other countries. For social workers, it is important to drill down into the impacts on the different groups and communities, so we can better tailor our support, during and after the pandemic, and these are summarised in the next section.

Black and global majority citizens

Excess mortality among Black and global majority people corresponded with higher infection rates due to people in this group being more likely in occupations where infection risk is higher. Again, Black and global majority people in Wales have been disproportionately adversely impacted by lockdowns, due to economic vulnerability (Platt and Warwick, 2020; Beaney et al, 2022).

Welsh Government (2020c) outlined a raft of measures aimed at mitigating the impact of these risks and challenges, while pointing to some already in place to address existing inequalities. These included recommencing work on the Race Equality Action Plan; developing a Welsh Workforce Risk Assessment Tool to identify workers most at risk of infection; support, advice, training and development for Black and global majority workers; and measures aimed at improving participation and leadership of Black and global majority people in public life in Wales.

Devakumar et al (2020: 234) criticise 'UK Government's "hostile environment" policy, including barriers to accessing the health service, such as upfront charging and the sharing of data with the Home Office, [which] has led to migrants avoiding healthcare' and highlight the particular vulnerabilities of Black and global majority people living in the UK who are not UK citizens.

While Wales is generally seen as a politically progressive country, this is all-too-often challenged by experiences of some Black and global majority people living there. Around 4 per cent of Wales' population is from a Black and global majority background. In 2016, anti-racism charity Show Racism the Red Card Wales, warned of rising racist attitudes among school children in Wales (BBC, 2016). Between 2017 and 2018, recorded hate crimes almost doubled from 2013 figures, to 3,932 (The Voice, 2021). These serve as a stark reminder of the work still to be done in tackling racism in Wales.

Gypsy, Roma and Traveller people

The social dimensions of the pandemic such as lockdowns and restrictions on social gathering had a disproportionate impact on Gypsy, Roma and Traveller people, who are more likely to be self-employed or small business owners, or musicians, entertainers and performers operating as part of the 'precariat' in the 'gig' economy (Marsh, 2020). These compounded pre-existing, chronic structural and historical discrimination and racism, ensuring the perpetuation of their economic exclusion and precarity (Marsh, 2020). There is clearly a need for targeted support, and Welsh Government (2020c) mentions three measures aimed at addressing issues faced by Gypsy, Roma and Traveller people: a dedicated advice and advocacy service; the convening of an expert Gypsy, Roma and Traveller stakeholder group to identify issues and advise Government and Public Health Wales, and additional funding to support Black and global majority school children experiencing loss of learning as a result of the pandemic.

Older people

Older people were at greater risk of infection and death from COVID-19 (Beaney et al, 2022). Despite claims that the UK Government had thrown a 'protective ring' around care homes in England (Merrick, 2021), the practice of discharging actually and potentially COVID-19-positive people from overstretched hospitals into care homes led to many thousands of excess deaths (Amnesty International, 2020), leading a subsequent High Court to rule that the UK Government had acted unlawfully in doing so (Dyer, 2022). The Welsh Government and Scottish Government have also been criticised for pursuing this policy (McKay et al, 2022; Thomas, 2022).

In addition, McGarrigle and Todd (2020: 1–2) found infection control measures were 'likely to have led to an increased sense of isolation and loneliness … established risk factors in mortality, cardiovascular disease, depression, and dementia'. Older people faced difficulties accessing health and social care, decline in their physical and mental health, increased loneliness, loss of confidence in engaging with the outside world, loss of income, increased cost of living, heightened risk of abuse and more bereavement (Age Cymru, 2020). Page et al (2021) argue changes in nursing practice aimed at countering the effects of social isolation and mask-wearing by focusing on relationship-based practice should be kept beyond the pandemic to promote well-being.

Women

In 2020, the Women's Equality Network (2020) Wales wrote to First Minister Mark Drakeford:

> [80%] of people employed in human health and social work activities in Wales are women. 42% of women in Wales are working part-time, compared to 14% of men. It is women who are at the forefront of responding to the virus as health workers, teachers and carers in the home. It is women who are at risk of being trapped at home with abusive partners. It will be women, particularly those who are disabled, black and global majority or on low incomes who are likely to be hardest hit by the pandemic.

Paterson (2020) found that women in Wales carried out a disproportionate amount of caring and home-schooling in the pandemic, impacting their ability to do paid work with consequences for their long-term career progression, and were also more likely to be working in the most impacted sectors and to be key workers in low-paid jobs.

A rise in domestic abuse is noted since the start of the pandemic (Piquero et al, 2021; Walklate et al, 2021) but Moore et al (2021) found that women were less likely to seek help during lockdowns, possibly indicative of a lack of opportunity for women confined with abusers to contact support services. This results in unmet need and increased exposure of children to domestic abuse. At the same time, Welsh Women's Aid (2020) found that domestic abuse support services suffered a 41 per cent loss of funding in the pandemic.

In March 2022, Welsh Government (2022b: 61) acknowledged the pandemic exacerbated existing risks and inequalities faced by particular groups, including women, signalling its intention to 'ensure that the policies we design to manage coronavirus and our response to future emergencies both maximise the protections for more vulnerable people and minimise the adverse impacts on those people as far as possible'. However, it has not developed a specific strategy for addressing the impact of COVID-19 on women in Wales.

Children

The Children's Commissioner for Wales (2020) consultation captured the experiences and views of 23,700 Welsh children and young people during the pandemic and found the majority felt 'happy most of the time' during the pandemic. A large majority reported feeling 'safe most of the time', with many reporting some advantages to staying at home more, such as increased time with family. The consultation involved a partnership between the then Children's Commissioner for Wales, Professor Sally Holland, Welsh Government, Welsh Youth Parliament and the charity Children in Wales. This suggests that, at the height of the pandemic, there was common shared purpose and synergy between the key state-mandated bodies and third sector organisations with responsibilities for promoting children's welfare, interests and viewpoints in Wales.

Children in care and care leavers

The legal system in Wales closely resembles that in England, where there were changes reducing 65 protections for children looked after using Statutory Instrument 445, which were eventually removed six months later following legal challenges by children's charity Article 39 (1). Rather than the same being applied in Wales, while recognising that the pandemic may make it hard for local authorities to comply with all existing requirements, Welsh Government clarified that all pre-existing legal requirements and duties remained in place during the pandemic: 'local authorities should make every effort to fully comply with the legislation and continue to fully take into account the needs and wishes of children in their care' (Welsh Government, 2020b: 20).

In producing its guidance, the Welsh Government consulted with other key individuals and agencies, including the Children's Commissioner for Wales. This approach served to undermine the UK Government's argument of necessity by which they argued that the diminution of rights enacted by SI445 was needed due to pandemic-related pressures.

The number of children looked after in Wales is likely to have increased during the pandemic (Welsh Government, 2021a), compounding the issue of Wales having one of the highest proportions of children in care in the UK (Taylor-Collins and Bristow, 2021). The social impacts of stringent lockdowns drove more children and families into contact with social services (Silman, 2020). Statutory child protection processes having to adapt to the 'new normal' of remote working and remote hearings has led to mixed outcomes for the children and families involved (Ferguson et al, 2022).

Children in care are particularly vulnerable to the myriad social impacts of the pandemic, from disruption to time with their birth families (Baginsky and Manthorpe, 2020) which, in turn, can impact on complex and delicate processes of reunification, to the rise in reported mental health issues among children and young people (Morris and Fisher, 2022). Roberts et al (2021) found that corporate parenting in Wales can either protect against or compound adversities arising from the pandemic for older care leavers, with marked differences between local authority responses in Wales. The pandemic therefore provided an opportunity to (re)consider the strengths and flaws of corporate parenting in Wales and reaffirmed the enduring importance not only of resources, but of relationships, in ensuring good support for children in care and care leavers (Roberts et al, 2021).

Disabled people

For disabled people, the disproportionate impact of COVID-19 includes increased risk from the disease itself, reduced access to routine health and social care, and the adverse social implications of isolation, social distancing and lockdowns (Shakespeare et al, 2021). The Disability Equality Forum in Wales (Welsh Government, 2021b) found that disabled people were 'locked out' from society during the pandemic. They highlighted inequalities, such as 68 per cent of deaths from COVID-19 were among disabled people in Wales, disabled people feel their lives are less valued in Welsh society, experiencing exclusion and discrimination when trying to access public services, including health services. The pandemic has negatively impacted on disabled people's human rights, including the right to independent living, and had a disproportionately negative impact on their mental health and well-being. It was felt the principles of 'Voice, Choice and Control' enshrined in the Social Services and Well-being (Wales) Act 2014 were abandoned during the pandemic.

The Welsh Government committed to setting up a ministerial task force to address the issues raised by the report and implement its recommendations. This task force is to be co-chaired by disabled people and has been broadly welcomed by disabled people's organisations.

Professionals and workers

Health and care workers and professionals are at the forefront of the pandemic response while facing their own particular challenges arising from intersecting inequalities. Women and Black and global majority people, for example, are overrepresented in the health and social care workforce and therefore are at greater risk from exposure to the virus itself (Welsh Government, 2022b). Additionally, these groups are more likely to be in more financially precarious positions due to part-time working and casualisation, which confers fewer workers' rights (Welsh Government, 2022b).

McFadden et al (2021a and 2021b) found that organisational and management support for UK social care workers in stressful times encouraged positive coping and help-seeking and were associated with improved mental health and well-being. In Wales, Cardiff University instigated the Health for Health Professionals Wales service, offering 'self-help, guided self-help, peer support, and virtual face-to-face therapies with accredited specialists' (Canopi, 2022), which was extended to include social care workers in April 2022.

Social work has a critical role to play in any public health crisis, yet social work does not appear to have been integral to the pandemic response and planning within the Welsh Government, leading to lack of specific government guidance for social workers as public health responders. However, in conversation, the director of the British Association of Social Workers Cymru stated she met regularly with the Health and Social Services Minister, communicating key challenges and messages from practice and raising questions and issues as they arose.

The Welsh Government's valuing of social workers' contributions in the pandemic was not just a matter of warm words of thanks, such as those contained in an open letter to social workers issued by the Chief Social Workers in England (Trowler et al, 2020) but involved making a payment of £500 to each social worker practising in the pandemic (Welsh Government, 2021b) and continued funding for the British Association of Social Workers (BASW) Professional Support Service providing free pastoral support to social workers for professional and personal issues (BASW, 2021).

A lack of capacity in the social work workforce that pre-existed the pandemic prompted BASW Cymru to call for an independent review of social work in Wales (BASW Cymru, 2020). This lack of capacity was then compounded by the pandemic, leading the Welsh social work regulator to set up a temporary register (Social Care Wales, 2022) aimed at re-engaging qualified social workers currently out of practice to address rising demand and worker absences. However, only 79 social workers were on the temporary register as of December 2021 (Samuel, 2022). The more recent call for an independent review of children's social care in Wales echoes similar concerns about the ongoing social work staffing crisis (Forrester, 2022). Values-driven innovation in leadership was also something social workers in Wales contributed, epitomised by BASW Cymru's decision to extend the organisation's offer of support and resources during to the pandemic to all Welsh social workers and student social workers, regardless of BASW membership.

Such leadership and partnership working were also demonstrated in decision making about practising social work safely through the pandemic. Initially, social work providers tried to maintain their services as normal, though increasing understaffing due to sickness and shielding soon saw services reduced. Rotas were introduced in social work offices to allow social distancing. As organisations became more equipped and confident using technology, hybrid working practices developed, including home-working and, where suitable and appropriate, communicating with people using services via mobile phones and video calling.

Concerns that students' placements were becoming less about learning and development and more about managing host organisations' workloads, which was not only detrimental to students but also possibly exposed people to risks associated with inexperienced practitioners carrying out complex work with little or no supervision, led to suspension of student placements and a more flexible approach to assessing students on their work so far (see Chapter 5). This allowed students to progress while recognising this cohort would require consolidation work later. At the same time, social work programmes moved much of their teaching online. Following discussions with employers, higher education institutions (HEIs), students and Social Care Wales, this blended approach will continue in the future for postgraduate students, who often have work and family and caring commitments and responsibilities, and because it reflects the approach in contemporary social work practice.

Community and grassroots responses

The pandemic saw an upturn in the number of people registering as volunteers (Taylor-Collins et al, 2021). This highlighted a long-standing reliance on the voluntary sector to provide many services to people in vulnerable situations in Wales (Senedd Cymru, 2021). Rees et al (2021) identified some key themes in respondents' views on learning from their experiences to support post-pandemic recovery. One was the retention of new services, such as befriending, which was key to combatting the social isolation brought on by infection control measures such as lockdowns, and aligns with the Welsh Government's Connected Communities strategy (2020a). Another was the retention of blended or hybrid ways of working, such as online meetings and activities, which some people found more inclusive, accessible and convenient, echoing aspects of social workers' experiences of online and hybrid working during the pandemic, and also those of people who access social support services. Respondents also highlighted the need for cooperation and coordination of community and civic response to make best use of available resources.

A study by Burrows et al (2021: 4) found 'the responsibilities of unpaid carers have increased considerably. There are more unpaid carers than ever before, and most of those who provided unpaid care before the pandemic are now spending more time on providing care for another person'. This was attributed to factors such as 'loss of respite, personal space, activities or external support' (p 5). However, notably absent were any announcements from the All–Wales Heads of Adults' Services Group like that of the English Association of Directors of Adult Social Services (2021) which spoke of a 'national emergency for social care' and asked people to 'provide care and support for family members who need it'. Unacknowledged in this plea, however, was the backdrop of years of politically chosen austerity that had local authorities struggling to meet the social care needs of their populations long before the onset of the global pandemic.

Learning and future direction of travel

There appear many parallels and similarities between the responses of the Welsh and the UK Governments to the COVID-19 pandemic, with both talking of taking opportunities to secure lasting change, and the UK COVID-19 Inquiry (2022) aims to uncover learning from the various approaches taken by countries in the UK in response to the crisis, to evaluate effectiveness.

There also appear key differences in the ideological underpinnings of countries' responses. The Welsh Government is widely held to have been appropriately responsive to risks associated with COVID-19 and to have had people's best interests at the heart of its decision making (Coslett, 2020). This stands in stark contrast to how many in the UK feel about the UK Government's handling of the pandemic (People's Covid Inquiry, 2021).

The Welsh way

Respect

Was demonstrated materially in the Welsh Government's £500 payment to social care and social workers who practised through the pandemic, and in its continued funding of the BASW professional support service, sending a powerful message that these professionals and workers are valued and valuable.

Cooperation

Cooperation and synergy between bodies and agencies is essential to mitigating the impacts of COVID-19. This has been modelled by Welsh agencies and organisations fostering mutual support and alliances between themselves, underpinned by ease and openness of communication.

Community

Wales has a proud history of strong community-mindedness, in no small part due to its industrial heritage. This came to the fore in the uptick in registered volunteers during the pandemic. It was also evident in the Welsh ACE Support Hub #TimeToBeKind campaign launched in March 2021, aimed at promoting the value of acts of kindness between people in difficult times.

Ambiguity

While the Welsh Government's pandemic response is generally viewed positively as being 'COVID-competent' and driven by a commitment to the rights and interests of its people and communities, this has not been sufficient to adequately protect some groups and communities notably women, Black and global majority people and Gypsy, Roma and Traveller people. Children in Wales continue to experience higher rates of poverty and there are more children entering care in Wales than elsewhere in the UK. There are worrying signs that Black and global majority people in Wales are experiencing increasing racism. These issues and vulnerabilities predate the pandemic, and in many cases have been compounded by it. While it does appear the Welsh Government is taking substantive steps to address these inequalities, this will be cold comfort to those acutely affected.

In Wales, policy and rhetoric appear characterised by a commitment to embedding learning from the pandemic to achieve its established vision of a more just and equal society. The UK Government has peddled the empty rhetoric of 'levelling up' while making lucrative contract awards to private companies, some with close connections to the government ministers, via a 'VIP express lane' later ruled unlawful (Good Law Project, 2022). Of direct relevance to social workers is how this preferential approach plays out in services and support for people in vulnerable situations. This is starkly apparent in children's services in England, where policy and the flow of public funds are greatly influenced by interconnected networks of key individuals and organisations (Hanley et al, 2021) such as the appointment of Josh MacAlister to lead the Review of Children's Social Care in England. MacAlister, at the time of the appointment, was the most connected individual within the current policy networks shaping children's services in England (Hanley et al, 2021). With England, Scotland and Northern Ireland either having, or having recently completed, children's care reviews, there have been recent calls for an independent review of children's social care in Wales. These calls must surely be accompanied with a demand that such a review is truly independent and led by someone without any vested interests in the system under review, beyond the requisite knowledge and experience, and the desire for a system that delivers what children need, whatever that may be.

Messages for practice

- The COVID-19 pandemic has brought many, often seemingly overwhelming, challenges, many of which persist, not least the ongoing agenda to dismantle and remove legal protections for people facing vulnerability and precarity, to which social workers need to be acutely alive.
- As elsewhere, professionals and workers in public service roles in Wales, as well as unpaid carers, have been impacted in myriad ways by the pandemic. Predictably, these impacts are not distributed evenly across groups.
- A key effect of the pandemic was to exacerbate and compound existing inequalities so that already marginalised people have borne a disproportionate share of its toll. COVID-19 is a wake-up call to the devastating impacts of the health, wealth and social inequalities facing minoritised and marginalised groups, providing further proof of the need to view the challenges people and communities face through the 'social lens'.
- It is more important than ever to promote the social model within multi- and interdisciplinary/agency contexts and to apply this lens to understanding the challenges faced by colleagues who hold diverse identities, so we can better support them.

Social workers stand up for the rights and interests of oppressed and marginalised people daily. At the same time, we decry a lack of a strong, collective voice for the profession. In this narrative, social workers are not very good at standing up for themselves. It is, sadly, a truism to say that social workers are too often vilified for dreadful outcomes they have little or no control over, and too infrequently celebrated for the positive ones they do. The pandemic has shown, again, that a necessary strength of social work is in standing up, individually and collectively, for the rights and interests of the people we support. If we extend this to those workers and professionals we work in partnership with every day, we may in turn find they step forward to stand up for us too. The pandemic has taught us that in such mutual support and solidarity, alliances and coalitions are forged, and we need those more than ever to fight the many injustices and inequities the pandemic has brought into sharp focus.

Welsh Government has, at least outwardly, sought to foster community cohesion and pursue equality. There is evidence of Welsh state-mandated institutions working far more cooperatively together in the interests of the individuals, families and communities with whom social workers most frequently work. While this institutional harmony is welcome, serious concerns remain. Despite an explicit policy goal of reducing the numbers of children in care, the numbers continue to rise and remain considerably higher in Wales than in England (Taylor-Collins and Bristow, 2021). And, despite a Welsh Government priority of 'ending' child poverty in Wales by 2020, in 2021, Wales had the highest rates of child poverty in the UK (BBC, 2021). As we hopefully move beyond the crisis, it remains to be seen whether policy makers and social work practitioners in Wales can make good on the rhetoric and policy aims to achieve a more just and equal post-pandemic society.

Further resources
1. The Health Foundation (2020) *Build Back Fairer: The COVID-19 Marmot Review*. https://www.health.org.uk/publications/build-back-fairer-the-covid-19-marmot-review
2. Burrows, D., Lyttleton-Smith, J., Sheehan, L. and Jones, S. (2021) *Voices of Carers during the COVID-19 Pandemic: Messages for the Future of Unpaid Caring in Wales*. https://phw.nhs.wales/publications/publications1/voices-of-carers-during-the-covid-19-pandemic-messages-for-the-future-of-unpaid-caring-in-wales/
3. Marsh, A.R. (2020) 'The impact of the novel coronavirus pandemic upon Romani and Traveller communities in Wales, 2020'. Romani Cultural & Arts Company. http://www.romaniarts.co.uk/the-impact-of-the-novel-coronavirus-pandemic-upon-romani-and-traveller-communities-in-wales-2020/

References
Age Cymru (2020) *Creating an Age Friendly Wales*. https://www.ageuk.org.uk/globalassets/age-cymru/documents/covid-19-survey/experiences-of-people-aged-50-or-over-in-wales-during-the-first-covid-19-lockdown-and-the-road-to-recovery---october-2020-eng.pdf
Amnesty International (2020) *Care Homes Report*. https://www.amnesty.org.uk/care-homes-report
Association of Directors of Adult Social Services (2021) 'Press release: A national emergency for social care'. https://www.adass.org.uk/adass-press-release-a-national-emergency-for-social-care
Baginsky, M. and Manthorpe, J. (2020) 'The impact of COVID-19 on children's social care in England', *Child Abuse & Neglect*, 116(2): 104739.
BASW Cymru (2020) *BASW Cymru Social Work Manifesto: Senedd Elections 2021*. https://www.basw.co.uk/resources/basw-cymru-social-work-manifesto-senedd-elections-2021
BBC (2016) 'Action call over racism by school children in Wales'. https://www.bbc.co.uk/news/uk-wales-37417006
BBC (2021) 'Wales "has highest child poverty rates in UK" says Save The Children', 20 May. https://www.bbc.co.uk/news/uk-wales-57157436
Beaney, T., Neves, A.L., Alboksmaty, A., Ashrafian, H., Flott, K., Fowler, A., et al (2022) 'Trends and associated factors for Covid-19 hospitalisation and fatality risk in 2.3 million adults in England', *Nature Communications*, 13: 2356. https://doi.org/10.1038/s41467–022–29880–7

British Association of Social Workers (2021) *Social Work Support Service to Be Launched Wales Wide as Survey Reveals Pandemic Has Left Social Workers 'Exhausted and Seeking Professional Help'*. https://www.basw.co.uk/media/news/2021/sep/social-work-support-service-be-launched-wales-wide-survey-reveals-pandemic-has#:~:text=The%20service%2C%20funded%20by%20Welsh%20Government%20will%20be%20delivered%20by%20BASW%20Cymru&text=A%20free%20peer%20support%20service

Burrows, D., Lyttleton-Smith, J., Sheehan, L. and Jones, S. (2021) *Voices of Carers during the COVID-19 Pandemic: Messages for the Future of Unpaid Caring in Wales*. https://phw.nhs.wales/publications/publications1/voices-of-carers-during-the-covid-19-pandemic-messages-for-the-future-of-unpaid-caring-in-wales/

Canopi (2022) 'About us'. https://canopi.nhs.wales/about-us/

Children's Commissioner for Wales (2020) *Coronavirus and Me*. https://www.childcomwales.org.uk/wp-content/uploads/2020/06/FINAL_formattedCVRep_EN.pdf

Coslett, L. (2020) 'Wales's Covid competence is inspiring many of us to thoughts of independence'. https://www.theguardian.com/commentisfree/2020/oct/27/wales-covid-competence-inspiring-independence-trust

Daniels, J. (2022) 'Many people are still shielding from COVID – and our research suggests their mental health is getting worse'. https://theconversation.com/many-people-are-still-shielding-from-covid-and-our-research-suggests-their-mental-health-is-getting-worse-186287

Devakumar, D., Bhopal, S.S. and Shannon, G. (2020) 'COVID-19: the great unequaliser', *Journal of the Royal Society of Medicine*, 113(6): 234–235.

Duffy, S. (2022) 'Figuring out the stats on coronavirus in Wales'. https://www.bbc.co.uk/news/uk-wales-52380643

Dyer, C. (2022) 'Covid-19: policy to discharge vulnerable patients to care homes was irrational, say judges', *British Medical Journal*, 377: o1098. https://doi.org/10.1136/bmj.o1098

Ferguson, H., Pink, S. and Kelly, L. (2022) 'The unheld child: social work, social distancing and the possibilities and limits to child protection during the COVID-19 pandemic', *The British Journal of Social Work*, 52(4): 2403–2421.

Forrester, D. (2022) 'Why we need an independent review of children's social care in Wales'. ExChange. https://www.exchangewales.org/why-we-need-an-independent-review-of-childrens-social-care-in-wales/

Good Law Project (2022) 'BREAKING: High Court finds Government PPE "VIP" lane for politically connected suppliers "unlawful"'. Good Law Project. https://goodlawproject.org/update/high-court-vip-lane-ppe-unlawful/

Hanley, J., Webb, C., Bald, C., Sen, R. and Kerr, C. (2021) 'Interdependence CSC: the interdependence of independence: a network map of children's services'. https://www.childrensservices.network/

Marsh, A.R. (2020) 'The impact of the novel coronavirus pandemic upon Romani and Traveller communities in Wales 2020'. http://www.romaniarts.co.uk/the-impact-of-the-novel-coronavirus-pandemic-upon-romani-and-traveller-communities-in-wales-2020/

McFadden, P., Neill, R.D., Mallett, J., Manthorpe, J., Gillen, P., Moriarty, J., et al (2021a) 'Mental well-being and quality of working life in UK social workers before and during the COVID-19 pandemic: a propensity score matching study', *The British Journal of Social Work*, 52(5): 2814–2833.

McFadden, P., Ross, J., Moriarty, J., Mallett, J., Schroder, H., Ravalier, J., et al (2021b) 'The role of coping in the wellbeing and work-related quality of life of UK health and social care workers during COVID-19', *International Journal of Environmental Research and Public Health*, 18(2): 1–15.

McGarrigle, L. and Todd, C. (2020) *The Adverse Effects of Social Isolation and Loneliness on Psychological and Physical Health Outcomes in Care Home Residents during COVID-19*. https://assets.publishing.service.gov.uk/government/uploads/system/uploads/attachment_data/file/1012417/S0584_Adverse_effects_of_social_isolation_and_loneliness_in_care_homes_during_COVID-19.pdf

McKay, C., McKay, E., Stavert, J., Murray, J., Johnston, L. and MacDonald, A. (2022) *Research Report for COVID-19 Public Inquiry: Corrected Draft, May 2022*. Scottish COVID-19 Inquiry.

Merrick, R. (2021) 'Matt Hancock denies making "protective ring around care homes" claim, despite saying it live on TV'. 6 June. https://www.independent.co.uk/news/uk/politics/matt-hancock-care-homes-protect-claim-b1860484.html

Moore, G., Buckley, K., Howarth, E., Burn, A.-M., Copeland, L., Evans, R. and Ware, L. (2021) 'Police referrals for domestic abuse before and during the first COVID-19 lockdown: an analysis of routine data from one specialist service in South Wales', *Journal of Public Health*, 44(2): e252–e259.

Morris, J. and Fisher, E. (2022) *Growing Problems, in Depth: The Impact of COVID-19 on Health Care for Children and Young People in England*. https://www.nuffieldtrust.org.uk/resource/growing-problems-in-detail-covid-19-s-impact-on-health-care-for-children-and-young-people-in-england

Page, S., Davies-Abbott, I. and Jones, A. (2021) 'Dementia care from behind the mask? Maintaining well-being during COVID-19 pandemic restrictions: Observations from Dementia Care Mapping on NHS mental health hospital wards in Wales', *Journal of Psychiatric and Mental Health Nursing*, 28(6): 961–969.

Paterson, L. (2020) *COVID-19 Women, Work and Wales*. Chwarae Teg. https://chwaraeteg.com/wp-content/uploads/2020/10/Covid-19-Women-Work-and-Wales-Research Report.pdf

People's Covid Inquiry (2021) *Misconduct in Public Office. Why Did So Many Thousands Die Unnecessarily? Report of the People's Covid Inquiry*. https://36085122–5b58–481e-afa4-a0eb0aaf80ca.usrfiles.com/ugd/360851_14d399accc1848cbb7649ad101546e66.pdf

Piquero, A.R., Jennings, W.G., Jemison, E., Kaukinen, C. and Knaul, F.M. (2021) 'Domestic violence during the COVID-19 pandemic: evidence from a systematic review and meta-analysis', *Journal of Criminal Justice*, 74. https://doi.org/10.1016/j.jcrimjus.2021.101806

Platt, L. and Warwick, R. (2020) 'COVID-19 and ethnic inequalities in England and Wales', *Fiscal Studies*, 41(2): 259–289. https://doi.org/10.1111/1475-5890.12228

Rees, S., Lundie, J., Crawford, L. and Dafydd, R. (2021) *Mobilising Voluntary Action in Wales: Learning from Volunteering Activity to Support Post COVID-19 Recovery*. September 2021 Briefing Paper.

Research Senedd (2022) *Looked After Children: Five Key Statistics*. https://research.senedd.wales/research-articles/looked-after-children-five-key-statistics/

Roberts, L., Rees, A., Mannay, D., Bayfield, H., Corliss, C., Diaz, C. and Vaughan, R. (2021) 'Corporate parenting in a pandemic: considering the delivery and receipt of support to care leavers in Wales during Covid-19', *Children and Youth Services Review*, 128.

Samuel, M. (2022) 'Temporarily registered social workers urged to restore full registration to remain in practice'. https://www.communitycare.co.uk/2022/03/08/temporarily-registered-social-workers-urged-to-restore-full-registration-to-remain-in-practice/

Sen, R., Kerr, C., MacIntyre, G., Featherstone, B., Gupta, A. and Quinn Aziz, A. (2021) 'Social work under COVID-19: a thematic analysis of articles in "SW2020 under COVID-19 Magazine"', *The British Journal of Social Work*, 52(3): 1765–1782.

Senedd Cymru (2021) *Impact of Covid-19 on the Voluntary Sector*. Welsh Parliament Equality, Local Government and Communities Committee. https://senedd.wales/media/d4jh52zz/cr-ld14075-e.pdf

Shakespeare, T., Ndagire, F. and Seketi, Q.E. (2021) 'Triple jeopardy: disabled people and the COVID-19 pandemic', *The Lancet*, 397(10282): 1331–1333.

Silman, J. (2020) '"Before, there were peaks and troughs – with Covid, it's relentless": Social work eight months into the pandemic'. https://www.communitycare.co.uk/2020/12/18/peaks-troughs-covid-relentless-social-work-eight-months-pandemic/

Social Care Wales (2022) *Temporary Register of Social Workers to Close to New Applicants*. https://socialcare.wales/news-stories/temporary-register-to-close#:~:text=On%2026%20March%202020%2C%20we

Taylor-Collins, E. and Bristow, D. (2021) *Evidence Briefing Paper: Children Looked After in Wales*. https://www.wcpp.org.uk/wp-content/uploads/2021/03/WCPP-Evidence-Briefing-Children-looked-after-in-Wales.pdf

Taylor-Collins, E., Havers, R., Durant, H., Passey, A., Bagnall, A.-M., South, J. and Boelman, V. (2021) *Volunteering and Wellbeing during the Coronavirus Pandemic*. https://www.wcpp.org.uk/publication/volunteering-and-wellbeing-during-the-coronavirus-pandemic/

The British Academy (2021) *The COVID Decade: Understanding the Long-term Societal Impacts of COVID-19.* https://www.thebritishacademy.ac.uk/publicati ons/covid-decade-understanding-the-long-term-societal-impacts-of-covid-19/ #:~:text=There%20are%20ongoing%20health%20impacts

The Voice (2021) 'Is Wales the most racist part of the UK?' https://www.voice-online.co.uk/news/uk-news/2021/11/17/is-wales-the-most-racist-part-of-the-uk/

Thomas, N. (2022) 'Untested patients discharged to care homes with "catastrophic consequences"'. https://www.southwalesargus.co.uk/news/20100477.care-boss-slams-wales-covid-discharge-policy-care-homes/

Trowler, I., Harvey, M. and Leddra, F. (2020) 'Open letter to social workers from Chief Social Worker for Children and Families and Joint-Chief Social Workers for Adults'. https://socialworkwithadults.blog.gov.uk/wp-content/uploads/sites/70/2020/09/200911-CSW-Open-Letter-to-Social-Workers-Sept-2020.pdf

UK Covid-19 Inquiry (2022) *Covid-19 Public Inquiry,.* https://covid19.public-inquiry.uk/

Walklate, S., Godfrey, B. and Richardson, J. (2021) 'Changes and continuities in police responses to domestic abuse in England and Wales during the Covid-19 "lockdown"', *Policing and Society,* 32(2): 1–13.

Welsh ACE Support Hub (2021) 'Time to be kind'. Ace Aware Wales. https://aceawarewales.com/time-to-be-kind/

Welsh Government (2020a) *Connected Communities: A Strategy for Tackling Loneliness and Social Isolation and Building Stronger Social Connections.* https://gov.wales/sites/default/files/publications/2020-02/connected-communities-strategy-document.pdf

Welsh Government (2020b) *Children's Social Services during the COVID-19 Pandemic: Guidance.* https://gov.wales/sites/default/files/pdf-versions/2021/1/2/1611048962/childrens-social-services-during-covid-19-pandemic-guidance.pdf

Welsh Government (2020c) *COVID-19 BAME Socio-economic Sub Group Report: Welsh Government response.* https://gov.wales/covid-19-bame-socio-economic-subgroup-report-welsh-government-response-html

Welsh Government (2021a) *Children Looked After by Local Authorities: April 2020 to March 2021.* https://gov.wales/children-looked-after-local-authorities-april-2020-march-2021

Welsh Government (2021b) *Locked Out: Liberating Disabled People's Lives and Rights in Wales Beyond COVID-19.* https://gov.wales/locked-out-liberating-disabled-peoples-lives-and-rights-wales-beyond-covid-19-html

Welsh Government (2022a) *Coronavirus Timeline: The Response in Wales.* https://research.senedd.wales/research-articles/coronavirus-timeline-the-response-in-wales/

Welsh Government (2022b) *Wales' Long-term COVID-19 Transition from Pandemic to Endemic.* https://gov.wales/wales-long-term-covid-19-transition-pandemic-endemic

Women's Aid (2020) *Impact of COVID-19 on Violence Against Women, Domestic Abuse and Sexual Violence Specialist Services in Wales: June Report Summary*. https://www.womensaid.org.uk/evidence-hub/research-and-publications/evidence-briefings-impact-of-covid-19-on-survivors-and-services/

Women's Equality Network Wales (2020) *Impact of Covid-19 on Women's Rights*. https://wenwales.org.uk/impact-of-covid-19-on-womens-rights/

22

Emerging social work practice in Wales

Rhoda Emlyn-Jones

Chapter objectives

- To reflect on the way in which complex organisational processes have defined Welsh social work practice.

- To explore the resulting loss of freedom of choice and decision-making for our staff and service users.

- To propose another Welsh way built upon core principles of the uniqueness of each person and the skill and insights of our staff, collaboratively working toward meaningful outcomes.

Introduction

This is a moment for meaningful change in Wales. We are talking to each other, challenging our thinking, and creating a critical mass, a tipping point, for change in culture and approach to social work provision. There is no better time, no better place and no better ambition. Much of this ambition is reflected in the preceding chapters.

Looking back over more than four decades of my social work practice in Wales I can reflect on the key elements that result in effective outcomes for those we are here to serve and support. I have had the privilege of working with many talented, committed workers. I have learned from them and from the people, families and communities who are facing and overcoming challenges. I worked for many decades developing services specifically designed to meet people in the uniqueness of their lives, working from where they are toward a better, improved future. The proven effectiveness of our models resulted in me being invited to support local authorities across Wales to develop family-focused services. These services focus on building relationships and understanding the challenges people face as they transition to a new way of managing their difficult circumstances. They invest in people, both at a preventative level and at moments of extreme risk or crisis. This chapter reflects that journey and the messages I have taken from it.

The key, I believe, is to step in closer, to understand the unique nature of each person, and to support the skilled staff who take that step closer and build insight and understanding as they work together with people and families. Throughout my working life, I have cautioned myself to ensure that we can evidence a clear link between the good intentions of our services and the lived experience of those we are seeking to support. People we meet are not problems to be solved, they are facing challenges that need to be overcome. As service providers, professional humility and courage are truly essential qualities.

The Social Services and Well-being (Wales) Act 2014 (SSWWA) came into force on 6 April 2016. As I had recently retired, I was able to assist Social Care Wales as part of their improvement agenda. I was glad to work closely alongside an organisation I respected, an organisation that had achieved real impact in Wales, providing national leadership and expertise in social care and early years. The task was to build upon previous evidence-based approaches to develop a transformational programme for local authorities who were keen to advance the opportunities the SSWWA gave them.

With the introduction of the SSWWA, a new philosophy and approach emerged in Wales. The Act is popular and has represented a breath of fresh air and optimism for workers across Wales. However, the change required to deliver it is challenging for organisations. Social Care Wales recognised this struggle and set in motion a range of resources to support the transformation. The Act requires a shift toward outcomes-focused social care; it supports and expects the sector to practise within a coproductive and strengths-based model of social work/care (see Chapters 1, 2, 6 and 7).

At the request of the Social Services Improvement Agency (SSIA) now Social Care Wales (SCW), I began the design of what became named the 'Collaborative Communications Skills Training, and Transformational Programme'. Our organisation, Achieving Sustainable Change Ltd, worked in partnership with SCW to refine and deliver the programme, initially through a series of pilot areas, then rolled out across Wales to those authorities keen to engage in the transformation. The programme consists of four phases, and councils across Wales have engaged with this process over the past eight years and continue to do so through the strategic partnership. It supports local authorities in moving to an outcome-focused approach.

Key elements of the transformation

This holistic approach aims to help organisations and all their personnel to think about the how, why and what of their engagement with individuals, families and colleagues and learn to build on their most effective practice. The programme also supports the development of mentors who champion change and continue to build confidence with their colleagues, embedding the practice. They influence the wider system through multi-agency workshops and address practicalities in system change.

The programme is delivered in phases. It begins with focusing on leadership to gain a clear vision and a shared view of the strengths of their organisation and the challenges they will need to overcome. The programme supports middle managers in the same way. Once a shared agreement is in place, the programme focuses on the skills and approaches of the practitioners and their view on how best they can be supported by managers, and importantly the system, to allow them to work differently.

We learn from the teams throughout, listening to what helps and what hinders their most effective practice. Throughout the programme, mentors and champions are identified and supported. They, in turn, support the reflective practice of the teams while ensuring a close connection between the senior management vision and the day-to-day practice on the ground. Crucially this requires a holistic approach where every process is subjected to scrutiny and dismantled if it proves to be an obstacle to best practice. The programme input includes the theories of human behaviour that inform professionals in their responses, and the teaching of skills and strategies that effective practitioners utilise in engaging with people at times of challenge and stress. Importantly it raises vital questions about how organisational systems must change to support effective practice. The programme maximises collaborative communication skills at every level in the organisation. Communication that directs people less and instead maximises a shared understanding and collaboration toward shared outcomes.

As the old culture diminishes, a slower deeper more meaningful and effective culture grows. A change of such depth and magnitude does not happen overnight and commitment is needed at every level. Llewellyn et al's (2021) work in evaluating the impact of the SSWWA five years on reinforces that one of the distinguishing features of the Act is that it purposefully states that the functions and duties of the SSWWA are to be performed to give effect to certain principles, including well-being, prevention, coproduction, voice and control, and multi-agency working. They highlighted the same feeling of optimism about the Act but also the struggle authorities were experiencing in the reality of its implementation. Llewellyn et al (2021) highlight that in its abstract form, the SSWWA is held up as an exemplar, but the challenge remains in the delivery and implementation of its ambitious agenda.

In a climate of high challenge and significant change, there is a need for the challenge to be understood and matched by the level of support needed at every level as we move from one way of functioning to another, support that crucially builds upon the strengths of the organisation. We have observed that as our programme unfolds clarity emerges in terms of a shared view of best practice. Skills are released and grow as workers feel freed up to utilise their communication skills and to recognise that the quality of each conversation is an important part of their role and influence. Staff and mentors begin to influence best practice across professional groups, actively and skilfully engaging other partner professionals to focus upon collaborative exploration of outcomes. Crucially, people begin to work together to dismantle old systems and build less complex more meaningful processes. Many authorities who have embraced the programme have changed their practice and realigned their forms and processes; ensuring that best practice leads, and the organisational systems we build backs it up.

This chapter explores the context within which local authorities and all their staff are attempting to create a proud future for social work in Wales (see Chapters 8, 9, 13, 14 and 15) working to the SSWWA and its core principles. Effective and sustainable implementation needs a whole systems approach. It requires strong leadership support, both strategic and operational, at a senior level but also dispersed through the organisation by mentors and other champions. The following key elements in effective leadership of the transformation has been evidenced by our learning over the past ten years of delivering the programme:

- Protect workers' time for training and reflective practice.
- Appoint someone to oversee implementation; model the approach in their communications.
- Help to engage partner agencies in a collaborative approach where each partner agency, alongside the person or family, is clear about the potential outcome and their contribution to it.
- Recognise the need to review systems; listen actively to the experiences of people – both staff and citizens – at the centre of the process.
- Link the approach to a vision and set of values which is coherent, convincing and unifying.
- Recognise that this should link to the SSWWA at a national level, and to other models and initiatives being implemented at an organisational level.
- Make sense on the ground, linking meaningfully with the purpose of teams and roles at a local level.
- Align systems, processes and structures, so that they support rather than obstruct the approach.

The problems we face

As I have said, this culture change is enshrined within the spirit of the SSWWA and supported by a National Outcomes Framework (Welsh Government, 2016) developed and promoted by SCW (Social Care Wales, 2022). It is crucial that we approach the transition from a position of system change, to address the culture and leadership of whole organisations, understanding the impact of systems that busy staff are compelled to follow and the policies and procedures they work within. We need to actively support the skills and approaches of all our staff to work toward a cohesive, collaborative culture. Our culture and approach shape our relationships and influence our conversations. The need to challenge the culture and to address the overly complex and sometimes overpowering nature of the proliferation of targets, guidelines, policies and procedures is commonly acknowledged and accepted by the organisations we have worked with; they also acknowledge the power of the old system and their need to stay focused on the change.

The implementation of the SSWWA places us in the middle of a significant culture change. Throughout Wales, local authorities are attempting to redefine their targets, guidelines, policies and procedures as they endeavour to shift to approaches that are collaborative and empowering for people, families and communities. There is increasing recognition that such an approach can be more effective and less wasteful, leading to better outcomes overall.

Over time, the increased attention on how well organisations and their workers were doing in adhering to processes, became more prominent than how well we were doing in our relationships with the people we served. Clear and accountable systems need to be in place in healthy organisations, but as we move toward true implementation of the principles of the Act each element of our current process needs to be subjected to scrutiny and explored from a new position of strengths-based outcome-focused practice. This requires a significant rethink and shift in practice and approach within a context of decades of complex systems that have been built into our organisations over time. For example, we ask busy social workers to engage with people, children and families at time of stress and difficulty and require them to fill in large assessment documents, through which the headings and required information gathering lead the conversation rather than allowing an intuitive unfolding of a meaningful conversation. The result is often far less meaningful and more uniform content. Workers and managers often comment that recorded and written care plans share uniform elements and prevent them from seeing, through the recording, to the heart of the matter restricting line of sight to unique family circumstances.

Busy staff are required to fill in risk assessment forms but rarely get the chance to explore the risk in depth with the family using an approach that would increase empathy and understanding of the most important parts of their lives, sharing insights and enabling families to build on their strengths to offset the priority risks in their lives. Staff spend precious time cutting and pasting information from one required field to another, sometimes blocked by systems, sometimes redirected, serving to take them further away from the emerging picture of the unique family functioning they are gaining insight into, further away from their own decision-making skills. We have built more and more paperwork that explores problems, needs and risks before any exploration of strengths, and narratives emerge that distort the view of the reader and result in a risk-averse decision-making culture.

Over the decades the culture of public service has moved more and more toward these approaches. We have confused concepts, replacing quality assurance measures with quality control measures, controlling the process rather than exploring our impact. Only by measuring impact and outcomes from a family's perspective can we claim true quality assurance. These are unintended consequences; processes were designed to improve quality, but have often resulted in reducing the autonomy, skill and decision-making of staff and, as a result, paradoxically reduced their effectiveness and the quality of their work. Limiting the sense of ourselves and our ability to recognise that our skills are the intervention, we became very 'service led', and while access to appropriate services is vital, services need to be perceived, by all involved, as a means to an end not as an end in themselves.

Service users experience a multitude of assessments. Each profession's specialist assessment became linked to the gatekeeping of vital, limited resources and we noticed a shift, over time, to releasing resources only to those in greatest need. This approach had a rationale but gradually led to people's circumstances being tested against ever-rising thresholds and tightening criteria. As a result of these deficit-focused processes, service users and referring professionals learned over time that if you could not prove you were 'bad enough' you could not get a service. We inadvertently created a culture of risk-focused conversations and elevated the status of 'services' to the detriment of skilled and engaging conversations that concentrated on the dilemmas, challenges, strengths and resources of each individual family member. The quality of the relationship between the worker and the person/family reduced in status, and the ability to empower and enable, to 'be the service', gradually became less valued or understood.

Risk-averse practice increased over time. Fearful of risks being missed, risk assessment documents were introduced as a prompt for staff, reminding staff to be 'tuned in' to possible risk factors. This was a useful tool but in many cases the document ended up being seen as an end in itself. We were often trying to understand what we could *do for* people, and what services we could offer, rather than gaining insight into what we could *do with* people (see Chapters 6, 10 and 12).

The dominance of the processes reduced the contact between a skilled professional and the person or family. Skilled conversations were squeezed out in favour of processes that needed to be completed. Care plans often focused on services rather than how the service could contribute to the overall outcome for the family. Plans were often based on addressing people's deficits rather than building on their competencies. The monitoring stage of the plan became overly focused on services and how much was being delivered.

Multiple assessments, deficit-focused care plans and monitoring/reviewing service-led plans were a recipe that often resulted in increases in: service user fear and resistance; crisis and dissatisfaction; the inappropriate use or overuse of resources; and the risk of creating dependency. This dominant culture takes time and effort to unpick as we work toward a new, very different way of working.

The Welsh way

The SSWWA has provided the opportunity to create our most empowering, engaging and effective public service, including social work. This begins with some shared ideologies. It looks for transformation in individuals, organisations and practice. This involves strengths-based rather than deficits-based approaches, where social work is working with rather than unto people.

The emerging solutions

Throughout the implementation of the collaborative communication programme, workers described how much they hoped to develop a shared, collaborative approach that grows self-efficacy and autonomy in individuals and families. They were keen to remain true to a process that has the best evidence of effectiveness. This wish aligns with the evidence of what people report they need and want from their services. The many stories from citizens captured by Measuring the Mountain (2020) evaluating the impact of social services in Wales reveal an incredible range of people's experiences and highlight the complexity of many people's lives as well as the enormous efforts people will go to in support of a family member, friend or loved one (see Chapter 10). Many of the stories illustrate the importance of good relationships and thoughtful interactions between people using services and people delivering services. Fostering trust, creating networks of support, and establishing relationships with a balance of power were seen to contribute to positive experiences and good outcomes. Further evidence from Measuring the Mountain revealed that both workers and people receiving services wanted to work in this positive way, but processes and organisational pressures resulted in them becoming procedural, risk-averse and overly service oriented.

These findings resonate with the beliefs and principles generated by our programme, and those underpinned by the key principles articulated within the SSWWA. Throughout our programme, the following concepts become the guiding principles that inform our approach and decision-making, it is important that they are embraced at all levels in the organisations we work with. These emerging principles in the programme include:

- Safer families result when the worker and the family feel confident that they have insight into the risks they face and feel equipped to manage the risks.
- Human beings have a natural capacity to find their own solutions however complex their challenges are.
- When we harness this natural human condition and respond thoughtfully to it, enhancing this innate capacity, families, communities, teams and organisations grow in their impact and effectiveness.
- The concept of well-being is naturally invested in and dependent on relationships, self-respect and self-determination and should be explored from that perspective.

How we think about something affects what we do, and we need to embed a new narrative. Continuity of approach is key, whether we are a worker engaging with a family, a manager engaging with their team, a leader of the organisation or those inspecting it and holding it to account, we need to be open, humble and curious. We need to foster trust through trustworthiness and truly respect the rights of human beings to determine their own lives in a wide range of diverse ways (see Chapters 2, 6, 19 and 20).

We will not easily recognise the most vulnerable or the most at risk in families and communities unless we support our staff in their most effective communication styles and develop safe places to deepen their insights and analyse dynamics. Staff should be encouraged to share the stories of their work to provide real and meaningful evidence of their impact on families and the changes people are managing to achieve in their challenging lives. Frontline practitioners should be freed up to embrace strengths-based values and learn afresh skills such as listening, empathy, storytelling, reflection, facilitation and collaboration to build knowledge of communities and trust within them, to confidently share best practice through reflective groups that are strengths-based and outcome-focused, appreciating that people are experts in their own lives and can take the lead in developing solutions. This represents a significant shift in thought and action and a willingness to share power and resources (see Chapter 12).

Transforming organisations need to demonstrate strong, visible leadership while modelling strengths-based behaviours and adopting strengths-based values to motivate staff. They need to support the skills in staff to engage with people and view them as resourceful, and to see people as part of the solution. This requires them to ensure that every element of the organisation is designed to maximise the likelihood of engagement and collaboration. Ways need to be found to actively share best practice stories. Organisations should be willing to lead on culture change – pushing boundaries, rethinking the concept of risk, and exploring with workers the principles that underpin their sense of duty and accountability.

It is important to recognise that investing in these new approaches and embedding them may take time; organisations need to put in place the systems and processes to facilitate culture change. At every level in the organisation there needs to be a sense of championing the change. There needs to be investment in and commitment to multi-agency working, promoting a shared approach and negotiating collaboration across all services and organisations. This is an efficient and effective way of working that produces better outcomes and achieves positive feedback from service users. Utilising collaborative outcome-focused approaches, staff are evidencing how they have helped the person or family overcome their fears and ambivalence about new ways of functioning in the light of living with ill health or disability, changes in family relationships or risks of family breakdown. They are supporting children, young people and older generations to build their own futures and manage their independence (see Chapters 13 and 14).

Collaboration is key, creating partnerships where people and families are recognised as the experts in their own lives and can explore their competencies and their values to assist them in challenging and changing their lives. We are interested in outcomes and knowing, together, what autonomy looks like and when it has been achieved.

As our public service system adjusts, we often find ourselves at odds with the old culture; so we need to share and support our common approach in order to maintain our position. All staff can be supported to apply the principles and skills to their wide range of functions. We need to maintain support for all our skilled staff. The unintended consequences of the vast number of quality control structures put in place over the decades have been counterproductive, creating an illusion of control over quality while reducing the quality assurance that comes from a clear line of sight through our staff's eyes to the needs of the families and communities they serve. Our work is complex and unpredictable, so we need a framework and organisational culture that allows us to explore our best practice and best decision-making. Skilled conversations need to lead and the system needs to follow. The culture change can be inspired by the SSWWA; the approach must be led by the conversation.

We start with what we can discover and consider strengths, priority risks and good enough outcomes from the family's perspective, strengthening families as they face huge challenges, deep sadness and loss, overwhelming past trauma or fears for uncertain futures.

Messages for practice

For our systems to change to better represent the emerging culture we need to consider:

- the tone of our letters and leaflets and emails, which need to be more human: the overemphasis on information undermines engagement and empowerment;
- placing more emphasis on how our communication makes people feel;
- the way we make and receive referrals needs to exploit the massive potential for relationship-building at the front line;
- reviewing the way we record our interactions, articulating family outcomes from the family's perspective;
- collecting the most meaningful data linked to outcomes.

Every one of our new workers, whatever their role and function, must be trained in the spirit and principles and skills underpinning their approach. Strengths-based, outcomes-focused practice becomes the accepted approach of the whole organisation and the spirit is upheld within the culture of each team.

It is vital to retain and support our skilled workforce. Tyrrell et al (2019), in an evaluation of the programme, focused upon the impact of strengths-based, outcome-focused practice underpinned by collaborative communication skills. They noted that practitioners felt our programme, and the wider changes to outcomes-based work, had improved their job satisfaction, helping them to feel:

- energised and reconnected with their original motivation to join the profession;
- more rewarded in their work, because they feel they are making a positive difference to individuals and families;

- excited and empowered by being liberated from the forms and traditional structures;
- more confident in using the skills of collaborative communication in professional and personal relationships;
- the value of their own strengths.

During the programme there are key moments to gather feedback from staff and report their views to management. Feedback from thousands of participants in the programme is captured and shared. They reflect the best hopes of staff working to make a positive difference as they enter people's lives. The work is complex and unpredictable and requires a trusted, safe environment to explore their insights and decision-making; when we create that environment, they feel re-energised. The following quotes from practitioners participating in the evaluation illustrate some of these points:

> 'We came into the job to make a difference and this way [of working] lets me do that.'

> 'Being able to be the social worker I have wanted to be.'

> 'We loved the programme; this is the work we have always wanted to do.'

> 'The leadership buy-in is so valuable, we feel as if we are working together.'

> 'I used to feel responsible for fixing things, now I have the skills and approaches to work with families in a different way and get much better outcomes.'

There can be no more important moment to consider the well-being of our staff. We need to value their skill, commitment and energy, build upon their principles and values and support them in pursuing their best practice.

Conclusion

Within the pages of this book, you will hear the voices of Welsh ambitions to create our most empowering, engaging and effective public service. We must strive to create safe ways in which services, staff and communities can thrive and grow in the face of unprecedented and unexpected pressures.

By considering the ways in which organisational processes have become over complex, inhibiting the freedom of choice and decision-making skills of staff and service users, a new approach has been developed. This new way of working has resulted in enabling service users and staff to acknowledge the uniqueness of each person and situation, and to work toward meaningful outcomes for all concerned.

The ambition in Wales is to start with a shared ideology and understanding of the psychological and dynamic nature of our work and equip staff with the best communication skills to engage and explore change. Setting these skilled staff within strong and empowering social services signifies the future for effective, efficient, high-quality public services.

Further resources
1. Cottam, H. (2018) *Radical Help*, London: Virago Press.
2. Gawande, A. (2014) *Being Mortal: Illness, Madness and What Matters in the End*, New York: Metropolitan Books.
3. Hohmom, M. (2021) *Motivational Interviewing in Social Work Practice* (2nd edn), New York: Guilford Press.

References
Llewellyn, M., Verity, F., Wallace, S. and Tetlow, S. (2021) *Evaluation of the Social Services and Well-being (Wales) Act 2014: Process Evaluation.* GSR report number 2/2021. Cardiff: Welsh Government.
Measuring the Mountain (2020) 'The stories'. http://mtm.wales/the-stories
Social Care Wales (2022) *Using the Outcomes Approach.* https://socialcare.wales/resources-guidance/improving-care-and-support/personal-outcomes/using-the-outcomes-approach
Tyrrell, H., Blood, I., Goulding, J. and Day, S. (2019) *Collaborative Communication Evaluation Report.* https://socialcare.wales/cms-assets/documents/Collaborative-Communications-Skills-Programme-evaluation-report.pdf
Welsh Government (2016) *Social Services: The National Outcomes Framework for People Who Need Care and Support and Carers Who Need Support.* Cardiff: Welsh Government.

Conclusion

Abyd Quinn Aziz, Jo Redcliffe and Wulf Livingston

In concluding this book, it feels useful to revisit what we hoped for when we started our first conversations on this. In the preface, we outlined how the three of us came together to put this together. We were clear in wanting an edited volume of diverse contributions, and not a formulaic textbook, capturing the variety of voices of people involved in social work in Wales. We wanted in this, to reflect the Welsh way and to highlight giving expression, coproduction, partnership working, prevention and looking at well-being as central to social work values, legislation and policy.

We also wanted to acknowledge the journey that those involved in social work in Wales are on, as outlined in Part I, and recognise the mountain (Cooke et al, 2019) we still face, rather than suggesting that we have arrived at the destination of all our ambition. Within this we wanted to look at what is distinctive, the Welsh ambition for social work by government, the social work regulator, academics, practitioners, students and, last but not least, people using services and carers. In doing so, our intention was to create something that would lead to discussions about and inform rather than direct practice.

This book has succeeded in being more than either just an academic or classroom textbook, while also taking significant account of both these important considerations. Each chapter offers unique perspectives combined with resources for readers to further explore these ideas. They achieve a range of different snapshots involved in using, delivering, teaching and legislating social work and many areas of practice. In this context it begins and ends with the very distinct personal voices of Plack and Emlyn-Jones. Looking back at the process, it has been all that we could have hoped for both in the working to create the book and the 'product'.

Wales has a long-standing commitment to the public sector and has pride in the aspiration of partnership, collaboration and sustainability, with some radical thinking in government. Much of this history has resonated in the chapters throughout this book with accounts of the aspirations for inclusivity, rights-based approaches and social justice orientations of the newer devolved legislation and practices. The turn of the 20th century saw inward and outward migration attracted by thriving industrialisation. Toward the end of the century, these industries declined and, together with the closures of mining, this led to a need for self-reliance for communities to survive, with higher unemployment rates and lower wages compared to other British nations. In 1997 the vote for devolution led to the establishment of the National Assembly, now the Welsh Parliament, which has enabled Wales to make some decisions on social care for itself. These more recent socioeconomic developments are also resonated throughout the book and, as the final chapter by Emlyn-Jones describes, this has created aspirations for and beginnings of change which have yet to be fully achieved.

In terms of the special nature of Wales, its relatively small population enables us to have conversations across the nation and profession. We have a small number employed in the social work workforce, just under 4,000 registered social workers according to recent reports (Social Care Wales, 2021). Devolution and the ability to make laws and policy has led to some divergence from the English model, and more so in social care. This is also supported by the principles of the Social Services and Well-being (Wales) Act 2014 (SSWWA), which brought into legislation good social work values, such as working in partnership, giving voice and control and coproduction.

The shift to the models of neoliberalism, care management and providers, which created the notion of 'customers', on the assumption that competition would lead to better services, has been seen as perhaps not the best option. Welsh social care and work had become embroiled in these perspectives. More recently, Wales has begun to focus on a values-based approach, embedding citizens' rights and services, working in partnership both with each other and with people using the services. Across the sector, we have worked to see people in the round and take an intersectional approach that informs assessment, planning and service provision.

That is why we have sought to capture 'the Welsh way' within each chapter and summarised these out of the chapters. Part I of the book provides the context of social work practice in Wales. At its heart is the importance of coproduction and the involvement of people using services, notably in contributions such as those from Waters and Lefroy. This core approach is then also reflected in Gwilym's summary of the Welsh policy framework, and the analysis of the rights-based legal approach by Ennis. Thomas's exploration of social work regulation and Redcliffe and Oritiz's examination of social work education brings focus to social work. The rights-based approach and attention to Welsh context (see Prysor's chapter) are constant themes, as they are reinforced by codes and regulations directing the workforce, students and social work education in this approach. The core theme here is the forging of a distinct Welsh framework.

From here we moved on, in Part II, to looking at some practice examples that explore how these are enacted. We consciously chose not to attempt to cover all the different services provided, rather to offer a snapshot from different perspectives that reflect the central principles and values of social work in Wales. At its heart is Buckley et al's focus on the experiences of people using services in social care and social work education. The themes are echoed across Wilkins' reflections on child and family social work in Wales, and Douglas and Barlow's analysis of the bringing together of the Children and Adult Approach to Safeguarding. In addition we see the application of the Welsh way through examples of practice experiences of and with unpaid carers and older people, through the contributions of Burrows and Lyttleton-Smith, and Alexander et al describe novel innovative approaches to working with older people. In the final two examples, Versey et al discuss peer-led work in alcohol and drug services, and Brierley-Sollis review taking a trauma-informed perspective in youth justice. The chapters within Part II have offered a flavour, a snapshot of how the diverse community (of practice) is coming to terms with the post-SSWWA environment.

Part III has looked forward to some of the challenges we face as a nation and some of the areas that Welsh social work needs to better develop in addressing. Thus, Thompson suggests a holistic approach to well-being and then we look more specifically with Parry and Davies' chapter on how social work needs to respond to the changing experiences of transgender children and their families, and young people's intimate relationships. Four huge topics of anti-racist social work, sanctuary seekers, COVID-19 and community development then provide rich exploration of how Wales grapples with issues that transcend boundaries and devolution and forges an emerging sense of a bespoke national response. Forbes and Quinn Aziz, Maegusuku-Hewett et al, Kerr et al, and Verity, through these topics, highlight how social work is still of the personal and political, and by consequence how the Welsh way is emerging into the myriad arenas of the micro, meso and macro. The messages of Part III about aspiring for change, grappling with complexity through individual, community, organisational, governmental and societal partnerships are then reflected in the final contribution from Emlyn-Jones in her candid reflections on supporting direct changes with social work practitioners.

As noted earlier, in inviting contributions we attempted to capture a flavour of what is going on and can be said at this moment in time, and by a range of people directly involved. We do not suggest that this is the totality of all perspectives and voices. We also anticipate that as the Welsh journey continues, others will inevitably be better placed to help contribute to the developing tale.

Creating the book involved hard work and we must recognise the time and effort put aside by busy people, in putting this together, who all shared the positivity of having their say. In the book we wanted to record these different ways of working and their underpinning aspirations so that we can learn together and continue the conversations that are supported by policy and legislation. We want to continue with the culture change and continue to hear the voices of people using services and, as Waters says in her chapter, 'disrupt the system'.

The commitment by Welsh Government to ensuring equal treatment of people in Wales and their human rights is enshrined in legislation, and many reports have evidenced the disparity between this intention and structural inequalities in the nation, such as by Future Generations Commissioner's report (2020), Race Council Cymru's report (Offord, 2016) and Equality and Human Rights Commission research reports (EHRC, 2021), as well as the Welsh Government's numerous reports on inequalities. Developments such as the government discussions on a National Care Service hold on to the values of working in a coproduced manner, focusing on 'what matters' to people, to take preventative approaches, with a focus on outcomes and to the notion of services free at the point of need. These are positive aspirations which require action and evaluation to support the nation's journey in achieving them.

In concluding with our thanks to the engaging contributions from the many voices involved in social work, that have let us celebrate where we have got to but who have also recognised the challenges of what more is to be done, we have been left pondering if Wales is at a tipping point in terms of fulfilling the aspirations of people using services, workers, students, policy makers and the nation, to make a change for the better for our future generations to come?

References

Cooke, K., Iredale, R., Williams, R. and Wooding, N. (2019) *Measuring the Mountain: What Really Matters in Social Care to Individuals in Wales*, Pontypridd: University of South Wales.

Equality and Human Rights Commission (2021) *Wales Impact Report 2021–22* . EHRC. https://www.equalityhumanrights.com/sites/default/files/3539_wales_impact_report_english_access_dv10a.pdf

Office of the Future Generation Commissioner of Wales (2022) *Annual Report.* Cardiff: Tramshed Tech.

Offord, P. (2016) *Report on the Results of a 2016 Survey Conducted by the Race Council Cymru.* Cardiff: Race Council Cymru.

Social Care Wales (2021) *Social Care Workforce Report.* Cardiff: Social Care Wales.

Index